Smart Hospitals

Scrivener Publishing
100 Cummings Center, Suite 541J
Beverly, MA 01915-6106

Publishers at Scrivener
Martin Scrivener (martin@scrivenerpublishing.com)
Phillip Carmical (pcarmical@scrivenerpublishing.com)

Smart Hospitals

5G, 6G and Moving Beyond Connectivity

Edited by

Arun Kumar

Manoj Gupta

Sanjeev Sharma

Er. Himanshu Sharma

and

Khursheed Aurangzeb

Scrivener Publishing

WILEY

This edition first published 2024 by John Wiley & Sons, Inc., 111 River Street, Hoboken, NJ 07030, USA and Scrivener Publishing LLC, 100 Cummings Center, Suite 541J, Beverly, MA 01915, USA

For more information about Scrivener publications please visit www.scrivenerpublishing.com.

Wiley Global Headquarters
111 River Street, Hoboken, NJ 07030, USA

For details of our global editorial offices, customer services, and more information about Wiley products visit us at www.wiley.com.

Library of Congress Cataloging-in-Publication Data

ISBN 9781394275441

Front cover images supplied by Adobe Firefly
Cover design by Russell Richardson

Set in size of 11pt and Minion Pro by Manila Typesetting Company, Makati, Philippines

Printed in the USA

10 9 8 7 6 5 4 3 2 1

Contents

1

Smart Hospitals: Integrating Connectivity and Intelligence

Yashwanth S., Varshini Kulkarni, Chethana H. T.* and Chaitra N. C.

Department of Computer Science and Engineering, Vidyavardhaka College of Engineering, Mysuru, India

Abstract

Health is a crucial part of every person; sometimes, a person may have an unstable condition such as a disease or illness. For people to revert to good condition, they may need intensive care provided by hospitals. Nowadays, hospitals have become busier because of rapid growth in population. Due to this, doctors, nurses, paramedics, and administrative staff are struggling to handle them. A solution to this problem is the use of technology such as the Internet of Things (IoT) to upgrade hospitals to smart hospitals including doing medical works like monitoring patients' data and performing various scanning tasks at a faster rate.

The "smart hospitals" concept is a comprehensive integration of 5th generation (5G) technology with cloud computing, big data analytics, IoT, and artificial intelligence (AI). The integration of 5G in smart hospitals encompasses several key elements—5G healthcare terminals, including medically integrated terminals, information collection and display terminals, and auxiliary terminals. The 5G healthcare-dedicated network employs network slicing, a dedicated user plane function (UPF), and multi-access edge computation for tailored medical networks, efficient data transmission, and low-latency processing. The healthcare-dedicated cloud manages network capabilities, computation resources, and medical applications. 5G healthcare applications showcase production efficiency and smart medical services. The healthcare-dedicated network architecture includes local, wide-area, and dynamic networks for intra- and inter- hospital services along with out-of-hospital medical services. The integration with existing medical systems and a unified platform management layer ensures seamless cloud–network integration, gradual migration, and efficient resource management. The aim of

**Corresponding author*: chethanaht@vvce.ac.in

Arun Kumar, Manoj Gupta, Sanjeev Sharma, Er. Himanshu Sharma and Khursheed Aurangzeb (eds.) Smart Hospitals: 5G, 6G and Moving Beyond Connectivity, (1–22) © 2024 Scrivener Publishing LLC

the chapter is to create a flexible ecosystem utilizing 5G technology for enhanced healthcare services and patient outcomes.

Keywords: 5G, IoT, AI, integration, patients, cloud, hospital, medical

1.1 Introduction

Health is defined as a state of complete physical, mental, and social well-being; it is not just the absence of disease or illness [1]. The word "hospital" is derived from the Latin word "hospice," which means guest. Hospitals are institutions that provide medical and surgical treatment along with nursing care for any sick or injured people [22]. Ensuring that those in need of receiving comprehensive healthcare, including preventive and curative treatments, is a fundamental role of social and medical organizations. It serves as a center for biosocial research, as well as a training center for health workers [21].

Hospitals are part of a social structure, which again have a subsystem, like supportive and utility services, clinical services with heterogeneous group of people like doctors, nurses, paramedics, and administrative staff all working together to provide medical care to patients [2]. The pandemic has brought to our attention and intensified the challenges faced by the healthcare industry. Numerous problems exist such as excessive doctor workloads, disgruntled patients, and disorganized facilities where staff members spend hours looking for essential equipment [3]. The rise of "informed patients," who reject passive treatment, is another significant issue. They expect greater details and a vote during treatment [24]. To be able to transform their facilities into "smart hospitals," which will enable them to handle the pandemic and center their offerings on the patient, numerous healthcare facilities have already turned to healthcare technology businesses [23].

The main contributions of this chapter are as follows:

1. A new method is defined to implement smart hospitals.
2. This method involves a layered approach using 5G.
3. Comfort and convenience can be improved through this method.
4. A detailed description of this framework is provided.
5. As a result, we can observe that 5G can support high-resolution medical imaging and diagnostic tools.

1.1.1 Exploring the Concept of Smart Hospitals

Smart hospitals are designed to leverage optimized and automated processes based on the information and communication technology (ICT) environment to improve current patient care methods and introduce new features at a minimal cost [3]. Data and technology are used by smart hospitals to increase patient care and operational efficiency. They work in a setting that is highly optimized and automated. These healthcare facilities use data analytics, artificial Intelligence (AI), 5G, and linked equipment. Each hospital will have different designs and common functions for its smart room, but they all enhance patient experience, expedite the clinical process, and promote collaboration.

The patients are clients and should receive personalized attention from healthcare facilities, which serve as the basis for smart hospitals. Since the word "customer" connotes a more engaged and exacting consumer, astute hospitals try their hardest to provide a distinctive experience rather than only concentrate on medical care. They even provide their services to the carers of their patients. For example, a health librarian employed by Stanford Hospital will assist family members [2].

1.1.2 Working of Smart Hospitals

A crowded hospital has many moving components such as patients, hospital employees, medicine, and medical equipment. Artificial intelligence automation offers a chance to streamline the operations throughout the institution. Even while a patient cannot always have a doctor or nurse by their side, patients can be closely monitored by a mix of smart sensors and intelligent video analytics, which can notify medical professionals when a patient is in distress and needs care. For example, patients in an intensive care unit (ICU) are linked to monitoring equipment that takes their vital signs continuously. Many of these beep repeatedly with different alerts, which occasionally causes medical professionals to miss the alarm from a single sensor. The smart hospital can be compared to an octopus. The secure server of the organization, which houses and manages all the facility's data, serves as its brain. Every department within its tentacles—radiology lab, ICU, emergency room (ER), and operating room, for example—is covered in sensors, or "octopus' suckers," that gather information from their environment. It would be impossible for the octopus to respond quickly throughout its entire body based on information sensed by a single arm if each tentacle functioned independently. The octopus can adapt to its changing surroundings because each tentacle relays data back to the central brain.

Similar to this, the smart hospital is a hub-and-spoke system with sensors placed throughout the building that may relay important information back to a central hub, assisting in the making of choices that affect the entire facility. Artificial intelligence would notify personnel in the recovery room to get ready for the patient's arrival, for example, if video feeds in the operating room indicate that a surgical procedure is almost finished.

Medical device companies, academic medical centers, and startups are using an end-to-end AI platform that integrates with the entire hospital network to power smart hospital solutions. This platform powers everything from medical devices running real-time applications to secure servers that store and process data over an extended period. It is compatible with several software libraries, cloud, edge, and data center infrastructure, as well as international partner ecosystem. Data are compiled by smart hospitals using intricately linked systems. The different systems like lighting, climate control, and shading are combined in one infrastructure (total room automation) at the ward level, where integration begins. Smart hospitals are patient-focused establishments that exchange data with other organizations and are integrated into an ecosystem. Programmers for healthcare management are offered in a variety of settings within this ecosystem, such as patient homes and gyms. Hospitals are generally designed to handle sophisticated treatments, such as critical care and surgery. Technology-wise, smart hospitals use the Internet of Things (IoT) and employ a variety of new technologies such as big data analytics, 5G, AI, augmented reality (AR), and cloud platforms. The architecture of smart hospitals is shown in Figure 1.1.

1.2 Implementation of Smart Hospitals

The implementation of 5G in smart hospitals involves the integration of 5G technology across various layers and devices of the healthcare system. The key aspects of how 5G is implemented in smart hospitals are given here:

1. 5G Healthcare Terminals

   Medically Integrated Terminals: These serve as a gateway to 5G access, enabling medical devices without the inbuilt 5G capability to access the 5G-based healthcare dedicated network.

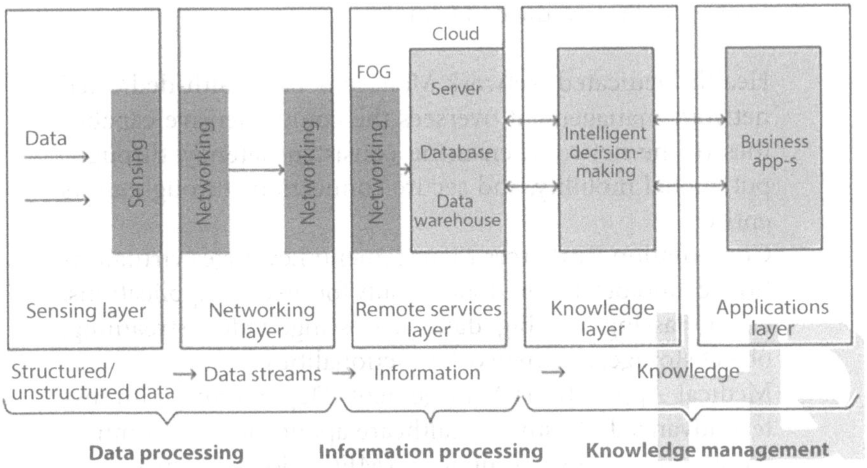

Figure 1.1 Architecture of smart hospitals [15].

Information Collection and Display Terminals: These include wearable devices, smart boxes, video terminals, first-aid kits, and imaging equipment, which gather and display data.
Auxiliary Terminals: Modern devices like ambulances, robots, and drones enhance the flexibility and efficiency of remote medical services.

2. 5G Healthcare-Dedicated Network

Network Slicing: A specialized 5G network designed for healthcare purposes employs network slicing, enabling the establishment of distinct virtual medical networks on a shared physical infrastructure. These slices are customized to meet various application needs within the healthcare sector.
Dedicated UPF: A dedicated UPF facilitates the seamless transmission of medical data between healthcare-specific terminals and the cloud infrastructure dedicated to healthcare services.
Multi-Access Edge Computation (MEC) Technology: Ensures efficient low-latency processing for healthcare applications by enabling computation at the network's edge.

3. 5G Healthcare-Dedicated Cloud

   Health-Dedicated Network Management: Health-dedicated network management oversees the comprehensive capabilities of the network, ensuring consistent latency, throughput, global mobility, and secure connections throughout its entirety.
   Computation Resources Management: Leverages virtualization technology tailored specifically for medical applications, encompassing AI, big data processing, video streaming, object storage, and network functionalities.
   Medical Applications Management: Deploys and administers advanced 5G smart healthcare applications, accommodating mobile edge computing (MEC) alongside private or alternative cloud architectures.

4. 5G Healthcare Applications

   5G Basic Applications: Showcase the experience of 5G in improving hospital production efficiency and transmission capacities.
   Medical Applications: This builds a full-scenario, smart medical service ecosystem, covering all the components like smart hospitals, telemedicine, and emergency rescue applications under various medical scenarios.

5. Healthcare Dedicated Network Architecture

   Local Healthcare Dedicated Network (LHDN): Facilitates wireless surgery, medical handcart operations, service robots, and seamless data sharing within the hospital premises, enhancing intra-hospital medical services.
   Wide-Area Healthcare Dedicated Network (WHDN): Facilitates broad-scale interconnectivity among multiple hospitals, enabling remote diagnosis, surgery, inspections, checkups, and collaborative efforts across distant locations.
   Dynamic Healthcare Dedicated Network (DHDN): Responds to medical requirements beyond hospital settings, including 5G ambulances, drones, home medical care, and

remote consultations, through dynamic adjustments of network slicing to accommodate various needs effectively.

6. Healthcare-Dedicated Cloud Integrating with Network and Existing Medical Systems

   Integration with Health-Dedicated Network: This takes the help of the industry gateway for cloud-network integration, supporting authentication to access, controlling of network, data transmission, and wide-area interconnection.
   Integration with Existing Medical Systems: Implements a strategy for the mutual existence of 5G and traditional hospital information infrastructures, allowing gradual migration of applications to 5G.

7. Unified Platform Management Layer: Manages the life cycle, status monitoring, access authority, and self-service resource management of the 5G healthcare dedicated cloud.

Overall, the implementation of 5G in smart hospitals shown in Figure 1.2 involves creating a seamless, efficient, and flexible ecosystem that leverages the capabilities of 5G technology for improved healthcare services to patients.

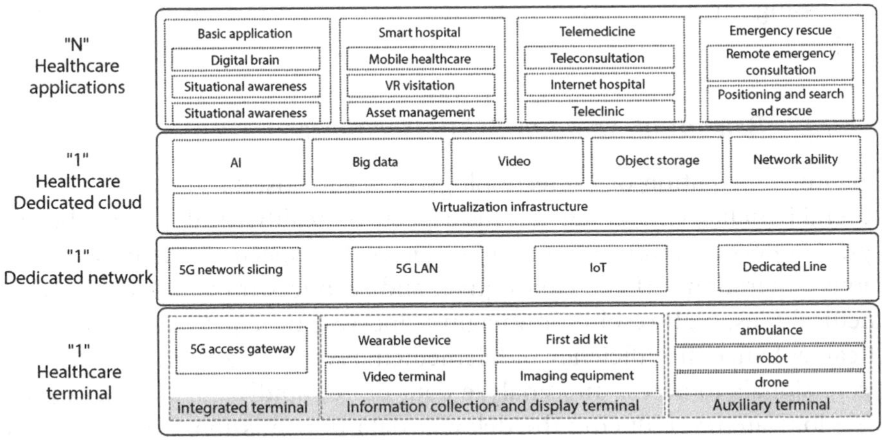

Figure 1.2 Implementation of smart hospitals using 5G [16].

1.2.1 Benefits of Smart Hospitals

In the past few years, the healthcare industry has witnessed a transformative shift with the advent of smart hospitals innovative healthcare facilities that make use of the power of connectivity and intelligence to increase the efficiency of patient care, streamline operations, and enhance overall efficiency. The benefits of smart hospitals extend across various dimensions, reshaping the landscape of healthcare delivery. This introduction aims to highlight the key benefits of smart hospitals, showcasing the profound impact they have on both patient outcomes and healthcare system dynamics.

1.2.1.1 Benefits of Implementing IoT in Healthcare

Enhanced patient comfort and convenience are achieved through IoT technologies, leading to heightened patient satisfaction and quicker recovery times. Healthcare professionals utilize IoT devices and data for efficient patient monitoring and optimal therapy delivery [18–20]. Furthermore, IoT security systems ensure the safety of patients, doctors, and hospital staff [21]. Sanitization through UV lights maintains a clean environment, promoting overall health [22]. Telemedicine, as defined by the International Society for Telemedicine and eHealth, utilizes information and communication technology to deliver healthcare services, facilitating accurate data sharing among physicians for improved diagnosis, treatment, and prevention of diseases and injuries. Telemedicine offers a solution for the complexity of patient records and helps reduce patient travel costs while addressing emergency care challenges faced by rural healthcare clinics [23].

1.2.1.2 Benefits of Adopting 5G in Healthcare

The implementation of 5G technology in smart hospitals can bring about several benefits, enhancing various aspects of healthcare delivery. The 5G system offers a significant amount of faster data speeds compared to previous generations. This enables quick and seamless transmission of large medical files, high resolution imaging, and real-time patient monitoring. It can enhance the efficiency of telemedicine services, allowing healthcare professionals to access and analyze data more rapidly. 5G networks provide low latency, reducing the delay in data transmission. This is critical for applications that require real-time communication, such as remote surgery to the patient, where even a slight delay can have serious consequences. Low latency is also beneficial for applications such as AR and virtual reality (VR) in medical training and education. With the increased capacity and connectivity of 5G networks, smart hospitals can seamlessly integrate a multitude of IoT devices and sensors. This enables the continuous monitoring of patients, medical equipment, and hospital facilities. The connectivity can also support the use of smart wearables for patient monitoring and management of chronic conditions. 5G facilitates more comprehensive and real-time remote patient monitoring. This is particularly beneficial for patients who are dealing with chronic conditions, allowing healthcare providers to monitor vital signs and other health metrics remotely. This can lead to early detection of potential issues, reducing the need for hospital admissions and improving overall patient outcomes. The high data speeds and low latency of 5G enable the healthcare providers to process and analyze a huge amount of patient data rapidly. This can contribute to the advancement of precision medicine by tailoring treatment plans based on individual patient characteristics and genetic makeup. Big data analytics can also help identify patterns and trends in health data for better disease management and prevention strategies. Networks come with improved security features, including advanced encryption and authentication protocols. This is crucial in healthcare settings where the privacy and security of patient data are of utmost importance. Robust security measures can help protect sensitive medical information from unauthorized access and cyber threats. 5G can support the use of advanced imaging technologies, such as high-resolution medical imaging and diagnostic tools. This can lead to more accurate and timely diagnoses, improving the overall quality of healthcare services.

5G networks are designed to accommodate the increasing demands of emerging technologies. As new healthcare innovations and technologies continue to evolve, the scalability and adaptability of 5G make it well-suited to support future advancements in smart hospitals.

1.2.2 Challenges of Smart Hospitals

Smart hospitals hold immense promise for revolutionizing healthcare delivery through the integration of connectivity and intelligence, but they are not without their set of challenges. The journey toward implementing and sustaining a smart hospital ecosystem is marked by obstacles that span technological, organizational, and ethical dimensions. While the implementation of 5G in smart hospitals offers numerous benefits, there are also challenges and considerations that need to be addressed. This introduction outlines some of the key challenges faced by smart hospitals as they strive to redefine healthcare in the digital age.

Challenges encountered in implementing the Internet of Medical Things (IoMT) network designs within smart hospitals include:

1. Body Movements: Patient movements can alter the topology of the body sensing network (BSN), requiring IoMT routing protocols capable of adapting to such changes while maintaining communication quality [13].
2. Temperature Fluctuations: Absorption of radiation by antennas and power consumption by node circuitry can elevate the temperature of IoMT devices. Elevated temperatures in wearables or implants can damage patient cells or organs, necessitating consideration of device power consumption.
3. Energy Efficiency: The lifespan, usability, and size of IoMT devices are contingent upon energy efficiency. Routing protocols should optimize device energy consumption, aiming for a battery life of 10 – 15 years for implant devices to minimize the need for repetitive surgeries and avoid associated physical and financial burdens. Frequent battery changes for wearable devices decrease device utilization.
4. Transmission Range: Short data transmission ranges can result in sensor node disconnections due to patient postural movements within the IoMT system [14].
5. Heterogeneous Environments: Data from various sensors within IoMT systems are heterogeneous, requiring routing protocols capable of managing the diverse environment of BSN applications, such as the Dexter Net.
6. Quality of Service (QoS): Real-time BSN applications, such as ECG monitoring, demand increased QoS to address time-critical situations and sensitivity to data loss effectively.
7. Security: Cloud storage of user data enables doctors' accurate and prompt responses to remotely monitored patients. However, this advancement poses the risk of user data being vulnerable to hacking or misuse.

Challenges faced in implementing 5G are as follows:

1. Infrastructure Costs: Upgrading to 5G requires significant investment in new infrastructure, including the installation

of 5G base stations and antennas. The initial costs of deploying 5G networks can be substantial, and healthcare organizations may need to allocate resources for these infrastructure upgrades [10].

2. Security Concerns: As with any advanced technology, 5G networks may pose security challenges. The increased connectivity and reliance on IoT devices in smart hospitals create more potential entry points for cyber threats. Ensuring robust cybersecurity measures is crucial to protect patient data and the integrity of healthcare systems.
3. Interoperability Issues: Integrating 5G technology with existing healthcare systems and devices can be complex. Ensuring interoperability between different medical devices, electronic health record (EHR) systems, and other hospital infrastructure is essential for a seamless and efficient operation. Standardization efforts are needed to address these interoperability challenges [11].
4. Regulatory Compliance: Healthcare is a highly regulated industry, and the deployment of 5G in smart hospitals must comply with various regulations related to patient privacy, data security, and healthcare standards. Adhering to these regulations while implementing new technologies can be a complex process.
5. Privacy Concerns: The increased use of IoT devices and sensors for patient monitoring and data collection raises concerns about patient privacy. Healthcare providers must implement robust privacy policies and mechanisms to safeguard patient information and ensure compliance with data protection regulations [12].
6. Health Concerns: There have been public discussions about potential health effects associated with exposure to electromagnetic fields (EMFs) from 5G technology. While scientific studies generally indicate that 5G technology is safe, addressing public concerns and ensuring transparent communication about the technology's safety is important.
7. Data Management and Storage: The high-speed data transfer capabilities of 5G generate large volumes of data in smart hospitals. Managing, storing, and analyzing this massive amount of data can strain existing IT infrastructure and require investments in advanced data storage and processing capabilities.

8. Workforce Training and Education: The adoption of 5G in smart hospitals necessitates training healthcare professionals to effectively use new technologies. Ongoing education is essential to ensure that staff can leverage the full potential of 5G and associated technologies for improved patient care.
9. Limited Coverage: While 5G networks are expanding, there may still be areas with limited 5G coverage. Smart hospitals in remote or underserved areas may face challenges in accessing the full benefits of 5G technology until coverage becomes more widespread.
10. Spectrum Allocation: The availability of suitable radiofrequency spectrum is crucial for 5G deployment. Issues related to spectrum allocation and interference can impact the performance of 5G networks in certain locations.

Addressing these challenges requires collaboration between healthcare providers, technology vendors, regulatory bodies, and other stakeholders. As technology continues to evolve, ongoing efforts are essential to overcome these challenges and fully realize the potential of 5G in smart hospitals.

1.2.3 Opportunities

In 2016, the smart hospital market was valued at $13.52 billion, and it is projected to reach $63.49 billion by 2023, reflecting a remarkable compound annual growth rate of 24.00% from 2017 to 2023 [25]. This market is categorized based on wireless connectivity, application types, services offered, service components, technology types, and geographic regions [25]. Smart hospitals must integrate smart hardware, software, and related technologies to optimize their operations. These technologies encompass smart mobility and systems for patients, staff, and equipment. Key technological drivers for smart hospitals include blockchain, biotelemetry, 5G and 6G technologies, drug development, precision medicine based on genomics and big data, and virtual rehabilitation in orthopedics [1]. The smart hardware component comprises WIFI, active radio frequency identification (RFID), IoT sensors, wearables, dashboards, and 5G networking, among others. Factors propelling the growth of the smart hospital market involve the increasing demand for healthcare infrastructure modernization, efficient solutions in hospitals, advancements in IoT technologies in healthcare, rising incidence of chronic diseases, and the expanding use of connected devices and instruments in hospital settings [25]. The integration of the Internet of Health Things (IoHT) and 5G technology, with their intelligent devices, equipment, applications, and buildings, holds significant promise for enhancing smart hospitals [17]. This integration improves healthcare delivery efficiency and cost-effectiveness by optimizing asset utilization. The current utilization of information technology in healthcare stands to benefit greatly from the incorporation of 5G technologies. The integration of 5G technology in smart hospitals presents a myriad of opportunities to revolutionize healthcare delivery and elevate patient outcomes. This advancement enables high-speed, low-latency communication, fostering the expansion of telemedicine services and facilitating real-time video consultations and remote monitoring, particularly benefiting those in remote or underserved areas. With enhanced connectivity and low latency, smart hospitals can implement advanced remote patient monitoring systems, continuously tracking vital signs for patients with chronic conditions. The capabilities of 5G, such as low latency and high bandwidth, support groundbreaking enhancements in surgical procedures, including advanced robotic surgery and real-time collaboration among experts in different locations. The improved connectivity of 5G also allows for seamless integration of IoT devices and wearables, enabling the collection of valuable data for patient health monitoring and preventive care. Additionally, 5G's low latency and high data speeds make it conducive to immersive experiences like AR and VR in healthcare, applicable to medical training, surgical simulations, and patient education. The rapid transfer and analysis of large datasets facilitated by 5G contribute to the implementation of big data analytics and predictive medicine, empowering healthcare providers to make informed, data-driven decisions for improved patient outcomes. The technology also supports real-time smart imaging and diagnostics, enhancing the accuracy of medical imaging and expediting the interpretation of results. Beyond clinical applications, 5G improves hospital operations by enabling smart technologies for asset tracking, inventory management, and facility monitoring, resulting in streamlined workflows, reduced costs, and optimal resource utilization. Furthermore, the increased connectivity and data transfer capabilities contribute to the advancement of personalized and precision medicine, allowing healthcare providers to tailor treatment plans based on patient-specific data, including genetic information. Smart hospitals with 5G can enhance the overall patient experience through technologies like virtual health assistants, smart patient rooms, and interactive portals, fostering patient engagement and participation in their own care. In summary, the deployment of 5G in smart hospitals signifies a transformative shift, offering a comprehensive and efficient approach to healthcare services while driving innovation in the industry. These opportunities collectively contribute to the evolution of healthcare systems, promoting efficiency, personalization, and accessibility in patient care.

1.3 Literature Review

In this section, a literature review on different approaches adapted by different authors is discussed.

Anuj Raghav and Paliwal [1] introduced a comprehensive conceptual framework for smart architecture, emphasizing energy conservation and security/interoperability. Central to their approach is the building management system (BMS), a multi-layered design consisting of cameras and end-of-system components at the field layer, middleware for the integration of physical and cyber systems, and the efficient management layer for decision-making based on intelligent network insights. In addressing security and interoperability, Raghav *et al.* leveraged IoT technologies, employing a hybrid network architecture that blends star and mesh topologies. Each floor and room feature sensor and actuator networks (Internet protocol version 6 over low-power wireless personal area networks: 6LoWPANs) linked to microcontrollers. These microcontrollers collect data from network nodes, transmitting it to gateways through IPv6 connections. Gateways, comprising local databases and routers, then relay the data to remote cloud platforms. The cloud platform, housing a database and server, serves as the ultimate destination for data storage and analysis. This system enhances a hospital's energy efficiency while ensuring a robust security framework through interconnected IoT technologies.

Arun Kumar *et al.* [2] advocated for the implementation of MicroStation technology to address the high data rates, ranges from 112 Mbps to 1.8 Gbps, required for medical applications like remote surgery and emergency clinic. The MicroStation includes microcells, femtocells, and picocells, which function as small cells compared to large-scale cells. Femtocells enhance coverage and capacity in confined spaces, while picocells extend wireless coverage in small areas. Microcells, similar to picocells, differ in coverage area and support more users. These small cells increase area range efficiency through higher frequency reuse. The architecture incorporates body area networks (BANs) comprising IoT devices to monitor health parameters. Due to the growing reliance on connected medical devices, the risk of cyberattacks on patient data transmission increases. Patient data from BANs are transmitted to macro base stations (MBS) in three scenarios: directly through a millimeter (mm) link backhaul if the BAN is close to MBS, via MBS transmission line if the BAN is far, and through small base stations (SBS) if the BAN is much farther. The MBS, equipped with smart antennas and 5G technology, uses massive multiple input multiple output (MIMO) for efficient data transfer to the 5G network, which is directly linked to a central data center. The data center stores and analyzes all patient information to provide accurate outputs to users. This comprehensive system ensures the secure and efficient transmission of medical data for improved healthcare outcomes.

Abdul Ahad *et al.* [3] presented a comprehensive 5G-based smart healthcare architecture incorporating key enabler technologies such as advanced MIMO, software-defined networking (SDN), device-to-device (D2D) communication, mm waves, small cells, network functions virtualization (NFV), and edge computing. Addressing security concerns, the system focuses on authentication, confidentiality, availability, nonrepudiation, and integrity. Given the high data rates demanded by smart healthcare applications, small cells, including femtocells, picocells, and microcells, are utilized to enhance capacity and coverage in limited areas. Security measures include primary and secondary authentication for mutual verification between medical devices and networks, with primary authentication supporting non-3G partnership project (3GPP) technologies. Confidentiality is ensured through key generation and exchange, involving the master base node (MeNB) and secondary next-generation base node (SgNB), providing privacy and authenticity for radio resource control (RRC) messages and user plane (UP) data. The incorporation of these components is intended to fulfill the data transfer speed needs of sophisticated healthcare applications, all the while ensuring the network's resilience against possible security risks and attacks.

In the development of smart hospitals, Suganthi *et al.* [4] employed IoMT and introduced an innovative approach. The system was organized into three main facets: the patient side, nurse side, and doctor side. On the patient side, various sensors, including a temperature sensor for room temperature control, an ultrasonic sensor for monitoring saline levels in a Trips bottle, and a light- dependent resistor (LDR) for light monitoring, were integrated. The sensor data were directly transmitted to a universal serial bus (USB), which served as the conduit for transmitting data to the Arduino Circuit. The collected data were then formatted using MQ telemetry transport (MQTT), a crucial element for data subscription awareness. The MQTT played a pivotal role in managing electronic devices such as fans. The doctors received sensor data through an Android application connected to the server, and prescriptions were sent from the server to the patients via Android Apps. All these data transfers were facilitated through the WIFI module. Subsequently, the acquired data were uploaded to the doctors' app, aiding in the administration of patient treatment. The prescribed medication from the doctor was then dispatched to the patients by the nurse, completing the integrated healthcare system.

A system developed by Aditi Khekale *et al.* [5] operates exclusively on IoT and a WIFI module, which serves the dual purpose of keeping patient information up to date. This module enables prompt actions by doctors and hospital staff based on the patient's condition, allowing for immediate medical interventions. The initial component includes a fan, light, and ultrasonic sensor that gather patient data, transmitting it to an Arduino mega (ATMEGA Atmel328PU) integrated with an Ethernet shield (W5100) via USB. An essential intermediary in this setup is the web server, which acts as a bridge between users and the Arduino. The server's primary functions include storing, processing, and delivering web pages to users through the hypertext transfer protocol (HTTP). These pages primarily consist of HTML documents containing images, style sheets, and scripts. In cases of high website traffic, multiple servers may be employed. The sensors generate data, transmitted to the Arduino mega board via USB, and then forwarded to the server using the WIFI module. To monitor the received data, individuals need to subscribe to the web server, allowing hospital staff to oversee the information. The web platform is utilized for switch control, managing electrical appliances and lighting. If the room temperature surpasses a predetermined level, the data are sent to the webpage, where it can be accessed either from the webpage itself or a mobile device [26].

This paper by Jyoti Srivastava *et al.* [6] summarized the vision of IoMT, a framework based on smart healthcare system, designed in different stages. The first stage is to gather real-time data from patients using various digital electronic devices like smart watches or implemented devices connected using a BSN or wireless sensor network (WSN). The second stage focuses on transferring data from a BSN to remote center over the Internet for future analysis. The help of AI-based data transmission and interpretation technique is employed, but in case of serious situations, healthcare professionals or other medical necessities can be alerted through AI-based applications on smartphones [25]. For less critical cases, patients can implement self-preventive measures.

Bingwen Zhou and Zhang [7] presented a smart medical framework that uses the advantages of resource integration and provide real-time health and medical services. The smart framework consists of the software, business, and hardware frameworks. Their idea is to keep all medical resources in the cloud. Patients can benefit from various medical services through the platform integrated with the help of medical institutions; they provide accurate medical-records editing services for patients through the same platform. From a business perspective, they provide online outpatient services. Patients can register an online appointment and pay in advance from this platform. Telemedicine service is designed for users in areas with underdeveloped medical facilities. Based on the symptoms, patients can consult doctors by text chatting. Doctors will then confirm the time of online diagnosis and treatment time.

Naik *et al.* [8] introduced a groundbreaking initiative in the realm of Diabetes 2.0 expenditure targeting the average user. They have proposed a 5G-Smart Diabetes application, representing an intelligent and cost-effective solution for diabetes diagnosis that ensures easy accessibility for users. This innovative approach capitalizes on 5G technologies, incorporating elements such as smart textiles, AI models, and the analysis of medical data [27]. The primary objective is to deliver a reliable detection and analysis platform for individuals dealing with diabetes. In their comprehensive study, the authors also outlined a data exchange mechanism among patients and introduced a personalized model utilizing medical data specifically tailored for the 5G-smart Diabetes application. The culmination of their efforts resulted in the development of a prototype system, consisting of smart textiles, smartphones, and medical data clouds. The research findings indicate the system's effectiveness in successfully providing personalized diagnostic and therapeutic assistance to patients, showcasing the potential of the 5G-Smart Diabetes initiative in enhancing the overall management of diabetes.

J. Lloret *et al.* [9] stressed the critical importance of 5G technologies for real-time patient monitoring. They highlight that the deployment of 5G networks is essential due to their ability to provide low latency and ensure sufficient bandwidths for all users. The suggested system architecture comprises distinct elements, including wearable technology equipped with sensors for gathering body measurements. A smartphone positioned next to the patient processes the data obtained from the wearable technology. Additionally, there is a database incorporating a smart engine for diagnosis, which triggers alarms using machine learning algorithms applied to extensive big data sourced from diverse hospitals and patient records. Table 1.1 shows the comparison of the survey on smart hospitals.

Table 1.1 A comparison of the survey on smart hospitals.

Authors	Methodology	Limitations	Accuracy
Anuj Raghav and Paliwal [1]	It uses building management system (BMS) and IoT technologies like star and mesh topologies along with sensors, actuators, and microcontrollers. For analytics and data storage, they used cloud environment.	High cost, and implementation and maintenance are difficult.	85%
Arun Kumar *et al.* [2]	They used IoT gadgets, massive multiple input and multiple output (MIMO) integrated smart antenna, wire backhaul, mm link backhauls, and radio wires.	Valid system integration, significant latency, limited range, and data speed issues, and elevated expenses.	73%
Abdul Ahad *et al.* [3]	This approach encompasses the utilization of edge computing, device-to-device (D2D) communication, sophisticated multiple-input and multiple-output (MIMO) technology, software-defined networking (SDN), millimeter waves (mm waves), non-orthogonal multiple access (NOMA), network function virtualization (NFV), and small cells.	High cost, limitations in resources, susceptibility to a single-point-of-failure, and restricted scalability.	77%
Suganthi *et al.* [4]	Combination of various sensors like temperature, ultra-sonic, heart-beat sensor, and blood pressure sensors along with LDR to acquire data from patients. Arduino UNO (ATMEGA328) for Processing with WIFI module.	Limited scalability, single-point-of-failure, no security provided.	65%
Aditi Khekale *et al.* [5]	This method uses various sensors like temperature, ultra-sonic, heart-beat sensors and Arduino mega (ATMEGA Atmel328U) +Ethernet shield (W5100), WIFI module.	Availability is low. The model is not robust. No security provided.	57%

(*Continued*)

Table 1.1 A comparison of the survey on smart hospitals. (*Continued*)

Authors	Methodology	Limitations	Accuracy
Jyoti Srivastava *et al.* [6]	Uses various sensors, BSN, WSN, or RFID.	Continuous power supply is required. Implementation is difficult.	91%
Bingwen Zhou and Zhang [7]	This approach comprises MongoDB, web technologies, and cloud infrastructure.	Able to reach small regions only.	83%
Naik *et al.* [8]	They used cloud infrastructure, smart textiles, and artificial intelligence models	Limited scalability, single-point-of-failure, and high cost.	62%
J. Lloret *et al.* [9]	Combination of various sensors to measure different patient parameters, cloud facility, and web app technology.	Difficulty in maintenance	69%

The limitations of this research study are as follows:

1. There may be accessibility issues for certain regions, especially in rural areas or underserved areas with limited access to high-speed Internet or advanced facilities.
2. The integration of 5G technology across multiple layers and devices of the healthcare system adds complexity to the infrastructure.
3. Ensuring seamless communication and data exchange between different devices can be challenging.
4. Protecting sensitive patient data and ensuring the security of medical devices connected to the 5G network is crucial.
5. The healthcare system must adhere to strict regulations and compliance standards to ensure patient safety and privacy.
6. Implementing terminals, networks, and cloud systems can be expensive.

1.4 Conclusion

In conclusion, the integration of 5G technology and IoT in smart hospitals has revolutionized healthcare delivery. Smart hospitals, leveraging connectivity and intelligence, offer a myriad of benefits that reshape patient care and operational efficiency. The implementation of 5G technology enables faster data transmission, seamless connectivity, and low latency, enhancing telemedicine services, and real-time patient monitoring. The adoption of IoT in healthcare within smart hospitals has significantly improved patient comfort, safety, and physician capabilities. The IoT devices, wearable technologies, and data access have contributed to higher patient satisfaction, faster recovery times, and safer environments. The use of IoT security support systems and UV light sanitation systems has also enhanced safety measures within healthcare facilities. Furthermore, telemedicine, facilitated by IoT, has played a crucial role in overcoming barriers for rural healthcare clinics, providing accurate data sharing for prevention, diagnosis, and treatment of diseases, while reducing patient travel costs. Moreover, the transformative shift toward smart hospitals has had a profound impact on patient outcomes and healthcare system dynamics. The combination of 5G technology and IoT has not only improved the efficiency of telemedicine services but has also facilitated quick and seamless transmission of large medical files and high-resolution imaging. This technological advancement marks a significant milestone in the healthcare industry, emphasizing the crucial role of connectivity and intelligence in enhancing patient care and overall operational effectiveness.

References

1. Anuj Raghav, and Mrinal Paliwal "*An Overview of Inter-Connectivity and Security in a Smart Hospital Building*", February 2022, India.
2. Arun Kumar, R. Dhanagopal, Mahmoud A. Albreem, Dac-Nhuong Le "*A comprehensive study on the role of advanced technologies in 5G based smart hospital*", 2 April 2021.
3. Abdul Ahad, Zahra Ali, Abdul Mateen, Mohammad Tahir, Abdul Hannan, Nuno M. Garcia, Ivan Miguel Pires "*A Comprehensive review on 5G-based Smart Healthcare Network Security: Taxonomy, Issues, Solutions and Future research directions*", 3 May 2023.
4. S.T Suganthi, Arangarajan Vinayagam, Veerapandiyan Veerasamy, A. Deepa, Mohamed Abouhawwash, Mariammal Thirumeni, Detection and classification of multiple power quality disturbances in Microgrid network using probabilistic based intelligent classifier, *Sustain. Energy Technol. Assess.*, Volume 47, 2021, 101470, https://doi.org/10.1016/j.seta.2021.101470.
5. Aditi Khekale, Piyush Anjankar, Jagdish Pimple "*Implementation of Smart Hospital Using Internet of Things for Healthcare System*", 5, May-2018, India.

6. Jyoti Srivastava, Sidheswar Routray, Sultan Ahmad "*Internet of Medical Things (IoMT)-Based Smart Healthcare System: Trends and Progress*", 16 July 2022, India.
7. Bingwen ZHOUa and Xiaohua ZHANG "*Hospital Information Platform Based on Internet and Intelligent Treatment*", China.
8. Ramachandra Naik, S.C. Prashantha, H. Nagabhushana, S.C. Sharma, H.P. Nagaswarupa, K.S. Anantharaju, B.M. Nagabhushana, H.B. Premkumar, K.M. Girish, A single phase, red emissive Mg2SiO4:Sm3+ nanophosphor prepared via rapid propellant combustion route, *Spectrochim. Acta, Part A*, Volume 140, 2015, Pages 516-523, https://doi.org/10.1016/j.saa.2015.01.011.
9. J. Lloret, L. Parra, M. Taha, and J. Tomás, "*An architecture and protocol for smart continuous eHealth monitoring using 5G*", May 2017, Spain.
10. S. Akshatha, S. Sreenivasa, L. Parashuram, V. Udaya Kumar, S.C. Sharma, H. Nagabhushana, Sandeep Kumar, T. Maiyalagan, Synergistic effect of hybrid Ce3+/Ce4+ doped Bi2O3 nano-sphere photocatalyst for enhanced photocatalytic degradation of alizarin red S dye and its NUV excited photoluminescence studies, *J. Environ. Chem. Eng.*, Volume 7, Issue 3, 2019.
11. Ramachandra Naik, S.C. Prashantha, H. Nagabhushana, Effect of Li+ codoping on structural and luminescent properties of Mg2SiO4:RE3+ (RE = Eu, Tb) nanophosphors for displays and eccrine latent fingerprint detection, *Opt. Mater.*, Volume 72, 2017, Pages 295-304, https://doi.org/10.1016/j.optmat.2017.06.021.
12. Mohd Javaid, Abid Haleem, Ravi Pratap Singh, Rajiv Suman "*5G technology for healthcare: Features, serviceable pillars, and*", December 2023, India.
13. Sebastian MP, "*Smart Hospitals: Challenges and Opportunities*", March 2019, India.
14. Fatimah Al-Jawad, Raghad Alessa, Sukainah Alhammad, Batoola Ali, Majd Al-Qanbar and Atta-ur-Rahman, "*Applications of 5G and 6G in Smart Health Services*", March 2022, Saudi Arabia.
15. Banu Çalı¸s Uslu, Ertug Okay and Erkan Dursun, "*Analysis of factors affecting IoT-based smart hospital design.*"
16. Hora SK, Poongodan R, de Prado RP, Wozniak M, Divakarachari PB. Long Short-Term Memory Network-Based Metaheuristic for Effective Electric Energy Consumption Prediction. *Appl. Sci.*, 2021; 11(23):11263. https://doi.org/10.3390/app112311263.
17. G. Ramakrishna, Ramachandra Naik, H. Nagabhushana, R.B. Basavaraj, S.C. Prashantha, S.C. Sharma, K.S. Anantharaju, White light emission and energy transfer (Dy3+→Eu3+) in combustion synthesized YSO: Dy3+, Eu3+ nanophosphors, *Optik*, Volume 127, Issue 5, 2016,Pages 2939-2945, https://doi.org/10.1016/j.ijleo.2015.11.234.
18. https://itrexgroup.com/blog/smart-hospitals-market-overview-trends-considerations/.
19. https://iimk.ac.in/uploads/publications/3052smartHospitals_MPS2019.pdf.

20. S. Akshatha, S. Sreenivasa, L. Parashuram, V. Udaya Kumar, S.C. Sharma, H. Nagabhushana, Sandeep Kumar, T. Maiyalagan, Synergistic effect of hybrid $Ce3+/Ce4+$ doped $Bi2O3$ nano-sphere photocatalyst for enhanced photocatalytic degradation of alizarin red S dye and its NUV excited photoluminescence studies, *J. Environ. Chem. Eng.*, Volume 7, Issue 3, 2019.
21. Arun Kumar, Aziz Nanthaamornphong, R. Selvi, J. Venkatesh, MohammedH. Alsharif, Peerapong Uthansakul, Monthippa Uthansakul, "*Evaluation of 5G techniques affecting the deployment of smart hospital infrastructure: Understanding 5G, AI and IoT role in smart hospital*", November 2023.
22. A. Kumar, M. A. Albreem, M. Gupta, M. H. Alsharif and S. Kim, "Future 5G Network Based Smart Hospitals: Hybrid Detection Technique for Latency Improvement," in *IEEE Access*, vol. 8, pp. 153240-153249, 2020, doi: 10.1109/ACCESS.2020.3017625.
23. *A comprehensive study on the role of advanced technologies in 5G based smart hospital Author links open overlay panel* Arun Kumar, R. Dhanagopal, Mahmoud A. Albreem, Dac-Nhuong Le, December 2021.
24. *Evaluation of 5G techniques affecting the deployment of smart hospital infrastructure: Understanding 5G, AI and IoT role in smart hospital* Author links open overlay panel Arun Kumar, Aziz Nanthaamornphong, R. Selvi, J. Venkatesh, Mohammed H. Alsharif, Peerapong Uthansakul, Monthippa Uthansakul, November 2023.
25. *5G-Based Smart Hospitals and Healthcare Systems Evaluation, Integration, and Deployment*. Edited By Arun Kumar, Sumit Chakravarty, Aravinda K, Mohit Kumar Sharma.
26. *Analysis of FBMC Waveform for 5G Network Based Smart Hospitals*, Balamurali Ramakrishnan, Arun Kumar, Sumit Chakravarty, Mehedi Masud, Mohammed Baz.
27. *Analysis of Hybrid Spectrum Sensing for 5G and 6G Waveforms*, Arun Kumar, J Venkatesh, Nishant Gaur, Mohammed H. Alsharif, Abu Jahid, Kannadasan Raju.

2

Evolution of 5G and 6G Cellular Systems

Kama Ramudu[1]*, Bodla Rushikesh[1], Pingili Shiva Chandana[1], B. Jagadish Kumar[2] and Venkat Tulasi Krishna Gannavaram[3]

[1]Department of ECE, Kakatiya Institute of Technology and Science, Warangal, India
[2]Department of EEE, Kakatiya Institute of Technology and Science, Warangal, India
[3]School of Electrical, Computer and Energy Engineering, Arizona State University, Tempe, United States

Abstract
The evolution of cellular communication systems from 4G to 5G marked a significant leap in wireless technology, emphasizing enhanced mobile broadband, low latency communications, and massive machine type communications. Fifth-generation technology introduced advanced antenna technologies, network slicing, and spectrum innovations to meet the demands of emerging applications such as augmented reality and the Internet of Things. As the telecommunications landscape advances, the prospective trajectory towards 6G anticipates groundbreaking developments. While still in its early stages, 6G envisions terahertz communication, quantum technologies, and a seamless integration of artificial intelligence. This evolution aims for ubiquitous connectivity, sustainability, and novel applications like holographic communication and a bio-integrated connectivity. The abstract nature of 6G emphasizes the potential for transformative changes in wireless communication, fostering a future where connectivity becomes more immersive, intelligent, and integrated into everyday life.

Keywords: 5G and 6G cellular systems, enhanced mobile broadband, massive MIMO, IoT, AI

**Corresponding author*: ramudukama@@gmail.com; ORCID: 0000-0002-8585-9396

Arun Kumar, Manoj Gupta, Sanjeev Sharma, Er. Himanshu Sharma and Khursheed Aurangzeb (eds.) Smart Hospitals: 5G, 6G and Moving Beyond Connectivity, (23–44) © 2024 Scrivener Publishing LLC

2.1 Introduction

The Evolution of 5G and 6G Cellular Systems starts off evolved with an exploration of the background, tracing the historic trajectory of mobile era. History sets the level by means of elucidating the foundational shifts from 1G to the contemporary era of 5G and the emerging prospect of 6G. Commencing with the advent of 1G in the early 1980s, which liberated communiqué from stressed constraints, the heritage highlights the successive generations—2G, 3G, and 4G—every bringing pivotal improvements in virtual conversation. This adventure underscores the transformative impact of cell structures on international connectivity, shaping the way individuals communicate, work, and engage. The narrative then pivots to the progressive era of 5G, emphasizing the call for a driven need for higher data speeds, extremely low latency, and connectivity for an ever-growing array of devices. The history segment illuminates how 5G has ended up the linchpin of contemporary connectivity, fostering innovations in industries starting from healthcare to smart cities. As the discussion transitions in the direction of the burgeoning idea of 6G, history points at the demanding situations and possibilities that lie ahead. It invites readers to realize the non-stop evolution spurred by technological improvements, societal shifts, and the perpetual pursuit of extra efficient and shrewd communication systems. In essence, history provides a contextual framework, inviting readers to delve into the subsequent sections with the know-how of the interconnected evolution that has brought us to the cusp of 6G [1, 2].

"Evaluating 5G Techniques Affecting Deployment of Smart Hospital Infrastructure: Understanding the Role of 5G, AI, and IoT in Smart Hospital" begins with the growing importance of 5G, artificial intelligence (AI), and the Internet of Things (IoT) technologies that may transform the healthcare industry. These can emphasize the critical role of systems and the need for seamless integration of these technologies. The introduction may discuss the specific focus of the research, such as analyzing the impact of 5G strategies on smart hospital design strategies. It can also name the authors, indicating a concerted effort to explore the intersection of 5G, AI and IoT in healthcare, potentially establishing the methodology and key findings in [3].

With reference to [4], "Future 5G Network Based Smart Hospitals: Hybrid Detection Technique for Latency Improvement" can address the increasing importance of 5G networks in a smart hospital in addition to the challenge of latency in healthcare functionally and the need for innovative solutions to improve communication efficiency. A hybrid introduction program on the new concept of the delayed problems in the paper should be proposed to increase the 5G network intelligently and astronomically and for the cycle to increase in a real-time application of the latest low ground. Significant infrastructure exists for the provision of health services.

A comprehensive study of the role of advanced technologies in 5G-based smart hospitals can be opened by the increasing integration of advanced technologies in healthcare, especially in smart hospitals based on 5G. It can bring the transformative power of these technologies, such as AI, IoT and 5G, to transform healthcare. The introduction may outline the scope of the research, aiming to provide a comprehensive review of how this technology can improve patient care, enhance surgical outcomes, and improve overall health care outcomes in smart hospitals. This may indicate the methodology and significant contribution in the research work [5] to healthcare technology and management.

"Assessing 5G Techniques Affecting the Deployment of Smart Hospital Infrastructure: Understanding the Role of 5G, AI, and IoT in Smart Hospitals [6]" perhaps begins with the increasing adoption of 5G, AI, and IoT technologies in healthcare. This may make it difficult to implement these technologies in smart clinical environments and a greater understanding of their function is needed. The introduction may indicate the objectives of the study, such as assessing the impact of 5G techniques on smart clinical system implementation policies. It can also name the authors, indicating a joint effort to analyze the interface of 5G, AI and IoT in healthcare, potentially establishing the methodology and key findings in this work.

"5G-Based Smart Hospitals and Healthcare Systems: Evaluation, Integration and Deployment" may open by highlighting the transformational potential of 5G technology in healthcare. It could increase the demand for advanced communications infrastructure in healthcare settings and the role of 5G in meeting these needs. The introduction may outline the objectives of the study, such as 5G integration challenges in smart hospitals and health systems, and implementation strategies. It can also name the authors, meaning a joint effort to explore the practical applications and implications of 5G technology to improve patient care, efficiency, and overall healthcare delivery [7].

In this research work [8], the analysis of Filter Bank Multicarrier (FBMC) waveforms for 5G network-based smart hospitals perhaps brings a focus on FBMC waveform analysis in 5G networks of smart hospitals. It can address the unique needs of smart hospitals, such as low latency and high reliability, addressed by waves of FBMC. The paper can outline the objectives, such as testing the performance of the FBMC wave in smart hospitals. It can also name the authors, indicating a concerted effort to explore technological aspects and implications of using the FBMC waveform in 5G networks for smart hospitals.

Finally, the analysis of hybrid spectrum sensing in 5G and 6G waveforms begins by discussing the critical importance of efficient spectrum sensing techniques in future wireless communication systems [9]. The introduction may indicate the motivation for the research, such as the need to investigate the performance of hybrid spectrum sensing techniques on 5G and 6G waveforms. It may also indicate a concerted effort to find new spectrum-sensing solutions.

2.2 Objectives of the Study

Within the framework of the Evolution of 5G and 6G Cellular Systems, the phase on targets serves as a guiding beacon, elucidating goals and purposes that propel the examination ahead. The number one purpose is to provide clarity on the purpose and focus of the research. The targets embody a multifaceted exploration. Firstly, the analysis seeks to resolve the technological intricacies that outline every stage of mobile evolution, presenting a comprehensive knowledge of the advancements from 1G to the current 5G panorama. This includes dissecting the key features, architectures, and deployment nuances that represent every technology. Secondly, the research endeavors to shed light on the challenges encountered at some stage in the transition to 5G. This includes an exam of the hurdles faced in deploying 5G networks, know-how the intricacies of migrating from non-standalone (NSA) to standalone (SA) architectures and comparing the performance enhancements achieved within the 5G atmosphere. Furthermore, the goals extend into the uncharted territory of 6G. The study ambitions to outline the concept of 6G, exploring the expected programs and use cases, which are anticipated for the subsequent technology of cell generation. This involves investigating the technological necessities and capability breakthroughs that may symbolize the 6G panorama. In essence, the goals of the analysis are threaded with a twin cause: to offer a comprehensive retrospective evaluation of the evolution from 1G to 5G and to solidify a forward-searching gaze into the but-to-be-realized realm of 6G. By gratifying those objectives, the analysis is aimed to be equipped by researchers, enterprise professionals, and policymakers with a nuanced know-how of the beyond, gift, and destiny of cellular structures, fostering knowledgeable discourse and strategic selection-making in the dynamic subject of telecommunications [10, 11].

2.3 Scope and Significance

The Evolution of 5G and 6G Cellular Systems intricately defines its scope and significance, shaping the bounds and significance of the examination. The scope is meticulously mentioned, focusing on the exploration of 5G technology and the initial research into the emerging landscape of 6G. This delineation ensures a concentrated examination, delving into the complexities of 5G even as supplying a preliminary glimpse into the predicted future of cellular structures. The importance of the observation lies in its potential impact on numerous fronts. Understanding the evolution of 5G is vital for industries, policymakers, and researchers as the spine of present-day communication. Simultaneously, the exploration of 6G is tremendous for its capability to revolutionize connectivity similarly. The observation is seen to provide insights large beyond technical realms, addressing societal, economic, and international implications, thereby contributing to the ongoing discourse at the transformative strength of cell generation [12, 13].

2.4 Basics of Cellular Technology

2.4.1 Overview of 1G to 4G

The section Overview of 1G to 4G in the Evolution of 5G and 6G Cellular Systems offers a foundational knowledge of the development in cell era from the first to the fourth generation. It serves as a comprehensive primer, tracing the ancient improvement and key functions of every generation. Commencing with 1G's leap in cellular communication all through the early 1980s, the assessment navigates through subsequent generations, highlighting the pivotal transition from analog signals in 1G to the virtual talents of 2G, the introduction of cell information in 3G, and the high-velocity information transmission of 4G. This retrospective evaluation elucidates the technological milestones, including the shift to virtual and the combination of the mobile internet that has shaped our modern-day cellular landscape. By encapsulating the essence of every technology, this section prepares readers for the subsequent exploration of 5G and the emerging ideas of 6G, fostering a contextual understanding of the continuous evolution in cellular technology [14–16].

2.4.2 Key Features and Advancements

In the Evolution of 5G and 6G Cellular Systems, section 2.4.2 delves into important features and advancements, which have propelled the cellular generation from its nascent ranges to the sophisticated landscape of 4G. This section serves as a focal point, dissecting the transformative factors that distinguish every technology. The exploration begins with an in-intensity evaluation of the important thing functions that described 1G to 4G. From the initial strides in cellular voice verbal exchange with 1G to the digital revolution delivered by means of 2G, the introduction of mobile records in 3G, and the excessive velocity records transmission abilities of 4G, a reader's advantage is the perception into successive improvements, which have shaped the evolution. Crucially, the phase elucidates the technological advancements using these capabilities, presenting nuanced information of the improvements that have propelled mobile systems ahead. By comprehending the important functions and underlying technological leaps, readers are primed for a deeper exploration into the specifics of 5G technology and the anticipated advancements inside the realm of 6G [17].

2.5 5G Technology

2.5.1 Introduction to 5G

Within the complete exploration of the Evolution of 5G and 6G Cellular Systems, section 2.5.1 serves as a gateway into the transformative era of 5G. This segment gives an important introduction, outlining the fundamental principles and targets of 5G era. The narrative begins by elucidating the essence of 5G, emphasizing its progressive capabilities, which include stronger information speeds, extremely low latency, and strong device connectivity. It delves into the motivations riding the development of 5G, rooted in the escalating demand for advanced connectivity to help a myriad of programs, from augmented truth to the IoT. This advent lays the groundwork for the next sections through fostering a clear understanding of the defining traits and objectives of 5G. It sets the stage for a deeper exploration into the additives, deployment challenges, and real-world programs of 5G technology, inviting readers to navigate the intricacies of this cutting-edge cell machine [18].

2.5.2 Key Features and Components

The narrative navigates via the pillars of 5G, highlighting better facts speeds, ultra-low latency, and massive tool connectivity as key capabilities. It similarly dissects the complicated additives of 5G networks; along with superior antennas, software program-defined networking (SDN), and community function virtualization (NFV). By unravelling those factors, readers gain insight into the technological infrastructure that enables the unparalleled competencies of 5G. Understanding the important functions and additives of 5G units shows a comprehensive comprehension of the network's skills and functionalities. This knowledge bureaucracy is the premise for subsequent discussions on deployment demanding situations, use cases, and the evolving landscape that paves the way for the anticipated generation of 6G [19].

2.5.3 Deployment Challenges

In the context of the Evolution of 5G and 6G Cellular Systems, section 2.5.3 delves into the elaborate landscape of deployment demanding situations encountered during the implementation of 5G era. This phase serves as an essential exam of the realistic hurdles and complexities faced with the aid of the industry in bringing the guarantees of 5G to fruition. The narrative unravels multifaceted demanding situations, encompassing issues like infrastructure improvement, spectrum allocation, and the combination of recent technologies. It scrutinizes the complexities of upgrading existing networks and the coexistence with legacy technologies. Additionally, the section addresses regulatory issues and public issues surrounding the deployment of 5G infrastructure. By comprehending the deployment challenges, readers take advantage of a holistic perspective at the actual global impediments that have an impact on the adoption and growth of 5G networks. This nuanced expertise lays the foundation for discussions on mitigations, destiny advancements, and the overarching evolution closer to the predicted 6G cellular systems [20].

2.5.4 Use Cases and Applications

The Evolution of 5G and 6G Cellular Systems explores the various landscapes of use instances and applications delivered forth with the aid of 5G era. This section serves as a charming adventure into the practical implications of 5G across various industries and everyday eventualities. The narrative unfolds the transformative potential of 5G, showcasing its function in permitting augmented reality (AR), virtual reality, self-reliant automobiles, and clever cities. It highlights the implications for healthcare, production, education, and beyond, illustrating how 5G acts as a catalyst for innovation and efficiency. By delving into the actual global programs of 5G, readers take advantage in a profound understanding of its effect on improving personal stories and revolutionizing industries. This knowledge serves as a precious precursor to discussions at the evolutionary direction toward 6G, hinting at the growing integration of advanced technologies into the cloth of our interconnected international.

2.6 Towards 6G

2.6.1 Definition and Concept of 6G

The Evolution of 5G and 6G Cellular Systems embarks on an exploration of the nascent concept and definition of 6G, imparting readers with a glimpse into the anticipated frontier of cell technology. This section serves as a pivotal second inside the narrative, ushering within the prospect of the subsequent generation of wi-fi communication. The narrative unfolds with the aid of defining the foundational ideas underpinning 6G, delving into the anticipated capabilities, and outlining the targets that power its improvement. It explores the anticipated want for unparalleled facts speeds, ultra-dependable low latency, and intelligence beyond the abilities of 5G. By presenting a conceptual framework, this section invites readers to contemplate the transformative capacity of 6G, setting the stage for deeper explorations into the technology and challenges with the intention to form its emergence. The dialogue at the definition and concept of 6G acts as a beacon, illuminating the uncharted territories of destiny cellular structures and fostering anticipation for the technological marvels that lie beforehand [21, 22].

2.6.2 Envisioned Applications and Use Cases

The Evolution of 5G and 6G Cellular Systems navigates into the area of predicted applications and use cases that define the conceptual panorama of 6G. This segment serves as a visionary exploration, offering readers an insight into the transformative potential and societal effect that 6G is predicted to deliver. The narrative unfolds with the aid of envisioning programs that go past the skills of present-day technology, exploring scenarios together with holographic conversation, immersive extended reality studies, and seamless integration of synthetic intelligence into ordinary life. It examines the potential for 6G to revolutionize industries like healthcare, transportation, and education, laying the basis for unheard of levels of connectivity and automation. By delving into the envisaged applications and use cases of 6G, readers are triggered to ponder a future wherein connectivity transcends limitations, and technological innovation reshapes the manner we stay and have interaction. This visionary exploration units the stage for a deeper knowledge of the technological requirements and demanding situations to define the evolution toward the subsequent frontier of cellular systems [23].

2.6.3 Key Technology Requirements

The Evolution of 5G and 6G Cellular Systems section 2.6.3 delves into the vital realm of key technological requirements to be able to underpin the improvement of 6G. This segment serves as a technological compass, guiding readers via the critical elements had to comprehend the bold imaginative and prescient of the next generation of wireless conversation. The narrative elucidates the expected conditions, such as advancements in information speeds, extremely low latency, and the capacity to seamlessly connect a fair larger range of devices. It explores the need for breakthroughs in areas along with synthetic intelligence, quantum verbal exchange, and Terahertz (THz) communication, forming the spine of 6G's abilities. By dissecting the important thing technological requirements for 6G, readers gain a profound expertise of the technological frontier that lies beforehand. This exploration unit the stage for discussions on the demanding situations, possibilities, and the collaborative efforts required to materialize the transformative guarantees of 6G cellular structures [24].

2.7 Technologies Enabling 6G

2.7.1 Artificial Intelligence and Machine Learning

The Evolution of 5G and 6G Cellular Systems shifts the focal point to the pivotal role of AI and machine learning (ML) as foundational technology using the evolution towards 6G. This section serves as a gateway into the transformative capacity of wise structures in shaping the destiny of mobile conversation. The narrative unfolds by exploring how AI and

ML are expected to play an imperative role in improving the talents of 6G networks. It delves into the prospects of leveraging AI for community optimization, predictive analytics, and dynamic useful resource allocation, paving the manner for relatively adaptive and self-optimizing communiqué systems. By dissecting the packages of AI and ML inside the context of 6G, readers advantage insight into the symbiotic courting among superior intelligence and the evolution of mobile era. This exploration sets the level for a deeper information of the complicated interaction among technological advancements, laying the inspiration for the expected technology of 6G cellular systems [25].

2.7.2 Terahertz Communication

The Evolution of 5G and 6G Cellular Systems makes a specialty of the current realm of THz verbal exchange, a pivotal era anticipated to shape the panorama of 6G. This section serves as a lens into the transformative capability of THz frequencies in advancing wi-fi communiqué. The narrative unfolds via exploring the unique traits of THz frequencies, known for their extremely excessive facts costs and capability applications in high-capacity, quick-range conversation situations. It delves into the challenges and possibilities associated with harnessing THz communication for 6G networks, paving the manner for advancements in information transmission speeds and capacity. By dissecting the position of THz communiqué within the context of 6G, readers benefit insight into the guarantees and complexities of employing this superior era. This exploration sets the degree for deeper information of the technological landscape, laying the muse for the expected era of 6G cell structures driven via improvements in THz communication [26].

2.7.3 Quantum Communication

In the Evolution of 5G and 6G Cellular Systems, the focus shifts to the groundbreaking area of quantum communication, an instrumental technology anticipated to underpin the cloth of 6G networks. This segment serves as a portal into the potential of quantum advancements in revolutionizing secure and excessive-performance conversation. The narrative unfolds via exploring the particular attributes of quantum verbal exchange, offering unheard of security through quantum key distribution and the capability for an extremely fast and efficient information switch. It delves into the challenges and guarantees related to integrating quantum communication into the 6G framework, paving the manner for quantum-secure, steady, and green communication networks. By dissecting the role of quantum communication inside the context of 6G, readers gain perception into the quantum revolution poised to redefine the limits of communiqué technologies. This exploration sets the level for a profound knowledge of the transformative landscape, laying the inspiration for the anticipated generation of 6G mobile structures driven by way of the concepts of quantum communication.

2.8 Challenges in 6G Developments

2.8.1 Technical Challenges

The Evolution of 5G and 6G Cellular Systems illuminates the tricky panorama of technical demanding situations that encapsulate the development of 6G. This segment serves as a critical examination of the hurdles and complexities that researchers and enterprise experts need to navigate to result in the conclusion of 6G networks. The narrative dives into multifaceted challenges, starting from the harnessing of advanced technologies like AI, THz communiqué, and quantum communication, to addressing problems of interoperability, safety, and strength efficiency. It explores the intricacies of optimizing network structure, handling spectrum sources, and ensuring the seamless integration of numerous technologies. By scrutinizing the technical demanding situations in 6G improvement, readers benefit from a complete expertise of the formidable barriers that should be conquer. This exploration now not handiest highlights the complexities but additionally underscores the need for revolutionary solutions and collaborative efforts to pave the way for the predicted generation of 6G cell systems [27].

2.8.2 Regularity and Standardization Challenges

The Evolution of 5G and 6G Cellular Systems navigates the nuanced terrain of regulatory challenges imperative to the improvement of 6G. This section serves as a crucial exploration of the felony and coverage hurdles that shape the trajectory in the direction of 6G networks. The narrative delves into the complexities of spectrum allocation, international standardization, and regulatory frameworks important for the deployment of 6G. It addresses the demanding situations posed by the worldwide nature of telecommunication requirements, emphasizing the need for harmonized policies to facilitate seamless implementation. By scrutinizing the regulatory demanding situations, readers gain insight into the problematic interplay between technological innovation and the felony panorama. This exploration highlights the imperative for international cooperation, standardization bodies, and regulatory frameworks that balance innovation with ethical concerns, paving the way for the anticipated era of 6G mobile systems.

2.8.3 Security and Privacy Concerns

The Evolution of 5G and 6G Cellular Systems delves into the moral and societal implications inherent within the improvement of 6G. This section serves as a reflective exploration of the broader impact that the deployment of superior cell technology might also have on society. The narrative navigates via considerations inclusive of privacy concerns, records safety, and the ability societal shifts added about with the aid of the mixing of pervasive connectivity. It scrutinizes the moral dilemmas posed by advanced technology like AI, quantum communiqué, and the large deployment of sensors inside the 6G panorama. By dissecting the moral and societal implications, readers get advantage from a nuanced understanding of the obligations and challenges that accompany technological innovation. This exploration emphasizes the significance of ethical frameworks, regulatory oversight, and inclusive talk to ensure that the advent of 6G aligns with societal values and fosters nice influences on a worldwide scale.

2.9 Future Prospects and Industry Impacts

2.9.1 Anticipated Benefits of 6G

The Evolution of 5G and 6G Cellular Systems ventures into the speculative realm of future outlooks, extending beyond the horizon of 6G. This section serves as a contemplative exploration, inviting readers to check the trajectory of cellular structures and the opportunities that lie in advance. The narrative explores potential scenarios, advancements, and improvements that could manifest in the post-6G generation. It contemplates the integration of emerging technology, societal shifts, and the ever-accelerating tempo of innovation so one can shape the future of wireless conversation. By delving into future outlooks, readers are induced to not forget the evolving dynamics of connectivity, looking forward to how technological landscapes, societal needs, and business imperatives might also converge within the cellular systems that observe 6G. This speculative exploration serves as each a reflective end and a catalyst for ongoing discussions surrounding the perpetual evolution of telecommunications.

2.9.2 Potential Disruptions in Industries

The Evolution of 5G and 6G Cellular Systems delves into the tricky interaction between technology, society, and industry, projecting future trajectories beyond 6G. This phase serves as a contemplative exam of the dynamic relationships with a purpose to shape the cellular landscape in the years to come. The narrative unfolds via scrutinizing how technological improvements catalyze societal shifts and influence commercial landscapes. It contemplates the symbiotic dating between innovation and societal desires, acknowledging the function of industry in guidance the trajectory of destiny cell systems. By exploring the interaction of technology, society, and industry, readers benefit from seeing complicated dynamics on the way to define the publish-6G generation. This contemplative exploration serves as a roadmap, inviting stakeholders to navigate the evolving panorama collaboratively, ensuring that destiny cellular structures align with the values and aspirations of society at the same time as assembly the needs of a dynamic business landscape.

2.9.3 Economic and Social Implications

The narrative of the evolution from 5G to 6G cellular systems focuses on the crucial themes of continuous collaboration and global cooperation, both essential for steering the future of mobile technology. These elements are pivotal in shaping the trajectory and ensuring seamless progression towards advanced cellular networks. This section serves as a realistic exploration, highlighting the importance of collective efforts in shaping the trajectory beyond 6G. The narrative delves into the necessity for ongoing collaboration amongst industry stakeholders, researchers, policymakers, and worldwide bodies. It emphasizes the role of worldwide cooperation in placing standards, addressing demanding situations, and fostering surroundings conducive to innovation. By spotlighting non-stop collaboration and worldwide cooperation, readers are entreated to understand the shared duty in steerage the route of future cellular systems. This exploration serves as a name to motion, advocating for concerted efforts to make certain that the cell future is fashioned through collective wisdom, inclusivity, and a shared commitment to advancing the technology for the advantage of worldwide society.

2.10 Comparative Analysis: 5G Versus 6G

2.10.1 Speed and Latency

The narrative of the Evolution of 5G and 6G Cellular Systems weaves collectively the threads of technological progress, societal impact, and the collaborative efforts that have described the exploration. This section serves as a reflective synthesis, inviting readers to contemplate the adventure from 1G to the estimated frontiers beyond 6G. The narrative revisits the important thing milestones, challenges, and breakthroughs that mark the evolution of cell technology. It reflects at the transformative impact on society, industries, and communiqué paradigms. Moreover, the conclusion underscores the non-stop nature of this evolution, emphasizing the need for adaptability, resilience, and forward-questioning inside the dynamic area of telecommunications. By providing a retrospective lens and projecting ahead, this conclusion serves as a milestone itself, encapsulating the collective understanding and envisioning a destiny in which mobile structures seamlessly combine with the cloth of global connectivity. It leaves readers with anticipation for the uncharted territories that look forward to in the ever-evolving panorama of wi-fi conversation.

2.10.2 Network Capacity

The Evolution of 5G and 6G Cellular Systems extends beyond belief, presenting insights into the results that the discussed evolution holds for the destiny. This segment serves as an ahead-searching exploration, charting the course ahead and contemplating the wider outcomes on era, society, and global connectivity. The narrative delves into the capability ramifications of mobile evolution, acknowledging its profound impact on numerous sectors. It anticipates the acceleration of technological innovation, societal modifications, and the elaborate interplay among connectivity and numerous industries. By exploring future results, readers are prompted to not forget the ripple results of mobile improvements. This ahead-searching exploration serves as a guide, encouraging stakeholders to navigate the evolving panorama with foresight, adaptability, and a proactive stance, ensuring that the cell structures of the destiny align with the needs and aspirations of a dynamic and interconnected global.

2.10.3 Energy Efficiency

In the Evolution of 5G and 6G Cellular Systems, the narrative underscores the essence of continuous studying and modeling in embracing the mobile frontier. This segment serves as a name to movement, advocating for a mindset of perpetual mastering and versatility inside the face of evolving telecommunications landscapes. The narrative delves into the dynamic nature of generation, emphasizing the need for professionals, researchers, and enterprise stakeholders to remain vigilant, responsive, and open to ongoing improvements. It highlights the position of adaptability in navigating the complexities of destiny mobile structures, urging a commitment to staying informed and engaged with the ultra-modern developments. By spotlighting the ethos of non-stop gaining knowledge and adaptation, this phase empowers readers to proactively embody the cell frontier. It encourages a lifestyle of interest, innovation, and resilience, ensuring that people and businesses are properly prepared to make contributions meaningfully to the ever-evolving tapestry of wi-fi communiqué.

2.10.4 User Experience

In the Evolution of 5G and 6G Cellular Systems, the narrative converges at the subject of collaborative endeavors in shaping the destiny of mobile evolution. This section serves as a rallying name for collective motion, underlining the importance of unified efforts in propelling the trajectory of cell structures. The narrative explores the synergies among numerous stakeholders, urging enterprise leaders, researchers, policymakers, and communities to collaborate in charting the route beforehand. It emphasizes the significance of shared visions, open communication, and cross-disciplinary cooperation in addressing the challenges and possibilities that lie at the horizon. By spotlighting the ethos of shaping the future together, this section instills a sense of shared duty. It encourages a tradition of inclusivity, expertise alternation and mutual aid, envisioning a future wherein the evolution of cellular systems is a collaborative tapestry woven by using the collective efforts of a worldwide community.

2.11 Main Contribution of 5G and 6G Evolution

This book chapter mainly focuses on the evolution of 5G and 6G cellular systems and their potential contributions and expectations. As of today, 5G technology was the latest standard in cellular networks. However, this chapter provides some potential contributions and expectations regarding the evolution of 5G to 6G. Keep in mind that developments may have occurred since the last update. Contributions of the Evolution from 5G to 6G Cellular Systems are explained in detail in this section.

Increased Data Rates: 6G is expected to offer significantly higher data rates compared to 5G. This will enable faster download and upload speeds, leading to improved user experiences and support for emerging applications like holographic communication and AR at an unprecedented level.
Lower Latency: 6G aims to achieve ultra-low latency, reducing the time it takes for data to travel between devices and networks. This is crucial for applications like real-time communication, autonomous vehicles, and remote surgery.
Enhanced Connectivity: 6G is likely to provide better connectivity in challenging environments, including rural and remote areas. This could involve improved satellite communication integration, extending the reach of high-speed networks to underserved regions.
Advanced Spectrum Usage: 6G is expected to leverage higher frequency bands, including THz frequencies. This would allow for increased bandwidth and support for a massive number of connected devices.
Artificial Intelligence Integration: AI is likely to play a more prominent role in 6G networks. AI could be used to optimize network resource allocation, enhance security, and provide intelligent network management.
Sustainable and Green Technologies: 6G may focus on energy-efficient and environmentally friendly technologies. This could involve optimizing power consumption in network infrastructure and devices, aligning with global efforts for sustainable technology development.
Ubiquitous Connectivity: 6G aims to provide seamless and ubiquitous connectivity, ensuring that users experience consistent and reliable network performance regardless of their location or the density of connected devices.
Tactile Internet: The evolution from 5G to 6G may introduce the concept of the "tactile internet," allowing for highly responsive and interactive communication. This could enable applications such as remote tactile sensing and control, benefiting fields like healthcare and manufacturing.
New Use Cases and Services: 6G is expected to unlock new use cases and services that were not feasible with previous generations. This could include innovations in areas like immersive extended reality (XR), advanced automation, and transformative applications in various industries.

It is important to note that the above-stated contributions are based on expectations and predictions, and the actual development and deployment of 6G technologies may evolve differently based on technological, regulatory, and market factors.

2.12 Limitations of 5G and 6G Cellular System

In this section, focuses on 5G and the potential 6G cellular systems bring about significant advancements; they also come with certain limitations and challenges. Here are some limitations associated with both 5G and the anticipated evolution towards 6G:

2.12.1 Limitations of 5G

Infrastructure Costs: Deploying 5G infrastructure, especially the small cells required for high-frequency bands is expensive. The cost of upgrading or building new networks can be a significant barrier, especially for smaller service providers.

Limited Coverage in Rural Areas: 5G deployment is initially concentrated in urban areas, and rural regions may not receive the same level of coverage. The rollout in less populated areas could be slower due to economic considerations.

Interference and Signal Range: Higher-frequency bands used in 5G have shorter wavelengths, leading to reduced signal range and increased susceptibility to obstacles and interference. This can impact coverage and reliability, especially in densely populated urban environments.

Device Compatibility: Older devices may not be compatible with 5G networks, requiring users to upgrade their devices to take advantage of the new technology. This can be a constraint for some users.

Security Concerns: As with any new technology, 5G introduces new security challenges. The increased number of connected devices and the use of virtualization in network architecture can potentially expose new attack vectors.

2.12.2 Potential Limitations of 6G (Anticipated)

Extreme Frequency Challenges: The use of extremely high-frequency bands in 6G, such as THz frequencies, may present challenges related to signal propagation, atmospheric absorption, and hardware development. Overcoming these challenges will be critical for widespread deployment.

Energy Consumption: The integration of new technologies and services in 6G networks may increase energy consumption. Balancing the demand for higher data rates and low latency with energy efficiency will be a key challenge.

Global Standardization: Achieving global standardization for 6G may be complex, as different regions and countries may have varying requirements, regulatory environments, and priorities. Harmonizing these aspects is crucial for seamless global connectivity.
Privacy Concerns: With increased reliance on AI and data analytics, privacy concerns may intensify. Striking a balance between providing personalized services and safeguarding user privacy will be a critical consideration.
Regulatory and Policy Challenges: The rollout of 6G will likely face regulatory and policy challenges, including spectrum allocation, licensing, and international cooperation. Addressing these issues is essential for the successful deployment of 6G networks.
Integration with Existing Technologies: Integrating 6G with existing infrastructure and technologies may pose challenges, particularly in managing backward compatibility with older generations of networks and devices.

It is important to note that these limitations are based on current expectations and potential challenges. As technology develops and standards evolve, some of these limitations may be mitigated, while new challenges may arise. Additionally, ongoing research and innovation are essential to addressing these limitations and ensuring the successful evolution of cellular networks.

2.13 Conclusion

2.13.1 Summary of Findings

In the Evolution of 5G and 6G Cellular Systems, the Summary of Findings serves as a crucial synthesis, encapsulating the important thing insights garnered at some stage in the exploration. This phase distills the complete examination, emphasizing pivotal discoveries regarding the evolution from 1G to the anticipated 6G frontier. The precise delves into the transformative milestones, demanding situations, and technological advancements characterizing each generation. It provides a holistic view of the dynamic interaction between mobile era, societal influences, and the collaborative efforts shaping the trajectory of wireless verbal exchange. Crucially, the summary highlights the innovative capabilities of 5G and gives glimpses into the predicted landscape of 6G. By distilling the findings, this section enables readers to comprehend the overarching narrative, reinforcing the significance of technological evolution in telecommunications. It serves as a beacon, guiding readers through the elaborate evolution of cellular structures and laying the groundwork for destiny contemplation and exploration inside the ever-evolving realm of wi-fi connectivity.

2.13.2 Future Research Directions

In the Evolution of 5G and 6G Cellular Systems, the narrative pivots towards unexplored frontiers, guiding the trajectory of next investigations. This phase serves as a compass, charting paths for researchers, industry professionals, and policymakers to delve into uncharted territories and address rising challenges. The dialogue probably outlines avenues for further exploration, which includes in-intensity analyses of unique technological additives, the societal effect of evolving cell structures, or strategies for overcoming persisting challenges. It may emphasize the need for interdisciplinary collaboration, inspire investigations into ethical issues, or propose novel approaches to optimize the deployment and integration of 6G technology. By delineating future studies instructions, this section invites a collective undertaking to extend information, innovate, and shape the continued evolution of cell structures. It sets the degree for a dynamic and collaborative studies panorama, making sure that scholars and practitioners contribute meaningfully to the continual development of telecommunications technology.

References

1. Mahdi, M.N.; Ahmad, A.R.; Qassim, Q.S.; Natiq, H.; Subhi, M.A.; Mahmoud, M. From 5G to 6G Technology: Meets Energy, Internet-of-Things and Machine Learning: A Survey. *Appl. Sci.*, 2021, *11*, 8117. https://doi.org/10.3390/app11178117.
2. L. Lu, G. Y. Li, A. L. Swindlehurst, A. Ashikhmin, and R. Zhang, "An overview of massive MIMO: Benefits and challenges." *IEEE J. Sel. Topics Signal Process.*, vol. 8, no. 5, pp. 742–758, Oct. 2014.
3. Arun Kumar, Aziz Nanthaamornphong, R. Selvi, J. Venkatesh, Mohammed H. Alsharif, Peerapong Uthansakul, Monthippa Uthansakul, Evaluation of 5G techniques affecting the deployment of smart hospital infrastructure: Understanding 5G, AI and IoT role in smart hospital. *Alex. Eng. J.*, Volume 83, 2023, Pages 335-354, ISSN 1110-0168, https://doi.org/10.1016/j.aej.2023.10.065.
4. A. Kumar, M. A. Albreem, M. Gupta, M. H. Alsharif and S. Kim, "Future 5G Network Based Smart Hospitals: Hybrid Detection Technique for Latency

Improvement." in *IEEE Access*, vol. 8, pp. 153240-153249, 2020, doi: 10.1109/ACCESS.2020.3017625.

5. Arun Kumar, R. Dhanagopal, Mahmoud A. Albreem, Dac-Nhuong Le, A comprehensive study on the role of advanced technologies in 5G based smart hospital. *Alex. Eng. J.*, Volume 60, Issue 6, 2021, Pages 5527-5536, ISSN 1110-0168, https://doi.org/10.1016/j.aej.2021.04.016.
6. Arun Kumar, Aziz Nanthaamornphong, R. Selvi, J. Venkatesh, Mohammed H. Alsharif, Peerapong Uthansakul, Monthippa Uthansakul, Evaluation of 5G techniques affecting the deployment of smart hospital infrastructure: Understanding 5G, AI and IoT role in smart hospital. *Alex. Eng. J.*, Volume 83, 2023, Pages 335-354, ISSN 1110-0168, https://doi.org/10.1016/j.aej.2023.10.065.
7. Arun Kumar, Sumit Chakravarty, Aravinda K, Mohit Kumar Sharma, *5G-Based Smart Hospitals and Healthcare Systems Evaluation, Integration, and Deployment*, 1st Edition, ISBN:781032515274, 266 Pages 127 B/W Illustrations, Published December 13, 2023 by CRC Press.
8. Ramakrishnan, B.; Kumar, A.; Chakravarty, S.; Masud, M.; Baz, M. Analysis of FBMC Waveform for 5G Network Based Smart Hospitals. *Appl. Sci.*, 2021, *11*, 8895. https://doi.org/10.3390/app11198895.
9. Kumar, A.; Venkatesh, J.; Gaur, N.; Alsharif, M.H.; Jahid, A.; Raju, K. Analysis of Hybrid Spectrum Sensing for 5G and 6G Waveforms. *Electronics*, 2023, *12*, 138. https://doi.org/10.3390/electronics12010138.
10. M. Simsek, D. Zhang, D. Öhmann, M. Matthé, G. Fettweis, "On the Flexibility and Autonomy of 5G Wireless Networks" in *IEEE Access*, 2017.
11. P. Schulz *et al.*, "Latency Critical IoT Applications in 5G: Perspective on the Design of Radio Interface and Network Architecture" in *IEEE Commun. Mag.*, 55(2): 70-78, 2017.
12. Rohde & Schwarz. "*5G Evolution—On the Path to 6G: Expanding the Frontiers of Wireless Communications, White Paper.*" Aug. 2020. [Online]. Available: https://www.mobilewirelesstesting.com/wpcontent/uploads/2019/10/5G-evolution-on-the-path-to-6G-_wp_en_3608-3326-52_v0100.pdf.
13. Hora SK, Poongodan R, de Prado RP, Wozniak M, Divakarachari PB. Long Short-Term Memory Network-Based Metaheuristic for Effective Electric Energy Consumption Prediction. *Appl. Sci.*, 2021, 11(23):11263. https://doi.org/10.3390/app112311263.
14. Sun, Y.; Liu, J.; Wang, J.; Cao, Y.; Kato, N. When machine learning meets privacy in 6g: A survey. *IEEE Commun. Surv. Tutor.*, 2020, *22*, 2694–2724.
15. Pouttu, A.; Burkhardt, F.; Patachia, C.; Mendes, L.; Brazil, G.R.; Pirttikangas, S.; Jou, E.; Kuvaja, P.; Heikkilä, M.; Päivärinta, T.; *et al.* 6G *White Paper on Validation and Trials for Verticals towards 2030's; 6G Research Visions*. 2020. Available online: https://www.6gchannel.com/items/6g-white-paper-validation-trials/ (accessed on 15 July 2021).
16. Zhang, S.; Zhu, D. Towards artificial intelligence enabled 6G: State of the art, challenges, and opportunities. *Comput. Netw.*, 2020, *183*, 107556.

17. M. Agiwal, A. Roy, N. Saxena Next generation 5G wireless networks: A comprehensive survey. *IEEE Commun. Surv. Tutorials*, 18 (3), (2016), pp. 1617-1655.
18. Arshad, A. Farooq, A. Shah Evolution and development towards 4th generation (4G) mobile communication systems. *J. Am. Sci.*, 6 (12), (2010), pp. 63-68.
19. L. Bariah, L. Mohjazi, S. Muhaidat, P.C. Sofotasios, G.K. Kurt, H. Yanikomeroglu, O.A. Dobre A prospective look: Key enabling technologies, applications and open research topics in 6G networks. *IEEE Access*, 8, (2020), pp. 174792-174820.
20. Q. Bi, Ten trends in the cellular industry and an outlook on 6G. *IEEE Commun. Mag.*, 57 (12), (2019), pp. 31-36.
21. S. Chen, Y.C. Liang, S. Sun, S. Kang, W. Cheng, M. Peng Vision, requirements, and technology trend of 6G: How to tackle the challenges of system coverage, capacity, user data-rate and movement speed. *IEEE Wirel. Commun.*, 27 (2), (2020), pp. 218-228.
22. D. Chandramouli, P. Andres-Maldonado and T. Kolding, "Evolution of Timing Services From 5G-A Toward 6G," in *IEEE Access*, vol. 11, pp. 35150-35157, 2023, doi: 10.1109/ACCESS.2023.3265213.
23. C.-X. Wang *et al.*, "On the Road to 6G: Visions, Requirements, Key Technologies, and Testbeds," in *IEEE Commun. Surv. Tutorials*, vol. 25, no. 2, pp. 905-974, Secondquarter 2023, doi: 10.1109/COMST.2023.3249835.
24. Cristina Emilia Costa; Fabrizio Granelli, "Wireless 5G (The 5G Mobile Network Standard)," in *IEEE Technology and Engineering Management Society Body of Knowledge (TEMSBOK)*, IEEE, 2024, pp.219-231, doi: 10.1002/9781119987635.ch14.
25. Wei Jiang; Fa-Long Luo, "The Vision of 6G: Drivers, Enablers, Uses, and Roadmap," in *6G Key Technologies: A Comprehensive Guide*, IEEE, 2023, pp.89-130, doi: 10.1002/9781119847502.ch3.
26. Z. Chen, X. Ma, B. Zhang, Y. Zhang, Z. Niu, N. Kuang, S. Li, A survey on terahertz communications. *China Commun.*, 16 (2), (2019), pp. 1-35.
27. Ramachandra Naik, S.C. Prashantha, H. Nagabhushana, S.C. Sharma, H.P. Nagaswarupa, K.S. Anantharaju, B.M. Nagabhushana, H.B. Premkumar, K.M. Girish, A single phase, red emissive Mg2SiO4:Sm3+ nanophosphor prepared via rapid propellant combustion route. *Spectrochim. Acta, Part A*, Volume 140, 2015, Pages 516-523, https://doi.org/10.1016/j.saa.2015.01.011.

3

A Review on Augmented Reality and Virtual Reality Technologies in the Field of Healthcare

Deekshitha S. Nayak[1,2*] **and R. Shivarudraswamy**[1,2]

[1]*Department of Electronics & Communication Engineering, Mangalore Institute of Technology & Engineering, Moodabidri, Karnataka, India*

[2]*Department of Electrical and Electronics Engineering, Manipal Institute of Technology, Manipal Academy of Higher Education, Manipal, Karnataka, India*

Abstract

Immersion technologies are quickly changing the healthcare industry, particularly augmented reality and virtual reality. Augmented reality enhances the real world with digital information, and virtual reality replaces the real world with a simulated environment. Virtual reality and augmented reality present a multitude of opportunities for medical diagnosis, treatment, education, and rehabilitation. Virtual reality can generate completely immersive and simulated settings, while augmented reality superimposes digital information onto the real world. This article examines the state of augmented reality and virtual reality in healthcare today, stressing the technologies many uses, future advantages, and current challenges.

Keywords: Augmented reality, virtual reality, medical diagnosis, industrial implementation

Abbreviation

AR	Augmented Reality
VR	Virtual Reality
M-IoT	Medical Internet of Things

**Corresponding author*: deekshitha.nayak06@gmail.com

Arun Kumar, Manoj Gupta, Sanjeev Sharma, Er. Himanshu Sharma and Khursheed Aurangzeb (eds.) Smart Hospitals: 5G, 6G and Moving Beyond Connectivity, (45–60) © 2024 Scrivener Publishing LLC

3.1 Introduction

The term augmented reality (AR) refers to the understanding of contemporary technology, which operates by identifying and detecting crucial intuitive cues and offering competing services. These days, AR is regarded as one of the most cutting-edge technologies available worldwide [1]. The augmentation prototype increased its efficacy and had an impact on nearly every facet of life, including industrial implementation, emergency response, and healthcare administration. Numerous studies have been conducted and have produced impressive results in the effort to create AR prototypes that are more successful. Augmented reality improves the way a three-dimensional (3D) holographic image appears on expensive glasses [2]. Because AR technology has so many uses, its advancement in healthcare has taken on great significance. Computer vision, object recognition and identification, image processing, picture segmentation, and cloud computing technologies are being integrated into AR-based healthcare systems. The world's population is getting older every day, and as they make up over 60% of the global population, they require special attention and round-the-clock medical supervision. It has been observed that many patients can be saved if prompt medical attention is provided. However, a number of factors, including excessive latency, the cost of medical care, the time it takes to travel from a rural area to a town multispecialty hospital, a lack of infrastructure, a shortage of personnel, and others, are lowering the standard of care and severely harming patients. One of the major issues facing the modern world is medical health care. Concerns about the standard of care are raised by inadequate funding, inadequate infrastructure, and unfavorable healthcare laws. In addition, it is believed that the electromagnetic waves produced by mobile towers are dangerous and have the potential to trigger a number of fatal illnesses in people. In medical applications, battery life is critical because it affects patient safety, health, and the dependability of medical equipment. Batteries are necessary for the operation of numerous medical devices, such as portable monitors, infusion pumps, and pacemakers. Extended battery life lowers the possibility of potentially fatal pauses in monitoring or treatment by ensuring continuous device operation. By extending cell life, surgical procedures for battery replacements can be minimized, which will lessen discomfort and problems for patients. Furthermore, consistent battery performance is essential for life-saving actions during emergencies. Strong battery management and low-power designs are necessary to maintain medical devices' efficacy and integrity, which will eventually improve patient outcomes. In order to facilitate communication between patients and healthcare professionals, a smart hospital integrates cutting-edge technology like 4G, 5G, the Internet of Things, artificial intelligence, and more. The development of cellular communication, including 4G radio, has already helped the health care sectors. It offers telehealth care services including online patient monitoring via video conferencing and the use of wearable technology and GPS positioning in various emergency scenarios. But services like remote surgery, patient video monitoring, report sharing, controlling large wearables, and patient medical history storage necessitate low latency, high spectral access, quick data rates, and high-power efficiency from the cellular framework. A number of significant improvements have been made to AR-based healthcare solutions, including faster, more reliable, and more secure connectivity and privacy for each patient, all while offering high-quality diagnosis and treatment. Wireless services, early diagnosis, real-time monitoring, online consultation, tumor detection, diagnosis specialty, medical health service and personal assessment are the growing prototypes of AR-based healthcare solution. One of the most important factors in enhancing the standard of medical treatment and keeping medical imaging is spectral availability. There are more and more wireless apps, which means that more bandwidth is needed to support more applications with higher service quality. It is seen, therefore, that a significant portion of the bandwidth is squandered and improperly used. Therefore, the key to the successful implementation of the 5G and B5G radio frameworks is the optimal use of bandwidth. By creating an efficient, contemporary healthcare system, 5G can aid in expanding the use of remote health monitoring. The prerequisites for health will differ from public appeals. When building a network for smart health care, the main concerns will be low latency, improved network coverage, improved access to remote locations, and a secure network. The smart health-commerce application will grow and expand into mobile. Enhancing latency and stability is seen to be essential for supporting health monitoring service-related services. A highly accessible service should be provided along with a high data rate measured in gigabytes. In order to support the enormous number of devices, effective spectrum management is also required. In developing nations, access to medical treatment is a major issue, particularly in rural areas. The development of wireless telecommunications has greatly enhanced medical care in a number of ways, such as easing the burden on patients of traveling from remote areas to modern health care facilities for remote health diagnoses and by guaranteeing that patients receive quality care without having to pay exorbitant fees. High data-rate, low latency, and high spectrum are required for the remote health monitoring to make use of the high-standard hospital's medical resources. The study unveiled a brand new healthcare system that incorporates cognitive resources and the 5G data model. In a similar vein, its application has improved medication adherence and rehabilitative care. The usage of VR in healthcare settings is growing as new technical developments open new avenues for diagnosis and treatment [3]. Virtual reality is a kind of technology that simulates reality by immersing the user in a virtual environment, giving the idea that the user is physically present in that virtual place. This is done with the use of a headset. Virtual reality presents a multitude of opportunities for the user to engage with a virtual world or virtual avatars. Avatars, or virtual characters, have the potential to enhance the user's perception of reality and enable significant communication [4]. Virtual reality interventions have been trailed in a number of healthcare settings, including the treatment of chronic pain, the management of depressive symptoms, the improvement of symptom burden in patients with terminal cancer, and the application of VR within the treatment of forensic psychiatric patients. These research demonstrate VR's potential as a cutting-edge technology that could improve healthcare. Both urban and rural residents will benefit from improved medical facilities thanks to the smart hospitals. In the current situation, receiving high-quality medical care is seen as one of the most important concerns. The use of 4G wireless is raising the bar for medical care. On the other hand, minimal latency is seen to be among the most crucial factors for both surgical procedures and remote monitoring. Experiments have demonstrated that the use of VR is beneficial in enhancing the treatment of a variety of conditions, including eating disorders, psychosis, and anxiety disorders. However, further research is required to fully understand the effectiveness of VR in healthcare. Because this technology is not used often, the extra value of virtual reality is frequently overlooked in practice. Technological innovations in 5G, block chain, and the Medical Internet of Things (M-IoT) offer standard amenities and a patient-friendly system in the healthcare industry. The demand from industry, subscribers, and operators is increasing, which is accelerating the development of next-generation technology. It is anticipated because, owing to various services and applications, the 5G network will not be accessible. Thus, smart hospitals based on 5G networks might not be able to reach the necessary latency. The current cloud architecture, however, was created specifically for the 5G network. The Internet of Things uses a number of sensors to gather patient medical data. Using artificial intelligence algorithms, a recommendation or medication can then be made. But putting in place a fully developed smart hospital costs more money, which raises the cost of medical care, which must be kept to a minimum for greater public advantages.

The current contribution of the work of VR and AR in healthcare emphasizes the technologies, future advantages, and current challenges associated with it.

3.2 Augmented Reality in Healthcare

By superimposing digital data over the actual world, AR improves our understanding of and ability to interact with it. Augmented reality has several uses in the medical field, such as:

3.2.1 Surgical Guidance

Augmented reality in surgery is more than just showing pre-operative images. Using special glasses or headsets, it superimposes digital data, such as 3D representations of blood veins, bones, and nerves, right onto the surgical field. This real-time visualization provides crucial guidance during crucial surgeries, similar to having a transparent textbook on human anatomy hovering just over the patient. By enabling surgeons to precisely identify vital tissues, AR reduces the possibility of injuring delicate organs, blood arteries, or nerves. Consider a scenario where a neurosurgeon operates on a patient's brain while projecting a 3D map of the patient's neural connections onto the brain. When used with augmented reality, haptic feedback gloves can provide a tactile sense within the virtual world, improving surgical accuracy even more. Artificial reality-based solutions have the potential to encourage users to complete their physical therapy exercises and gather objective data on things like range of motion through immersive and engaging settings. It provides patients with interactive, realistic settings that mimic physical rehabilitation activities. Virtual reality can reduce stress for patients who have partial immobility of a limb by projecting an image of the non-functional limb that is moved by the patient using their working right hand. Augmented reality makes it possible to precisely locate tumors and other targets, resulting in smaller incisions and quicker recuperation periods. This is especially advantageous for delicate surgeries such as treatments involving the brain, spine, and eyes. Augmented reality simulations allow residents and medical students to perform difficult surgery on virtual patients. This gives them a realistic and safe setting in which to practice before operating on actual patients. This degree of accuracy may result in reduced surgical complications, minimal invasive procedures [5].

3.2.2 Enhancement of Decision-Making

During surgery, AR gives doctors immediate access to vital information. Reading a patient's medical history while not losing sight of the surgery is possible. Surgeons are empowered by this real-time data stream to make well-informed judgments on the spot and modify their strategy as necessary for the best results. Augmented reality can create dynamic 3D models from complex medical data, including MRIs, X-rays, and genetic information. This makes it possible to evaluate data intuitively and spot minute irregularities that could go unnoticed in more conventional two-dimensional representations. With the use of AR, patients can see intricate medical diagnoses such as tumors or fractures inside their own bodies, leading to a more thorough comprehension of their health and increased autonomy in making decisions. By giving the appropriate information, enhancing comprehension, encouraging collaboration, and promoting improved communication, AR enables decision-making in the healthcare industry. Better decision-making, better patient outcomes, and a health-care system that is more patient-centered result from this.

3.2.3 Improved Collaboration and Training

Augmented reality can completely change surgical training by offering life-like simulations that resemble the real world. In a secure virtual setting, residents and medical students can rehearse intricate procedures before entering the operation room. By superimposing vital signs, images, and even 3D models on top of the patient, surgeons may virtually "scrub in" and provide real-time advice using AR headsets. This is especially helpful for difficult treatments or places where there are not many specialists available. In order to promote a more knowledgeable and cooperative decision-making process, doctors can provide patients with AR visualizations of diagnosis and available treatments during consultations. By enabling virtual connections between medical personnel and patients in distant places, AR enhances accessibility and minimizes the need for travel by facilitating immersive telemedicine experiences. Augmented reality can also ease communication between surgeons, enabling specialists in various locations to provide during intricate procedures [6].

3.2.4 Medical Diagnosis and Visualization

Augmented reality turns two-dimensional pictures of medical images into interactive 3D representations. These models can be rotated, zoomed in on particular regions, and even superimposed in real time onto the patient's body by medical professionals. An innovative method to diagnosis and treatment planning is provided by this immersive experience. With the use of AR, medical professionals may see pathological lesions and intricate anatomical structures in three dimensions, giving them a far better grasp of their position, size, and relationship to surrounding tissues. Suppose you could virtually dissect a tumor during an MRI scan and observe all its intricate connections to neurons and blood arteries. This degree of specificity permits: through the ability to identify small anomalies and comprehend their spatial context, AR can assist medical professionals in diagnosing patients more quickly and accurately, which can lead to early interventions and better patient outcomes. Augmented reality gives medical professionals the ability to plan operations and other procedures more precisely. By simulating several surgical techniques on a 3D model, they can maximize their strategy and reduce any risks. It is possible to make items that are haptic, auditory, visual, tactile, and olfactory. Physical data from many sources can be integrated into a virtual environment to be integrated instantaneously. Three-dimensional anatomical data can now be shown overlaid on a patient following years of development. They are frequently made using eyewear exhibits that superimpose data on the observer's environment. Physicians can decrease treatment regimen challenges and increase productivity, safety, and cost-effectiveness by utilizing a single AR display while maintaining eye contact with the patient. In the medical field, augmented reality has promised cost savings through safer procedures and the removal of unnecessary screens, among other benefits.

3.2.5 Remote Assistance and Collaboration

By enabling remote collaboration, AR can help healthcare workers support and guide colleagues who are in different locations in real-time. Remote surgeons can instantly see a specialist's 3D annotations superimposed on their patient's anatomy. To ensure maximum precision during a delicate brain surgery, picture a neurosurgeon in a rural hospital getting step-by-step instructions from a famous neurologist in a major city. By removing the need for experts to physically visit isolated locations, AR can save time, money, and possibly even avoid delays in essential care. With AR-guided treatments, medical personnel can learn from more seasoned colleagues virtually, obtaining essential expertise without having to leave their own clinics shown in the Figure 3.1.

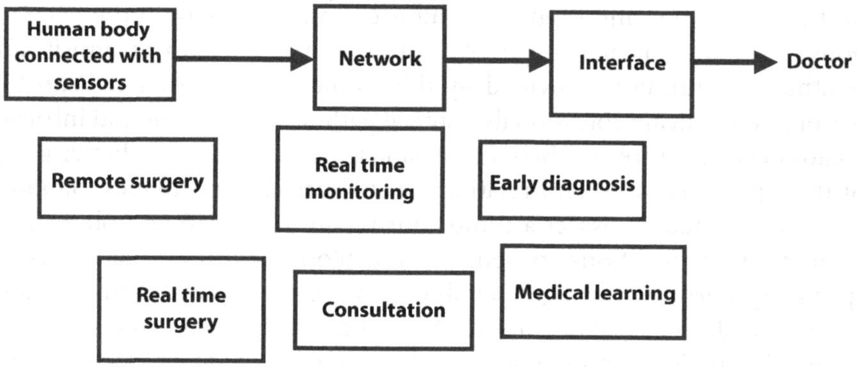

Figure 3.1 Augmented reality in the platform of healthcare.

3.3 Virtual Reality in Healthcare

Virtual reality transports viewers into computer-generated settings that either recreate or mimic real-world events; it has many uses in the medical field, such as:

3.3.1 Medical Training and Education

Virtual reality simulations can offer medical professionals and students a safe, lifelike setting in which to perform surgery, identify illnesses, and understand difficult medical concepts. Through VR simulations that imitate actual surgeries, trainees can perform difficult procedures on virtual patients in a secure setting. Before ever setting foot in an actual operating room, picture mastering suturing procedures, developing your laparoscopic skills, or even practicing a delicate brain surgery [7]. This hands-on instruction increases self-assurance, sharpens dexterity, and reduces the likelihood of mistakes in practical situations. Students can interact in VR settings with virtual patients who display a variety of symptoms and presentations. In a risk-free environment, students can practice taking medical histories, doing exams, and coming to diagnoses. Imagine dissecting a virtual heart as a cardiology resident to see a valve defect or investigating a virtual patient's lungs as an intern to diagnose pneumonia. Diagnostic skills are improved, and active participation is fostered by this interactive learning.

3.3.2 Exposure Therapy

With the right tools, VR exposure therapy can be carried out at home or in the convenience of a therapist's office. This makes traditional treatment less stigmatized and more accessible to people who would be reluctant or unable to attend in-person sessions. Because VR is immersive, it is compelling by nature. Instead of just listening to therapy sessions, patients actively work to overcome their concerns. Better results are achieved through increased motivation and treatment adherence when using this interactive strategy. Rather, it uses a ladder technique, whereby the virtual scenarios' realism and intensity are progressively increased from a light exposure point. Through gradual mastery of their concerns, patients can develop resilience and confidence through this controlled exposure. Biofeedback sensors and VR therapy can be used together to track a patient's physiological reactions in real time. Utilizing this data will allow interventions to be more effectively tailored and the virtual environment made uniquely. In order to enhance balance and coordination, patients can engage in activities like strolling through virtual forests or climbing mountains in VR. These simulated environments are designed to mimic real-world situations. Conventional therapy may be monotonous, which lowers motivation and causes boredom. Virtual reality adds enjoyment and novelty to exercises, making them more dynamic and engaging, which improves adherence and results. By using VR to divert patients' attention from their discomfort, therapy sessions can be longer and more productive. Furthermore, some VR experiences might encourage awareness and relaxation, which can lessen the sense of pain [8].

3.3.3 Painless Treatment

Virtual reality takes patients to relaxing or interesting virtual settings, such as busy cityscapes, serene beaches, or even magical realms. By drawing patients' attention away from the physical aspects of pain, this immersed shift of focus provides a much-needed break and lessens the perceived intensity of the pain. Virtual reality is more than just static landscapes. In such virtual environments, patients can engage in guided meditations, play games, and solve puzzles. This active participation increases diversion even more, keeping the mind occupied and lowering awareness of pain. Real-time tracking and analysis of patient movements via VR systems allows for quick feedback on form and progress. Patients can modify their motions and enhance their technique more successfully with the assistance of this tailored feedback. With the increasing portability and affordability of VR equipment, therapeutic sessions can now take place at home or in other remote locations. For patients who might find it difficult to travel to traditional therapy visits, this improves accessibility.

3.3.4 Physical Rehabilitation

Physical treatment activities become thrilling sports and challenges when done in virtual reality. To strengthen their hand dexterity, patients can punch robots, navigate obstacle courses to improve their balance, or develop coordination by playing virtual basketball. This playful, game-like approach to therapy improves adherence to treatment goals and makes it enjoyable. Virtual reality environments can be tailored to meet the needs and skills of each user. Exercises can be modified to meet specific objectives, virtual worlds can be selected to pique the patient's attention, and difficulty levels can be changed. In addition to ensuring that therapy targets the appropriate areas for maximum recovery, this personalization raises engagement.

3.4 Advantages of AR and VR in the Healthcare

Augmented reality and virtual reality have a much wider impact on healthcare than just futuristic situations and gaudy devices. These innovations have the potential to positively impact every facet of the medical field and, in the end, improve results for both patients and medical personnel. Better patient outcomes will result from AR and VR's ability to facilitate better diagnosis and treatment. More timely diagnosis, more successful treatments, and more seamless recovery processes are all made possible by precise surgical guidance, interactive diagnostic tools, and customized rehabilitation programs. This therefore has an impact on medical education, which is the cornerstone of healthcare. Before entering the real world, medical professionals and students can refine their abilities, perform difficult operations, and acquire essential experiences in an entertaining and safe setting via immersive simulations. This results in a new generation of healthcare professionals who are more capable and self-assured [9, 10].

That is not where the ripple ends. Augmented reality and virtual reality have the potential to lower healthcare costs by improving resource allocation, decreasing errors, and expediting workflows. This would enable a greater number of patients to receive necessary care. At last, the ripple touches the core issue: patient happiness and engagement. Interactive VR can help patients feel less anxious and uncomfortable during treatments while also educating them about their ailments and empowering them to take an active role in their own care. As a result, AR and VR provide several advantages beyond their immediate uses. They have a beneficial knock-on impact that lowers costs, increases patient-centeredness, empowers medical staff, and enhances patient outcomes. The skyrocketing expense of healthcare is a global concern, putting a burden on finances and limiting access to necessary care. However, during the growing tide, AR and VR are coming to the rescue, providing creative solutions for streamlining the system and cutting excess. Patients may no longer need to travel great distances for specialized opinions or routine check-ups because of AR-powered remote consultations. Imagine saving time, money on travel, and hospital resources by having a rural patient consult with a cardiologist hundreds of miles away. By increasing precision and efficiency, AR surgical guidance can cut down on operating time and the requirement for expensive follow-up procedures. Imagine a world in which surgeons may reduce complications and decrease hospital stays by viewing important anatomy in real-time. By projecting real-time data on medical supplies, AR overlays help optimize inventory levels and save waste. Nurses could rapidly check stock levels and expiration dates by scanning a medication cabinet, which would cut down on resource waste and avoid the need for needless refilling [11, 12].

Medical workers can receive immersive training using virtual reality simulations, which eliminates the need for costly real-world tools and resources. Imagine surgeons practicing intricate procedures in a virtual operating room, reducing the possibility of errors and the resulting expenses, or nurses improving their suturing techniques. Regardless of location, AR can enable real-time data sharing and visualization between healthcare practitioners. Imagine a physician in a rural clinic working together with a major city specialist to diagnose a patient, saving money on transfers, and accelerating decision-making. By superimposing paperwork and checklists directly onto patients or equipment, AR can expedite data entry and administrative duties. Envision nurses recording vital signs or surgeons directly annotating X-rays in the field, reducing paperwork errors and boosting productivity shown in Figure 3.2.

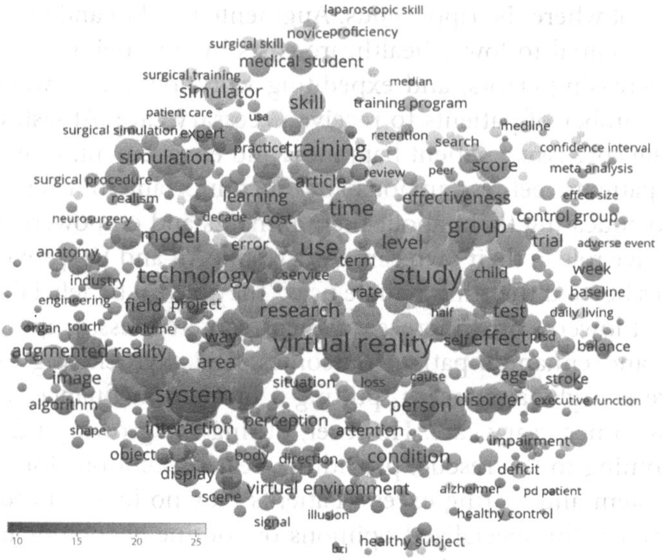

Figure 3.2 Application of AR and VR in the medical field reproduced by the Ref [21].

3.4.1 Possible Remedies for Bridging the Gap

Innovation and Price Reductions: As a result of growing competition and technological advancements, the cost of VR and AR equipment is decreasing, opening it out to a larger spectrum of healthcare practitioners.

Creative Financing Models: By spreading out the expense of implementing VR and AR, healthcare institutions can make it more manageable. Creative collaborations, grants, and subscription models can help.

Payment Reform: More providers may find VR and AR technologies to be financially feasible if advocacy efforts are directed on amending healthcare payment regulations to allow coverage for these technologies.

Virtual Reality Clinics: Underserved communities can have more access to these technologies through shared VR facilities in community centers or mobile VR units.

AR App Development: One way to increase the use of these technologies is to concentrate on creating AR apps that are easily accessible and affordable, utilizing smartphones or basic wearables.

Training and Support Programs: By providing healthcare professionals with technical assistance and training, obstacles can be addressed, and VR and AR can be successfully incorporated into their practices.

3.5 Challenges and Future Scope

Although there is no denying that VR and AR have a lot of potential in the healthcare industry, two major obstacles to their mainstream adoption are cost and accessibility. These technologies are now only available to well-funded organizations and affluent individuals because of their high equipment and software costs. Smaller hospitals, clinics, and solo practitioners may find it unaffordable to purchase VR and AR equipment, software licenses, and infrastructure modifications. Updating software licensing and maintaining VR and AR hardware increases the continuous cost burden. The price of VR and AR technologies may not be sufficiently covered by the healthcare reimbursement systems in place, which would discourage their widespread use. The price of VR and AR technologies may not be sufficiently covered by the healthcare reimbursement systems in place, which would discourage their widespread use [13].

The limitations are:

Digital Divide: Inequitable access to infrastructure and technology exacerbates already-existing healthcare inequalities, possibly keeping low-income neighborhoods and rural areas from taking advantage of VR and AR's benefits.
Physical Restrictions: Not all patients may find VR headsets or AR tools comfortable or feasible to use, which could prevent some patient populations from benefiting from these technologies.
Lack of Support and Training: It is possible that healthcare personnel lack the knowledge and tools necessary to successfully incorporate VR and AR into their daily operations and patient care plans.

While VR and AR offer a bright future for healthcare, navigating this unexplored area requires careful consideration of a number of ethical issues that may be present [14, 15]. These possible obstacles necessitate careful consideration and proactive fixes to guarantee the moral application of these potent technologies: massive volumes of private patient data, such as biometric data, medical histories, and even emotional responses, are gathered via VR and AR. To avoid abuse and privacy violations, it is essential to have strong data security safeguards and explicit patient consent procedures [16, 17]. It is imperative to create strong ethical frameworks tailored to VR and AR healthcare applications that address user safety, data privacy, and informed consent [18]. Giving patients accurate information about data gathering, any hazards, and their rights over their data gives them the power to choose VR and AR experiences that best suit their needs. For responsible development and adoption, it is essential to conduct honest research on the effectiveness and ethical implications of VR and AR in healthcare, guaranteeing varied patient representation and open sharing of results [19, 20].

3.6 Conclusion

Virtual reality and augmented reality have the potential to completely transform healthcare, but doing so will require thoughtful planning and proactive measures. We can negotiate the ethical minefield and clear the path for a future in which VR and AR empower people, revolutionize healthcare, and serve everyone in an ethically and responsibly manner by embracing these technologies with prudence, transparency, and a dedication to patient well-being. Though there may be brief barriers due to technical issues, VR and AR promise in healthcare is yet unbounded. We can ensure that these technologies shine the brightest, illuminating a future where technical glitches fade away and are replaced by a seamless, immersive, and transformative vision of healthcare for all, by addressing these challenges through innovation, collaboration, and a commitment to user-centered design. Even while technology may occasionally malfunction, the goal is still evident: a time when healthcare is not only effective but also interesting, empowering, and available to everyone. Virtual reality and augmented reality not only transform healthcare but also make it a more personal, connected, and ultimately healthier experience for each and every person by cooperating to overcome technological obstacles.

References

1. Allard, J., Gouranton, V., Lecointre, L., Limet, S., Melin, E., Raffin, B., *et al.* (2004). "Flowvr: A Middleware for Large Scale Virtual Reality Applications," in *European Conference on Parallel Processing* (Springer), 497–505.
2. Andone, D., and Frydenberg, M. (2019). "Creating Virtual Reality in a Business and Technology Educational Context," in *Augmented Reality and Virtual Reality* (Springer), 147–159.

3. Arlati, S., Greci, L., Mondellini, M., Zangiacomi, A., Santo, D., Franchini, F., *et al.* (2017). "A Virtual Reality-Based Physical and Cognitive Training System Aimed at Preventing Symptoms of Dementia," in *International Conference on Wireless Mobile Communication and Healthcare* (Springer), 117–125.
4. Hora SK, Poongodan R, de Prado RP, Wozniak M, Divakarachari PB. Long Short-Term Memory Network-Based Metaheuristic for Effective Electric Energy Consumption Prediction. *Appl. Sci.*, 2021; 11(23):11263. https://doi.org/10.3390/app112311263.
5. Allard, J., Lesage, J.-D., and Raffin, B. (2010). Modularity for Large Virtual Reality Applications. *Presence: Teleoperators and Virtual Environments*, 19, 142–161.
6. Balog, A., and Pribeanu, C. (2009). Developing a Measurement Scale for the Evaluation of Ar-Based Educational Systems. *Stud. Inform. Control*, 18, 137–148.
7. Bierbaum, A., Just, C., Hartling, P., Meinert, K., Baker, A., and Cruz-Neira, C. (2001). "Vr Juggler: A Virtual Platform for Virtual Reality Application Development," in *Proceedings IEEE Virtual Reality 2001* (IEEE), 89–96.
8. Allard, J., Gouranton, V., Lecointre, L., Melin, E., and Raffin, B. (2002). "Net Juggler: Running Vr Juggler with Multiple Displays on a Commodity Component Cluster," in *Proceedings IEEE Virtual Reality 2002* (IEEE), 273–274.
9. Chardonnet, J.-R., Mirzaei, M. A., and Merienne, F. (2021). Influence of Navigation Parameters on Cybersickness in Virtual Reality. *Virtual Real.*, 25, 565–574.
10. Currie, J., Bond, R. R., McCullagh, P., Black, P., Finlay, D. D., Gallagher, S., *et al.* (2019). Wearable Technology-Based Metrics for Predicting Operator Performance during Cardiac Catheterisation. *Int. J. CARS*, 14, 645–657.
11. Fussell, S. G., and Truong, D. (2021). Accepting Virtual Reality for Dynamic Learning: an Extension of the Technology Acceptance Model. *Interact. Learn. Environ.*, 3, 1–18.
12. Garcia-Palacios, A., Botella, C., Hoffman, H., and Fabregat, S. (2007). Comparing Acceptance and Refusal Rates of Virtual Reality Exposure vs. *In Vivo* Exposure by Patients with Specific Phobias. *Cyber Psychology Behav.*, 10, 722–724.
13. Greenbaum, D. (2015). Expanding Elsi to All Areas of Innovative Science and Technology. *Nat. Biotechnol.*, 33, 425–426.
14. Groth, C., Tauscher, J.-P., Heesen, N., Castillo, S., and Magnor, M. (2021). "Visual Techniques to Reduce Cybersickness in Virtual Reality," in *2021 IEEE Conference on Virtual Reality and 3D User Interfaces Abstracts and Workshops (VRW)* (IEEE), 486–487.
15. Hamzeheinejad, N., Roth, D., Götz, D., Weilbach, F., and Latoschik, M. E. (2019). "Physiological Effectivity and User Experience of Immersive Gait

Rehabilitation," in *2019 IEEE Conference on Virtual Reality and 3D User Interfaces (VR)* (IEEE), 1421–1429.
16. Kumar, Arun, Aziz Nanthaamornphong, R. Selvi, J. Venkatesh, Mohammed H. Alsharif, Peerapong Uthansakul, and Monthippa Uthansakul. (2023) "Evaluation of 5G techniques affecting the deployment of smart hospital infrastructure: Understanding 5G, AI and IoT role in smart hospital." *Alexandria Eng. J.*, 83, 335-354.
17. Kumar, Arun, Mahmoud A. Albreem, Manoj Gupta, Mohammed H. Alsharif, and Sunghwan Kim. (2020) "Future 5G network based smart hospitals: Hybrid detection technique for latency improvement." *IEEE Access*, 8, 153240-153249.
18. Kumar, Arun, R. Dhanagopal, Mahmoud A. Albreem, and Dac-Nhuong Le. (2021) "A comprehensive study on the role of advanced technologies in 5G based smart hospital." *Alexandria Eng. J.*, 60, no. 6, 5527-5536.
19. Ramakrishnan, Balamurali, Arun Kumar, Sumit Chakravarty, Mehedi Masud, and Mohammed Baz. (2021) "Analysis of FBMC waveform for 5G network based smart hospitals." *Appl. Sci.*, 11, no. 19, 8895.
20. Kumar, Arun, J. Venkatesh, Nishant Gaur, Mohammed H. Alsharif, Abu Jahid, and Kannadasan Raju. (2022) "Analysis of Hybrid Spectrum Sensing for 5G and 6G Waveforms." *Electronics*, 12, no. 1, 138.
21. Yeung, Andy Wai Kan, Anela Tosevska, Elisabeth Klager, Fabian Eibensteiner, Daniel Laxar, Jivko Stoyanov, Marija Glisic. (2021) "Virtual and augmented reality applications in medicine: analysis of the scientific literature." *J. Med. Internet Res.*, 23, no. 2, 25499.

4

Compressed Sensing Reconstruction Algorithms for Medical Images – A Comparison

Kavitha K. J.[1*], Vishwaraj B. Manur[1], Suprith P. G.[1], Mahendra S. Naik[2] and Chaitra S. N.[1]

[1]*ECE Department, GM Institute of Technology, Davangere, India*
[2]*New Horizon College of Engineering, Bangalore, India*

Abstract
The Internet of Things (IoT) is a rapidly developing field of technology that has the potential to revolutionize healthcare, smart cities, daily human activities, manufacturing and other industries. Incorporating compressive sensing (CS) into the design of IoT platforms is a highly appealing paradigm. The medical imaging community has been very interested in CS because of its potential to produce high-quality picture reconstructions with less data by taking use of compressibility. In this paper, we have discussed various compressing reconstruction algorithms that could be used in the medical imaging application for better image construction by eliminating unnecessary redundant bits. The orthogonal matching pursuit algorithm (OMP), sparsity-adaptive matching pursuit algorithm (SaMP), adaptive step-size SaMP algorithm (AS-SaMP) and dynamic-step-size SaMP (DSS-SaMP) are discussed, evaluated and compared with each other in terms of bit error rate (BER), signal error rate (SER), and mean square error (MSE).

Keywords: IoT, CS, OMP, SaMP, AS-SaMP, DSS-SaMP, BER, SER, MSE

4.1 Introduction

The Internet of Things (IoT) is a rapidly developing field of technology with the potential to revolutionize a wide range of industries. The IoT is made

**Corresponding author*: kavithakj219@gmail.com

Arun Kumar, Manoj Gupta, Sanjeev Sharma, Er. Himanshu Sharma and Khursheed Aurangzeb (eds.) Smart Hospitals: 5G, 6G and Moving Beyond Connectivity, (61–90) © 2024 Scrivener Publishing LLC

up of a network of wireless communication protocols, actuators, sensors, and data processing technologies that work together to deliver a particular application. Numerous extremely dynamic heterogeneous devices, each with unique and constrained computational and communication capabilities, are frequently used to characterize the IoT.

In an IoT scenario, a vast number of autonomous smart devices gather data from the real world and use wireless links to connect to the cloud and each other to share information and perform particular functions. Nevertheless, these IoT-powered devices' compute capability and battery life are constrained by the high energy consumption of wireless communication [7, 8]. Therefore, a variety of strategies, including cooperative transmission, multi-hop network designs, and advanced compression techniques, need to be investigated to maximize data transfer [11]. Incorporating compressive sensing (CS) into the design of IoT platforms [9] is a highly appealing paradigm for the latter.

In a smart hospital environment leveraging IoT, various devices and sensors are interconnected to enhance healthcare services, improve patient outcomes, and streamline hospital operations [13]. Compressed sensing [12] reconstruction algorithms play a crucial role in efficiently collecting and reconstructing data from these sensors, especially in scenarios where bandwidth and energy constraints are significant concerns.

An IoT scenario in a smart hospital employing CS reconstruction algorithms:

❖ *Sensor Deployment:*
- Various sensors are strategically deployed throughout the hospital to monitor different aspects of healthcare, such as patient vital signs, environmental conditions, and equipment status.
- Examples of sensors include wearable devices for patients, environmental sensors for temperature and humidity control, and equipment sensors to monitor the condition of medical machinery.

❖ *Data Acquisition:*
- Sensors continuously collect data in real-time, generating a significant amount of raw data.
- Traditional methods of transmitting raw data from sensors to a central processing unit can be

resource-intensive, leading to increased bandwidth usage and energy consumption.

❖ *Compressed Sensing Implementation:*
- Compressed sensing is employed to reduce the amount of data transmitted and processed while maintaining the essential information.
- Instead of transmitting raw data, sensors perform *in situ* compression by sampling the data at a rate much lower than the Nyquist rate. This compressed data is then sent to a central processing unit or a cloud server.

❖ *Central Processing Unit (CPU)/Cloud Server:*
- The central processing unit or a cloud server receives the compressed data from various sensors.
- Compressed sensing reconstruction algorithms are applied to reconstruct the original data from the compressed measurements accurately.

❖ *Advantages of Compressed Sensing:*
- *Bandwidth Efficiency:* CS reduces the amount of data that needs to be transmitted, optimizing the utilization of available bandwidth.
- *Energy Savings:* Transmitting less data also leads to reduced energy consumption, which is critical in IoT devices with limited power resources.
- *Real-time Monitoring:* Despite the reduced data transmission, CS allows for near real-time monitoring of vital signs and other parameters.

❖ *Applications in Healthcare:*
- The reconstructed data can be used for various healthcare applications, such as continuous monitoring of patient health, early detection of abnormalities, and predictive analytics for disease prevention.
- The hospital staff can receive alerts and notifications based on the reconstructed data, enabling prompt responses to critical situations.

- *Security and Privacy Considerations:*
    - Implementing secure communication protocols and encryption is crucial to protect patient data and maintain privacy.
    - Compliance with healthcare data regulations, such as the Health Insurance Portability and Accountability Act of 1996 (HIPAA), is essential to ensure the confidentiality and integrity of patient information.

In a smart hospital scenario, the integration of IoT devices with CS reconstruction algorithms enable efficient data acquisition, transmission, and analysis, leading to improved healthcare outcomes and operational efficiency.

Compressed sensing, also known as compressive sensing, compressive sampling, or sparse sampling, is a signal processing technique that efficiently acquires and reconstructs a signal by solving underdetermined linear equations. Compressed sensing is an alternative approach to the Shannon – Nyquist sampling theorem. This method uses several nonlinear ways to reconstruct a signal from a few random observations, provided that the original signal was sparse or compressible. The majority of the coefficients in a sparse signal are zero, and only a few of them hold all the information. This kind of signal can be acquired by means of a basis transformation. The idea behind this is that by optimizing, one may recover a signal from considerably less samples than those needed to satisfy the Nyquist – Shannon sampling theorem [10] by taking advantage of the signal's sparsity. Redundancy in many important signals is exploited by CS.

The aforementioned theorem shows that, provided the continuous signal is uniformly sampled at a rate that is at least twice its Fourier bandwidth, it may be reconstructed from a discrete sequence of collected samples. However, even the most sophisticated samplers may not be able to achieve the required sampling rate for some applications, such as radar imaging or other imaging modalities outside of visible wavelengths. Additionally, because so many samples were gathered, they must be compressed. Research and business have shown a great deal of interest in CS as a potent signal processing technique for audio and image compression.

Imaging plays a critical role in various aspects of medicine, such as identifying diseases and diagnosis, treatment planning, and therapy response monitoring. A broad spectrum of contrast mechanisms and radiological imaging techniques has found therapeutic use due to the complexity of the human body and the variety of potential disease states. Computed tomography (CT) and magnetic resonance imaging (MRI) are two of the most used techniques.

While handling the large volume of medical data becomes a major difficulty, the necessity of comprehensively monitoring all key signals and pictures in the medical system becomes more urgent. There are various benefits to using CS with a solid theoretical foundation in data reconstruction using several less sampled signal vectors, particularly in health monitoring. Additionally, it lessens the adverse effects of patients being exposed to radio waves and electromagnetic fields, which are employed in medical equipment like CT and MRI redundantly and needlessly. The first benefit of the low data samples is that MRI and CT imaging may now be completed considerably more quickly in a couple of seconds as opposed to the several minutes it takes now.

For instance, there have been enormous efforts made in the healthcare industry to investigate the many uses of CS. According to experts, CS has a lot of potential applications in pathology and medical laboratory testing, especially in settings where a lot of data is collected.

Although these modalities' image generation processes differ substantially, they share a number of frequently incompatible system design objectives [6].

- ❖ Medical Image Quality: Medical imaging is used to support clinical assessments. Imaging systems are made to optimize image quality in order to accomplish this goal. In actuality, clinical task performance with a medical imaging system is the best indicator of its quality. Therefore, task performance—the goal of medical imaging—should be reflected in picture quality metrics.
- ❖ Patient security: Although clinical imaging is done to help patients, there is always some risk associated with every modality. Because X-ray CT uses ionizing radiation, which can raise a patient's chance of developing some cancers [1], it is best to reduce the amount of radiation exposed to patients.

In certain cases, even the non-ionizing radiation used in an MRI can induce thermal harm because it produces heat within the body [2]. Patient safety must be minimized, even if lowering radiation exposure could lead to an unacceptably poorer quality of image.

- Medical Imaging Speed: Faster imaging has a number of benefits. Patients are dynamic entities, and movements throughout the process of image production may result in artifacts that compromise the quality of the image. By decreasing the chance of patient mobility, faster imaging speeds naturally lessen the severity of these distortions. In addition to improving patient comfort and throughput, faster imaging can maximize the use of imaging hardware, which is frequently costly. Speed is especially important in dynamic imaging, where a series of images must be captured swiftly one after the other to reflect the dynamics of a time-varying contrast agent or a physiological activity. However, the requirement to obtain sufficient data to produce satisfactory image quality limits the speed at which images may be captured.

Similar to other imaging data, medical imaging data is not free of charge. Compressive sensing is naturally of interest to those who wish to minimize this expenditure. The adoption of CS is encouraged by the numerous intrinsic benefits of medical imaging. Users can modify the radiation source to make the system more receptive to CS reconstruction since they have control over it. Furthermore, the raw data from medical imaging is oblique. The imaging community is very interested in CS due to its potential to produce high-quality images from acquisitions of sparse data sampling.

This may contribute to achieving the above-specified design objectives. Excitement and a rapid growth in publications on what is called "compressive sensing" have somewhat sidestepped the typical methodical, methodical approach to scientific research, even though there is potential for faster, safer image acquisitions without sacrificing image quality if the prior knowledge that medical images are compressible, if not truly sparse, is properly utilized. Specifically, a great deal of important work that was done in the literature before the big bang of CS has mostly been forgotten or ignored.

This is partly due to many of the ideas that have been reinterpreted under the banner of CS in recent years that have first originated in journals dedicated to particular applications, and CS may be applied to any area of imaging science, which has a wealth of literature.

- *IoT in Smart Hospitals:*
  Patient Monitoring: IoT devices can be used for continuous patient monitoring, collecting real-time data on vital signs, medication adherence, and other relevant health metrics. Wearable devices, smart sensors, and medical implants can transmit data to a centralized system.
  Asset Tracking: IoT can help track medical equipment, such as infusion pumps, wheelchairs, and monitoring devices. This ensures that equipment is readily available when needed, reducing delays in patient care and improving resource utilization.
  Environment Monitoring: IoT sensors can monitor environmental factors such as temperature, humidity, and air quality within hospital facilities. This is crucial for maintaining optimal conditions for patient comfort and equipment functionality.

- *Compressed Sensing Algorithms:*
  Data Compression: CS allows for efficient data compression and transmission of large volumes of medical data. This is particularly important in IoT applications, where bandwidth may be limited. By compressing data at the source, the communication and storage requirements are reduced.
  Sparse Signal Reconstruction: CS enables the reconstruction of sparse signals from a reduced set of measurements. In healthcare, this can be applied to signals such as medical images (e.g., CT scans, MRI) and physiological signals (e.g., ECG, EEG), allowing for faster transmission and reduced storage needs.
  Energy-Efficient Sensing: CS can be used to optimize energy consumption in IoT devices by reducing the amount of data that needs to be processed and transmitted. This is especially relevant for battery-operated medical devices.

- *Integration of IoT and CS in Smart Hospitals:*
  Real-time Monitoring and Analytics: IoT devices can collect a vast amount of data from various sources. Compressed sensing algorithms can help efficiently process and analyze this data in real-time, providing actionable insights to healthcare professionals.

Remote Patient Monitoring: CS allows for the transmission of compressed health data from wearable devices to central servers, enabling remote patient monitoring without overwhelming network bandwidth.
Privacy-Preserving Data Sharing: CS techniques can be employed to share aggregated and anonymized patient data securely, ensuring privacy compliance while still allowing for valuable data analysis.

- *Challenges and Considerations:*
  Security: As with any IoT application, security is a critical concern. Implementing robust encryption and authentication mechanisms is essential to protect sensitive medical data.
  Interoperability: Ensuring that IoT devices and CS algorithms can seamlessly integrate with existing healthcare systems is crucial for the success of smart hospitals.
  Regulatory Compliance: Adhering to healthcare regulations and standards is essential to ensure patient safety and data integrity.

The combination of IoT and CS in smart hospitals holds great potential for improving healthcare delivery, patient outcomes, and resource efficiency. However, it is crucial to address security, interoperability, and regulatory considerations for successful implementation.

When considering CS reconstruction algorithms for medical images in an IoT context, several key features should be taken into account to ensure effective and efficient image recovery. Here are some essential features to consider:

- ❖ *Sparsity-Promoting Techniques:* CS relies on the assumption that the underlying signal (medical image) is sparse or compressible in a certain domain. Look for algorithms that effectively promote sparsity, as medical images often exhibit sparse characteristics.
- ❖ *Adaptability to Different Image Modalities:* Medical imaging encompasses various modalities (MRI, CT, X-ray, etc.), each with their own unique characteristics. An ideal CS algorithm should be adaptable to different image modalities, providing robust performance across a range of medical imaging applications.
- ❖ *Efficiency in Real-Time Processing:* In the context of IoT and medical applications, the algorithm should be computationally efficient and capable of real-time or near-real-time

processing. This ensures timely delivery of reconstructed images for prompt medical decision-making.

- *Low Energy Consumption:* IoT devices are often resource-constrained, particularly in terms of energy. A CS algorithm for medical images in IoT should be designed to minimize energy consumption, making it suitable for deployment on devices with limited power resources.
- *Robustness to Noise and Artifacts:* Medical images may be subject to noise and artifacts due to various factors such as equipment limitations or patient movement. The CS algorithm should exhibit robust performance in the presence of noise and artifacts, ensuring reliable reconstruction in less-than-ideal conditions.
- *Adaptive Sampling Strategies:* Adaptive sampling strategies can enhance the efficiency of CS algorithms by dynamically adjusting the sampling rate based on the image content. This allows for better utilization of resources and improved reconstruction quality.
- *Scalability:* Consider the scalability of the CS algorithm, especially when dealing with large-scale IoT deployments in a hospital setting. The algorithm should be able to handle a growing number of sensors and devices without sacrificing performance.
- *Data Compression and Transmission:* Given the constraints of IoT networks, an effective CS algorithm should contribute to data compression during image acquisition and support efficient transmission of compressed data. This helps in optimizing bandwidth usage and reducing communication latency.
- *Security and Privacy Considerations:* Ensure that the CS algorithm incorporates secure communication protocols and encryption methods to protect sensitive medical data. Compliance with healthcare data regulations, such as HIPAA, is essential for maintaining patient privacy.
- *Compatibility with IoT Communication Protocols:* To enable communication between sensors and the central processing unit or cloud server, the CS algorithm should effortlessly interface with popular IoT communication protocols (such as message queuing telemetry transport (MQTT), constrained application protocol (CoAP)).
- *Reconstruction Quality Metrics:* Implement mechanisms to assess and quantify the quality of reconstructed images

using appropriate metrics (e.g., PSNR, SSIM) to ensure that the algorithm meets the required standards for medical imaging applications.

- *Adherence to Regulatory Standards:* Ensure that the CS algorithm adheres to regulatory standards for medical devices and healthcare information systems to guarantee its suitability for clinical use.

By considering these key features, a CS reconstruction algorithm for medical images in an IoT environment can be tailored to meet the specific requirements of healthcare applications, providing efficient and reliable image reconstruction for improved patient care and diagnosis. In the next section, we will discuss the concept of the CS theory and various reconstruction CS algorithms.

The implementation of 5G technology in the context of CS algorithms has several potential implications and benefits. Here are some ways in which 5G can impact and enhance CS applications [13–16]:

- High Bandwidth and Low Latency: Benefit: 5G networks offer significantly higher data transfer rates and lower latency compared to previous generations. This high bandwidth and low latency facilitate the efficient transmission of compressed data, enabling faster and more responsive communication between sensors, devices, and CPUs.
- Improved Real-time Data Transmission: CS algorithms often involve the transmission of data from sensors to a central processing unit or cloud server. The low latency and high bandwidth of 5G networks support real-time or near-real-time transmission of compressed data, making it particularly advantageous in applications where timely data processing is critical, such as healthcare and IoT.
- Enhanced IoT Connectivity: 5G networks are designed to support a massive number of connected devices simultaneously. In the context of CS in IoT, this capability is crucial for handling the large-scale deployment of sensors and devices, facilitating seamless communication and data exchange.
- Edge Computing Support: 5G enables edge computing by bringing computational resources closer to the source of data generation. This can be advantageous for CS applications, allowing some processing tasks to be performed at the edge of the network, reducing the need for transmitting

large amounts of raw data and improving overall system efficiency.

- Network Slicing for Quality of Service (QoS): 5G introduces the concept of network slicing, which allows the creation of virtualized, customized network segments tailored to specific applications or services. This can be leveraged for CS applications to ensure the desired QoS and prioritization of data traffic.
- Flexibility in Network Deployment: 5G supports different deployment models, including public networks, private networks, and hybrid solutions. This flexibility can be advantageous for implementing CS algorithms in various scenarios, such as healthcare, industrial settings, and smart cities, where specific deployment requirements may differ.
- Dynamic Resource Allocation: 5G networks feature dynamic resource allocation capabilities, allowing resources to be allocated based on demand. This adaptability is beneficial for CS applications, where the resource needs may vary depending on factors such as the number of connected devices, data complexity, and processing requirements.
- Network Security and Reliability: 5G incorporates advanced security features, including encryption and authentication protocols. This ensures the secure transmission of compressed data in applications where data privacy is paramount, such as medical imaging and healthcare monitoring.
- Network Synchronization: CS often involves the synchronization of sensors or devices to optimize data acquisition. The precise timing and synchronization capabilities of 5G networks can contribute to improved coordination and collaboration among distributed sensors.
- Support for Massive Machine-Type Communications (mMTC): 5G is designed to support mMTC [18], making it well-suited for scenarios involving a large number of IoT devices. In CS applications, this capability is essential for handling the diverse data sources and sensors contributing to the overall reconstruction process.

While 5G brings several advantages to CS applications, it is important to consider the associated challenges, including the potential increased energy consumption in devices and the need for infrastructure upgrades to fully leverage the benefits of 5G technology. Additionally, careful consideration of security and privacy aspects remains crucial in sensitive applications like medical imaging.

4.2 Concept of Compressed Sensing Theory

The process of creating an image using measurements is called image reconstruction. Sensor encoding, or the representation of an object in the sensor domain that is subsequently transformed into an image by inverting the encoding function, is a step in the image reconstruction process. Because of sensor non-idealities and noise, precise inverse transform analytical information may not be known beforehand, making image reconstruction a difficult operation.

A new approach in signal processing called CS intends to acquire a compressed form of sparsely patterned signals during the sensing stage, hence facilitating high-quality reconstruction during the receiver stage [6, 7]. An alternative paradigm provided by the CS algorithm replaces the conventional acquisition rules, which state that an exact recovery can only be ensured if the number of measured samples is at least equal to the number of samples in the original signal. These requirements, however, do not account for the signal's structure.

Therefore, according to CS, if the signal of interest is sparse, that is if it can be represented by fewer non-zero coefficients than its original dimension, then capturing the salient information in the signal through a small number of random linear measurements or projections of the sparse signal is sufficient to yield an acceptable reconstruction quality. The goal of CS is to move the complexity from the sensors, which are typically self-powered and resource-constrained to the receiver side, which is typically deployed on computer platforms with less restriction.

With the right transformation, it is always possible to find a compressible or sparse representation for signals of interest in the majority of real-world applications. As a result, CS has been widely used in many different applications, including wireless communications, image processing, radar, bio-signal compression, and many more.

For example, there have been significant initiatives in the healthcare industry to investigate the various uses of computer science. According to experts, CS has a lot of potential applications in pathology and medical laboratory testing, especially in settings where a lot of data is collected.

Figure 4.1 shows the overall block diagram of CS acquisition and reconstruction methods usually employed in almost all applications. The benefit

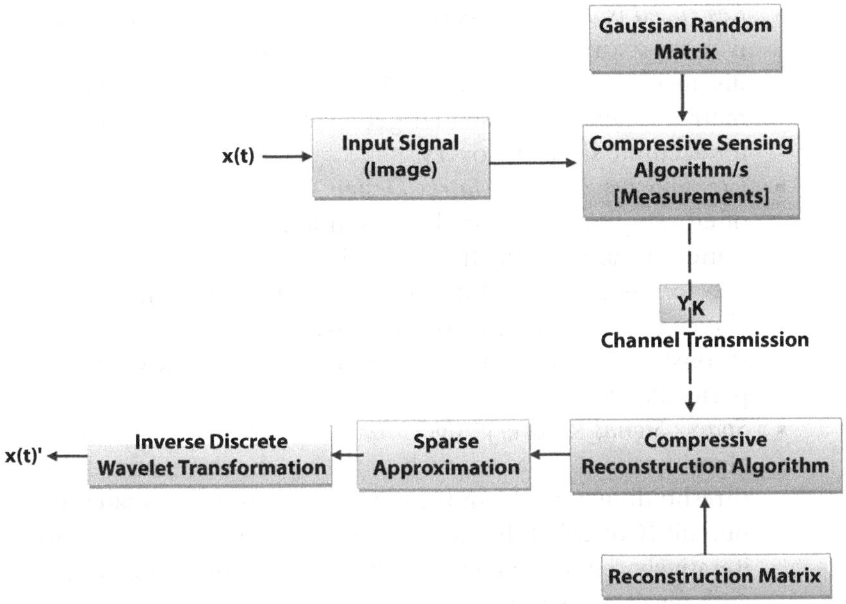

Figure 4.1 Compressive sensing acquisition and reconstruction system.

of the CS approach is that compression occurs during the data acquisition process rather than later.

Compressed sensing reconstruction algorithms exhibit several key properties that make them suitable for efficiently recovering signals or images from a reduced set of measurements. Some important properties of CS reconstruction algorithms are mentioned below:

- *Sparsity:* The underlying signal or image is sparse, meaning that only a small number of non-zero coefficients are needed to represent it on a certain basis or transform domain. Sparsity is a fundamental assumption in CS. Many natural signals, including medical images, are sparse or compressible in the right representation.
- *Incoherence:* The sensing matrix (measurement matrix) used in CS reconstruction should be incoherent with the sparsity basis. Incoherence ensures that the measurements capture diverse information about the sparse signal. Higher incoherence improves the chances of accurately reconstructing the original signal from a small set of measurements.

- *Restricted Isometry Property (RIP):* A matrix satisfies the RIP if it approximately preserves all k-sparse vectors' pairwise distances for a small k. The RIP ensures that the sensing matrix retains the essential geometric properties required for accurate signal recovery.
- *Compressive Sensing Matrix Design:* Efficient CS algorithms often employ structured or random sensing matrices. Random matrices, such as Gaussian or Bernoulli matrices, are commonly used for their theoretical guarantees. The choice of the sensing matrix is critical for the success of CS reconstruction, influencing both algorithmic efficiency and performance.
- *Sparse Signal Recovery Algorithms:* Many CS reconstruction algorithms are iterative, such as basis pursuit, iterative hard thresholding (IHT), and compressive sampling matching pursuit (CoSaMP). Iterative algorithms exploit sparsity and iteratively refine the reconstruction, achieving better results with fewer measurements.
- *Stability and Robustness:* CS algorithms should be stable against noise and small perturbations in the measurements.
- *Robustness:* The ability to handle deviations from ideal conditions, such as noisy or incomplete measurements, is crucial for practical applications.
- *Adaptive Sampling:* Adaptive sampling strategies dynamically adjust the sampling rate based on the observed signal characteristics during the reconstruction process. Adaptive sampling improves efficiency by focusing on capturing important signal features, reducing the number of measurements required.
- *Computational Efficiency:* Efficient CS reconstruction algorithms, such as fast iterative shrinkage-thresholding algorithms (FISTA), aim to reduce computational complexity. In real-world applications, especially in IoT and medical imaging contexts, computational efficiency is crucial for real-time or near-real-time processing.
- *Low-Dimensional Representations:* CS algorithms often provide low-dimensional representations of signals, facilitating storage, transmission, and analysis. Compact representations contribute to data compression, reducing storage and communication requirements.

Guarantees and Theoretical Foundations: Robust CS algorithms often come with theoretical guarantees, such as stability and convergence, providing a solid foundation for their application.

Understanding and leveraging these properties help in the design and implementation of effective CS reconstruction algorithms for diverse applications, including medical imaging and IoT scenarios.

In this paper, we will discuss the various CS reconstruction algorithms used for regenerating the transmitted medical images and their comparison in terms of evaluation of metrics bit error rate (BER), signal error rate (SER), mean square error (MSE) against signal-to-noise ratio (SNR).

4.3 Comprehensive Sensing Reconstruction Algorithms

Compressed sensing is a signal processing technique that has found applications in various fields, including medical imaging. In the context of medical imaging, CS is particularly valuable for its ability to acquire and reconstruct images with fewer data points than traditional methods, leading to reduced acquisition time and potentially lower radiation exposure. The overview of CS theory applied in medical imaging is explained below:

- *Sparse Representation:*
  Assumption of Sparsity: The underlying principle of CS in medical imaging assumes that the image to be reconstructed has a sparse representation in some domain (e.g., wavelet, Fourier, or spatial domain).
  Sparse Transform: The transformation of the image into a sparse representation is a key step in CS. This sparsity assumption implies that most of the information in the image can be represented with a small number of coefficients in the chosen domain.

- *Random Sampling:*
  Non-Uniform Sampling: Instead of uniformly sampling the entire image, CS employs non-uniform or random sampling of the data. This means that only a subset of measurements is acquired, reducing the amount of data collected during the imaging process.

Incoherent Sampling: The sampling pattern should be incoherent with the chosen sparse transform to ensure that a small number of random measurements can capture the essential information for image reconstruction.

- *Reconstruction Algorithms:*
  L1 Minimization: CS typically involves solving an optimization problem, where the objective is to minimize the L1 norm of the sparse representation. This is often done through algorithms like basis pursuit, FISTA, or other iterative optimization techniques.
  Iterative Reconstruction: The reconstruction process is iterative and involves updating the sparse coefficients and refining the image estimate in each of the iteration process.

- *Applications in Medical Imaging:*
  MRI: CS has been successfully applied in accelerating MRI scans. By undersampling k-space (spatial frequency domain) data and using CS algorithms, it is possible to reconstruct high-quality images with fewer measurements, reducing scan times.
  CT: In CT imaging, CS can be employed to reduce the number of X-ray projections needed for image reconstruction. This can potentially lead to lower radiation exposure for patients.
  Positron Emission Tomography (PET) and Single Photon Emission Computed Tomography (SPECT): CS can be used to reduce the number of acquired projections in nuclear medicine imaging, improving imaging efficiency.

- *Challenges and Considerations:*
  Algorithm Complexity: Some CS algorithms can be computationally demanding, requiring careful consideration of computational resources.
  Optimal Sampling Patterns: The choice of the sampling pattern plays a crucial role in CS. Designing optimal sampling patterns for specific imaging modalities is an ongoing research area.
  Noise Sensitivity: CS methods can be sensitive to noise. Incorporating techniques to handle noise during reconstruction is essential.

❖ *Benefits:*
Reduced Acquisition Time: CS enables faster imaging by acquiring fewer measurements, which is particularly beneficial for imaging modalities with longer acquisition times.
Lower Radiation Dose: In modalities like CT, CS can potentially reduce radiation exposure to patients by requiring fewer X-ray projections.

Evaluating the performance of CS reconstruction algorithms in medical image recovery involves the use of various quality metrics to assess the accuracy and fidelity of reconstructed images compared to the original ones. Here in this paper, some common quality metrics used in the evaluation of CS reconstruction algorithms for medical image recovery are discussed [17]:

❖ *Peak Signal-to-Noise Ratio (PSNR):* The power of the corrupting noise (the difference between the original and reconstructed images) is measured by PSNR, a commonly used metric that compares the maximum possible power of a signal (the original image). Superior reconstruction quality is indicated by higher PSNR values.
❖ *Structural Similarity Index (SSI or SSIM):* The structural similarity between the original and reconstructed images is evaluated using a metric called SSIM. It considers contrast, structure, and brightness. Perfect similarity is denoted by a value of 1, while SSIM values range from -1 to 1.
❖ *Mean Squared Error (MSE):* MSE measures the average squared differences between corresponding pixels in the original and reconstructed images. Lower MSE values indicate better reconstruction quality.
❖ *Normalized Root Mean Squared Error (NRMSE):* NRMSE is the normalized version of MSE, taking into account the dynamic range of the pixel values in the images. It provides a normalized measure of the error between the original and reconstructed images.
❖ *Peak Absolute Error (PAE):* PAE measures the maximum absolute difference between corresponding pixels in the original and reconstructed images. It provides insight into the worst-case scenario in terms of reconstruction error.
❖ *Mean Absolute Error (MAE):* MAE calculates the average absolute differences between corresponding pixels in the original and reconstructed images. It provides a measure of the average error across the entire image.

- *Visual Inspection:* While quantitative metrics are essential, visual inspection by medical professionals remains a crucial aspect of evaluating image quality. Radiologists or clinicians can assess the clinical relevance and diagnostic utility of the reconstructed images.
- *Computational Complexity:* Consideration of the computational complexity of the algorithm is important, especially in real-time or resource-constrained environments. This includes analyzing the time and memory requirements of the reconstruction process.
- *Robustness to Noise and Artifacts:* Evaluating the algorithm's performance under different noise levels and the presence of artifacts is essential to ensure its robustness in practical medical imaging scenarios.
- *Convergence Analysis:* For iterative CS algorithms, examining convergence behavior, convergence rate, and stability during the reconstruction process are important.

When evaluating CS reconstruction algorithms in medical image recovery, a combination of these metrics provides a comprehensive understanding of the algorithm's performance in terms of accuracy, efficiency, and clinical relevance. It is often beneficial to use multiple metrics to gain a more holistic view of the reconstruction quality.

Compressed sensing in medical imaging is an active area of research, and ongoing developments aim to address challenges and optimize its application across different imaging modalities. The potential benefits in terms of faster imaging and reduced radiation exposure make CS a promising approach for the future of medical imaging.

Managing the massive amount of medical data becomes a major difficulty, even as the necessity of comprehensively monitoring all key signals and pictures in the medical system at all times grows more and more necessary. Particularly in health monitoring, CS with a solid theoretical foundation in the reconstruction of data by many less sampled signal vectors offers various benefits. Additionally, it lessens the adverse effects of patients being exposed to radio waves and electromagnetic fields, which are employed in medical equipment like CT and MRI redundantly and needlessly.

When integrating CS with medical imaging, it is critical to acknowledge that CT and MRI are quite advanced technology. Because of this, even in cases where CS is enhanced with assurances of precise picture recovery, it is impractical to anticipate sudden disruptive technical change in MRI or CT. This is for an easy reason:

Although mathematically perfect reconstruction does not always equate to the usefulness of real-world medical imaging equipment, CSGs pertinent to CT or MRI take exact image reconstruction of sparsely sampled data provided by idealized imaging systems into consideration [4, 5].

In this paper, we mainly discuss the following CS reconstruction algorithm used in the work:

- *Orthogonal Matching Pursuit algorithm (OMP):* One class of greedy algorithms is the OMP, an iterative algorithm used for sparse signal approximation and reconstruction. It is commonly employed in signal processing and CS applications where the goal is to represent a signal using only a small number of non-zero coefficients in a certain basis. The OMP is particularly useful when the signal is believed to have a sparse or compressible representation.

The greedy method attempts to compute the mismatch of the gathered data in order to estimate the growth in the rare signal in each of the iteration, or iteratively agrees on the signal coefficient until the signal converges. The OMP uses a straightforward technique to quickly create improvement indications.

It has to know the sparsity beforehand, which is usually equal to the number of iterations needed to get accurate results. Consequently, iteration and calculation time rise with sparsity. The pseudo code used for OMP algorithm is as shown below:

OMP Pseudo code:
Input sampled vector **y**, sensing matrix ϕ, sparsity K
Output K Space estimation of x
Initialization residual $r_0 = y$, index set Λ, iteration k = 1
1 while $k \leq K$
2 $\lambda k = arg\ max_{j=1\ to\ k} | < r_{k-1}, \phi > |$
3 update $\Lambda k = \Lambda_{k-1} \cup \Lambda_k$

$$\phi = \left[\phi_{k-1}, \phi_{\Lambda_k}\right]$$

4 solve $\hat{x} = arg\ max \,| y - \phi_k \hat{x} |_2)$ by LS method
5 update $r_k = y - \phi_k \hat{x}, \mathrm{k} = \mathrm{k} + 1$
6 if k > K **then** stop
7 else go to **step 1.**

The above pseudo code algorithm steps are explained below:

- Initialization:
  - Start with an initial guess for the sparse signal, often set to zero.
  - Initialize a residual signal, which is the difference between the original signal and the current approximation.

- Iteration:
  - At each iteration process, identify the atom (basis function) that has the highest correlation with the residual signal. This is done by calculating the inner products between the atoms and the residual signal.
  - Select the atom that maximizes the correlation, and update the support set (the set of indices corresponding to non-zero coefficients in the sparse signal).
  - Update the sparse coefficients using a least-squares minimization over the selected atoms.

- Update Residual:
  - Update the residual signal by subtracting the contribution of the selected atoms from the original signal.

- Convergence Criteria:
  - Repeat the iteration until a certain convergence criterion is met. This criterion could be a predefined number of iterations, a threshold for the residual norm, or other stopping conditions.

Overall, we may say that OMP is a greedy algorithm that selects one atom at a time based on its correlation with the residual. The algorithm stops when a predefined number of iterations is reached or when the residual is below a certain threshold. The OMP is widely used in applications such as CS; where the goal is to efficiently reconstruct a sparse signal from a limited number of measurements.

While OMP is effective in certain scenarios, it may not be suitable for all types of signals or sparse representations. The choice of the algorithm depends on the characteristics of the signal and the specific application requirements.

❖ Sparsity adaptive matching pursuit algorithm (SaMP):
The adaptive matching pursuit (AMP) algorithm is an extension of the matching pursuit algorithm, designed to address certain limitations and enhance performance, particularly in scenarios with sparsity constraints. Adaptive matching pursuit is iterative and seeks to find the sparse representation of a signal, often in the context of CS or sparse signal processing. The algorithm adapts its basis functions during each iteration process based on the observed residuals.
In 2008, N. Nguyn *et al.* developed the SaMP algorithm as a solution to the sparsity information need [2]. With an initial fixed step-size of 's' that is smaller than the sparsity ($s<k$), this technique approaches sparsity. Two tests are conducted on this algorithm: an initial test and a final test.
Sparsity is calculated step-by-step using the correlation test and a comparison between the current and prior residuals. Selecting the step-size is an important consideration since it affects both computing time and performance. The algorithm steps of SaMP is as shown below:

Initialization:

- Start with an initial guess for the sparse signal, often set to zero.
- Initialize a residual signal, which is the difference between the original signal and the current approximation.
- Choose an initial set of basis functions or atoms.

Iteration:

- At each iteration, calculate the correlation between the residual signal and the current set of basis functions (atoms).
- Update the coefficients of the basis functions based on the correlation and the residuals.
- Adaptively adjust the set of basis functions by including or excluding atoms based on their contribution to the signal reconstruction. This adaptability helps in handling sparsity more efficiently.

Update Residual:

- Update the residual signal by subtracting the contribution of the selected atoms from the original signal.

- *Convergence Criteria:*
  - Repeat the iteration until a certain convergence criterion is met. This criterion could be a predefined number of iterations, a threshold for the residual norm, or other stopping conditions.

The following pseudocode provides a simplified representation of the AMP algorithm. The pseudo code used in the work for SaMP CS reconstruction algorithm is as shown below:

SaMP pseudocode:
Input sampled vector **y**, sensing matrix ϕ, step-size S
Output Sparse estimation of x
Initialization residual $r_0 = y$, estimation $\hat{x} = 0$,
empty final list $F_0 = \emptyset$, step-size S= s, iteration k = 1
1 while (stopping condition is not true)
2 Preliminary selection $S_k = arg_m max\left(\left|\phi_{\mathrm{m}}^{*} r_{k-1}\right| S\right)$
3 Make candidate list $C_k = F_{k-1} \cup S_k$
4 Final select $F\ arg_m\ max\left(\left|\phi_{C_{km}}^{\dagger} y\right|, S\right)$
5 compute residue $\mathrm{r} = \mathrm{y} - \phi_F \phi_F y$
6 if halting condition is true **then** quit iteration
7 else if $\| r \| \geqslant \| r_{k-1} \|$ ***then***
Update the size of finalist S = S + s
8 else
Update the finalist $F_k = F$
Update the residue $r_k = r$
Update iteration index k = k + 1
9 end if
10 Repeat until halting condition true
Output: $\hat{x}_F = \phi_F^{\dagger} y$ estimation of non-zero coefficients

The adaptive nature of the algorithm involves dynamically updating the set of basis functions based on the observed correlations and the residuals. This adaptability helps in efficiently capturing the sparse structure of the signal.

- *Sparsity Handling:* By adaptively adjusting the set of basis functions, Adaptive Matching Pursuit is designed to handle sparse signals more effectively compared to some other pursuit algorithms.

- *Convergence Criteria:* The algorithm stops when a predefined number of iterations is reached or when the residual is below a certain threshold.

Adaptive matching pursuit, like other pursuit algorithms, is used in scenarios where signals can be represented sparsely in a certain domain and is particularly suitable for applications such as CS, sparse signal reconstruction, and feature selection in machine learning. The choice of the algorithm depends on the characteristics of the signal and the specific requirements of the application.

❖ Adaptive step-size SaMP algorithm (AS-SaMP)
Sequential approximate message passing is a framework used in CS for signal reconstruction. In SaMP algorithms, the idea is to iteratively refine the estimate of the signal by passing messages between variables. Each iteration process, involves updating the estimate of the signal and refining the probability distributions associated with the sparse coefficients. In the context of CS and signal reconstruction, combining an adaptive step-size strategy with a SaMP algorithm could involve dynamically adjusting the step size during each iteration process of the SaMP process.
This adaptation may be based on the local properties of the signal, the residual error, or other relevant metrics. The step-size determines the trade-off between computing time and performance. The SaMP algorithm becomes increasingly sophisticated with a fixed step-size. R. Venkatesan presented the AS-SaMP algorithm in 2015 [1, 3] to make step-size adaptable with sparsity. This takes into account the fact that as iteration goes on, the energy difference between the subsequent phases gets less. The AS-SaMP algorithm decreases the step-size when the signal drops at a predetermined pace. It begins with a bigger step-size. This is indicated by a specific threshold "σ." The pseudocode used in the work for AS-SaMP CS reconstruction algorithm is as shown below:

AS-SaMP Pseudo code:
Input Sampled vector **y**, sensing matrix ϕ, threshold σ, initial step-size S
Output Sparse estimation of x
Initialization residual $r_0 = y$, estimation $\hat{x} = 0$,
Empty final list $F_0 = \emptyset$, step-size $S = s, \hat{x}_{old} = \emptyset$ iteration k = 1

1 while (stopping condition is not true)
2 Preliminary selection $S_k = arg_m\ max\left(\left|\phi_m^* r_{k-1}\right|, S\right)$
3 Make candidate list $C_k = F_{k-1} \cup S_k$
4 Final select $F\ arg_m\ max\left(\left|\phi_{C_{km}}^{\dagger} y\right|, S\right)$
5 $\hat{x}(F_k) = \phi_F^{\dagger} y$
6 compute residue $\mathrm{r} = \mathrm{y} - \phi_F \phi_F^{\dagger} y$
7 if halting condition is true **then** quit iteration
8 else if $\| r \| \geqslant \| r_{k-1} \|$ **then**
9 if $\| \hat{x}(F_k) \| - \| \hat{x}_{old} \| < \sigma$ **then**

$$S = [s/2], \mathrm{S} = \mathrm{S} + \mathrm{s}, \hat{x}_{old} = \hat{x}(F_k), r_k = r_{k-1}, \mathrm{k} = \mathrm{k} + 1$$

10 else $\mathrm{S} = \mathrm{S} + \mathrm{s}, \hat{x}_{old} = \hat{x}(F_k), r_k = r_{k-1}, \mathrm{k} = \mathrm{k} + 1$
11 end if
12 else

$$Fk = F, r_k = r, \mathrm{k} = \mathrm{k} + 1$$

13 end if
14 end while
Output: $\hat{x}_F = \phi_F^{\dagger} y$ estimation of non-zero coefficients

- Dynamic step-size SaMP (DSS-SaMP)
  Dynamic step-size strategies involve adapting the step size during the iterations of an optimization or reconstruction algorithm. This adaptation is often based on the local behavior of the algorithm, the properties of the data, or other relevant criteria. The goal is to improve convergence and performance in varying conditions. When incorporating dynamic step-size strategies into a SaMP algorithm, the step size at each iteration could be adjusted based on the progress of the algorithm or the characteristics of the signal being reconstructed. Potential strategies might include:

  - Adaptive Step-Size based on Residuals: Adjust the step size based on the magnitude or characteristics of the residual error at each iteration process. Larger residuals might suggest a need for a larger step size, and vice versa.
  - Local Signal Characteristics: Modify the step size based on local signal characteristics or properties. For example,

if certain coefficients are changing rapidly, a smaller step size might be beneficial.

- Convergence Criteria: Adjust the step size dynamically based on the convergence behavior of the algorithm. If the algorithm is converging rapidly, the step size could be increased to expedite convergence.

The threshold $\sigma \leq \|h\|$, where h is the expected signal to accomplish fine tuning, is taken into consideration in the AS-SaMP algorithm. Greater performance and more iterations are indicated by a larger "}". Better estimate quality is thus the result of earlier fine tuning. Choosing this 'σ' is crucial since it directly affects step-size adjustment, quality, and the quantity of iterations. For step-size adaptivity, the suggested method takes into account both the new threshold model and the fundamental SaMP structure. The pseudocode used in the work for DSS-SaMP CS reconstruction algorithm is as shown below:

DSS-SaMP pseudocode:
Input Sampled vector **y**, sensing matrix ϕ, threshold σ, initial step-size S
Output sparse estimation of x
Initialization residual $r_0 = y$, estimation $\hat{x} = 0$,
empty final list $F_0 = \emptyset$, iteration k = 1, stage index j = 1
1 while (stopping condition is not true)
2 Preliminary selection $S_k = arg_m\ max\left(\left|\phi_m^* r_{k-1}\right|, S\right)$
3 Make candidate list $C_k = F_{k-1} \cup S_k$
4 Final select $F\ arg_m\ max\left(\left|\phi_{C_{km}}^{\dagger} y\right|, S\right)$
5 compute residue $r = y - \phi_F \phi_F^{\dagger} y$
6 if halting condition is true **then** quit iteration
7 else if $\|r\| \geqslant \|r_{k-1}\|$ **then** stage switching
8 if $\|r\| > \sigma\ \|y\|$ **then**

$$S = [s/2],\ j = j + 1,\ S = j * s$$

9 else j = j + 1, S = j * s
10 end if
11 else j = j + 1, S = j * s, $rk = r$, $Fk = F$
12 end if
13 update iteration k = k + 1
14 Repeat Until halting condition true
Output: $\hat{x}_F = \phi_F^{\dagger} y$ estimation of non-zero coefficients

The recommended algorithm is used at each stage to execute the first and final tests. Similar to the SaMP and AS-SaMP algorithms, these correlation tests imply a connection between the columns of the sensing matrix and the residual signal. The technique starts with a higher step-size to allow for faster convergence, and it dynamically reduces the step-size with fine-tuning in later stages as the estimated signal's energy decreases. In this case, the threshold parameter "σ" is specified so that multiplying it by the input signal's norm yields the new threshold. As a result, the step-size decreases in proportion to the percentage of the norm of "y."

The main concept is to update the step-size by fixing the threshold based on the energy of the input signal (new threshold $\text{I}=\sigma\|y\|$, as opposed to ~ khk. In addition, step-size is adjusted based on the stage number. As a result, the new threshold π is chosen in relation to 'y' rather than at random as in AS-SaMP, creating a controlled threshold environment. This suggested approach does not require any external criteria that other existing algorithms employ, and it also alters the SaMP algorithm that overcomes the fixed step-size problem. This makes things simpler. To preserve generality, "σ" is used here for both the DSS-SaMP and AS-SaMP algorithms.

4.4 Results and Discussion

This section will examine the steps involved in the decompression of any medical image into a binary image using the various approaches OMP, SaMP, AS-SaMP and DSS-SaMP algorithms to the respective medical image that has been compressed.

In this work, a medical image is converted to a binary image, and the image is compressed into a $m \times m$ matrix using a CS algorithm once it has been converted to a binary image during transmission over the channel. Next, choose a 4x4 matrix at random from the matrix. Then, this compressed image is reconstructed using the above-mentioned algorithms. All the algorithms are evaluated in terms BER, SER and MSE.

Signals that are "sparse" in comparison to standard signals draw attention in some applications, such as biological systems, high-speed analog-to-digital compression, and imaging. Let us say there are millions of pixels in a picture. However, only a small portion of the image's numerous pixels, roughly 100,000, are important for reconstructing the original image; the remaining pixels have little bearing on this process, hence most compression algorithms often reject the values in these pixels.

Compression and subsequent sampling are extremely inefficient and wasteful of resources, including energy and observation time. The goal of sparse representation is to extract a few significant or crucial signals that together may represent the complete signal to be taken with a non-zero value [8].

The majority of signals are zero or too tiny to be ignored, therefore they may be referred to as sparse signals [9]. Generally speaking, signals in the form of compressed and accurately projected pictures and sounds have a signal with non-zero coefficients. And a signal will cause the coefficient value to be dispersed rather than to accumulate in one area.

The MSE comparison of the OMP, SaMP, AS-SaMP, and DSS-SaMP algorithms is displayed in Figure 4.2. This illustrates that the adaptive sparsity algorithms outperform the well-known OMP sparsity technique. Furthermore, compared to the adaptive sparsity algorithms SaMP and AS-SaMP, the suggested method DSS-SaMP exhibits a lower MSE as shown in figure 4.2(a). It is evident that the DSS-SaMP algorithm outperforms the OMP, SaMP, and AS-SaMP algorithms in terms of BER as shown in figure 4.2(b).

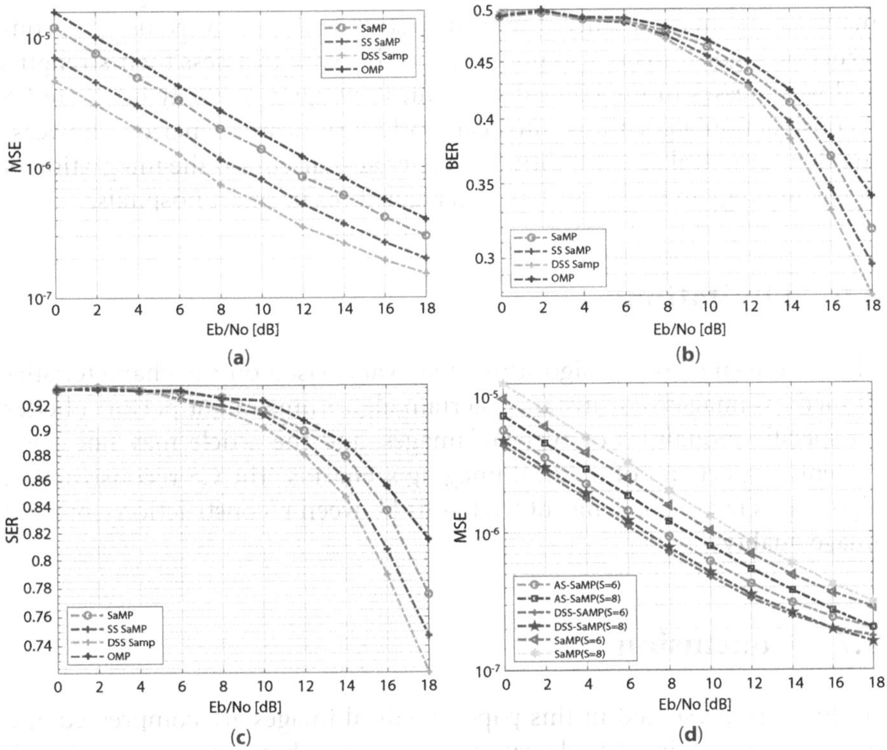

Figure 4.2 A comparison of OMP, SaMP, AS-SaMP and DSS-SaMP algorithms.

This demonstrates how the DSS-SaMP method functions as a reliable estimator with lower error bits. It is evident that the DSS-SaMP algorithm outperforms the OMP, SaMP, and AS-SaMP algorithms in terms of BER. This demonstrates how the DSS-SaMP method functions as a reliable estimator with lower error bits. It is evident that the OMP, SaMP, and AS-SaMP algorithms have higher SER values than the DSS-SaMP methods as shown in Figure 4.2(c). This demonstrates how the DSS-SaMP method functions as a reliable estimator with a lower error rate in symbols. Figure 4.2(d) shows the results of MSE for various step-sizes DSS-SaMP gives better results.

4.5 Contribution of the Work

The work proposed in the paper shows the demonstration of how the implementation of CS reconstruction algorithms enhances the efficiency of medical image reconstruction compared to traditional methods. This could include reduced data acquisition times or lower sampling rates while maintaining image quality. The comparative analysis of various CS reconstruction algorithms is also presented in the work to assess their strengths and weaknesses in the context of medical imaging. We may integrate CS reconstruction algorithms into real-world healthcare scenarios, showcasing their practical applicability. The paper also discussed the integration of 5G technology in CS reconstruction algorithms in smart hospitals.

4.6 Limitations

The effectiveness of CS algorithms may vary based on the characteristics of medical images. For instance, certain algorithms might perform better on specific modalities or types of images, and the article may not cover the entire spectrum of medical imaging scenarios. The CS reconstruction algorithms face a challenge of trade-offs between reconstruction time and image quality.

4.7 Conclusion

In the work presented in this paper, medical images are compressed and decompressed using CS algorithms. The algorithms are compared with each other using metrics BER, SER, and MSE against SNR. In the work, although sparsity level is practically difficult to achieve for OMP, SaMP increases performance with blind recoveries in addition to high computational time. Using a random threshold, AS-SaMP with an adjustable step-size executes a trade-off between computational time and performance. The DSS-SaMP method takes the input signal's energy into account, which further enhances performance and reduces computing costs.

References

1. Rani M, Dhok S B, Deshmukh R B, A Systematic Review of Compressive Sensing: Concepts, Implementations and Applications, *IEEE Access*, 2018, *6*, 4875–4894.
2. Chen Z, Huang C, Lin S, A new sparse representation framework for compressed sensing MRI, *Knowl. Based Syst.*, 2020, *188*, 104969.
3. Hora SK, Poongodan R, de Prado RP, Wozniak M, Divakarachari PB. Long Short-Term Memory Network-Based Metaheuristic for Effective Electric Energy Consumption Prediction. *Appl. Sci.*, 2021; 11(23), 11263. https://doi.org/10.3390/app112311263.
4. Majumdar A, *Compressed Sensing for Engineers*, Taylor & Francis Group: Abingdon, UK, 2019.
5. SherY, Review of Algorithms for Compressive Sensing of Images, arXiv 2019, arXiv:1908.01642.
6. Graff C G, Sidky E Y, Compressive sensing in medical imaging, *Appl Opt.*, 2015 Mar 10; 54(8), C23-44. doi: 10.1364/AO.54.000C23. PMID: 25968400; PMCID: PMC4669980.
7. Djelouat H, Amira A, Bensaali F, Compressive Sensing-Based IoT Applications: A Review, *J. Sens. Actuator Netw.*, 2018, *7*, 45. https://doi.org/10.3390/jsan7040045.
8. P S Mathew, Applications of IoT in healthcare, *Cognitive Computing for Big Data Systems over IoT*, pp. 263–288, Springer, Berlin, Germany, 2018.
9. Djelouat, Hamza "IoT Based Compressive Sensing for ECG Monitoring." *2017 IEEE International Conference o n Internet of Things (iThings) and IEEE Green Computing and Communications (GreenCom) and IEEE Cyber, Physical and Social Computing (CPSCom) and IEEE Smart Data (SmartData)* (2017): 183-189.
10. Shannon, C. Communication in the Presence of Noise. *Proc. IRE*, 1949, *37*, 10–21.
11. Ramakrishnan B, Kumar A, Chakravarty S, Masud M, & Baz M, Analysis of FBMC waveform for 5G network based smart hospitals, *Appl. Sci.*, 2021, 11(19), 8895.

12. Kumar A, Venkatesh J, Gaur N, Alsharif M H, Jahid A, & Raju K, Analysis of Hybrid Spectrum Sensing for 5G and 6G Waveforms, *Electronics*, 2022, 12(1), 138.
13. Higuchi K, & Benjebbour A, Non-Orthogonal Multiple Access (NOMA) with successive interference cancellation for future radio access, *IEICE Trans. Commun.*, 2015, E98B (3), 403–414.
14. Ding Z, Fan P, & Poor H V, Impact of User Pairing on 5G Nonorthogonal Multiple-Access Downlink Transmissions, *IEEE Trans. Veh. Technol.*, 2016, 65(8), 6010–6023.
15. Islam S M R, Avazov N, Dobre O A, & Kwak K S, Power-Domain Non-Orthogonal Multiple Accesses (NOMA) in 5G Systems: Potentials and Challenges, *IEEE Commun. Surv. Tutorials*, 2017, 19(2), 721–742.
16. Dai L, Wang B, Yuan Y, Han S, Chih-Lin I, & Wang Z, Non-orthogonal multiple access for 5G: solutions, challenges, opportunities, and future research trends, *IEEE Commun. Mag.*, 2015, 53(9), 74-81.
17. Kavitha K J & Shan P B, Medical image watermarking based on novel encoding for EHR and fusion based morphological watershed segmentation algorithm for medical images, *Multimed. Tools Appl.*, 2023, 1-28.
18. Suprith P G, & Mohammed R A, The Performance Evaluation of NOMA for 5G systems using Automatic Deployment of multi Users. *Int. J. Electron. Telecommun.*, 2022, 68.

5

Internet of Medical Things (IoMT)

Gobinath A.[1], Rajeswari P.[1]*, Suresh Kumar N.[2] and Anandan M.[3]

[1]Velammal College of Engineering and Technology, Madurai, Tamil Nadu, India
[2]R.M.K. College of Engineering and Technology, Thiruvallur District, Tamil Nadu, India
[3]Vel Tech Rangarajan Dr. Sagunthala R&D Institute of Science and Technology, Chennai, Tamil Nadu, India

Abstract

The Internet of Medical Things (IoMT) is transforming patient care, clinical processes, and healthcare outcomes by integrating interconnected medical devices, sensors, and applications, marking a paradigm shift in the healthcare industry. IoMT encompasses a wide range of interconnected devices, from smart home health monitors and wearable fitness trackers to implanted medical devices and remote patient monitoring systems. These devices collect real-time health data such as vital signs, activity levels, and medication compliance, enabling continuous monitoring and personalized treatments. Healthcare providers can reduce hospital readmissions and improve patient outcomes by remotely monitoring patients, detecting early warning signs of health deterioration, and taking proactive measures to intervene. One of the primary benefits of IoMT is its ability to facilitate telemedicine and remote patient monitoring, especially in underserved or remote areas with limited access to healthcare services. Wearable technology that tracks physiological parameters and instantly transmits data to medical professionals can assist patients with chronic conditions like diabetes, hypertension, or heart disease, allowing for immediate adjustments to treatment plans, medication dosages, and lifestyle recommendations, thereby enhancing disease management and patient engagement. Moreover, IoMT technologies play a crucial role in population health management and preventive medicine by enabling early detection of health risks and promoting healthy behaviors. Healthcare organizations can target interventions, health promotion campaigns, and resource allocation by identifying trends, patterns, and risk factors within patient populations

**Corresponding author*: pra@vcet.ac.in

Arun Kumar, Manoj Gupta, Sanjeev Sharma, Er. Himanshu Sharma and Khursheed Aurangzeb (eds.) Smart Hospitals: 5G, 6G and Moving Beyond Connectivity, (91–106) © 2024 Scrivener Publishing LLC

through the analysis of aggregated data from connected devices. IoMT also supports remote health monitoring for post-operative patients, individuals with disabilities, and the elderly, maintaining their independence and quality of life while reducing healthcare costs. Despite its transformative potential, several obstacles must be addressed for IoMT to achieve widespread adoption. Data privacy and security are paramount, given the sensitive nature of health information collected and transmitted by connected devices. Robust encryption, authentication protocols, and compliance with legal frameworks like the Health Insurance Portability and Accountability Act (HIPAA) are essential to protect patient privacy and prevent unauthorized access or data breaches. Another challenge is the interoperability and integration of IoMT with existing healthcare systems. The proliferation of diverse devices and platforms necessitates interoperable standards and seamless data exchange to facilitate clinical decision-making and comprehensive patient care coordination. Additionally, ongoing validation and calibration of IoMT devices are crucial to ensure data quality, reliability, and usability across various healthcare settings.

Keywords: Internet of Medical Things, IoMT, telemedicine, remote patient monitoring, healthcare transformation

5.1 Introduction: Internet of Medical Things

The Internet of Medical Things (IoMT) represents a transformative paradigm shift in healthcare delivery, leveraging interconnected devices, sensors, and systems to revolutionize patient care and clinical practice. In recent years, the proliferation of advanced technologies has ushered in a new era of connected healthcare, where medical devices seamlessly communicate, collect, and analyze health data in real-time. This introduction provides a comprehensive overview of the IoMT, delineating its definition, significance, applications, challenges, and implications for the future of healthcare [1].

5.1.1 Defining the IoMT

At its core, the IoMT refers to the integration of medical devices, wearables, and healthcare systems with network connectivity and data analytics capabilities. These interconnected devices form a vast ecosystem of smart healthcare solutions that enable remote patient monitoring (RPM), personalized medicine, and improved clinical outcomes. The IoMT encompasses a wide array of devices, including wearable fitness trackers, smartwatches, implantable sensors, and medical-grade monitoring equipment. By harnessing the power of connectivity, the IoMT enables seamless data exchange between patients, healthcare providers, and medical systems, facilitating proactive healthcare management and early intervention [2–4].

The emergence of the IoMT holds profound implications for healthcare stakeholders, including patients, clinicians, healthcare institutions, and policymakers. For patients, the IoMT offers unprecedented access to personalized healthcare services, empowering individuals to actively monitor their health status, manage chronic conditions, and make informed decisions about their well-being. Clinicians benefit from IoMT-enabled remote monitoring capabilities, allowing for proactive disease management, timely interventions, and improved patient outcomes. Healthcare institutions stand to gain from IoMT by enhancing operational efficiency, optimizing resource allocation, and delivering cost-effective, patient-centered care. Moreover, policymakers recognize IoMT as a catalyst for healthcare innovation, driving regulatory reforms, and shaping the future of healthcare policy [4–7]. Figure 5.1 shows the Internet of Things in medical care.

The applications of IoMT span across the healthcare continuum, encompassing preventive, diagnostic, therapeutic, and rehabilitative care. Remote patient monitoring represents a prominent application of IoMT, enabling healthcare providers to remotely monitor vital signs, medication adherence, and disease progression in real-time. Telemedicine platforms leverage IoMT technologies to facilitate virtual consultations, telehealth services, and remote patient education, bridging geographical barriers and improving healthcare access. The IoMT also supports precision medicine initiatives by enabling the collection of large-scale health data, genetic

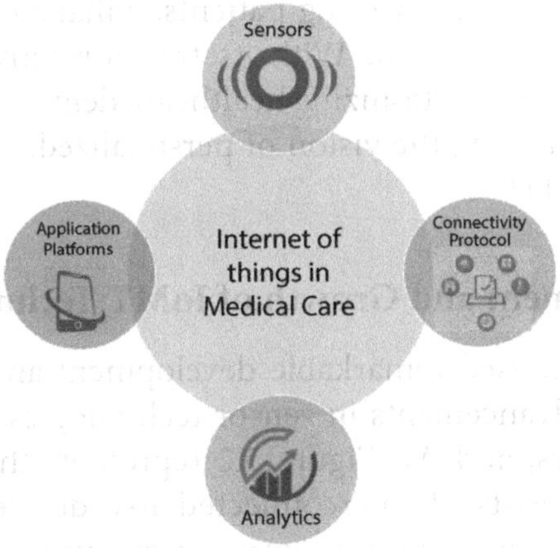

Figure 5.1 The Internet of Things in medical care.

information, and environmental factors, facilitating tailored treatment plans and predictive analytics [8].

Despite its transformative potential, IoMT implementation faces several challenges and considerations, including data security and privacy concerns, interoperability issues, regulatory compliance, and ethical considerations. The interconnected nature of IoMT devices raises cybersecurity risks, necessitating robust encryption protocols, data encryption, and access controls to safeguard sensitive health information. Interoperability challenges arise from the diversity of IoMT devices, protocols, and data formats, hindering seamless data exchange and integration across healthcare systems. Regulatory frameworks, such as the HIPAA, impose stringent requirements for data protection, privacy, and patient consent in IoMT deployments. Ethical considerations surrounding data ownership, consent, and patient autonomy underscore the need for transparent governance frameworks and ethical guidelines in IoMT applications [9].

Looking ahead, IoMT holds immense promise for shaping the future of healthcare delivery, driving innovation, and improving patient outcomes. The convergence of IoMT with emerging technologies, such as artificial intelligence (AI), machine learning, and edge computing, will further accelerate its adoption and transformative impact on healthcare. By harnessing the power of data-driven insights, IoMT has the potential to revolutionize clinical decision-making, disease management, and healthcare delivery models. However, realizing the full potential of IoMT requires collaborative efforts from healthcare stakeholders, policymakers, industry leaders, and technology innovators to address the challenges and harness the opportunities presented by this transformative paradigm shift in healthcare [10].

The IoMT represents a disruptive force that is reshaping the landscape of healthcare delivery, empowering patients, enhancing clinical care, and driving healthcare innovation. With its transformative potential, IoMT holds the promise of revolutionizing healthcare delivery, improving patient outcomes, and advancing the vision of personalized, proactive, and data-driven healthcare [11].

5.1.2 Development and Growth of IoMT Technologies

The IoMT has witnessed remarkable development and growth in recent years, driven by advancements in sensor technologies, connectivity solutions, data analytics, and AI. Figure 5.2 represents the The IoT deployment structure consists of interconnected IoT devices, which transmit data to gateway servers. These gateway servers process and forward the data to cloud storage, enabling centralized data management and analysis.

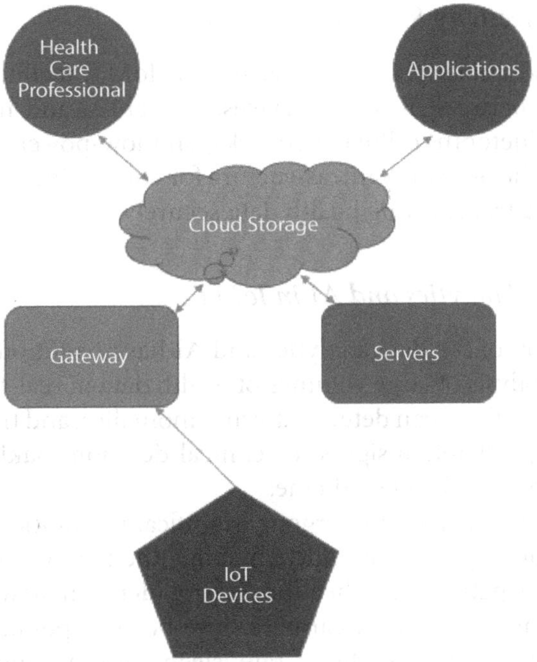

Figure 5.2 The IoT deployment structure.

This section provides an overview of the historical evolution and key milestones in IoMT technologies, highlighting their transformative impact on healthcare delivery, patient care, and clinical practice [12].

5.1.2.1 *Early Beginnings of IoMT*

The concept of IoMT traces its roots back to the early 2000s when researchers and innovators began exploring the potential of integrating medical devices and systems with internet connectivity. Early IoMT applications focused primarily on RPM, with the development of wearable devices for tracking vital signs, medication adherence, and disease progression [13].

5.1.2.2 *Advancements in Sensor Technologies*

One of the key drivers of IoMT growth has been the evolution of sensor technologies, enabling the development of smaller, more accurate, and cost-effective sensors for monitoring various physiological parameters. Sensors such as accelerometers, gyroscopes, heart rate monitors, and temperature sensors have become ubiquitous in wearable devices, allowing for continuous monitoring of patients' health status in real-time [14].

5.1.2.3 Connectivity Solutions for IoMT

Connectivity solutions play a critical role in IoMT, facilitating seamless data exchange between medical devices, wearables, and healthcare systems. Wi-Fi, Bluetooth, cellular networks, and low-power wide-area networks provide the necessary infrastructure for connecting IoMT devices to the internet and transmitting health data securely.

5.1.2.4 Data Analytics and AI in IoMT

The proliferation of big data analytics and AI has revolutionized IoMT by enabling the analysis of large volumes of health data in real-time. Artificial intelligence algorithms can detect patterns, anomalies, and trends in health data, providing valuable insights for clinical decision-making, predictive analytics, and personalized medicine.

Wearable devices have undergone significant evolution in terms of design, functionality, and usability, making them more accessible and user-friendly for patients and healthcare providers. Smartwatches, fitness trackers, and medical-grade wearables have become popular choices for monitoring physical activity, heart rate, sleep patterns, and other health metrics.

The development and growth of IoMT technologies have ushered in a new era of connected healthcare, transforming the way patients are monitored, diagnosed, and treated. With ongoing innovation and collaboration, IoMT is poised to revolutionize healthcare delivery, improve patient outcomes, and enhance clinical workflows in the years to come.

5.2 Wearable Devices and Sensors for IoMT

Wearable health surveillance devices have revolutionized healthcare by providing individuals with continuous monitoring of vital signs and health parameters. These devices, such as smartwatches, wristbands, neckbands, and belts, offer convenience, portability, and real-time data tracking capabilities. This article explores several wearable devices currently in use, their specific applications, and their impact on healthcare management [15].

5.2.1 Types of Wearable Devices

Wearable devices encompass a diverse range of gadgets that are capable of collecting, processing, and transmitting health-related data. These devices come in various forms, including smartwatches, fitness trackers, medical-grade wearables, and implantable sensors.

5.2.1.1 Smartwatches

Smartwatches have gained popularity for their multifunctionality and health monitoring features. They typically include sensors for tracking heart rate, activity levels, sleep patterns, and even electrocardiograms (ECG) in some cases. Applications such as Apple Health and Google Fit allow users to visualize their health data, set fitness goals, and receive insights into their overall well-being. Additionally, smartwatches can provide notifications for irregular heart rhythms, potentially aiding in the early detection of cardiac arrhythmias or other cardiovascular conditions.

5.2.1.2 Wristbands

Wristbands, also known as fitness trackers or activity monitors, are designed primarily for tracking physical activity and exercise metrics. They feature accelerometers and gyroscopes to measure movement, steps taken, distance traveled, and calories burned. Some wristbands also include heart rate sensors for monitoring exercise intensity and recovery. These devices are widely used by athletes, fitness enthusiasts, and individuals seeking to improve their physical fitness. Moreover, wristbands with sleep tracking capabilities can monitor sleep duration and quality, offering insights into sleep patterns and potential sleep disorders.

5.2.1.3 Neckbands

Neckbands are wearable devices worn around the neck that offer discrete health monitoring and communication capabilities. These devices may include sensors for tracking vital signs such as heart rate, respiratory rate, and skin temperature. Neckbands are particularly useful for RPM applications, allowing healthcare providers to monitor patients' health status in real-time and intervene promptly if abnormalities are detected. Additionally, neckbands equipped with communication features enable patients to stay connected with caregivers or emergency services, enhancing safety and peace of mind.

5.2.1.4 Belts

Smart belts are wearable devices worn around the waist that provide health monitoring and posture correction functionalities. These devices typically include sensors for measuring waist circumference, body movement, and posture alignment. Smart belts can analyze sitting, standing, and walking patterns to promote ergonomic posture and prevent musculoskeletal injuries. Moreover, some smart belts incorporate haptic feedback or vibrating alerts to remind users to maintain proper posture throughout the day. These devices are beneficial for individuals with sedentary lifestyles, office workers, and individuals recovering from back injuries.

5.2.1.5 Smart Clothing

Smart clothing integrates wearable technology directly into garments, offering non-intrusive health monitoring and activity tracking. These garments contain embedded sensors that measure vital signs such as heart rate, respiration rate, and body temperature. Smart clothing is particularly useful for athletes, military personnel, and individuals with chronic conditions who require continuous health monitoring without wearing additional devices. Furthermore, smart clothing can be seamlessly integrated into everyday attire, providing discreet health monitoring capabilities without compromising comfort or style.

5.2.1.6 Smart Rings

Smart rings are compact wearable devices worn on the finger, offering health tracking features similar to smartwatches in a more discreet form. These rings typically include sensors for monitoring heart rate, sleep quality, and activity levels. Additionally, some smart rings feature near-field communication technology for contactless payments and authentication purposes. Smart rings are ideal for individuals who prefer minimalist wearable technology or require inconspicuous health monitoring during daily activities.

5.2.1.7 Smart Glasses

Smart glasses, also known as augmented reality (AR) glasses, are wearable devices with integrated displays that overlay digital information onto the user's field of view. While primarily used for AR applications, smart glasses can also incorporate health monitoring features such as heart rate monitoring, step tracking, and visual cues for medication reminders or navigation assistance. Smart glasses have the potential to revolutionize healthcare by providing healthcare professionals with hands-free access to patient data, medical records, and procedural guidance during surgeries or clinical consultations.

5.2.1.8 *Smart Patches*

Smart patches are thin, flexible adhesive patches that adhere to the skin, offering continuous monitoring of various physiological parameters. These patches contain miniaturized sensors for monitoring vital signs, hydration levels, glucose levels, and skin conductivity. Smart patches are particularly useful for RPM, clinical trials, and research studies requiring long-term data collection without the need for bulky wearable devices. Furthermore, smart patches are comfortable to wear and can be worn discreetly under clothing, making them suitable for continuous health monitoring in various settings.

5.2.1.9 *Smart Earbuds*

Smart earbuds are wireless earphones equipped with biometric sensors for health monitoring and fitness tracking. These earbuds measure heart rate, blood oxygen saturation, and activity levels using optical sensors and accelerometers embedded within the earbud housing. Additionally, smart earbuds can provide real-time feedback on workout intensity, pace, and technique, enhancing the user's exercise experience. Smart earbuds are ideal for individuals who prefer audio-based feedback and motivation during workouts or outdoor activities.

5.3 Challenges Faced in Customizing Wearable Devices

Customizing wearable devices presents several challenges, ranging from technical complexities to user preferences, and regulatory considerations. These challenges can significantly impact the development, deployment, and adoption of personalized wearable solutions across various industries and applications.

One major challenge in customizing wearable devices is achieving a balance between functionality and form factor. Wearable devices must be compact, lightweight, and comfortable to wear, while also incorporating a diverse range of sensors, processors, and communication modules. Designing wearable devices that meet both technical requirements and user preferences can be challenging, especially when integrating multiple functionalities into a single device. Moreover, ensuring durability, water resistance, and battery life adds further complexity to the design process, requiring careful consideration of materials, manufacturing techniques, and power management strategies.

Another challenge in customizing wearable devices is addressing interoperability and compatibility issues. With a proliferation of wearable platforms, operating systems, and communication protocols, ensuring seamless integration and interoperability between wearable devices and other hardware and software systems can be challenging. Compatibility issues may arise when integrating wearable devices with existing healthcare systems, IoT platforms, mobile applications, or cloud services, hindering data exchange, communication, and data analytics. Standardization efforts and open-source frameworks can help address interoperability challenges, but achieving widespread adoption and compatibility remains a significant hurdle.

Furthermore, customization of wearable devices raises privacy and security concerns related to sensitive health data. Wearable devices collect a wealth of personal health information, including vital signs, activity levels, and sleep patterns, raising concerns about data privacy, confidentiality, and unauthorized access. Protecting sensitive health data from cyber threats, data breaches, and unauthorized use requires robust encryption, authentication, and access control mechanisms. Moreover, compliance with data privacy regulations such as HIPAA, GDPR, and CCPA adds regulatory complexity and compliance overhead to wearable device customization efforts, requiring careful attention to data protection and privacy-by-design principles.

Additionally, customization of wearable devices entails addressing diverse user preferences, needs, and demographics. User acceptance and adoption of wearable devices depend on factors such as design aesthetics, ease of use, comfort, and perceived value. Designing customizable wearable devices that cater to a broad range of user preferences and requirements requires user-centric design approaches, usability testing, and iterative feedback loops. Moreover, ensuring inclusivity and accessibility for users with diverse abilities, cultures, and languages adds further complexity to the customization process, requiring consideration of universal design principles and accessibility standards.

Moreover, customization of wearable devices presents challenges related to regulatory compliance and certification. Depending on the intended application and target market, wearable devices may be subject to regulatory requirements and standards governing medical devices, consumer electronics, and data privacy. Achieving regulatory compliance and obtaining necessary certifications such as FDA clearance, CE marking, or FCC certification requires thorough documentation, testing, and validation of wearable devices, adding time and cost to the customization process. Moreover, navigating evolving regulatory landscapes, changing compliance requirements, and jurisdictional differences can pose additional challenges for wearable device manufacturers and developers.

Customizing wearable devices presents several challenges related to technical complexity, interoperability, privacy and security, user preferences, and regulatory compliance. Addressing these challenges requires a multidisciplinary approach involving expertise in design, engineering, data science, cybersecurity, regulatory affairs, and user experience. By overcoming these challenges, personalized wearable solutions have the potential to transform healthcare, wellness, sports, and various industries, empowering individuals to monitor their health, enhance performance, and improve quality of life. However, continued innovation, collaboration, and investment are needed to realize the full potential of customized wearable devices in addressing global health challenges and advancing personalized medicine.

5.4 Real-World Examples of IoMT Implementation

Implementations of IoMT are increasingly prevalent across various sectors of healthcare, revolutionizing patient care, clinical workflows, and healthcare management. These real-world examples demonstrate the diverse applications and transformative impact of IoMT technologies in improving health outcomes, enhancing operational efficiency, and empowering both patients and healthcare providers.

5.4.1 Remote Patient Monitoring (RPM)

Remote patient monitoring enables healthcare providers to monitor patients' health status outside traditional clinical settings, facilitating timely interventions, and reducing hospital readmissions. For example, Philips Healthcare's "Telehealth Program" utilizes IoMT-enabled devices such as blood pressure monitors, pulse oximeters, and weight scales to remotely monitor patients with chronic conditions such as heart failure, chronic obstructive pulmonary disease, and diabetes. Healthcare providers receive real-time data from patients' home devices, enabling proactive management of their conditions, early detection of exacerbations, and personalized interventions based on individual health data.

5.4.2 Wearable Devices for Chronic Disease Management

Wearable devices equipped with sensors and wireless connectivity offer continuous monitoring of vital signs, activity levels, and other health parameters, empowering individuals to manage chronic diseases more effectively. For instance, Abbott's FreeStyle Libre system provides continuous glucose monitoring for patients with diabetes, eliminating the need for routine fingerstick blood glucose testing. The wearable sensor, worn on the back of the upper arm, measures interstitial glucose levels continuously and transmits data to a smartphone or reader device, enabling real-time glucose monitoring, trend analysis, and insulin dose adjustments.

5.4.3 Smart Hospitals and Healthcare Facilities

These IoMT technologies are transforming traditional healthcare facilities into smart hospitals, equipped with interconnected devices and systems for seamless data exchange, real-time monitoring, and predictive analytics. For example, GE Healthcare's "Edison" platform integrates medical devices, electronic health records, and AI algorithms to optimize clinical workflows, improve patient outcomes, and enhance operational efficiency. By harnessing data from IoMT-enabled devices such as patient monitors, ventilators, and infusion pumps, healthcare providers can gain actionable insights, automate routine tasks, and deliver personalized care to patients.

5.4.4 Telemedicine and Virtual Care

Telemedicine platforms leverage IoMT technologies to enable virtual consultations, remote diagnosis, and telemonitoring of patients, expanding access to healthcare services and improving care coordination. One notable example is Teladoc Health, a leading telemedicine provider that offers virtual visits with board-certified physicians, psychiatrists, and other healthcare professionals. Patients can connect with providers via video conferencing, secure messaging, or phone calls, eliminating geographical barriers and enabling timely access to medical advice, prescriptions, and referrals. The IoMT-enabled devices such as digital stethoscopes, otoscopes, and dermatoscopes further enhance the diagnostic capabilities of telemedicine providers, enabling remote examination and assessment of patients' health conditions.

5.4.5 Clinical Trials and Research

The IoMT technologies play a crucial role in accelerating clinical trials, enhancing patient recruitment, and improving data collection and analysis. For example, Medidata Solutions, a leading provider of cloud-based clinical research software, offers IoMT-enabled solutions for remote patient monitoring, electronic data capture, and clinical trial management. Wearable devices such as activity trackers, biosensors, and ECG monitors enable remote monitoring of study participants' health status, adherence to study protocols, and real-time collection of objective health data. By leveraging IoMT technologies, clinical researchers can streamline trial operations, reduce costs, and accelerate the development of new treatments and therapies for various diseases and medical conditions.

These real-world examples illustrate the wide-ranging applications and transformative impact of IoMT implementations in healthcare. From remote patient monitoring and chronic disease management to smart hospitals, telemedicine, and clinical research, IoMT technologies are reshaping the delivery of healthcare services, improving patient outcomes, and driving innovation in the healthcare industry. As IoMT continues to evolve, it holds the promise of revolutionizing healthcare delivery, promoting preventive care, and empowering individuals to take control of their health and well-being in the digital age.

5.5 Conclusions

In conclusion, the real-world implementations of IoMT represent a significant paradigm shift in healthcare delivery, with transformative implications for patient care, clinical workflows, and healthcare management. Through remote patient monitoring, wearable devices for chronic disease management, smart hospitals, telemedicine, and clinical research, IoMT technologies are revolutionizing how healthcare is accessed, delivered, and experienced.

These examples showcase the versatility and impact of IoMT across various healthcare sectors, from empowering individuals to manage chronic conditions more effectively to enhancing clinical decision-making, operational efficiency, and patient outcomes. By leveraging interconnected devices, sensors, data analytics, and telecommunication technologies, IoMT enables seamless data exchange, real-time monitoring, and predictive analytics, driving personalized, proactive, and patient-centered care. Moreover, IoMT implementations hold the promise of improving access to healthcare services, particularly in underserved communities and remote regions, by overcoming geographical barriers and expanding the reach of telemedicine and virtual care. Additionally, IoMT-enabled clinical trials and research initiatives are accelerating the development of innovative treatments and therapies, leading to advancements in medical science and improved patient outcomes.

As IoMT continues to evolve, it is essential to address challenges related to data privacy, interoperability, regulatory compliance, and user acceptance to realize its full potential in healthcare. Collaboration among stakeholders, including healthcare providers, technology vendors, policymakers, and patients, is crucial to ensuring the responsible and ethical use of IoMT technologies while maximizing their benefits for individuals and society. Overall, the real-world implementations of IoMT exemplify the convergence of healthcare and technology, offering unprecedented opportunities to revolutionize healthcare delivery, promote preventive care, and empower individuals to lead healthier lives. With continued innovation, investment, and collaboration, IoMT has the potential to transform the healthcare landscape, ushering in a new era of personalized, connected, and sustainable healthcare for all.

References

1. Joyia, G.J. and Liaqat, R.M., (2019) on Internet of Medical Things (IoMT): Applications, Benefits and Future Challenges in Healthcare Domain. *J. Commun.*, 12, 4, 240–247.
2. Rubí, J.N.S. and Gondim, P.R.L., (2019) on IoMT Platform for Pervasive Healthcare Data Aggregation, Processing, and Sharing Based on OneM2M and OpenEHR. *Sensors (Basel)*, 19, 1–25.
3. Sethi, P. and Sarangi, S., (2017) on Internet of Things: Architectures, Protocols, and Applications. *J. Electr. Comput. Eng.*, 2017, 1–25.
4. Kumar, A., Nanthaamornphong, A., Selvi, R., Venkatesh, J., Alsharif, M. H., Uthansakul, P., & Uthansakul, M. (2023). Evaluation of 5G techniques affecting the deployment of smart hospital infrastructure: Understanding 5G, AI and IoT role in smart hospital. *Alex. Eng. J.*, 83(15), 335-354.
5. Kumar, A., Nanthaamornphong, A., Selvi, R., Venkatesh, J., Alsharif, M. H., Uthansakul, P., & Uthansakul, M. (2023). Analysis of Hybrid Spectrum Sensing for 5G and 6G Waveforms. *Electronics*, 12(1).
6. Kumar, A., Nanthaamornphong, A., Selvi, R., Venkatesh, J., Alsharif, M., Uthansakul, P., & Uthansakul, M. (2023). Future 5G Network Based Smart Hospitals: Hybrid Detection Technique for Latency Improvement. *IEEE Access*, 8.

7. Kumar, A., Dhanagopal, R., Albreem, M. A., & Le, D. N. (2021). A comprehensive study on the role of advanced technologies in 5G based smart hospital. *Alex. Eng. J.*, 60(6), 5527-5536.
8. Kumar, A., Chakravarty, S., Aravinda, K., & Sharma, M. K. (Eds.). (2024). *5G-Based Smart Hospitals and Healthcare Systems: Evaluation, Integration, and Deployment*, CRC Press.
9. Ramakrishnan, B., Kumar, A., Chakravarty, S., Masud, M., & Baz, M. (2021). Analysis of FBMC Waveform for 5G Network Based Smart Hospitals. *Appl. Sci.*, 11(19).
10. Rajeswari, P., Suresh Kumar, N., & Gobinath, A. (2020). A Novel Trident shaped Ultra wide Band Textile Antenna. *Int. J. New Innov. Eng. Technol.*, 13(3).
11. G. Ramakrishna, Ramachandra Naik, H. Nagabhushana, R.B. Basavaraj, S.C. Prashantha, S.C. Sharma, K.S. Anantharaju, White light emission and energy transfer ($Dy^{3+} \rightarrow Eu^{3+}$) in combustion synthesized YSO: Dy^{3+}, Eu^{3+} nanophosphors, *Optik*, Volume 127, Issue 5, 2016, Pages 2939-2945, https://doi.org/10.1016/j.ijleo.2015.11.234.
12. Rajeswari, P., & Gobinath, A. (2020). Performance Analysis of Microstriplines Interconnect Structure with Novel Guard Trace as Parallel Links for High-Speed DRAM Interfaces. *Int. J. Wirel. Pers. Commun.*, 112(1).
13. Rajeswari, P., *et al.* (2017). Design of Koch Fractal Antenna for Wireless Applications. *Int. J. Eng. Res. Technol.*
14. Rajeswari, P., *et al.* (2017). Design of Ultra-wideband Textile Antenna for Wearable Applications. *Int. J. Eng. Res. Technol.*
15. P.K. Jisha, Ramachandra Naik, S.C. Prashantha, H. Nagabhushana, S.C. Sharma, H.P. Nagaswarupa, K.S. Anantharaju, B. Daruka Prasad, H.B Premkumar, Facile combustion synthesized orthorhombic $GdAlO_3{:}Eu^{3+}$ nanophosphors: Structural and photoluminescence properties for WLEDs, *J. Lumin.*, Volume 163, 2015, Pages 47-54, https://doi.org/10.1016/j.jlumin.2015.03.006.

6

The Impact of 5G and 6G on Healthcare

Rajeswari P.[1]*, Gobinath A.[1], Suresh Kumar N.[2] and Anandan M.[3]

[1]*Velammal College of Engineering and Technology, Madurai, Tamil Nadu, India*
[2]*R.M.K. College of Engineering and Technology, Thiruvallur District, Tamil Nadu, India*
[3]*Vel Tech Rangarajan Dr. Sagunthala R&D Institute of Science and Technology, Chennai, Tamil Nadu, India*

Abstract

The tremendous progress of telecommunications technology in recent times has incited innovative ideas in a multitude of sectors, including the healthcare industry. A new era of connectedness has been brought about by the rise of 5G and the exciting potential of 6G networks, presenting unprecedented opportunities to transform patient care, healthcare delivery, and medical research. Global healthcare systems are already starting to change due to the rollout of 5G networks, which enhance connectivity, speed, and reliability. 5G enables real-time data transfer with ultra-low latency and high bandwidth capabilities, facilitating telemedicine, remote patient monitoring, and virtual consultations. Regardless of geographic limitations, healthcare providers can now remotely check patients' vital signs, provide personalized treatment, and make timely interventions. Additionally, 5G-powered technologies such as virtual reality (VR) and augmented reality (AR) offer immersive training experiences for medical students and support complex surgical procedures remotely. Looking ahead, 6G networks hold even greater promise for healthcare. Sixth generation (6G) technology, expected to be several times faster than 5G, could lead to advancements in precision medicine, diagnostics, and medical imaging. Enhanced data speeds and network reliability would enable seamless integration of the Internet of Medical Things (IoMT), wearable technology, and biosensors, promoting continuous health monitoring and early disease detection. Furthermore, the proliferation of AI-powered algorithms and machine learning models on 6G networks may provide predictive analytics, aiding medication development, prognosis,

**Corresponding author*: pra@vcet.ac.in

Arun Kumar, Manoj Gupta, Sanjeev Sharma, Er. Himanshu Sharma and Khursheed Aurangzeb (eds.) Smart Hospitals: 5G, 6G and Moving Beyond Connectivity, (107–124) © 2024 Scrivener Publishing LLC

and treatment planning. The convergence of 6G with technologies like quantum computing and blockchain could address significant issues with data security, interoperability, and scalability in healthcare. Blockchain-based solutions could ensure the integrity and security of sensitive patient data, allowing healthcare providers to share electronic health records (EHRs) securely while protecting patient privacy. The unmatched processing power of quantum computing could revolutionize the resolution of complex medical problems, from drug discovery to genome sequencing, accelerating scientific discoveries and personalized treatments. However, several obstacles and ethical questions surround the widespread use of 5G and the eventual transition to 6G in healthcare. Issues of data privacy, regulatory compliance, and equitable access to advanced healthcare services must be addressed to reduce inequities and ensure inclusive healthcare delivery. Policymakers, industry partners, and healthcare professionals must collaborate, as integrating new technology requires significant investments in infrastructure, workforce training, and interoperable systems.

Keywords: 5G, 6G, telecommunications, healthcare transformation, telemedicine, remote patient monitoring, virtual reality

6.1 Introduction: The Evolution of Wireless Connectivity: A Journey from 4G to 6G

The world of wireless communication has undergone a remarkable transformation over the past few decades, evolving from 2G to the current state-of-the-art 4G networks. Each generation has brought about significant advancements, with 5G now making headlines and the conceptualization of 6G already on the horizon [1].

6.1.1 4G Technology: The Foundation of Mobile Broadband

Introduced in the late 2000s, 4G or fourth-generation technology marked a pivotal moment in the history of mobile communication. It brought about a paradigm shift by providing faster data transfer rates, lower latency, and enhanced multimedia capabilities compared to its predecessor, 3G. The deployment of 4G networks laid the groundwork for the widespread adoption of mobile broadband, empowering users to stream high-definition videos, engage in seamless video conferencing, and enjoy enhanced mobile gaming experiences. The ubiquity of 4G networks revolutionized how people interacted with digital content on their mobile devices [2, 3].

6.1.2 5G Technology: Unleashing the Power of Connectivity

The advent of 5G, or fifth-generation technology, took the promise of connectivity to unprecedented levels. Launched commercially in the early 2020s, 5G builds upon the foundation of 4G but introduces transformative features such as ultra-fast data speeds, extremely low latency, and massive device connectivity. These enhancements pave the way for revolutionary applications, including real-time communication for critical systems, augmented reality (AR) and virtual reality (VR) experiences, and the Internet of Things (IoT) on an unprecedented scale. The healthcare sector, in particular, benefits from 5G through telemedicine, remote patient monitoring, and the seamless integration of medical devices [4].

6.1.3 6G Technology: Envisioning the Future Frontier

Even as 5G continues to unfold its potential, researchers and industry experts are already envisioning the next frontier in wireless communication: 6G. While still in the conceptual stage, 6G is anticipated to push the boundaries of connectivity further. Expected to be commercially available by the end of the next decade, 6G aims to deliver even faster data rates, lower latency, and novel capabilities such as holographic communications and advanced artificial intelligence (AI) applications. The potential impact of 6G on sectors like healthcare, education, and industry is staggering, promising a world where connectivity is seamlessly integrated into every facet of our lives.

One of the key differentiators between these generations lies in their technical capabilities. Fourth generation technology focused on delivering high-speed internet to mobile devices, 5G expanded on this by providing ultra-reliable, low-latency communication and enabling a massive number of connected devices. Sixth generation is poised to take this a step further with advancements like terahertz-frequency communication, enabling unprecedented data rates and communication speeds.

Despite the promises of each new generation, challenges persist. The implementation of 5G has raised concerns about privacy, security, and the potential environmental impact. As we look towards 6G, addressing these challenges becomes crucial to ensure responsible and sustainable deployment. Beyond the technicalities, the societal impact of these wireless generations cannot be overstated. From changing how we communicate and consume information to enabling new forms of economic activity, each generation has shaped the way we live and work. The societal implications of 6G are yet to unfold, but they are likely to be profound, influencing everything from education and healthcare to smart cities and beyond.

The journey from 4G to 6G reflects the relentless pursuit of connectivity advancements that redefine the possibilities of the digital age. Each generation builds on the achievements of its predecessor, offering new capabilities and shaping the future of communication. As we stand on the cusp of 6G, the potential for transformative change is immense, promising a world where connectivity seamlessly integrates with every aspect of our lives, unlocking innovations we can only begin to imagine [5].

6.1.4 Revolutionizing Healthcare: Significance of 4G, 5G, and the Anticipated Impact of 6G

The evolution of wireless technologies, from 4G to the imminent arrival of 6G, holds profound implications for the healthcare sector. These advancements not only enhance the efficiency of existing healthcare practices, but also pave the way for innovative applications that have the potential to transform patient care and medical research.

6.2 Telemedicine and Remote Patient Monitoring

The advent of 4G laid the groundwork for telemedicine, allowing healthcare professionals to connect with patients remotely. However, it is with the deployment of 5G that telemedicine has truly come into its own. The ultra-fast data speeds and low latency of 5G facilitate real-time video consultations, enabling healthcare providers to conduct virtual examinations, offer diagnoses, and prescribe treatments from a distance. Remote patient monitoring, powered by 5G, allows continuous tracking of vital signs through wearable devices, ensuring timely intervention and personalized care [6]. This capability becomes particularly crucial in managing chronic conditions and post-surgery recovery, where constant monitoring can detect anomalies early, preventing complications and reducing hospital readmissions.

6.3 IoT in Healthcare and Advanced Medical Imaging

The integration of IoT devices into the healthcare ecosystem is significantly amplified with the capabilities of 5G networks. These networks can handle a massive number of connected devices simultaneously, paving the way for a plethora of applications. In healthcare, this means a proliferation of smart medical devices and sensors that collect real-time patient data. From smart pills that monitor medication adherence to wearable devices that track physical activity, 5G-enabled IoT devices contribute to a more comprehensive and accurate understanding of an individual's health. Furthermore, 5G facilitates the transmission of large medical imaging files, enabling remote access to high-quality imaging data for timely and accurate diagnoses. The faster data rates and low latency of 5G are particularly critical in fields like radiology, where rapid access to detailed images is paramount for making informed medical decisions.

6.4 Anticipated Impact of 6G in Healthcare

Looking forward, the anticipated arrival of 6G holds even greater promises for healthcare. The terahertz-frequency communication capabilities of 6G are expected to revolutionize medical applications, offering enhanced connectivity for devices within the human body, such as nanobots or implantable sensors. This could open new frontiers in personalized medicine, allowing for real-time monitoring and targeted interventions at the cellular level. Moreover, the integration of holographic communication facilitated by 6G could revolutionize medical education and collaboration, enabling healthcare professionals to share three-dimensional models

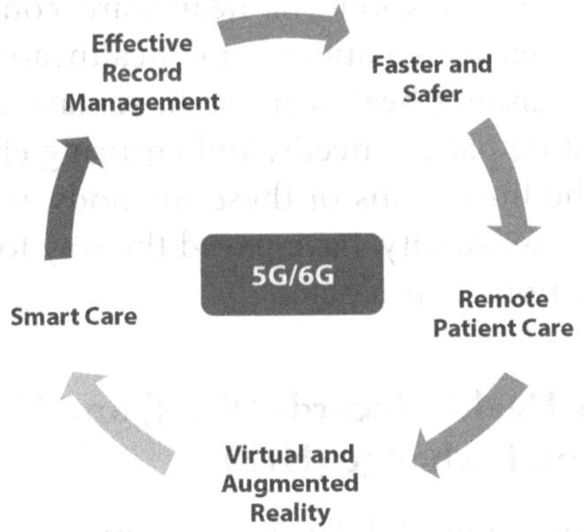

Figure 6.1 Capabilities and instruments of 5G for healthcare applications.

and visualizations, enhancing their understanding and decision-making capabilities.

Figure 6.1 shows the evidence of the capabilities and instruments of 5G for healthcare applications. The significance of 4G, 5G, and the anticipated impact of 6G in the healthcare sector is transformative. These advancements not only address the current challenges in healthcare delivery but also inspire new possibilities for personalized, efficient, and accessible healthcare solutions. As we move into the era of 6G, the boundaries of what is achievable in healthcare are poised to expand even further, holding the promise of a future where technology seamlessly integrates with healthcare, enhancing the quality of patient care and driving advancements in medical research and practice.

6.5 Current State of Healthcare Connectivity

The healthcare industry is undergoing a digital revolution, with communication technologies playing a pivotal role in enhancing patient care, optimizing workflows, and fostering collaboration among healthcare professionals. This comprehensive overview explores the existing communication technologies in healthcare, spanning a spectrum from traditional methods to cutting-edge innovations.

6.5.1 Traditional Communication Methods

Despite the influx of advanced technologies, traditional communication methods still form the backbone of healthcare communication. Face-to-face interactions between patients and healthcare providers, as well as verbal exchanges among healthcare staff, remain crucial for building rapport, understanding patient needs, and ensuring effective care coordination. However, the limitations of these methods, such as geographical constraints and time sensitivity, have paved the way for the integration of modern communication technologies.

6.5.2 Electronic Health Records (EHR) and Health Information Exchange (HIE)

The widespread adoption of EHR has revolutionized the way patient information is documented and shared among healthcare providers. The EHR systems centralize patient data, enabling seamless communication and information access across different departments and care settings. Health Information Exchange (HIE) goes a step further by facilitating the interoperable exchange of patient information between different healthcare organizations. This interoperability improves care coordination, reduces duplication of tests, and enhances the overall quality of patient care by providing a comprehensive view of a patient's medical history.

6.5.3 Telemedicine and Video Conferencing

Telemedicine has emerged as a transformative communication technology, especially in remote patient care. Through video conferencing, healthcare providers can conduct virtual consultations, enabling patients to receive medical advice from the comfort of their homes. This technology bridges geographical gaps, making healthcare services accessible to individuals in underserved or remote areas. Video conferencing also facilitates multidisciplinary team meetings, enabling specialists from different locations to collaborate on complex cases and share expertise in real-time [7–9].

6.5.4 Mobile Health (mHealth) Apps and Wearables

The rise of mobile health (mHealth) apps and wearables has empowered individuals to actively participate in their healthcare. These apps enable users to monitor their health metrics, schedule appointments, and receive medication reminders. Wearable devices, such as smartwatches and fitness trackers, collect real-time data, providing valuable insights into a user's physical activity, heart rate, and sleep patterns. Integration with healthcare providers and EHR systems allows seamless data sharing, fostering continuous engagement and enabling healthcare professionals to monitor patients remotely.

6.5.5 Unified Communication Platforms

Unified communication platforms integrate various communication channels into a single, cohesive system. In healthcare, these platforms streamline communication by combining voice, video, messaging, and collaboration tools. Healthcare professionals can securely communicate with each other in real-time, share documents, and access relevant patient information within a unified interface. This approach enhances care team collaboration, reduces communication silos, and ultimately improves the efficiency of healthcare delivery.

6.5.6 Challenges and Future Trends

While the integration of communication technologies in healthcare brings numerous benefits, it also presents challenges. Privacy and security concerns, interoperability issues, and resistance to change within traditional healthcare settings are hurdles that need to be addressed. The future of healthcare communication technologies includes the integration of AI, blockchain for enhanced security, and the potential impact of 5G and 6G networks, promising even faster and more reliable communication for healthcare applications.

The landscape of communication technologies in healthcare is diverse and evolving rapidly. From traditional face-to-face interactions to the integration of cutting-edge technologies like telemedicine and wearables, the healthcare industry continues to leverage communication tools to enhance patient care, improve efficiency, and foster collaboration among healthcare professionals. As technology continues to advance, the integration of these communication tools will play a crucial role in shaping the future of healthcare delivery and patient outcomes.

6.6 Limitations and Hurdles in Current Healthcare Communication Systems

Despite significant strides in integrating digital communication tools, several hurdles persist, impacting the efficiency, security, and accessibility of current healthcare systems.

6.6.1 Interoperability Issues

One of the primary challenges faced by current healthcare communication systems is interoperability. The existence of diverse EHR systems and communication platforms often leads to incompatible formats and standards. This lack of seamless data exchange hinders the fluidity of communication between different healthcare providers and institutions. Patients receiving care from multiple providers may find their medical records scattered across disparate systems, impeding comprehensive and timely healthcare delivery.

6.6.2 Security and Privacy Concerns

The paramount importance of patient data security in healthcare communication cannot be overstated. Current systems grapple with the constant threat of cyberattacks and data breaches. Protecting sensitive patient information becomes a formidable challenge as communication channels multiply. The need to balance accessibility and data security is an ongoing struggle, with healthcare providers striving to implement robust encryption measures and cybersecurity protocols. Compliance with regulatory frameworks, such as the Health Insurance Portability and Accountability Act (HIPAA), adds an additional layer of complexity to the already intricate landscape [10].

6.6.3 Fragmented Communication Channels

Healthcare communication often occurs across various channels, including emails, phone calls, secure messaging, and in-person interactions. The fragmentation of these channels can lead to communication silos, where crucial information remains confined within specific departments or individuals. This lack of integration hampers real-time collaboration and can result in delayed responses to patient needs, ultimately impacting the quality and continuity of care.

6.6.4 Resistance to Technology Adoption

The integration of new communication technologies faces resistance within traditional healthcare settings. Clinicians and staff accustomed to established practices may be hesitant to adopt digital tools, leading to a slower transition toward more efficient communication methods. Overcoming this resistance requires targeted training programs, highlighting the benefits of technology adoption for both patient care and workflow optimization.

6.6.5 Limited Patient Engagement

While healthcare communication technologies have made strides in facilitating communication between providers, patient engagement remains a challenge. Encouraging patients to actively participate in their healthcare journey through digital platforms, such as patient portals and telemedicine apps, encounters barriers such as varying levels of digital literacy and concerns about data privacy. Bridging this engagement gap is essential for realizing the full potential of patient-centered care.

6.6.6 Inadequate Infrastructure and Connectivity

Uneven access to robust internet connectivity and outdated infrastructure in certain regions poses a significant challenge. Rural areas, in particular, may struggle with limited bandwidth and unreliable connectivity, hindering the implementation of advanced telemedicine and remote patient monitoring solutions. Addressing these infrastructure gaps is crucial for ensuring equitable access to modern healthcare communication technologies.

It is evident that the current healthcare communication landscape is not without its share of limitations and challenges. Interoperability issues, security concerns, fragmented communication channels, resistance to technology adoption, limited patient engagement, and inadequate infrastructure collectively shape the complex environment in which healthcare communication systems operate. Tackling these challenges requires a multifaceted approach, encompassing technological innovations, education, and a commitment to addressing the unique needs of diverse healthcare settings. Only through concerted efforts can we navigate these hurdles and pave the way for a more efficient, secure, and patient-centric healthcare communication ecosystem.

6.7 Impact of 5G on Healthcare

The advent of 5G technology holds immense promise for numerous industries, and healthcare stands poised for transformative change. With superior speed, bandwidth, and reliability compared to its predecessors, 5G introduces innovative possibilities that can reshape the landscape of medical care delivery. Let us explore the potential impact of 5G on healthcare in the following section.

6.7.1 Enhanced Telemedicine and Remote Care

Improved Accessibility: The extensive reach of 5G extends healthcare services to remote and underserved areas, allowing specialists to conduct virtual consultations and monitor patients from a distance. This proves particularly beneficial for managing chronic diseases, post-surgical care, and mental health consultations.

Real-time Diagnostics and Interventions: High-speed data transfer enables seamless transmission of medical images and live video consultations, facilitating quicker and more accurate diagnoses. Real-time data from wearable devices can trigger timely interventions, especially in critical situations.

Remote Surgery and Procedures: With minimal latency and high reliability, 5G opens the door to advanced tele-surgery. Surgeons can operate robots remotely with precision, expanding access to specialized procedures in geographically limited areas.

6.7.2 Precision Medicine and Personalized Care

AI-powered Analytics: Massive data generated by connected devices and medical wearables can be analyzed in real-time by AI algorithms. This facilitates personalized treatment plans, early disease detection, and preventative measures.
Genomics and Remote Monitoring: 5G facilitates faster and more efficient transmission of large genomic datasets, enabling personalized medicine tailored to individual patients' genetic makeup. Continuous remote monitoring of vital signs and biomarkers aids in proactive healthcare management.
Connected Medical Devices: Implantable devices and sensors can transmit real-time health data to healthcare providers, enabling continuous monitoring and immediate intervention in emergencies.

Despite challenges, the undeniable potential of 5G to revolutionize healthcare demands responsible and collaborative adoption. By embracing this technology, we can create a more connected, efficient, and personalized healthcare system, ultimately improving the lives of both patients and healthcare professionals [11].

6.8 The 6G Horizon: Unveiling the Potential Frontiers of Advanced Connectivity

As we stand on the precipice of the next leap in wireless communication, the anticipated arrival of 6G technology heralds a new era with promises of unprecedented capabilities. Building upon the foundations laid by 5G, 6G is envisioned to revolutionize connectivity, offering advancements that extend beyond faster data speeds and lower latency. Let us delve into the anticipated advancements with 6G technology, exploring the potential frontiers that could reshape industries and societies.

6.9 Terahertz-Frequency Communication

One of the defining features of 6G technology is its utilization of terahertz-frequency communication. Unlike the lower-frequency bands used in previous generations, terahertz frequencies offer significantly higher data transfer rates. This leap in speed is anticipated to bring about revolutionary changes in how we transmit and receive information. The immense bandwidth provided by terahertz frequencies could facilitate near-instantaneous downloads of large files, high-definition video streaming without buffering, and real-time transmission of vast datasets. In healthcare, this could translate into rapid sharing of medical imaging, genomic data, and intricate virtual simulations for diagnostics and treatment planning.

6.10 Ultra-Reliable, Low-Latency Communication (URLLC)

Sixth generation technology is expected to further enhance the reliability and reduce latency compared to its predecessors. Ultra-reliable, low-latency communication (URLLC) is a cornerstone feature, catering to applications demanding real-time responsiveness. In healthcare, this could revolutionize telemedicine and remote surgeries. Surgeons operating remotely would experience minimal delay, ensuring precise control over robotic systems during procedures. Emergency response systems could benefit from instantaneous data transfer, enabling swift reactions in critical situations. The seamless integration of AR and VR in healthcare education and training is also on the horizon, providing immersive and real-time experiences for medical professionals.

6.11 Holographic Communication

A standout feature of 6G is its potential to enable holographic communication. This futuristic concept involves the transmission of three-dimensional holographic images in real-time. In healthcare, holographic communication could revolutionize telemedicine consultations. Imagine a scenario where medical professionals collaborate across the globe, viewing and discussing holographic representations of patient data, anatomy, and medical procedures. This level of visual collaboration could lead to more precise diagnostics, advanced surgical planning, and enhanced medical education. Holographic communication holds the promise of breaking down geographical barriers, fostering a new era of global collaboration among healthcare experts.

6.12 Advanced Artificial Intelligence Integration

Sixth generation technology is poised to integrate AI more deeply into the fabric of communication networks. The synergy between 6G and AI is expected to bring about unprecedented levels of automation, optimization, and customization. In healthcare, this could revolutionize diagnostics, treatment planning, and patient care. Artificial intelligence algorithms, empowered by the vast amounts of real-time data delivered by 6G, could analyze medical images with unmatched precision, predict disease trajectories, and recommend personalized treatment plans. The marriage of 6G and AI may usher in an era where healthcare systems become not just reactive but predictive, proactively addressing health issues before they manifest.

6.13 Massive Device Connectivity

Sixth generation technology is designed to support an enormous number of connected devices per unit area, surpassing the capabilities of previous generations. This massive device connectivity is fundamental to the vision of a fully interconnected world, often referred to as the Internet of Everything (IoE). In healthcare, this could translate into a proliferation of smart medical devices and wearables seamlessly integrated into patient care. From smart prosthetics that communicate directly with the nervous system to biosensors continuously monitoring health metrics, the possibilities are expansive. This interconnected ecosystem could facilitate comprehensive health monitoring, early detection of anomalies, and prompt interventions, contributing to a paradigm shift in preventive healthcare.

6.14 Environmental and Energy Efficiency

Beyond technical capabilities, 6G is anticipated to prioritize environmental sustainability and energy efficiency. As the world grapples with climate change, the development and deployment of technology need to align with eco-friendly principles. Sixth generation aims to minimize its environmental footprint by optimizing energy usage and exploring renewable energy sources for network operations. In healthcare, this commitment to sustainability could extend to the development of eco-friendly medical devices and digital health solutions. The integration of energy-efficient technologies in healthcare infrastructure would not only contribute to environmental conservation but also promote long-term sustainability in the delivery of healthcare services.

The anticipated advancements with 6G technology transcend the boundaries of conventional connectivity. From terahertz-frequency communication to holographic collaboration, the potential frontiers of 6G hold the promise of transforming industries and redefining the way we live, work, and receive healthcare. As we eagerly await the realization of 6G, the convergence of cutting-edge technology and human innovation opens doors to a future where connectivity is not just faster but smarter, more reliable, and intricately woven into the fabric of our daily lives.

6.15 Designing an Antenna for Healthcare Applications

As healthcare applications continue to leverage wireless technologies for enhanced communication, monitoring, and diagnostics, the design of specialized antennas becomes pivotal. Antennas play a crucial role in facilitating reliable and efficient wireless connectivity in healthcare devices. One notable and versatile option for healthcare applications is the microstrip antenna, known for its compact design, ease of integration, and adaptability to various frequencies.

A microstrip antenna is a type of planar antenna that consists of a radiating patch on one side of a dielectric substrate, with a ground plane on the other side. Its simplicity, low profile, and lightweight characteristics make it suitable for integration into small and portable healthcare devices. The microstrip antenna's design flexibility allows for tuning to specific frequency bands, making it an ideal choice for applications such as medical telemetry, wearable health monitors, and implantable medical devices. The frequency range is a critical consideration in healthcare applications. Depending on the specific use case, the antenna needs to operate within designated frequency bands for medical telemetry or communication with other healthcare devices. The microstrip antenna's dimensions can be adjusted to resonate at desired frequencies, ensuring compatibility with the targeted wireless communication standard [12, 13].

The designed antenna operating within the frequency range of 5.8 GHz is well-suited for medical telemetry systems and wireless medical devices communication. The 5.8 GHz band is commonly utilized for short-range

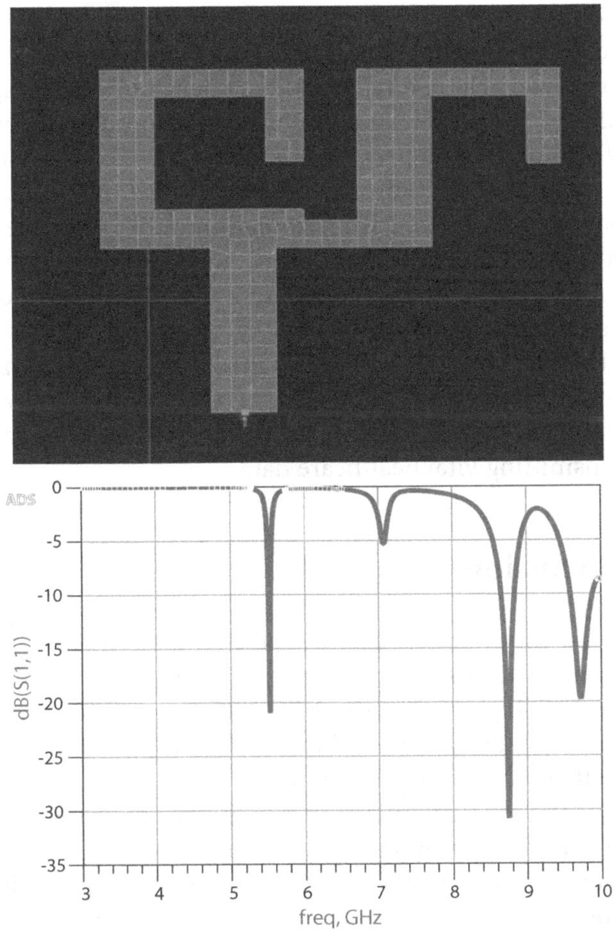

Figure 6.2 Proposed antenna for healthcare communications.

communication applications, offering several advantages for healthcare devices:

The 5.8 GHz band provides ample bandwidth for transmitting medical data, including physiological parameters, imaging data, and real-time monitoring information. Figure 6.2 will shows the proposed antenna performance. This allows for high-resolution data transmission without significant compression or loss of information. The 5.8 GHz band is less crowded compared to lower frequency bands like 2.4 GHz, reducing the likelihood of interference from other wireless devices operating in the same spectrum. This ensures reliable and consistent communication between medical devices, critical for accurate monitoring and diagnosis.

While the range of communication in the 5.8 GHz band is relatively short compared to lower frequency bands, this is often desirable for medical telemetry systems and wireless medical devices. Short-range communication reduces the risk of signal interference and unauthorized access, enhancing the security and privacy of medical data transmission. The 5.8 GHz band is allocated for industrial, scientific, and medical applications, making it suitable for medical device communication while complying with regulatory requirements. This ensures that healthcare devices operating within this frequency range adhere to established standards for safety and interoperability.

Overall, the use of an antenna designed for the 5.8 GHz frequency range aligns well with the needs of medical telemetry systems and wireless medical devices communication, providing a reliable, secure, and efficient means of transmitting vital healthcare data.

6.16 Conclusion

In conclusion, the chapter explores the transformative potential of advanced communication technologies, specifically 5G and 6G, in the healthcare sector. The emergence of 5G technology promises significant advancements, including enhanced telemedicine, precision medicine, and operational efficiency. Fifth generation's superior speed, bandwidth, and reliability pave the way for innovative healthcare applications, revolutionizing patient care delivery and medical diagnostics.

Furthermore, the anticipation of 6G technology brings forth even more ambitious possibilities, such as terahertz-frequency communication, holographic collaboration, and advanced AI integration. These anticipated advancements hold the promise of further elevating healthcare capabilities, fostering global collaboration, and enabling predictive, personalized patient care.

Throughout the chapter, key considerations and challenges in healthcare communication technology design and implementation are addressed. These include interoperability, security, accessibility, and infrastructure requirements. Despite these challenges, the potential benefits of embracing advanced communication technologies in healthcare are undeniable.

From the design of specialized antennas for healthcare applications to the measurement of antenna performance on unconventional substrates like jean fabric, the chapter underscores the importance of tailored solutions for the unique needs of the healthcare industry. Wearable antennas, in particular, offer opportunities for unobtrusive, yet effective, wireless communication in health monitoring devices.

In essence, as healthcare continues to embrace wireless connectivity and digital transformation, careful attention to design, regulation, and ethical considerations is paramount. By harnessing the capabilities of 5G, anticipating the possibilities of 6G, and designing tailored antennas for healthcare applications, the healthcare sector stands poised for unprecedented advancements in patient care, medical diagnostics, and operational efficiency.

References

1. Kumar, A., Nanthaamornphong, A., Selvi, R., Venkatesh, J., Alsharif, M. H., Uthansakul, P., & Uthansakul, M. (2023). Evaluation of 5G techniques affecting the deployment of smart hospital infrastructure: Understanding 5G, AI and IoT role in smart hospital. *Alex. Eng. J.*, 83(15), 335-354.
2. Kumar, A., Nanthaamornphong, A., Selvi, R., Venkatesh, J., Alsharif, M. H., Uthansakul, P., & Uthansakul, M. (2023). Analysis of Hybrid Spectrum Sensing for 5G and 6G Waveforms. *Electronics*, 12(1).
3. Kumar, A., Nanthaamornphong, A., Selvi, R., Venkatesh, J., Alsharif, M., Uthansakul, P., & Uthansakul, M. (2023). Future 5G Network Based Smart Hospitals: Hybrid Detection Technique for Latency Improvement. *IEEE Access*, 8.
4. Kumar, A., Dhanagopal, R., Albreem, M. A., & Le, D. N. (2021). A comprehensive study on the role of advanced technologies in 5G based smart hospital. *Alex. Eng. J.*, 60(6), 5527-5536.
5. Kumar, A., Chakravarty, S., Aravinda, K., & Sharma, M. K. (Eds.). (2024). *5G-Based Smart Hospitals and Healthcare Systems: Evaluation, Integration, and Deployment*. CRC Press.
6. Ramakrishnan, B., Kumar, A., Chakravarty, S., Masud, M., & Baz, M. (2021). Analysis of FBMC Waveform for 5G Network Based Smart Hospitals. *Appl. Sci.*, 11(19).
7. Rajeswari, P., Suresh Kumar, N., & Gobinath, A. (2020). A Novel Trident shaped Ultra wide Band Textile Antenna. *Int. J. New Innov. Eng. Technol.*, 13(3).
8. Rajeswari, P., *et al.* (2020). A Compact 2 element planar Canonical MIMO antenna design for IoT Applications. *J. Xidian Univ.*, 14(11).
9. Rajeswari, P., & Gobinath, A. (2020). Performance Analysis of Microstriplines Interconnect Structure with Novel Guard Trace as Parallel Links for High-Speed DRAM Interfaces. *Int. J. Wirel. Pers. Commun.*, 112(1).
10. Rajeswari, P., *et al.* (2017). Design of Koch Fractal Antenna for Wireless Applications. *Int. J. Eng. Res. Technol.*

11. Rajeswari, P., *et al.* (2017). Design of Ultra-wideband Textile Antenna for Wearable Applications. *Int. J. Eng. Res. Technol.*
12. T.N. Vinuth Raj, Priya A. Hoskeri, H.B. Muralidhara, C.R. Manjunatha, K. Yogesh Kumar, M.S. Raghu, Facile synthesis of perovskite lanthanum aluminate and its green reduced graphene oxide composite for high performance supercapacitors, *J. Electroanal. Chem.*, Volume 858, 2020, 113830, https://doi.org/10.1016/j.jelechem.2020.113830.
13. Kulandaivel, I.G. Rahamathullah, A.P. Sathiyagnanam, K. Gopal, D. Damodharan, De Poures Melvin Victor, "EGR on performance, combustion and emission characteristics of a CRDi diesel engine fueled with WHDPE oil/diesel blends", *Fuel*, Volume 278, 15 October 2020, 118304.

7

Design and Fabrication of Vehicle Automation Systems

Dhivya V.[1], Karthikeyan M.[2]* and Selvam M.[3]

[1]*Department of Electronics and Communication Engineering, VelTech MultiTech Dr. Rangarajan Dr. Sakunthala Engineering College (Autonomous) Avadi, Chennai, Tamil Nadu, India*

[2]*Centre for Advanced Wireless Integrated Technology, Chennai Institute of Technology, Kundrathur, Chennai, Tamil Nadu, India*

[3]*Department of Mechanical Engineering, VelTech MultiTech Dr. Rangarajan Dr. Sakunthala Engineering College (Autonomous) Avadi, Chennai, Tamil Nadu, India*

Abstract

Industry 4.0 has created a great revolution in technology, which includes the Internet of Things (IoT) and cloud computing. Several autonomous systems are developed, and recent research has been implemented in the automobile sector using Industry 4.0. One of its emerging concepts is autonomous cars. The work is based on vehicle motion using an ultrasonic sensor that can be associated with autopilot systems for obstacle avoidance. To ensure comfortable travels for passengers, a specialized frame design is proposed in this work. Road conditions in certain areas may not favor comfortable travels due to unexpected trenches and speed bumps. This may affect the vehicle, as well as the passengers. Our proposed design is used to encounter these problems, and it ensures smooth travel.

***Keywords*:** IoT, cloud computing, autonomous cars, ultrasonic sensor, autopilot, obstacle avoidance

**Corresponding author*: karthickm37@gmail.com

Arun Kumar, Manoj Gupta, Sanjeev Sharma, Er. Himanshu Sharma and Khursheed Aurangzeb (eds.) Smart Hospitals: 5G, 6G and Moving Beyond Connectivity, (125–138) © 2024 Scrivener Publishing LLC

Nomenclatures

IoT	Internet of Things
LIDAR	Light Detection and Ranging
YOLO	You Only Look Once
ISEE	International Society of Explosive Engineers
DC	Direct Current
AC	Alternating Current
RADAR	Radio Detection and Ranging
IDE	Integrated Development Environment
AUV	Autonomous Underwater Vehicle
SONAR	Sound Navigation and Ranging

7.1 Introduction

Autonomous cars are a widely trending topic in today's innovation. They can sense, actuate, and provide certain commands to move the vehicles towards their destination. These vehicles use sensors to detect the object before the vehicle and enable the mechanism to take respective actions to counter those objects. The commands are coded using certain complex algorithms that send the signals to the microprocessor. The processor then executes the command. Various sensors are associated with the vehicle. The radio detection and ranging (RADAR) sensor detects the position of nearby vehicles using radio waves. The light detection and ranging (LIDAR) sensor is a light sensor that measures the distance and detects the end of a road. Video sensors are inserted inside the vehicle to display the real-time motion of the vehicle through a camera. The ultrasonic sensor detects the crests and troughs in a road by sending sound waves and identifying their nearby distance. These various signals from sensors are then processed by the microprocessor, which executes certain commands using algorithms that have been programmed already. This project aims to understand the concept of an autonomous car through a simple model (Figure 7.1). This project also demonstrates the working of an autonomous car that uses an ultrasonic sensor, which detects any obstacles before them and provides a necessary signal to the controller to tackle those obstacles during their journey. A customized design frame is also discussed, which might be useful to absorb the shocks from the road surface and ensure safe travels for the passenger.

7.2 Related Work

7.2.1 Innovation in Autonomous Vehicles

The innovation of autonomous cars had started in 1920 with the invention of autopilot airplanes. Algorithms used in autopilot airplanes were followed the same for the autonomous cars. Various research and articles have been developed in this domain.

The autonomous car introduced by Apple uses the You Only Look Once (YOLO) algorithm, which consists of end-to-end neural networks that can be used for object detection. The YOLO algorithm has better accuracy and speed compared to other algorithms, so it is being used widely in the autonomous field. The YOLO algorithm works by dividing the image of the object into various numbers of grids. The grids then correspond to the signals to their connected coordinates, which recognize the object by drawing its image [1]. This algorithm works by probability to avoid duplicate images. Apple is currently developing a self-driving car under the project name "Titan." Electric cars have already been introduced, but the concept of autonomous cars is totally a different approach towards automation. So, firms like Tesla and GM Motors have currently developed autonomous cars that use an autopilot system, and it has been introduced for public use. Followed by Tesla, various firms like the International Society of Explosive Engineer (ISEE) also have been developing their cars based on automation [2].

The Motion of Autonomous Vehicle Using SONAR. This is mainly used in autonomous underwater vehicles (AUVs). SONAR mainly uses sound waves to detect objects. It is widely used in the marine field. The research article is based on the concept that the SONAR uses acoustic waves to detect objects under the water, and it reflects the signal to the microprocessor of the submarines so that it can identify the objects and detect them. The major advantage of using SONAR is that it can sense objects even in the dark where cameras cannot work efficiently. Also, weather conditions cannot affect SONAR [3–5].

Autonomous Mobile Robots. Mobile robots are tested in place of cars on how the autonomous systems work. There are two main aspects used in mobile robots Navigation and planning [6, 7]. A laser scanner is placed on the robot to detect obstacles and avoid them during their path. For this purpose, they have created an algorithm that makes the robot collision-free from the object. The laser sensor captures the signal from the object and then transports it to the cell grid. The cell then uses the algorithm and instructs to robot to avoid those obstacles and continue its motion until further objects are encountered [8].

The investigations into 5G, artificial intelligence (AI), and IoT applications in smart hospitals [9–11] elucidate the potential symbiosis between communication technologies and autonomous systems. While the referenced articles primarily focus on healthcare, the relevance of their findings extends to the broader field of automation. The exploration of 5G techniques [12], latency improvement in future networks and the role of advanced technologies [13] signifies a broader technological backdrop that may impact the design and deployment of vehicle automation systems. These insights serve as a foundation for understanding the intersectionality of technologies critical to the development of sophisticated automation systems.

The obstacle detection vehicle uses an ultrasonic sensor. It also further elaborated on the use of Bluetooth and Android that aid in this automation. The Android phones have acquired a major turnaround that even vehicle automation can also be controlled using Bluetooth technology [14]. This research is based on vehicle automation using ultrasonic sensors, but the movement can be controlled using Bluetooth incorporated in Android phones. This is similar to the voice recognition system used in Android phones. The user can control the vehicles by commanding them through their voice. These concepts have also been used in various fields including home automation systems, wheelchairs, and artificial assistant systems.

7.3 Design of the Project

The design of the system uses an Arduino Uno board (Figure 7.2). It is the main functional block for commanding vehicle movements. A motor driver is attached to the Arduino that controls the motion of the vehicle by transferring the commands from the Arduino to direct current (DC) motors. Then, the ultrasonic sensor is used in front of the vehicle to detect the obstacles during its path and to avoid them to ensure automatic control. The motors are connected to the driver for the smooth motion of the vehicle. The servo motor is used to control the ultrasonic sensor, which tends the motion of the sensor to scan the obstacles in its path during motion. The components used in this project are:

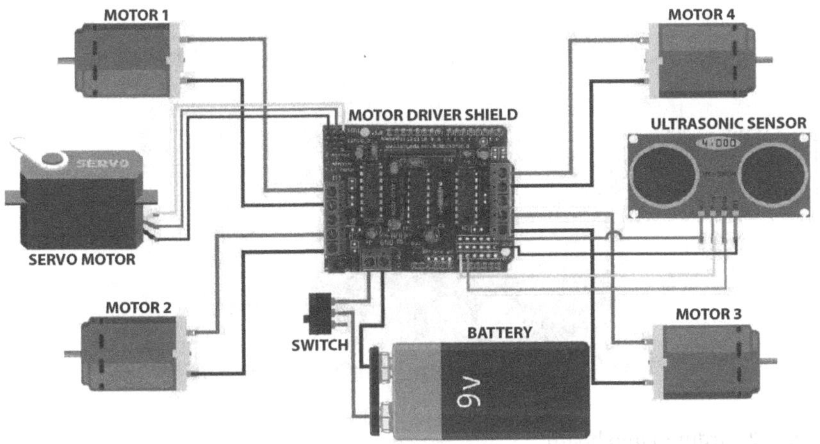

Figure 7.1 Layout of obstacle detection car.

- ARDUINO UNO BOARD
- ULTRASONIC SENSOR
- MOTOR DRIVER MODULE
- SERVO MOTOR
- BATTERY
- SWITCH
- DC MOTORS

7.3.1 Arduino Uno

An Arduino is a type of microcontroller that is primarily used in all types of electronic components. Arduino is an open-source controller, which means it can be coded using any type of programming language and is also easily available to download and use. Arduino uses an ATmega328P microcontroller, and it is developed by Atmel. The program can also be fed to the board from the website Arduino.cc. The board is equipped with various digital and analogue pins for input and output communications. The board consists of 14 digital pins and six analog pins, which are associated for various purposes. They are separately programmed using ARDUINO IDE. The board can be powered either by using a USB cable or using a voltage battery. The main purpose of using Arduino is that it is cost-effective, and the codes can be easily modified whenever the user needs a change.

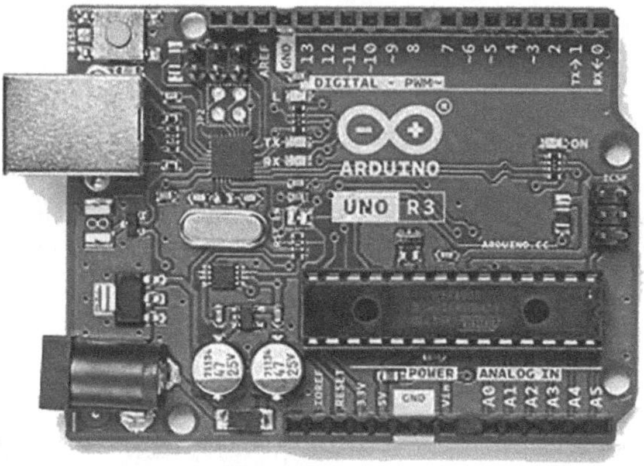

Figure 7.2 Arduino uno board.

7.3.2 Ultrasonic Sensor

An Ultrasonic sensor (Figure 7.3) is a special type of sensor that uses ultrasonic sound waves to detect the object and to find the approximate distance between them. Ultrasonic waves are waves that can travel faster than the speed of audible sound. These waves cannot be detected or heard by humans. Ultrasonic sensor uses two main components: transmitter and receiver. The transmitter transmits sound waves to detect the object. The receiver captures the incoming signal from the object and sends it to the microprocessor to process the signal. The distance between the object and the vehicle can be calculated using the formula.

$$D = 0.5TxC \quad (7.1)$$

(D-distance of the object T-time C-speed of sound in air (i.e.) 343 m/s).

Figure 7.3 Ultrasonic sensor.

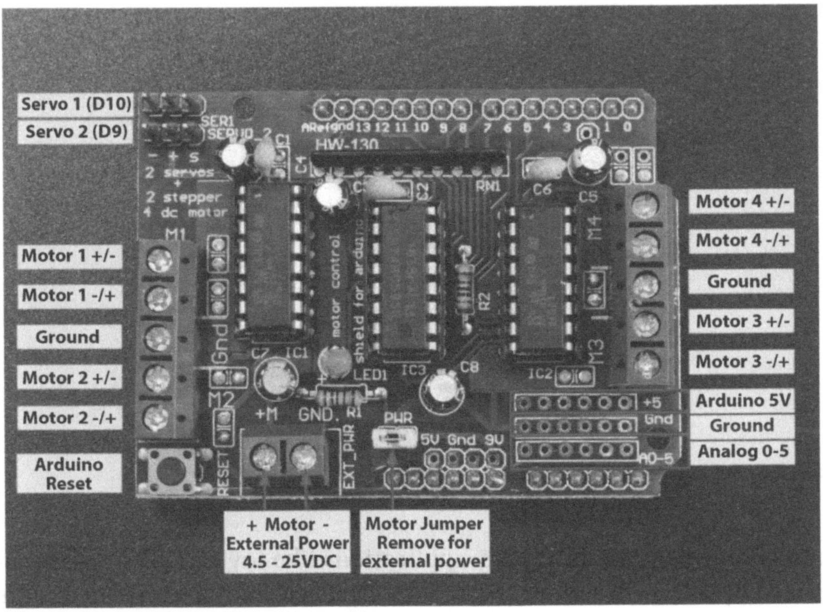

Figure 7.4 Motor driver shield.

7.3.3 Motor Driver Shield

The motor driver shield (Figure 7.4) is a special type of component that can control the motors attached to them. It can control the forward or reverse motion, starting and stopping, regulating the torque, and protecting the motor against overload. The driver shield used in this model is an L293D motor. It is a dual-channel H bridge motor driver that controls the DC motors and stepper motors. The motor is connected to the Arduino pins and uses a register to store and process the commands from Arduino to DC motors. The power connection from the motor to the Arduino is done through the jumper wires. So, the motor and Arduino are assembled in the circuit. The power is disconnected whenever the jumper wire is disconnected from the driver. The output of the driver is connected to the DC motors, which are attached to the wheels to assist in the vehicle's movement.

7.3.4 Servo Motor

Servomotors (Figure 7.5) are electro-mechanical devices that operate in angular rotation. This motor responds to the signals that are detected by the sensors. These motors are usually associated with sensors. The servo

Figure 7.5 Servo motor.

motors are widely used in many applications like toy cars, RC planes, and CD/DVD players. A servo motor is an electrical motor combined with a position-sensing device and controlled for specific angular rotation with the help of a servo mechanism. A Servo mechanism is a typical closed-loop control system. Servomotors are used when an object is required to rotate at some specific angles or distances. The servomotor works based on feedback received from the Arduino board. The sensor then initiates the Servomotor to rotate at an angle from where the signal is received. The motor is used as a base to hold the ultrasonic sensor.

7.3.5 Battery

An electric battery is a source of electric power consisting of one or more electrochemical cells with external connections for powering electrical devices. The battery has two terminals: cathode and anode. There are two kinds of batteries used AC and DC batteries.

7.3.6 Switch

An electric switch is a device that interrupts the electron flow in a current. It is mainly used to limit the flow of electrons. The electric switch is mainly used to regulate the flow of current between the load and the source of power.

7.3.7 DC Motors

The DC motors are used to convert the DC of electrical energy to mechanical energy. The DC motors are widely used in a variety of applications.

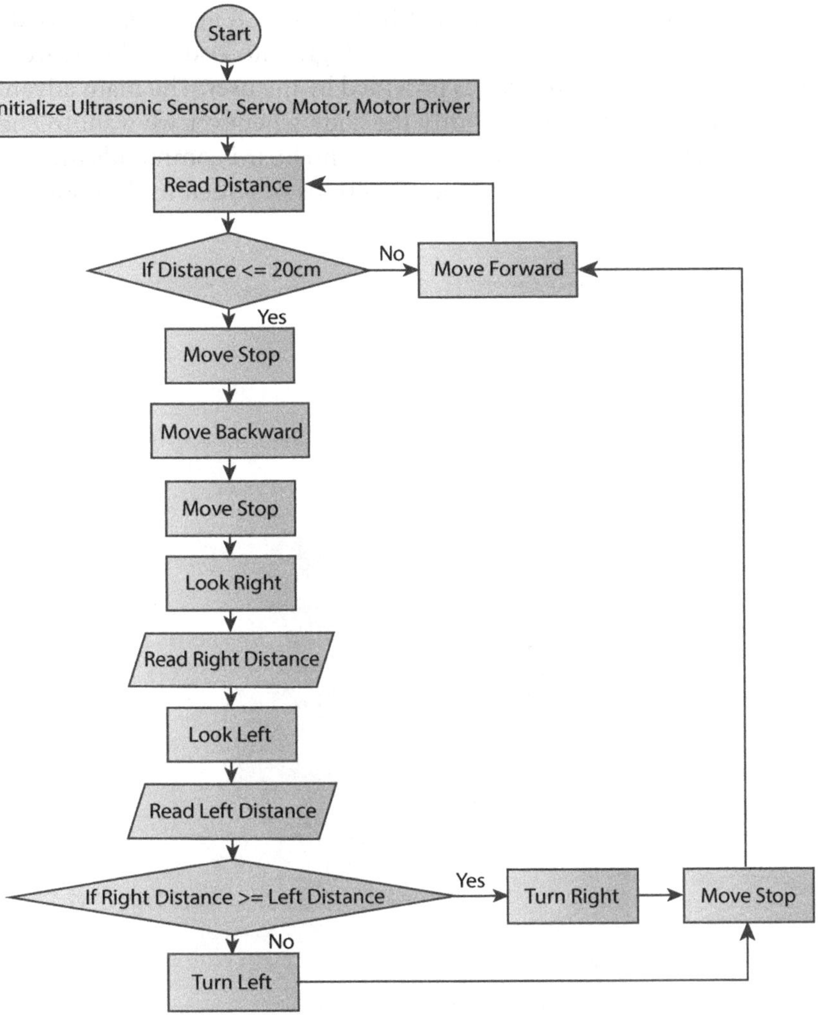

Figure 7.6 Algorithm of the obstacle detection car.

7.4 Fabrication

The method used for the working mechanism follows the algorithm (Figure 7.6). The C program is used as a basic platform for coding the Arduino board. The algorithm is the step-by-step instruction for solving a problem. The obstacle detection car (Figure 7.7) follows the following algorithm. The sectional views of the complete Design and Fabrication of Vehicle Automation Systems are illustrated in Figures 7.8 and 7.9. The Arduino board is used to convert the algorithm logic into codes. The board then performs according to the codes provided by the user. The main advantage of Arduino is being able to modify the code whenever we want to change its performance characteristics. The Arduino board commands the respective drivers to act according to the conditions provided in the code.

Figure 7.7 A prototype of an obstacle detection car.

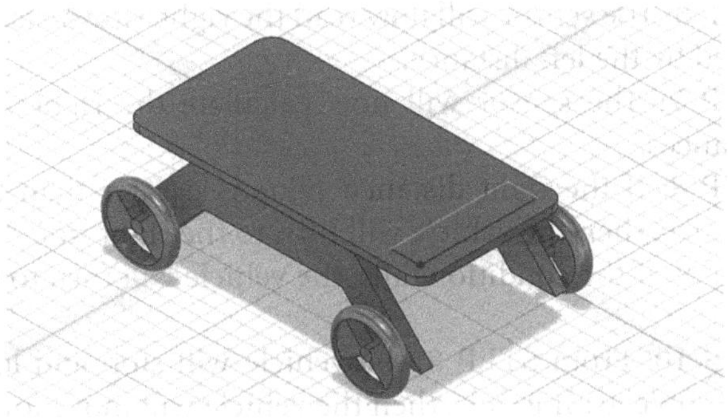

Figure 7.8 Isometric view of customized frame.

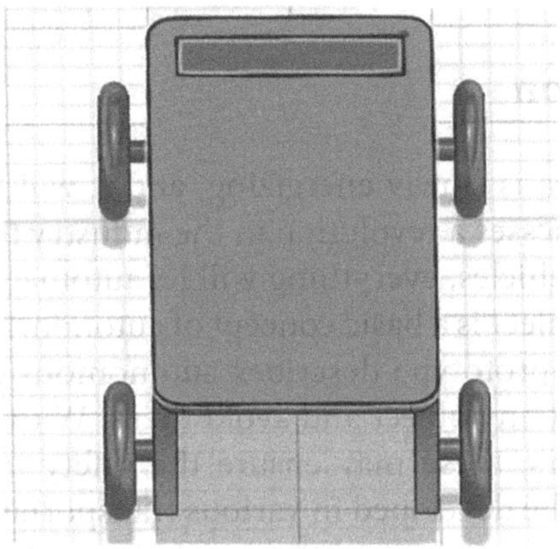

Figure 7.9 Front view of the customized frame.

7.4.1 Algorithm

- STEP 1: Start.
- STEP 2: The switch initializes the ultrasonic sensor, Servo motor and motor driver.
- STEP 3: The sensor will now read the distance.
- STEP 4: If the distance is less than 50 cm, the vehicle will stop.
- STEP 5: Then, the sensor will move backwards to detect the right-side distance.

- STEP 6: The sensor will now read the right-side distance followed by the left distance.
- STEP 7: The sensor will now calculate the right and left distances.
- STEP 8: If the right distance value is greater than the left distance, then the vehicle will turn to the right side.
- STEP 9: If the condition fails, the vehicle will turn to the left side.
- STEP 10: From STEP 8, the vehicle will stop and look for other objects. If it fails, then the vehicle will move forward.
- STEP 11: Again, the sensor will read the distance from STEP 3.
- STEP 12: The process from STEP 4 will continue again for the motion of the vehicle during its path.

7.5 Conclusion

The autonomous era is slowly energizing, and it will be a matter of time until the world witnesses a revolution in the industry towards automation. Starting from the vehicles, everything will be automatic in the future. The above-described project is a basic concept of autonomous cars using a simple prototype. This prototype describes autonomous cars that can travel on their own, detect any object and avoid them. With the use of Arduino and microcontrollers, these may ensure the safety travel of passengers. This concept might be developed in various transportation fields including railways, waterways, airways, and transportation of heavy vehicles. These inventions and research might slowly lead to a driverless era where people can travel without any manual intervention. Also, this might be the beginning of the autonomous world, which comes into effect in some more years.

7.5.1 Implementation

Obstacle avoidance may be useful in the field of automation, which makes the vehicle move easily without the need for humans to control them. However, the conditions will be easy for flat and smooth roads. But for damp and uneven surfaces, it is difficult to tackle the objects easily, so it requires enormous force and a sensing power to tackle them. So, in the end, we have created a design, which may be able to avoid these problems. The base of the vehicle has been raised to a certain height so that it may be able to transfer the vibrations of the pits and damped roads smoothly and ensure the safety of the passengers like in the case of off-road vehicles. So, our proposed design will satisfy the above problems and will ensure the safety of the passengers.

7.6 Future Scope

In the future, this concept can be enhanced by increasing the sensing range. As the sensor range increases, the efficiency of the vehicle also increases. We can also use more sensors around the vehicle so that it protects the vehicle without any damage. The use of a camera can detect the real-time motion of the vehicle, and it enables the user to be aware of their surroundings during the travel. Also, the status of the vehicle above and behind can be intimated by calculating the distance using sensors and by emitting a red light, which can be absorbed by the LIDAR of another vehicle to indicate that the previous vehicle has been halted, and it may avoid that vehicle without any collision; thereby, promoting the safeness in travel.

References

1. Couceiro, M.S., Figueiredo, C.M., Luz, J.M.A., Ferreira, N.M. and Rocha, R.P., 2012. A Low-Cost Educational Platform for Swarm Robotics. *Int. J. Robots Educ. Art.*, 2(1).
2. Freitas, G., Hamner, B., Bergerman, M. and Singh, S., 2012, October. A practical obstacle detection system for autonomous orchard vehicles. In *2012 IEEE/RSJ international conference on intelligent robots and systems* (pp. 3391-3398), IEEE.
3. T.N. Vinuth Raj, Priya A. Hoskeri, H.B. Muralidhara, C.R. Manjunatha, K. Yogesh Kumar, M.S. Raghu, Facile synthesis of perovskite lanthanum aluminate and its green reduced graphene oxide composite for high performance supercapacitors, *J. Electroanal. Chem.*, Volume 858, 2020, 113830, https://doi.org/10.1016/j.jelechem.2020.113830.
4. Jian, Z., Yan, Z., Lei, X., Lu, Z., Lan, B., Wang, X. and Liang, B., 2023, May. Dynamic control barrier function-based model predictive control to safety-critical obstacle-avoidance of mobile robot. In *2023 IEEE International Conference on Robotics and Automation (ICRA)* (pp. 3679-3685), IEEE.
5. Ajeil, F.H., Ibraheem, I.K., Azar, A.T. and Humaidi, A.J., 2020. Autonomous navigation and obstacle avoidance of an omnidirectional mobile robot using swarm optimization and sensors deployment. *Int. J. Adv. Rob. Syst.*, 17(3), p.1729881420929498.

6. Rishabh, K., 2021. Design of autonomous line follower robot with obstacle avoidance. *Int. J. Adv. Res. Ideas. Innov. Technol.*, 7(3), pp. 715-720.
7. Akilan, T., Srivastava, R., Chandraprabha, M., Chaudhary, A., Garg, A. and Verma, A.K., 2021, December. High secure wireless video surveillance robot using IOT technology. In *2021 3rd International Conference on Advances in Computing, Communication Control and Networking (ICAC3N)* (pp. 734-739), IEEE.
8. Venkatesh, S., 2021. Obsatacle Avoidance Robotic Vehicle Using Hc-Sr04 Ultrasonic Sensor. *Turk. J. Comput. Math. Educ.*, 12(12), pp. 2358-2362.
9. Kumar, A., Nanthaamornphong, A., Selvi, R., Venkatesh, J., Alsharif, M.H., Uthansakul, P. and Uthansakul, M., 2023. Evaluation of 5G techniques affecting the deployment of smart hospital infrastructure: Understanding 5G, AI and IoT role in smart hospital. *Alexandria Eng. J.*, 83, pp. 335-354.
10. Kumar, A., Albreem, M.A., Gupta, M., Alsharif, M.H. and Kim, S., 2020. Future 5G network based smart hospitals: Hybrid detection technique for latency improvement. *IEEE Access*, *8*, pp. 153240-153249.
11. Kumar, A., Dhanagopal, R., Albreem, M.A. and Le, D.N., 2021. A comprehensive study on the role of advanced technologies in 5G based smart hospital. *Alexandria Eng. J.*, *60*(6), pp. 5527-5536.
12. Ramakrishnan, B., Kumar, A., Chakravarty, S., Masud, M. and Baz, M., 2021. Analysis of FBMC waveform for 5G network based smart hospitals. *Appl. Sci.*, 11(19), p. 8895.
13. Kumar, A., Venkatesh, J., Gaur, N., Alsharif, M.H., Jahid, A. and Raju, K., 2022. Analysis of Hybrid Spectrum Sensing for 5G and 6G Waveforms. *Electronics*, 12(1), p.138.
14. Raza, M., 2018. Autonomous vehicles: levels, technologies, impacts and concerns. *Int. J. Appl. Eng. Res.*, 13(16), pp. 12710-12714.

8

Design and Optimization of Antennas with Improved ON–OFF Body Performance for Biomedical Applications

A.B. Gurulakshmi[1]*, Bhawna Khokher[1], G. Rajesh[1], Sanjeev Sharma[1], S. Meghana[1], Y. Veni[1], S. Bhavishya[1] and Mohammed H. Alsharif[2]

[1]New Horizon College of Engineering, Bangalore, Karnataka, India
[2]College of Electronics and Information Engineering, Sejong University, Gwangjin-gu, Seoul, South Korea

Abstract

This scholarly article investigates the design and optimization of antennas tailored for biomedical applications, emphasizing the enhancement of ON–OFF body performance. The study aims to address challenges related to ensuring robust signal transmissions in dynamic and variable body conditions. The design process intricately considers antenna geometry, materials, and optimization parameters within the frequency band ranging from 1 GHz to 7 GHz. Anticipated outcomes include advancements in signal quality, data accuracy, and adaptability to varying body conditions. The article underscores the significance of the designed patch antenna, measuring 18.25x18.25 mm^2, in contributing to the evolution of wireless biomedical technologies. Its tailored features aim to provide improved connectivity for medical sensing, monitoring, and diagnostic applications, showcasing its potential impact on enhancing biomedical device performance.

Keywords: Biomedical, phantom model, implantable phantom model, wearable phantom model, SAR- specific absorption rate

**Corresponding author*: gurulakshmiab@gmail.com

Arun Kumar, Manoj Gupta, Sanjeev Sharma, Er. Himanshu Sharma and Khursheed Aurangzeb (eds.) Smart Hospitals: 5G, 6G and Moving Beyond Connectivity, (139–168) © 2024 Scrivener Publishing LLC

8.1 Introduction

In the rapidly evolving field of biomedical applications [1], there is a growing demand for wireless technologies that can facilitate reliable and efficient communication within the human body [2].

Patch antennas find extensive use in biomedical [3, 4] applications for wireless communication in wearable health devices, biotelemetry systems, and implantable medical devices [5, 6]. Their compact design allows seamless integration into clothing and minimizes interference, making them ideal for continuous health monitoring [7]. Patch antennas in biomedical applications are employed for wireless communication in medical devices, while power dividers are utilized to efficiently distribute and manage power among multiple components [8, 9], enhancing signal reliability and device performance [10, 11]. Additionally, patch antennas enable remote healthcare monitoring and are employed in biomedical imaging applications, facilitating wireless transmission of data from devices such as wireless capsule endoscopes.

Overall, their versatility makes patch antennas crucial in advancing wireless connectivity in the biomedical field [12].

This research is centered on the design and optimization of antennas, with a particular emphasis on improving ON–OFF body performance. Ensuring consistent and robust signal transmission in dynamic and variable body conditions is crucial for the success of various wireless biomedical devices, including implantable sensors, health monitoring systems, and diagnostic tools.

The frequency range selected for antenna operation, spanning from 1 GHz to 7 GHz, is carefully chosen to strike a balance between signal penetration and data transmission. This frequency band is well-suited for applications where seamless communication within the human body is essential. The optimization process involves a detailed examination of antenna geometry, material selection, and key parameters to enhance overall performance. Utilizing advanced simulation tools and modeling techniques is critical for fine-tuning antennas to address challenges such as impedance matching, radiation pattern control, and polarization. These efforts aim to ensure reliable connectivity, even in the presence of body movements and surrounding biological tissues.

This study contributes to the advancement of wireless biomedical technologies [13] by developing antennas that not only operate within a specified frequency range but also exhibit improved ON–OFF body performance. An Internet of Things-based [14] smart monitoring system in hospitals utilizes connected sensors and devices to remotely monitor patient vital signs, streamline data collection, and enhance real-time communication for improved healthcare management [15, 16]. The ultimate objective is to design antennas that provide consistent signal quality, high data accuracy [17, 18], and adaptability to the dynamic conditions of the human body. These advancements are anticipated to play a transformative role in the development of future wireless biomedical devices, fostering innovation in medical sensing, health monitoring, and diagnostic applications.

8.2 Literature Review

The design and implementation of compact, dual-band patch antennas for body-centric relay communication have been explored in this work, with a focus on achieving efficient and reliable wireless communication.

In the utilization of coplanar waveguide, feed in compact antennas has been discussed. The study emphasizes the advantages of coplanar feeding structures for miniaturized antennas, providing insights into their impact on size reduction and performance.

The paper titled "Smart Hospital Infrastructure: Geomagnetic In-Hospital Medical Worker Tracking" [19] explores the application of geomagnetic technology for tracking medical workers within hospital environments. The study investigates the feasibility and implications of implementing such a system, aiming to enhance efficiency and workflow management in healthcare settings.

In summary, the proposed dual-band patch antenna for body-centric relay communication builds upon insights from existing literature on coplanar waveguide feeding, dual-band antennas, the impact of tissue thickness on resonance, slot etching for miniaturization, and comparative analysis with recent on-body antenna designs. The collective knowledge from these studies informs the design considerations and highlights the suitability of the proposed antenna for efficient and safe body-centric wireless communication.

8.3 Antenna Design

8.3.1 Antenna Without Phantom Model

Figure 8.1(a) represents the front view, and Figure 8.1(b) represents the back view of the proposed antenna. In this study, a meticulously designed antenna with dimensions of 18.25x18.25 mm^2 has been crafted and analyzed for its performance characteristics.

The substrate chosen for the antenna is FR4, a common material in the construction of printed circuit boards known for its stability and electrical properties. The comprehensive analysis of the antenna involves the calculation of various parameters, likely including impedance, bandwidth, and radiation patterns, to assess its suitability for practical applications.

To simulate real-world scenarios, the antenna is positioned inside a phantom model, replicating the human body, and further evaluated while being worn. The placement of the antenna at different distances, specifically at 10mm and 15mm gaps within the phantom model, introduces variations simulating different wearable conditions. This method facilitates a comprehensive examination of the antenna's functionality near the body, taking into account aspects like radiation efficiency, impedance matching, and potential detuning consequences. The study delves into how the antenna performs close to the body in wearable applications, contributing to the progress of on-body communication technologies.

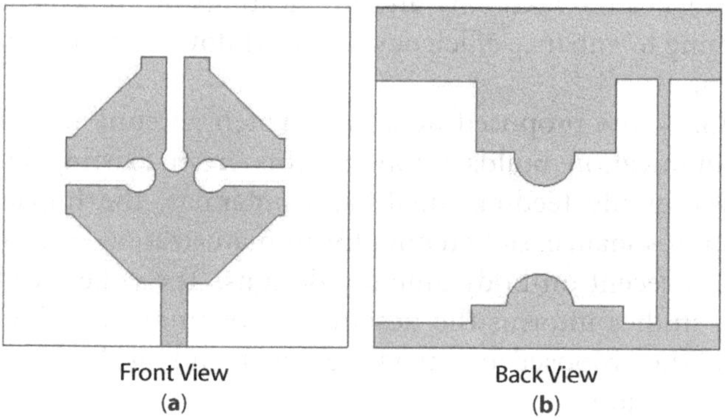

Figure 8.1 Patch antenna without a phantom model.

8.3.1.1 Parametric Analysis

Figure 8.2 details the physical dimensions of the proposed antenna design. The illustration highlights key components, including lengths and widths, providing insights into the antenna's structure. The figure serves as a visual reference for understanding the geometric and dimensional aspects critical to the antenna's functionality.

In Table 8.1, the parametric details corresponding to Figure 8.2 are provided, offering a comprehensive overview of dimensions of a proposed antenna.

8.3.1.2 Stack Diagram

In Figure 8.3, a stack view of the antenna is presented, showcasing various components and their arrangement. This visual representation provides insights into the internal structure of the antenna, highlighting the layering and spatial relationships of its different parts.

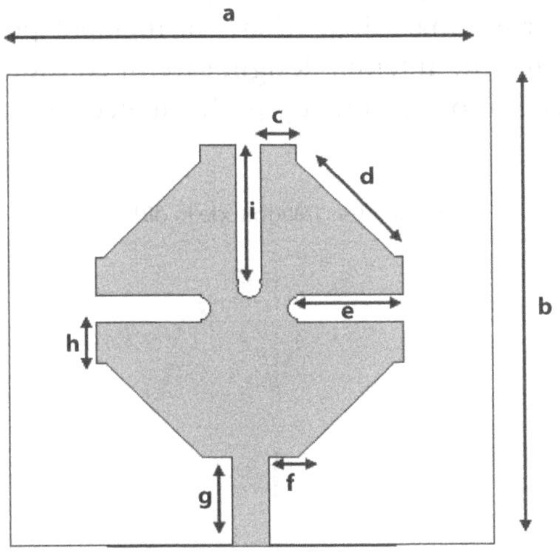

Figure 8.2 Dimensions of an antenna.

Table 8.1 Parametric list.

Parameters	a	b	c	d	e	f	g	h	i
Dimensions (mm)	18.25	18.25	1.37	5.16	3.97	1.12	3.42	1.55	5.25

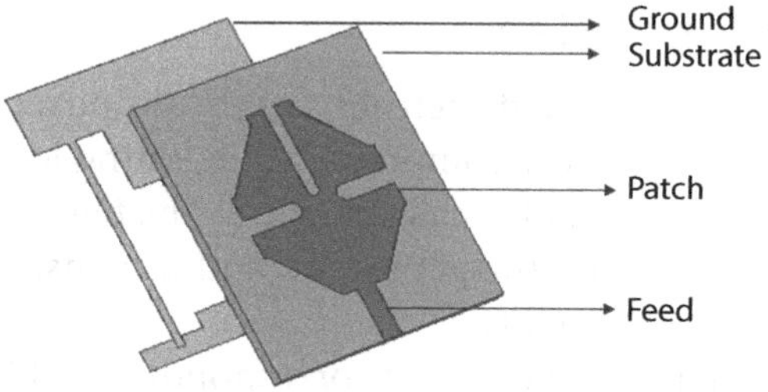

Figure 8.3 Stack representation of antenna.

8.3.1.3 Results Scattering Parameters (S-Parameters)

Figure 8.4 exhibits a reflection coefficient at its input port, denoted by the S11 parameter, with a magnitude of -30.64 dB at a frequency of 4.27 GHz. This S11 value signifies the proportion of an incident signal that is reflected to the source, and the negative dB value implies a 180-degree phase shift between the incident and reflected waves.

The magnitude of -30.64 dB suggests a relatively high level of reflection, indicating potential impedance mismatch or non-ideal matching conditions at the specified frequency. Achieving a reflection coefficient of 0 dB is indicative of perfect matching, where all incident power is absorbed, and none is reflected. In antenna design, careful consideration of the S11 parameter is essential for optimizing performance, and adjustments may

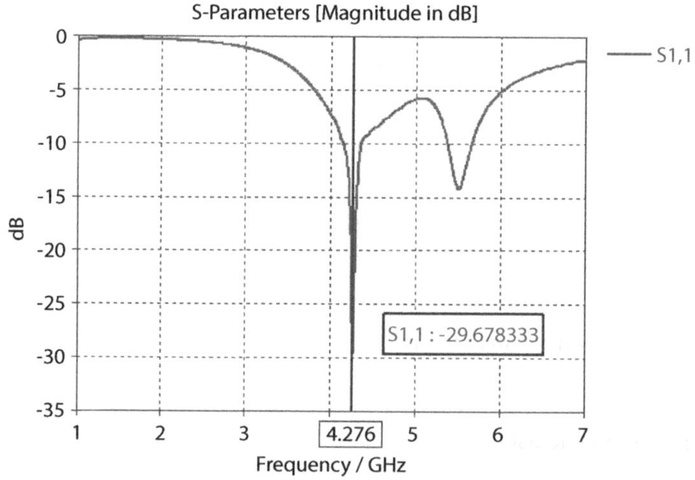

Figure 8.4 S-parameters of the antenna without the phantom model.

be needed to enhance impedance matching and reduce reflections, ensuring efficient power transfer and signal integrity, particularly in the targeted frequency range.

8.3.1.4 Voltage Standing Wave Ratio (VSWR)

The antenna in question exhibits a voltage standing wave ratio (VSWR) of 1.06 at a frequency of 4.27 GHz in Figure 8.5. The VSWR, a dimensionless ratio, serves as a crucial indicator of the antenna's matching efficiency with the connected system. A VSWR value of 1.06 is notably low, suggesting an exceptionally well-matched condition. This implies that the majority of the incident signal power is efficiently transferred to the antenna or radiated, while only a minimal amount is reflected towards the source. The specified frequency of 4.27 GHz is pivotal, indicating the specific point in the frequency spectrum where the antenna demonstrates optimal performance. The low VSWR underscores the antenna's capability for effective impedance matching, a critical factor for maximizing power transfer and minimizing signal reflections. This attribute is particularly advantageous in applications where signal integrity and power efficiency are paramount, affirming that the designed antenna excels in delivering efficient performance at the specified frequency.

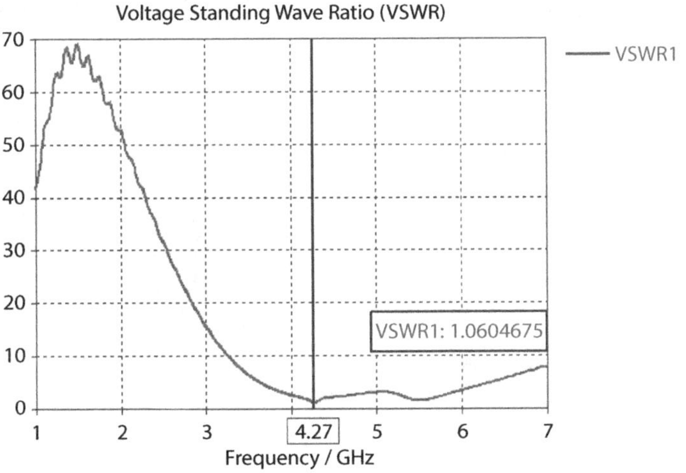

Figure 8.5 The VSWR of the antenna without a phantom model.

8.3.1.5 Radiation Pattern

The radiation pattern of the designed antenna at 4.27 GHz is quantified by a value of 1.36 in Figure 8.6(a) and (b). This numerical representation is indicative of the antenna's directional characteristics and how it distributes radiated energy in three-dimensional space. A radiation pattern value of 1.36 suggests that the antenna exhibits a certain level of directionality, focusing its radiated energy more strongly in specific directions compared to an isotropic radiator with a pattern value of 1. The specified frequency of 4.27 GHz is crucial, as it defines the point in the frequency spectrum where this directional behavior is observed. The radiation pattern value serves as a valuable metric for understanding the antenna's directivity and can be essential in applications where precise control over the spatial distribution of radiated energy is a critical factor.

8.3.1.5.1 Gain

The designed antenna, operating without a phantom model, demonstrates a gain of 1.41 at the frequency of 4.27 GHz in Figure 8.7. Antenna gain is a crucial parameter that denotes the directional efficiency of an antenna in concentrating its radiated power in specific directions. The gain value of 1.41 suggests a modest degree of directivity, indicating that the antenna can focus its radiated energy more effectively compared to an isotropic radiator. This directional characteristic is particularly relevant in applications where controlling the spatial distribution of the radiated signal is important. The specified frequency of 4.27 GHz is key, defining the point in the

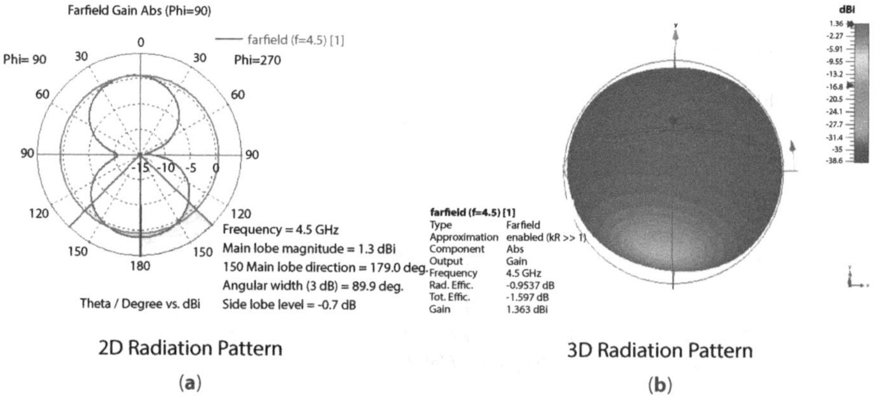

Figure 8.6 Radiation pattern of an antenna without a phantom model.

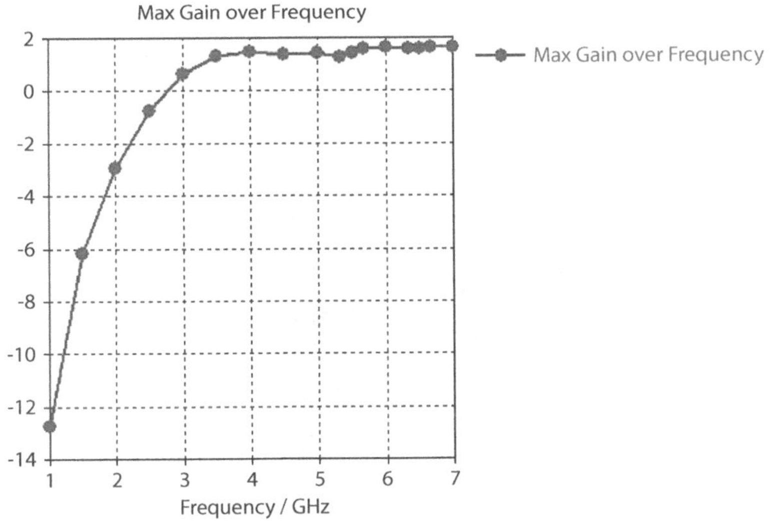

Figure 8.7 Gain of the antenna without a phantom model.

frequency spectrum where the antenna achieves this gain. Understanding and optimizing antenna gain is essential in various wireless communication systems and other applications where efficient radiation patterns and signal coverage are critical considerations.

8.3.2 Antenna with Implantable Phantom Model

In this experimental setup, the antenna under investigation was strategically placed within a simulated muscle environment. This placement within the muscle not only serves to mimic realistic on-body scenarios but also introduces a more intricate set of challenges and considerations. The presence of muscle tissue poses unique interactions with the antenna's electromagnetic field, impacting its performance characteristics such as impedance, radiation patterns, and efficiency.

Figure 8.8 illustrates the placement of the antenna within a phantom model, offering insight into the antenna's performance within a realistic human-body simulation. This visualization aids in assessing the antenna's behavior and efficiency in a context that simulates real-world conditions. By situating the antenna inside the muscle, the study aims to replicate conditions relevant to medical applications or other scenarios where communication devices may be integrated within or near bodily tissues.

Figure 8.8 Antenna inside the phantom model.

This approach gives valuable insights into how the antenna interacts with the muscle environment, contributing to the understanding of its suitability for applications requiring close integration with the human body as shown in Figure 8.8. The analysis within the muscle setting enhances the study's applicability to healthcare, biomedical, or wearable communication systems, where robust and reliable antenna performance is crucial for effective communication and data transmission.

8.3.2.1 Parametric List of the Phantom Model

Table 8.2 details the parametric information, specifically highlighting the thickness of individual layers in the antenna structure.

Table 8.2 Parametric list.

S.no	**Layers**	**Thickness**
A	Skin	1.5mm
B	Fat	5.5mm
C	Muscle	10mm

This table provides a comprehensive breakdown of the material layering, aiding in understanding the dimensional aspects crucial for the antenna's design and performance.

8.3.2.2 *Results S-Parameters*

The antenna, designed within a phantom model, exhibits a parameter with a magnitude of -30.16 dB at a frequency of 3.784 GHz in Figure 8.9. The negative sign indicates a level of attenuation or reflection in the antenna's behavior at this specific frequency. The magnitude of -30.16 dB suggests a notable degree of signal loss or reflection, pointing to potential impedance mismatch or other factors influencing the antenna's performance. The specified frequency is key, delineating the point in the frequency spectrum where this parameter manifests. Understanding and addressing such parameters are vital in antenna design, as they directly impact signal integrity and the efficiency of power transfer. Further analysis and adjustments may be necessary to optimize the antenna's behavior, ensuring that it meets the desired performance criteria within the specified frequency range.

8.3.2.3 *VSWR*

The antenna designed within a phantom model demonstrates a VSWR of 1.06 at 3.784 GHz in Figure 8.10. This low VSWR indicates efficient

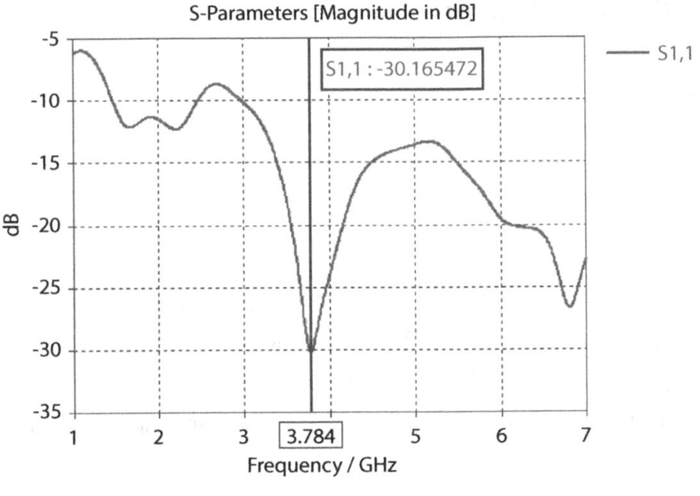

Figure 8.9 S-parameters of the antenna inside phantom.

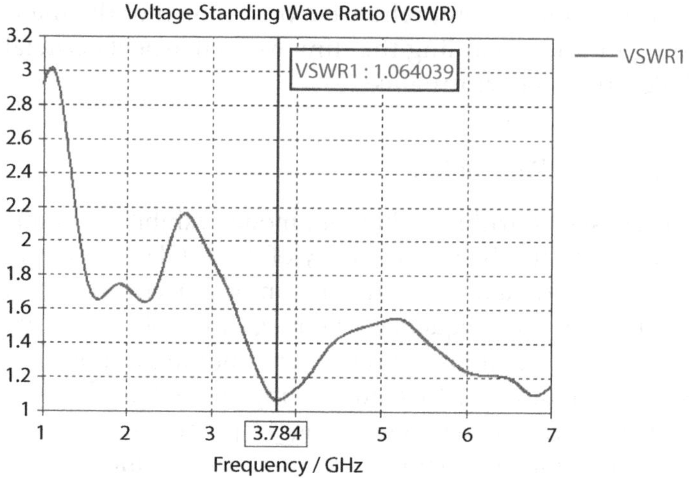

Figure 8.10 The VSWR of the antenna inside phantom.

impedance matching between the antenna and the simulated environment within the phantom model at the specified frequency. Attaining a VSWR approaching 1 implies minimal signal power reflection, indicating the antenna's effective power transfer. This characteristic is particularly beneficial in applications where precise impedance matching and minimal signal reflections are essential, such as in medical or communication systems with radiation patterns in 2D and 3D in Figure 8.11.

8.3.2.4 *Radiation Pattern*

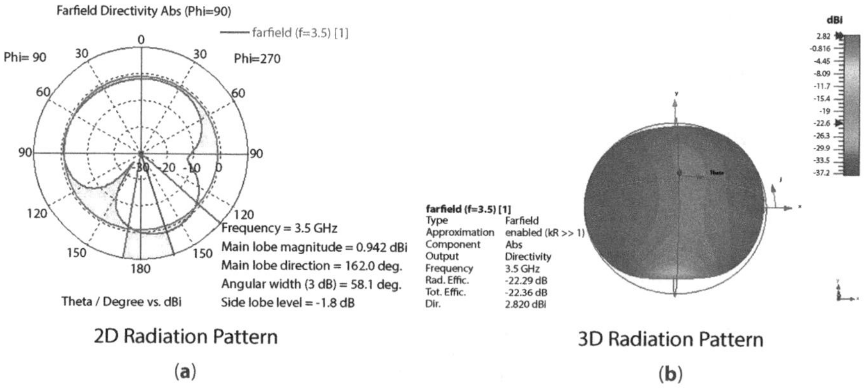

Figure 8.11 Radiation pattern of an antenna inside phantom.

8.3.2.5 *Specific Absorption Rate (SAR)*

Figure 8.12 shows the specific absorption rate (SAR) of 0.555 W/kg for the implantable phantom model signifies the rate at which electromagnetic energy is absorbed by body tissues when subjected to radiofrequency (RF) fields. The SAR, measured in watts per kilogram (W/kg), serves as a crucial metric in evaluating potential health impacts arising from electromagnetic radiation exposure, particularly in the context of implantable medical devices. In this scenario, the implantable phantom model represents a simulated human body used for testing and research purposes.

The SAR value indicates that the absorption rate is relatively low, suggesting a modest impact on body tissues. However, the interpretation must consider established safety guidelines set by regulatory bodies, such as the Federal Communications Commission, to ensure the SAR value falls within acceptable limits for human exposure. Implantable devices undergo rigorous testing using phantom models to assess safety and compliance with regulatory standards before actual deployment, emphasizing the importance of understanding and adhering to safety thresholds in electromagnetic exposure.

Figure 8.12 The SAR of the antenna inside the phantom.

8.3.3 Antenna with a Wearable Phantom Model

Placing the antenna on the skin is a deliberate choice to simulate practical scenarios in wearable communication technology, where devices are often in direct contact with the human body in Figure 8.13. This setup allows for a detailed exploration of how the antenna interacts with the skin's electromagnetic properties, considering factors such as impedance matching, radiation efficiency, and potential signal absorption. The skin, being a complex and varying medium, introduces challenges related to signal propagation and antenna performance. By closely examining the antenna's behavior when placed on the skin, the study aims to provide insights into the efficacy of the antenna in real-world applications like medical monitoring or body-worn communication devices. This placement choice is instrumental in assessing the antenna's performance under conditions that closely resemble its intended usage, contributing valuable data for the optimization of wearable and on-body communication technologies.

Figure 8.13 Antenna on the wearable phantom model.

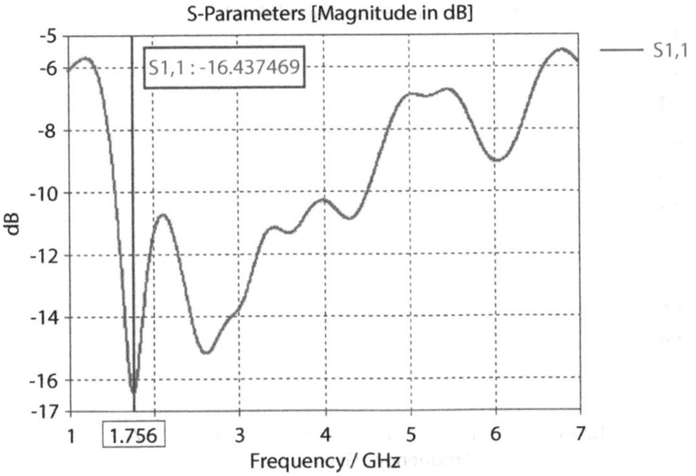

Figure 8.14 S-parameters of antenna on body.

8.3.3.1 *Results S-Parameters*

The antenna, simulated on a phantom model, exhibits S-parameters with a magnitude of -16.43 dB at a frequency of 1.75 GHz in Figure 8.14.

The negative value indicates a level of signal attenuation or reflection, suggesting potential impedance characteristics or performance considerations at this specific frequency within the phantom model.

8.3.3.2 *VSWR*

The antenna, tested on a phantom model, demonstrates a voltage standing wave ratio (VSWR) of 1.35 at a frequency of 1.75 GHz in Figure 8.15. A VSWR of 1.35 indicates a relatively low level of signal reflection, suggesting a reasonably efficient impedance match between the antenna and the simulated environment represented by the phantom model at the specified frequency with the radiation pattern shown in Figure 8.16. This parameter is significant in applications where precise impedance matching and minimal signal reflections are crucial, especially in scenarios involving interactions with biological tissues or other materials simulated by the phantom model.

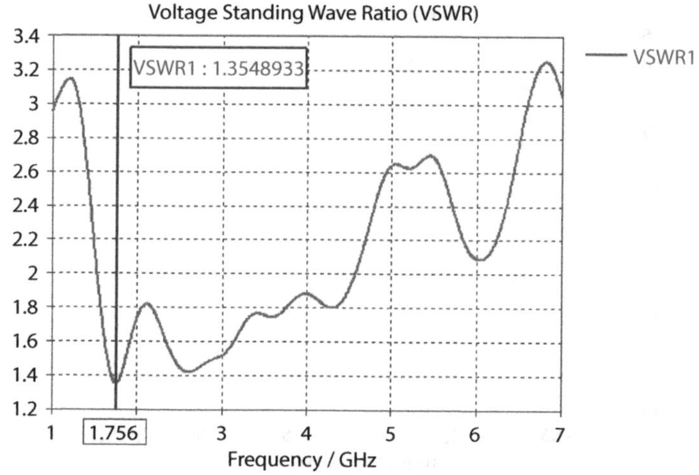

Figure 8.15 The VSWR of antenna on body.

8.3.3.3 *Radiation Pattern*

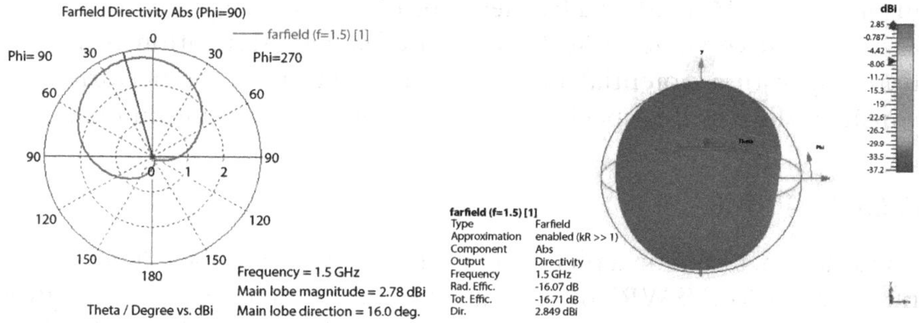

2D Radiation Pattern (**a**)

3D Radiation Pattern (**b**)

Figure 8.16 Radiation pattern of an antenna on a phantom model.

8.3.3.4 *SAR*

Figure 8.17 presents a SAR value of 0.274 W/kg for the wearable phantom model. The SAR quantifies the rate at which electromagnetic energy is absorbed by body tissues when exposed to radiofrequency fields. The recorded SAR value of 0.274 W/kg suggests a relatively low absorption rate,

Figure 8.17 The SAR of the antenna on a phantom model.

im- implying that the wearable phantom model has a moderate impact on body tissues. This information is crucial in assessing the safety profile of the wearable device, as lower SAR values are generally indicative of reduced potential health risks associated with radiofrequency exposure. However, the significance of this SAR value should be considered in the broader context of established safety guidelines and regulatory standards to ensure the device's compliance with safety measures and user well-being. The figure contributes valuable data for evaluating the device's safety and its potential deployment in real-world scenarios.

8.3.4 Antenna Placed 10mm Away from the Phantom Model

The below Figure 8.18 represents an antenna, which is placed 10mm away from the phantom model. In this experimental setup, the antenna was deliberately situated at a precise distance of 10mm away from a phantom model.

The placement at this specific distance is a crucial parameter in studying the antenna's performance. The phantom model, designed to mimic the electromagnetic properties of human tissues, serves as a surrogate for real-world scenarios. By situating the antenna at a 10mm distance, the study aims to analyze the effects of the body's electromagnetic influence on the

Figure 8.18 Antenna placed 10mm away from phantom model.

antenna's characteristics, such as impedance matching and radiation patterns.

8.3.4.1 Result S-Parameters

The antenna, placed with a 10mm gap within the phantom model, resonates strongly at 5.53GHz with an S-parameter of -25dB in Figure 8.19. This indicates a significant and efficient response at this specific frequency, making it suitable for applications requiring precise frequency performance, such as wireless communication or sensing systems.

8.3.4.2 VSWR

The antenna, with a 10mm gap in the phantom model, resonates sharply at 5.53GHz with a VSWR of 1.11 in Figure 8.20. This indicates excellent signal matching, crucial for reliable performance in applications like communication systems and sensing.

8.3.4.3 Radiation Pattern

When the antenna is positioned with a 10mm gap within the phantom model, it exhibits a radiation pattern of 6.14 as shown in Figure 8.21(a)

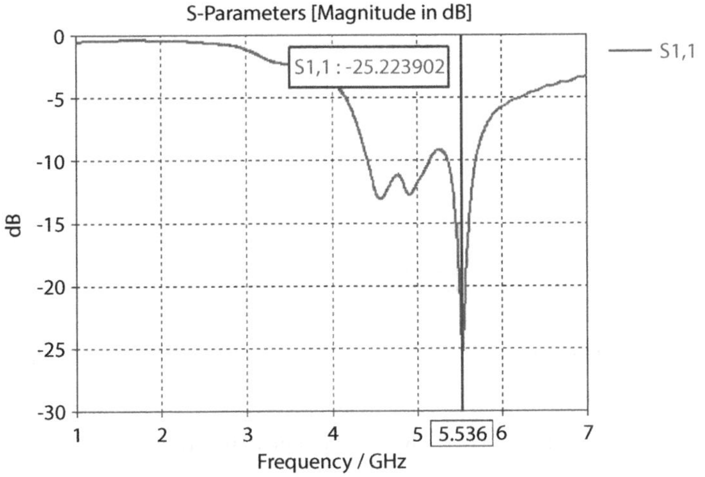

Figure 8.19 S-parameters of the antenna with 10mm gap.

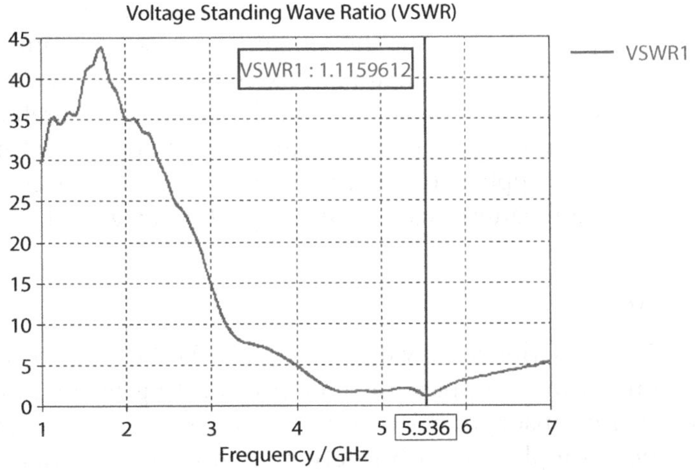

Figure 8.20 The VSWR of the antenna with 10mm gap.

and (b). The radiation pattern is a crucial parameter that describes how the antenna radiates electromagnetic energy in space. A value of 6.14 suggests a specific directional distribution of the emitted or received signals.

The gap between the antenna and the phantom model plays a significant role in shaping the radiation pattern. The size and configuration of the gap can affect the impedance matching, coupling, and overall performance of the antenna. In this context, the 10mm gap appears to influence the

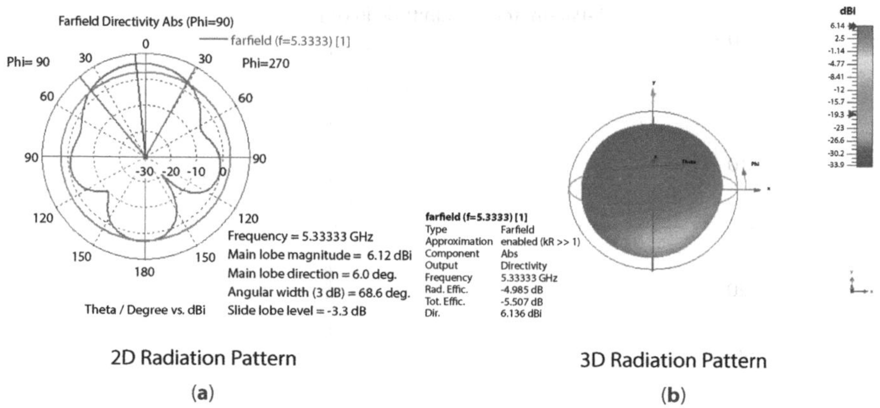

Figure 8.21 Radiation pattern of an antenna with 10mm gap.

radiation pattern, indicating a directional emission or reception of signals at the given frequency.

Optimizing the gap size is essential in antenna design, as it directly impacts the interaction between the antenna and its environment. The 10mm gap chosen for this configuration likely aligns with specific design considerations to achieve desired radiation characteristics. Careful adjustment of the gap allows engineers to fine-tune the antenna for optimal performance in various applications, such as communication systems, where directional radiation patterns can enhance signal coverage and reliability.

8.3.4.4 SAR

Figure 8.22 shows the SAR value of 0.0309 W/kg for the antenna located 10mm from the phantom model indicating minimal electromagnetic energy absorption by body tissues, suggesting a favorable safety profile. Compliance with safety guidelines is essential, but the assessment supports the responsible design and deployment of the antenna in wireless applications, minimizing potential health risks associated with RF exposure.

8.3.5 Antenna Placed 15mm Away from Phantom Model

In a deliberate deviation from the initial experimental setup, the antenna was intentionally placed at a different distance, specifically 15mm away from the phantom model, which is shown in Figure 8.23.

Figure 8.22 The SAR of the antenna placed 10mm away from phantom model.

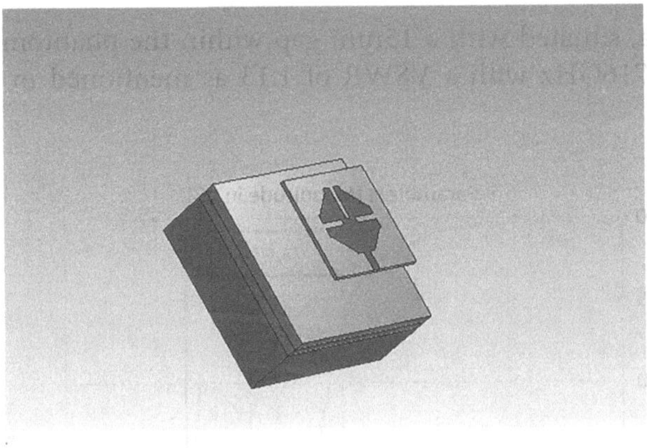

Figure 8.23 Antenna placed 15mm away from phantom model.

This deliberate variation in configuration serves as a critical parameter for evaluating the antenna's performance in conditions that more closely mimic real-world scenarios. The phantom model, designed to replicate the electromagnetic properties of human tissue, acts as a representative medium, introducing a level of realism to the experiment.

The choice of a 15mm separation allows for a detailed investigation into how the antenna's behavior is influenced by this extended distance in the presence of the phantom model. This setup aims to simulate scenarios where antennas may be positioned at varying distances from biological tissues in practical applications, such as medical devices or wireless communication systems used in healthcare. The results obtained under these conditions can provide valuable insights into the antenna's performance in environments resembling those encountered in real-world usage, enhancing the applicability of the findings to relevant technological contexts.

8.3.5.1 Results S-Parameters

The antenna, placed with a 15mm gap within the phantom model, resonates at 5.716GHz with an S-parameter of -23.83dB as shown in Figure 8.24. This highlights a strong and efficient response at this specific frequency, making it suitable for applications requiring precise frequency performance, such as wireless communication or sensing systems.

8.3.5.2 VSWR

The antenna, situated with a 15mm gap within the phantom model, resonates at 5.716GHz with a VSWR of 1.13 as mentioned in Figure 8.25.

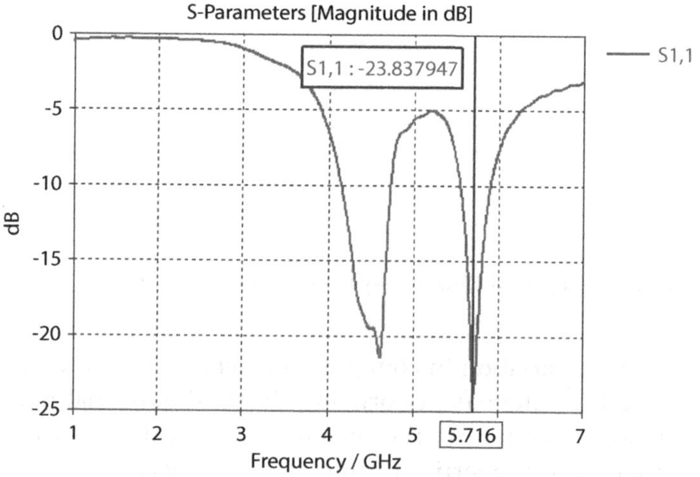

Figure 8.24 S-parameters of the antenna with 15mm gap.

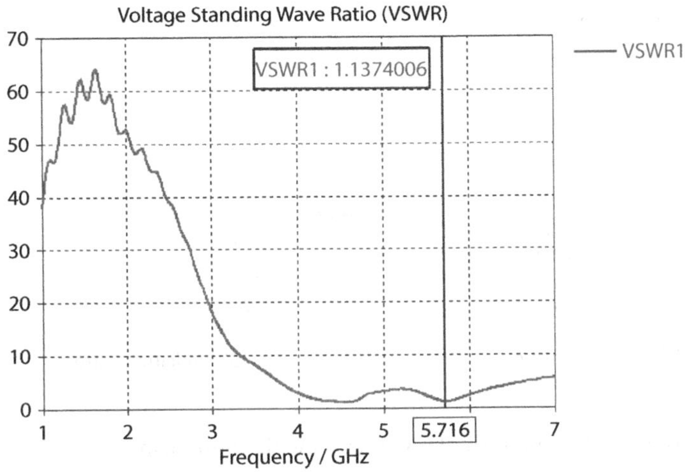

Figure 8.25 The VSWR of the antenna with 15mm gap.

This indicates excellent signal matching at the resonance frequency, crucial for reliable performance in applications such as communication systems and sensing.

8.3.5.3 Radiation Pattern

The comparison of the antenna's radiation patterns with a 10mm gap and a 15mm gap within the phantom model reveals distinct variations in Figure 8.26 (a) and (b). With a 10mm gap, the radiation pattern measures at 6.14, while the radiation pattern increases to 6.74 with a 15mm gap. This difference suggests that altering the gap size has a notable impact on the directional distribution of the antenna's emitted or received signals.

The 15mm gap configuration appears to influence the radiation pattern, resulting in a higher value. This change may be attributed to adjustments in impedance matching, coupling, or other factors affected by the increased separation between the antenna and the phantom model. The specific design choices in gap size are crucial, as they play a significant role in tailoring the antenna's performance for optimal functionality in practical applications. Further analysis and interpretation of these variations in radiation patterns can provide valuable insights into optimizing the antenna for specific use cases, particularly those that involve interactions with human tissues or other biological mediums.

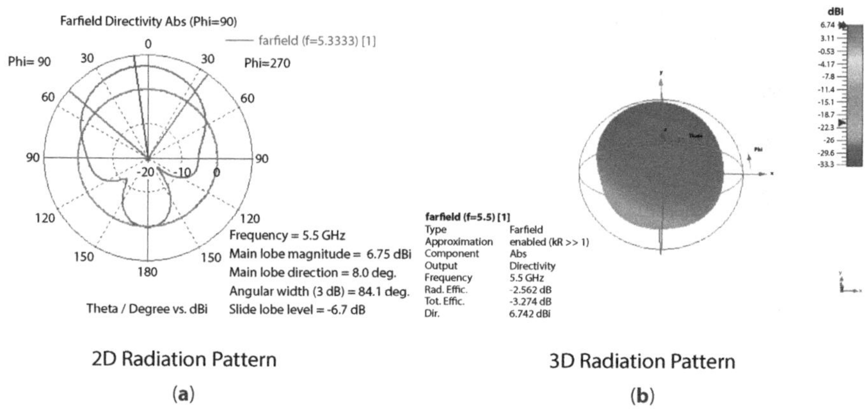

Figure 8.26 Radiation pattern of an antenna with 15mm gap.

8.3.5.4 *SAR*

Figure 8.27 shows the (SAR) value of 0.0309 W/kg for the antenna positioned 15mm away from the phantom model signifying minimal electromagnetic energy absorption by body tissues. This low SAR value suggests a negligible impact on human tissues at the specified distance, indicating a favorable safety profile for the antenna. While compliance with safety

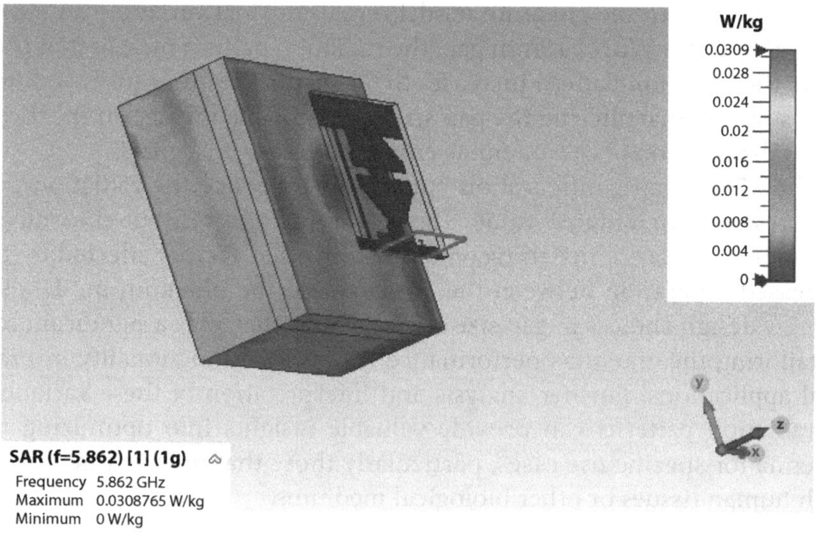

Figure 8.27 The SAR of antenna placed 15mm away from phantom model.

guidelines is crucial, the assessment supports the antenna's responsible use in wireless applications, emphasizing a minimized risk of potential health effects associated with radiofrequency exposure.

8.4 Comparison Results

8.4.1 S-Parameters

The S-parameter comparison analysis provides valuable insights into the antenna's performance under various conditions. Without the phantom model, the antenna exhibits an S11 value of -22.006 dB at 5.7 GHz in Figure 8.28. Upon introduction inside the phantom model, a notable shift is observed, with the resonant frequency decreasing to 3.78 GHz, accompanied by an increase in the reflection coefficient to -30.165 dB. This alteration suggests a considerable influence of the phantom model on the antenna's resonance characteristics and impedance matching.

When placed directly on the phantom model, the antenna demonstrates a resonance at 1.756 GHz, coupled with an S11 value of -16.43 dB. This shift in frequency and impedance further underscores the sensitivity of the antenna to its surrounding environment. Subsequent assessments involving a 10mm gap between the phantom model and the antenna reveal a resonant frequency of 5.53 GHz and an S11 value of -25.22 dB.

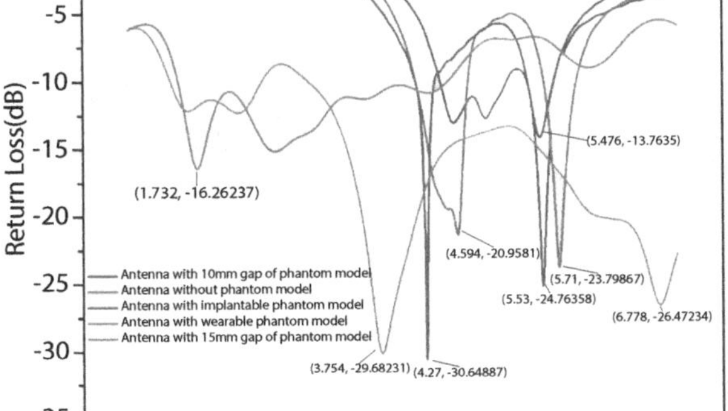

Figure 8.28 S parameter comparison.

Interestingly, the performance at this gap shows a level of recovery toward the characteristics observed without the phantom model, indicating a mitigated impact.

Extending the gap to 15mm gives a resonant frequency at 5.7 GHz with an S11 value of -23.83 dB. The gradual convergence of performance metrics towards the initial state without the phantom model suggests a diminishing effect with increased separation.

8.4.2 Gain

Figure 8.29 shows the antenna gain values for various scenarios providing insights into the performance characteristics in different environments. In an air medium, the gain is recorded at 1.3887, indicating the antenna's ability to amplify and focus the signal. However, when transitioning to implantable and wearable phantoms, the gain values experience significant reductions, standing at -17.833 and -11.989, respectively. These lower values may be attributed to the challenges posed by the phantom materials, impacting the antenna's efficiency in these simulated conditions. Interestingly, introducing gaps at 10mm and 15mm distances from the phantom model results in improved gain values of 2.800 and 4.641, respectively. This suggests that altering the proximity between the antenna and the phantom can positively influence the gain, potentially optimizing signal strength and reception. Overall, these comparisons highlight the dynamic nature of antenna gain concerning different mediums and

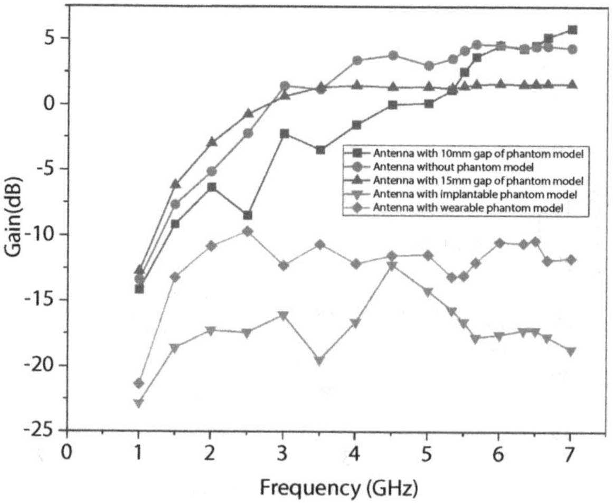

Figure 8.29 Gain comparison.

configurations, emphasizing the need for tailored designs based on specific application requirements and environmental conditions.

8.4.3 SAR

The SAR values provided offer detailed insights into how electromagnetic energy interacts with simulated human tissue in diverse scenarios.

The SAR is a critical metric used to gauge potential health implications of RF exposure, particularly in contexts involving human-like structures.

Moving on to scenarios involving simulated human tissue, the SAR values become significant. In an implantable phantom, the SAR is reported as 0.303 W/kg, indicating the rate at which electromagnetic energy is absorbed per kilogram of simulated tissue. This figure becomes essential when assessing potential health impacts associated with using the antenna in implantable devices.

In the case of a wearable phantom, the SAR is slightly lower at 0.274 W/kg. This value provides insights into the absorption rate in simulated human tissue for scenarios involving wearable devices. Understanding SAR in wearable contexts is crucial as these devices are near the body for extended periods.

As mentioned in Table 8.3, the SAR values take a different dimension when considering gaps between the antenna and the phantom. For both a 10mm and 15mm gap, the SAR is reported as 0.3039 W/g. This signifies the specific absorption rate per gram of simulated tissue. The uniformity of this value across different gap distances suggests that, within this range, the gap does not significantly alter the absorption rate per unit mass of tissue.

These SAR values are of paramount importance for assessing potential health risks associated with the antenna's usage. To ensure safety, these values should be compared against established safety limits set by regulatory

Table 8.3 SAR comparison.

S.no	Antenna	SAR value (1g tissue)
01	In air medium	NA
02	In implantable phantom	0.303 W/Kg
03	In wearable phantom	0.274W/Kg
04	10mm gap	0.3039W/g
05	15mm gap	0.3039W/g

bodies. Compliance with these limits is crucial to guarantee that electromagnetic exposure remains within acceptable thresholds, thereby mitigating any potential adverse health effects. The detailed breakdown of SAR values under various conditions provides a nuanced understanding of the potential impact on human health, aiding in making well-informed decisions regarding the deployment of such antennas in different applications.

8.5 Limitations

Sensitivity to Phantom Model Simplifications: The use of phantom models simplifies the complexity of the human body. The study acknowledges variations in antenna performance when using a phantom model, but the extent to which these simplifications affect real-world scenarios is not fully explored.

Limited Exploration of Body Variability: While the study addresses challenges related to signal transmission in dynamic and variable body conditions, the specific exploration of various body types, movements, and environmental factors is not detailed, potentially limiting the study's applicability to diverse scenarios.

Phantom Model Impact on Resonant Frequencies: The variations in resonant frequencies and S-parameters observed when using a phantom model may not fully capture the complexities of the human body. The study could further investigate the specific factors contributing to these variations for a more nuanced understanding.

8.6 Conclusion

The antennas designed without a phantom model exhibit favorable characteristics at different frequencies. At 4.27GHz, the antenna demonstrates the S-parameter of -30.64, a VSWR of 1.06, a radiation pattern of 1.36, and a gain of 1.41. Similarly, at 3.784GHz, the S-parameter is -30.16, and the VSWR remains at 1.06. In contrast, when antennas are designed within a phantom model, at 1.75GHz, the S-parameter is -16.43, and the VSWR is 1.35. Notably, the antenna resonates at 5.53GHz with a -25dB at a 10mm gap within the phantom model and 5.71GHz with a -23.8dB at a 15mm gap. These variations suggest that the phantom model affects the antenna performance, influencing resonant frequencies and S-parameters.

The inclusion of a phantom model introduces complexities to antenna design, leading to variations in resonant frequencies and S-parameters.

These findings emphasize the need for a comprehensive understanding of the surrounding environment when designing antennas for specific applications. As for applications in smart hospitals, antennas with enhanced performance characteristics can play a crucial role in facilitating seamless wireless communication for patient monitoring, asset tracking, and the integration of smart healthcare technologies within the hospital infrastructure. The adaptability of these antennas to different frequencies makes them suitable for diverse wireless applications, contributing to the advancement of communication systems in smart healthcare environments.

References

1. Suraj Kumar, Manisha Gupta, and Arun Kumar. Breast cancer detection based on antenna data collection and analysis. *Fog Computing for Healthcare 4.0 Environments: Technical, Societal, and Future Implications*, pages 481–497, 2021.
2. Sina Kiani, Pejman Rezaei, and Mina Fakhr. A cpw-fed wearable antenna at ism band for biomedical and wban applications. *Wireless Networks*, 27, 735– 745, 2021.
3. Arun Kumar and Manish Kumar Singh. Band-notched planar uwb microstrip antenna with t-shaped slot. *Radioelectron. Commun. Syst.*, 61(8), 371–376, 2018.
4. Zhi-Jie Yang, Shao-Qiu Xiao, Lei Zhu, Bing-Zhong Wang, and Hui-Lin Tu. A circularly polarized implantable antenna for 2.4-ghz ism band biomedical applications. *IEEE Antennas Wirel. Propag. Lett.*, 16, 2554–2557, 2017.
5. Zhi-Jie Yang and Shaoqiu Xiao. A wideband implantable antenna for 2.4 ghz ism band biomedical application. In *2018 International Workshop on Antenna Technology (iWAT)*, pages 1–3, IEEE, 2018.
6. Arun Kumar, Manoj Gupta, Mahmoud A Albreem, Dac-Binh Ha, and Er Mohit Kumar Sharma. *Wearable and Neuronic Antennas for Medical and Wireless Applications*, John Wiley & Sons, 2022.
7. Zhan Xia, Hua Li, Zongze Lee, Shaoqiu Xiao, Wei Shao, Xiao Ding, *et al.* A wideband circularly polarized implantable patch antenna for ism band biomedical applications. *IEEE Trans. Antennas Propag.*, 68(3), 2399–2404, 2019.
8. Arun Kumar, Aziz Nanthaamornphong, R Selvi, J Venkatesh, Mohammed H Alsharif, Peerapong Uthansakul, and Monthippa Uthansakul. Evaluation of 5g techniques affecting the deployment of smart hospital infrastructure: Understanding 5g, ai and iot role in smart hospital. *Alex. Eng. J.*, 83, 335–354, 2023.

9. Arun Kumar, Mahmoud A. Albreem, Manoj Gupta, Mohammed H. Alsharif, and Sunghwan Kim. Future 5g network based smart hospitals: Hybrid detection technique for latency improvement. *IEEE Access*, 8, 153240–153249, 2020.
10. Arun Kumar. A microstrip uwb antenna for next generation communication system. *Int. J. Wireless Mobile Comput.*, 15(3), 270–278, 2018.
11. Arun Kumar and Manish Kumar Singh. Dual band micro strip patch antenna for uwb application. In *Data Science and Analytics: 4th International Conference on Recent Developments in Science, Engineering and Technology, REDSET 2017, Gurgaon, India, October 13-14, 2017, Revised Selected Papers 4*, pages 434–441, Springer, 2018.
12. AB Gurulakshmi, G Rajesh, and Sanjeev Sharma. Numerical analysis on slinky 3 db power divider for high speed rf sensor system. In *2022 IEEE International Conference on Electronics, Computing and Communication Technologies (CONECCT)*, pages 1–4. IEEE, 2022.
13. Arun Kumar, R Dhanagopal, Mahmoud A Albreem, and Dac-Nhuong Le. A comprehensive study on the role of advanced technologies in 5g based smart hospital. *Alex. Eng. J.*, 60(6), 5527–5536, 2021.
14. Bhawna Khokher, M Dhivya, Devarasi Swetha, D Anila, Abhijit G Naik, and S Shwetha. Iot-based intelligent modeling of security monitoring system for human safety. In *2023 International Conference on Computer Communication and Informatics (ICCCI)*, pages 1–5, IEEE, 2023.
15. Konstantinos E Georgiou, Evangelos Georgiou, and Richard M Satava. 5g use in healthcare: the future is present. *JSLS: Journal of the Society of Laparoscopic & Robotic Surgeons*, 25(4), 2021.
16. Abdul Ahad, Mohammad Tahir, Muhammad Aman Sheikh, Kazi Istiaque Ahmed, Amna Mughees, and Abdullah Numani. Technologies trend towards 5g network for smart health-care using iot: A review. *Sensors*, 20(14), 4047, 2020.
17. Balamurali Ramakrishnan, Arun Kumar, Sumit Chakravarty, Mehedi Masud, and Mohammed Baz. Analysis of fbmc waveform for 5g network based smart hospitals. *Appl. Sci.*, 11(19), 8895, 2021.
18. Arun Kumar, J Venkatesh, Nishant Gaur, Mohammed H Alsharif, Abu Jahid, and Kannadasan Raju. Analysis of hybrid spectrum sensing for 5g and 6g waveforms. *Electronics*, 12(1), 138, 2022.
19. Keiko Yamashita, Shintaro Oyama, Tomohiro Otani, Satoshi Yamashita, Taiki Furukawa, Daisuke Kobayashi, Kikue Sato, Aki Sugano, Chiaki Funada, Kensaku Mori, *et al.* Smart hospital infrastructure: geomagnetic in-hospital medical worker tracking. *J. Am. Med. Inf. Assoc.*, 28(3), 477–486, 2021.

9

Beyond 5G-Based Smart Hospitals: Integrating Connectivity and Intelligence

Kiran Chand Ravi[1]*, G. Kavitha[2], Lakkakula Hari Prasad[3], Narni V. V. S. Srinivasa Rao[4], Shanmugavel Deivasigamani[5], Janjhyam Venkata Naga Ramesh[6] and Shams Tabrez Siddiqui[7]

[1]Department of ECE, MLR Institute of Technology, Hyderabad, India
[2]Department of ECE, Dr. MGR Educational and Research Institute, Chennai, India
[3]Department of ECE, Anurag Engineering College, Kodada, Telangana, India
[4]Department of EEE, Oxford College of Engineering, Tamil Nadu, India
[5]Department of Computer Science and Engineering, Sri Muthukumaran Institute of Technology, Anna University, Chennai, India
[6]Department of Computer Science and Engineering, Graphic Era Hill University, Graphic Era (Deemed to be University) University, Dehradun, India
[7]Department of Computer Science, College of Engineering and Computer Science, Jazan University, Jazan, Saudi Arabia

Abstract
The unfair delivery of medical resources, particularly in rural places around the world, has long contributed to digital era shortcomings in healthcare applications. The current healthcare system can be physiologically and psychologically transformed by utilizing cognitive data intelligence (CDI), which is the integration of cognitive computing (CC), massive data analytics, and tiny artificial intelligence (AI), particularly machine learning (ML), to assess a patient's health progress. The convergence of 6G-enabled tactile internet (TI), CDI, and the Internet-of-Healthcare enables remote detection of patients' emotional states during disease diagnosis. All these components are meant to come together as the 6GCIoHE system, which is going to make sure that patients get their treatment quickly, particularly for the haptic movements, by attaining worldwide abundant availability, very low latency, great dependability, and improved performance in cognitive healthcare in real-time. We propose a model-driven methodology to build and develop the 6GCIoHE system with care. This methodology takes into account the

**Corresponding author*: b4uchandu2011@gmail.com

Arun Kumar, Manoj Gupta, Sanjeev Sharma, Er. Himanshu Sharma and Khursheed Aurangzeb (eds.) Smart Hospitals: 5G, 6G and Moving Beyond Connectivity, (169–194) © 2024 Scrivener Publishing LLC

cognitive healthcare needs through the connections of knowledge sources, semantic and process management, and cognitive intelligence competences, and it uses different levels of refinement. The goal of this chapter is to build a new theoretical approach that would attract more research in the cognitive healthcare sector based on the 6GCIoHE architecture, applications, problems, and future directions.

Keywords: 6G, data intelligence, cognitive healthcare, ML, 6GCIoHE

9.1 Introduction

Since the last decade, the field of healthcare has observed a significant advancement in the treatment techniques and utilized approaches. The majority of its members are medical professionals, medical equipment, laboratories, and other related facilities, all of which are designed to offer patients the required medical facilities [1]. Patients are required to be physically present in order to communicate with their physicians for the purpose of receiving treatment in the conventional healthcare system [2]. However, according to the estimates provided in [3], the conventional healthcare system is finding it increasingly difficult to keep track of a large number of patients who are suffering from chronic diseases. According to the findings of the research study [4], older persons are likely to be the most impacted by a major sickness in the next 20 years. This is because of the significant growth in the population. As a consequence of this, they are required to meet with their physicians or undergo routine checkups, both of which require them to bear the burden of high costs associated with medical treatments. For the period of time spanning from 2017 to 2027, it is anticipated that the costs associated with healthcare in the United States will experience a significant rise, rising from 21% to 23% of the GDP [5].

It is therefore necessary for smart healthcare systems (SHS) to screen patients in order to manage a large number of patients who suffer from continuing diseases and to ensure these patients experience inexpensive and convenient treatment. If this does not occur, the patient might not receive the necessary medical therapy for their disease [6] due to delays in treatment or problems with cost. The Internet of Things (IoT), smart gadgets, and developing IT are all contributing to the gradual digitization of the out-of-date healthcare system, which is resulting in the transition to the SHS [7]. With the use of a SHS, physicians can remotely screen their patients. As was indicated before, patients are required to meet with their doctors or make an appointment in order to contact them on a regular basis, depending on the severity of their sickness. When a person with a corporeal impairment is dependent on another person to get their inspection done by the doctor, it might be challenging for them to access medical care [8]. As a result, SHS are able to assist in the monitoring of patients' health by enabling the early detection of illnesses, reducing the amount of time spent commuting, costs of hospitalization, and the amount of work that is required of hospital staff, among other benefits [9]. If a patient is suffering from an illness that cannot be cured, the patient can be self-confessed to the hospice without delay if the staff is informed about the circumstance. However, if the patient can be preserved remotely by supplying them with a prescription, then this can lessen the stress on the medicinal personnel. Additionally, it can lower the costs for patients to travel, which ultimately leads to a reduction in the overall expenditures that they incur [10]. The implementation of 6G technologies in various parts of the healthcare system is illustrated in Figure 9.1. This was done in order to overcome the difficulties associated with communication.

It is probable that future smart healthcare networks would incorporate a combination of 5G, 6G, and IoT-tools, as well as fog and cognitive computing (CC), Cloud of Things (CoT), and other technologies [11]. These technologies will help improve network coverage and performance while also addressing security concerns. There has been a quickening of the

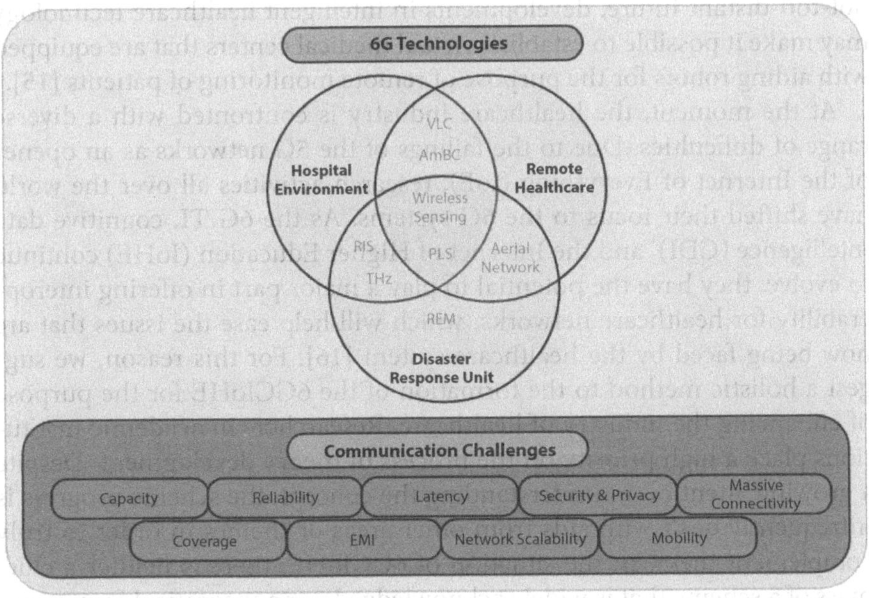

Figure 9.1 Technologies for 6G-enabled smart healthcare challenges.

deployment of 5G innovations worldwide. Because of its components, it is suitable for enabling large advancements in the insufficiency and asset of categorization humanoid services [12]. Sixth generation technology will most likely bring about changes in a number of industries, including healthcare. Our way of life will be altered because of the adoption of AI-driven healthcare that is dependent on the 6G connection. In the current state of affairs, time and place are the most momentous obstacles to healthcare, which will be resolved by 6G.

Using the radiofrequency classification method, we have developed an architecture that is based on artificial intelligence (AI) in order to facilitate the processing of patients' health data in a manner that is safe, effective, and dependable. It is possible to ensure that communication between patients and doctors is both effective and dependable thanks to the incorporation of a 6G communication network, which possesses characteristics such as low latency and high availability [13]. This assists in providing the medical personnel with the necessary information about the patient's health so that they can prescribe medications in accordance with the patient's condition. Figure 9.1 illustrates the technical revolutions that have occurred in the field of smart healthcare technology. These revolutions began in 2001, when the first telesurgery was done there [14]. After that, a number of innovations were implemented in the field of smart healthcare, including the introduction of telemedicine and AI in the years 2020 and 2021. In the not-too-distant future, developments in intelligent healthcare technology may make it possible to establish virtual medical centers that are equipped with aiding robots for the purpose of remote monitoring of patients [15].

At the moment, the healthcare industry is confronted with a diverse range of difficulties. Due to the failings of the 5G networks as an opener of the Internet of Everything (IoE), research activities all over the world have shifted their focus to the 6G systems. As the 6G TI, cognitive data intelligence (CDI), and the Internet of Higher Education (IoHE) continue to evolve, they have the potential to play a major part in offering interoperability for healthcare networks, which will help ease the issues that are now being faced by the healthcare system [16]. For this reason, we suggest a holistic method to the formation of the 6GCIoHE for the purpose of enhancing the industry of healthcare. Researchers in academic institutions place a high priority on the process of theory development. Despite a growing attention in understanding the concept, the scheme progress is infrequently dealt with aids from other areas or themes in order to truly complement them. In the situation of 6GCIoHE, there is neither a chief mass of a scheme that is widely acknowledged nor a theoretical framework that can be found in the existing body of literature [17]. Due to the fact that there is a gap in the literature on the development of theory in relation to 6GCIoHE for healthcare networks, this work provides extensive new information that can be used to design a fresh theoretic framework that makes a substantial influence of value.

A gap exists in the process of defining the CIoHE worldwide standards, even though the topics of privacy, security, and trust have been widely covered in the current body of literature. In order to examine security, privacy, and trust factors, CIoHE must be a part of a universal healthcare ecology. This would prevent the CIoHE from splintering into different sets of rules or standards. For the purpose of fostering innovation and promoting security and privacy solutions, it is necessary to engage with stakeholders in the healthcare industry in order to assist the creation of global standards.

This study has three main contributions and is important for healthcare because:

(i) It lays out the groundwork for the CIoHE framework, which automates patient care workflows, improves services and experiences, lowers costs, and promotes next-generation healthcare services.
(ii) The 6GCIoHE system architecture is the first of its kind to incorporate machine-to-machine communiqué, haptic-activities, interoperability, data-mobility, and information sharing; this facilitates efficiency in the healthcare industry.
(iii) We define the chances and issues that arise when implementing the 6GCIoHE, counting the CDI scalability obligation, data security, privacy concerns, and risk perceptions, and the CDI scalability obligation.

The rest of the chapter is as follows. The second section provides some context for smart healthcare technology and relevant literature. Section 9.3 delves into the suggested strategy for intelligent healthcare. In Section 9.4, we go over some of the ongoing issues, potential uses, and obstacles to smart healthcare research. Future directions and recommendations are presented in Section 9.5. The paper is concluded in Section 9.6.

9.2 Related Works

Within the context of rationally comprehending and evolving the various yet interrelated key components of the literature analysis, the state-of-art methods, latest models with limitations are inextricably tied to one another [18]. The bestowment of a solid foundation for the actuation of new information, the creation of theory development, and the identification of where the research gap exists are all outcomes that result from conducting a comprehensive evaluation of the relevant literature in any study attempt.

According to [19] the 4G network and communiqué technologies are being utilized extensively for applications that are related to intelligent healthcare practices. An increasing number of connected applications will generate data of varying kinds and types as the intelligent healthcare industry continues to expand. Consequently, this will put a considerable load on the network. It will be necessary for hospitals to implement remote operations in order to fulfill the linking needs for a wide variety of devices and machines that have sensor-based applications as the smart healthcare industry continues to go forward [20]. The current state of the art in terms of telecommunications is not sufficient to handle the intricate and ever-changing requirements that mobile healthcare apps place on communication networks.

In light of this, it is believed that the next 5G network, which will fulfill the majority of the necessities, would make it possible for intelligent healthcare apps to be implemented. There is a high probability that 5G and IoT tools will be utilized in the future SHS in order to improve cellular coverage, network performance, and address security issues. According to [21], the IoT would be beneficial to the health industry, as well as all other industries, in terms of both time and money. This is because the IoT integrates the functions of technology with everyday objects in the world. Patients who suffer from chronic diseases need to remain in the hospice for extended periods of time in order to receive monitoring. This type of hospitalization has a negative impact on the quality of life of patients and results in significant financial burdens for the healthcare system [22].

Numerous nations have initiated a variety of programs to encourage individuals to take responsibility for their own health management. The authors [23] underline that the utilization of 5G technologies is very necessary in order to implement a real-time monitoring system for patients. Low latency is provided by the 5G network technology, which also guarantees that all users will have access to the available capacity. The architecture that has been proposed is made up of a few different components. In order to provide patients with diabetes with a reliable detection and analysis service. In addition, the scientists developed a system for the transmission of data between patients, as well as a personalized model that makes use of medicinal data for the 5G smart diseases [24]. At some point in the future, the program will develop an architype system that will consist of medical data clouds, smartphones, and smart textiles. The findings of the study indicate that the system has the potential to successfully provide patients with individualized assistance in providing diagnostic and therapeutic services.

The authors of [25] thought there was reason to be optimistic about the precision of the approach, similar to the previous example. The article [26] suggests that a model for the prediction of cardiac disease that makes use of cloud computing and supervised machine learning (ML) could be developed. It was possible to forecast the sickness with a high degree of precision thanks to the technique's intelligence. Because of the current surge in the utilization of IT in the healthcare sector, which has led to the development of the Internet of Medical Things (IoMT), innovative e-health services are now accessible, particularly for the senior population that need daily support. The purpose of the study conducted by Cisotto and colleagues [27] was to determine the most common healthcare scenarios that could potentially benefit from 5G networks and to provide a summary of the communication requirements for these scenarios. The method of providing medical services using mobile devices is referred to as mobile health.

In [28], authors have written a study that provides a summary of the vision for beyond 5G networks and how it can overcome the difficulties that are currently face by the M-health industry. In addition to this, it intended to incorporate recent research on machine-to-machine and device-to-device sorts of communiqué in order to highlight the possibilities of these types of interactions. In order to provide answers to queries concerning the future of 6G network technologies, [29] provide an overview of the new characteristics of 6G, which includes the implementation of AI strategies. In addition to this, it provided a demonstration of the services that will soon be provided by 6G networking while also outlining the potential challenges that are linked with the integration of 6G technology. When it comes to 5G-oriented healthcare, the IoMT architecture is utilized in order to transmit medical data to the cloud for medical purposes.

It is possible that the future capabilities of 5G will make it possible to make significant breakthroughs in a wide range of health-related situations. These scenarios may include, but are not restricted to, the intelligent incessant nursing of patients who suffer from diseases, the authentication of patients' urgencies and emergency stages in 5G networks, and more. Diabetes that can be monitored by 5G, cognitive systems for healthcare that use 5G, the use of telesurgery, a robot, and 5G TI [30] are the basis for this. The idea that we would all be tired of these kinds of tools in the not-too-detached future is one that has been envisioned, gathering information from everything that we come across. The 6G network will aid the field of medicinal science by addressing individuals as a general system that incorporates both spiritual and environmental factors. As a prerequisite for continuous and mobile control, the exploitation of contemporary sensors of the body is essential. It is necessary to have a network that is dependable, secure, and adaptive, all of which can be accomplished with 6G [31].

It is dependent on the development of the infrastructure whether 5G services and applications will be of high quality. When it comes to the design of sophisticated network infrastructure, one of the most significant issues that needs to be reduced as much as possible is the cost that is involved [32]. In their presentation, the authors detailed a complete analysis on 5G networks and other modern technologies, both of which would be of critical importance during the implementation of smart hospitals. The work that is being presented examines the way modern technologies can be integrated with 5G for a variety of applications, including but not limited to healthcare, industrial, and remote monitoring. In addition, the article contains information regarding the 5G initiatives that have been implemented or are now being carried out throughout the universe [33]. In conclusion, it was determined that the 5G network might not be sufficient on its own to realize the goal of a smart hospital at this point. Therefore, the integration of 5G with both technological advancements and those that are already in existence becomes a serious concern [34]. This research concluded that the 5G network, in its capacity as an autonomous network, is unable to deliver the health services that were promised. Consequently, the 5G network will be a network of networks; it is merely an upgraded radio that is compatible with the radio that is already in use [35]. In this piece of work, the authors developed a novel architecture that has the potential to be applied in a sophisticated communication network. The architecture that has been described will manage the allocation of resources, as well as the interference problem that exists between the advanced radios and the existing radios. An additional conclusion that was reached was that the operation of the health care system that is based on the 5G network will be contingent on the various kinds of services [36].

The development of technologies of the next generation is accelerating at a quicker rate due to the increased demand from operators, industry, and subscribers. It is anticipated that the 5G network would not be accessible since various services and applications will consume it. So, it is possible that a smart hospital that is built on 5G networks would not reach the required latency [37]. On the other hand, the cloud architecture that is currently in use was developed specifically for the 5G network. This is because it will provide medical employment opportunities. In order to address the challenges that the 5G network presents, it is possible to implement the 6G network, which offers superior services and applications across all industries. On the other hand, if 5G is unable to live up to its promises, the concept of 6G will eventually become a reality [38].

9.3 Methodology

It is of the utmost importance to establish more solid foundations for the construction of theories by utilizing a more extensive and consistent research basis. As a result, this study took into account the fundamental difficulties that are associated with the investigation of information and communications technology (ICT), and it focused particularly on the 6GCIoHE in order to imitate the ideologies of the disciplined autopsy that is comprised of cognitive healthcare systems. The 6G network is a new technology that is characterized by discrete tools that grow to the consequent paradigm value-added activities [39]. This is accomplished through the progress of a scattered service 6G-enabled TI approach, which is illustrated in Figure 9.2. This framework reassures the development of tactile applications for the healthcare sector.

A significant amount of effort is being put forth by the research community in order to develop innovative remote processes in SHS. An entirely new era of the IoHE has been established, which is referred to as the "Cognitive IoHE." This new era aims to include cognitive skills into IoHE-based applications in order to guarantee intelligent management by facilitating collaboration and interaction between the IoHE and humans [40]. Through the automation of tasks based on certain patterns, the autonomic

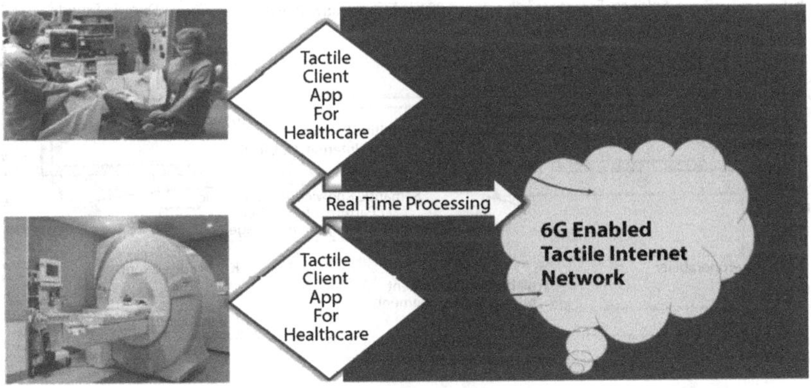

Figure 9.2 The TIF (Tag Image File Format) for healthcare apps using 6G.

CC throws light on prospects that have never been seen before for the development of intelligent CIoHE systems. Additionally, it places a heavy emphasis on the management of complex systems.

Taking into consideration the aforementioned, we devised a novel approach in order to map the functions of the 6GCIoHE that are responsible for monitoring and carrying out scrutiny, planning, and implementation of the organization process [41]. As part of this technique, a collection of cognitive design shapes was proposed as a means of guiding the 6GCIoHE system architect in the direction of delivering IoHE-based systems that are both flexible and intelligent. The 6GCIoHE system must have intelligent manageability, interoperability, and scalability in order to accommodate the patterns required. The proposed technique is depicted in Figure 9.3, which provides an overview of the methodology, which consists of two steps named (i) identification and (ii) formalization.

Based on the findings of the research, there is no agreement regarding the architecture of the 6GCIoHE system. In spite of the fact that the three-layer structure contains the fundamental concept of CIoHE, it is not adequate for the investigation of the 6GCIoHE. Due to the fact that healthcare applications have varying needs, the five-layer design was selected since it has a direct impact on the performance of the application. Additionally, the five-layer design is believed to be the most effective when a healthcare scheme is done using cutting-edge skills such as 6G TI, CDI, and IoHE, as well as diverse application domains. For this reason, we suggested the architecture consisting of five layers. It is the levels of dispensation in the hominid brain that served as inspiration for the five-layer 6GCIoHE

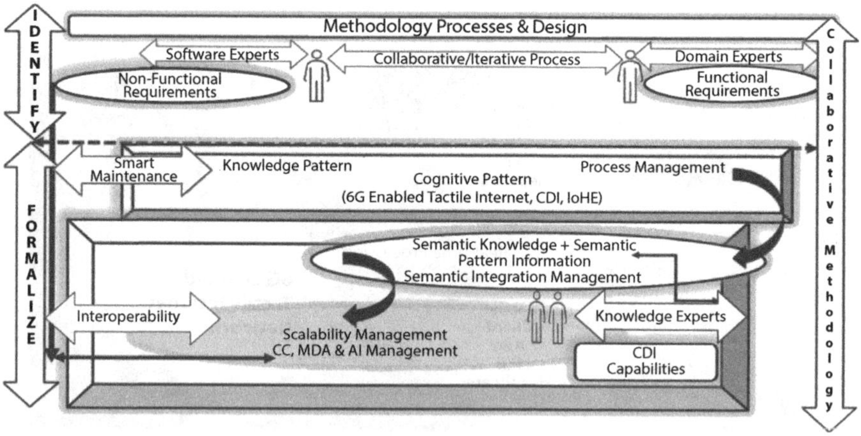

Figure 9.3 Structure of the proposed approach.

architecture that was presented. This architecture was also inspired by the abilities of human beings to think, feel, remember, make decisions, and react to the physical environment. The latency problems that are associated with cloud-based solutions are addressed by the 6GCIoHE system architecture that has been presented.

9.4 6G-Enabled SHS Applications and Challenges

9.4.1 Applications

Every 81 days, the volume of data pertaining to healthcare increases by a factor of two. The CC is classified as a system that is capable of learning at a large scale, which enables it to intermingle with humans in a more natural manner. By gaining deep province perceptions and delivering this knowledge to patients in a way that is serviceable, ordinary, and timely, cognitive systems can provide advice to individual patients, as well as caregivers. To ensure data protection and robust security, the information and communications technology infrastructure needs to be sufficiently pliable to allow for the harmonization of tenders with distributed strategies and the acceleration of digital submissions with IoHE systems [42]. In order to improve treatment and save money, there are a number of innovative IoHE solutions that enable doctors and patients to connect with one another without the need for in-person visits [43]. As compared to patients who had routine in-person visits, patients who received remote symptom monitoring have had improvements in both their outcomes and their overall experience. In addition to easing the process of data gathering and transmission between a patient and a physician, the function of monitoring symptoms can also make it possible to make adjustments to therapy in real time.

Better patient condition tracking, the creation of automated healthcare warnings, and real-time, relevant engagement with all health professionals are all benefits of combining 6G with algorithms powered by AI. There will be less death and illness, shorter hospital stays, and fewer medical expenses as a result of all of this. Here we'll take a look at a handful of the 6G technologies that will be used in healthcare in the near future.

9.4.1.1 In-Body, On-Body, Off-Body Communications

By leveraging ICT capabilities, this strategy aims to remotely monitor people's health. From in-body to on-body to off-body, it is all covered in the body layer. Data transferred in real-time to edge devices and the cloud is made possible by off-body communications. Biological communication networks consist of nanostructures or molecules, which act as sensors in the body [44].

9.4.1.2 *Intelligent Nanoscale Inner Body Communications*

The advent of biomedical cells has ushered in a new era known as the Internet of Bio-Nano Things (IoBNT), which will allow for the possibility of intra-body monitoring and manipulation. The system gathers medical data, sends it to the doctor or nurse, and then remotely triggers the necessary actions. Here, 6G technology is crucial, as it will enable the connecting of IoBNT and IoNT [45].

9.4.1.3 *Human Bond Communications*

In this approach, data is detected and transmitted using all the human senses. The potential for one person's "thoughts" or experiences to be transmitted to another is rapidly approaching. Sixth generation technology could be seen as a "material" technology that provides an engaging user experience by analyzing the data stored by the sensors of emotions [46]. It is feasible to provide improved services, including patient monitoring, diagnosis, support, and treatment.

9.4.1.4 *Visible Light Communication*

Visual light communication is a subset of optical wireless technology; it transmits data by means of light beams. Utilizing the infrastructure that can offer a downlink channel for improved connectivity, acquiring data from the body, and engaging in extensive user communication are all possible uses [47]. Cognitive computing applications in SHS are displayed in Figure 9.4.

As the transition from digital to cognitive occurs, a new era is beginning for applications in the healthcare industry. This new era will allow doctors to work together with CC systems to expand healthcare. Over the course of their lifetime, a single individual is projected to generate more than one million terabytes of data pertaining to their health. This is due to the ever-increasing amount of healthcare information that is collected by linked medical devices. It is vital to have a smart monitoring system in order to control the progression of patients' health based on WBS (Work Breakdown Structure). Some samples of such a system include: (i) When it comes to the management of diabetes, the WBS can be utilized to quantity

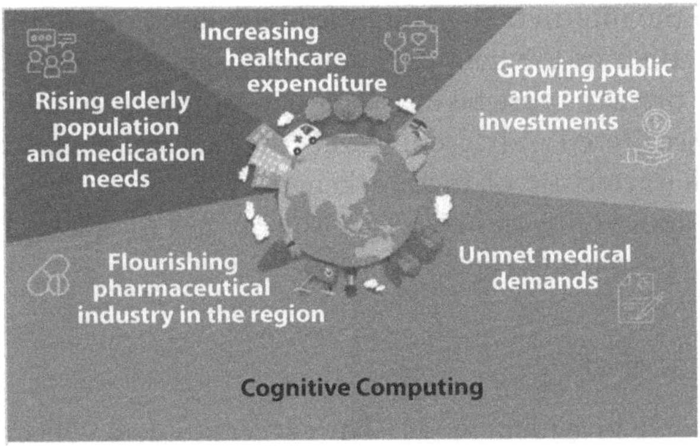

Figure 9.4 The CC for a populace smart healthcare system.

the "blood sugar of the patient." The CC outline, for example, is responsible for identifying the interactions that take place between the WBS and the physicians for the purpose of anomaly recognition and visualization.

9.4.2 Research Challenges

Here, we compiled all the current smart healthcare technology research obstacles and open security risks.

9.4.2.1 Security and Privacy

Due to the potential sharing of personally identifiable information among multiple members of the medical staff prior to transmission to physicians, the data produced by the numerous wearable devices and BANs poses a number of security and privacy concerns within the smart healthcare system. Furthermore, data must be protected from a variety of sensors and wireless technologies that could be used by hackers to obtain sensitive information. So, to ensure privacy and safety in the smart healthcare system, new counter security measures are required [48].

Wireless interface assaults, including unauthorized data access, integrity issues, and Denial of Service (DoS) to healthcare applications and data centers, are a real concern when healthcare devices are integrated into 6G-enabled IoT networks. There are increasing security and privacy concerns with the proliferation of interconnected gadgets. In particular, data communications and data management centers are susceptible to DoS, hijacking, spoofing, and eavesdropping assaults. One example is the potential for hackers to gain control of implantable cardiac devices that are linked to the internet. This might lead to alterations in their functionality and the theft of the data they communicate. Consequently, 6G–IoT security and privacy must take risk reduction into account. Because IoT networks are scattered and decentralized, they are well-suited to the decentralization characteristic of the blockchain, which also provides security features like anonymity and integrity. This makes the blockchain method more important in the 6G age.

9.4.2.2 Data Sharing

While healthcare providers in SHS have access to data collected from IoT devices, patients and their families have no idea who processes their data or how long it takes before it reaches them. As an example, patients may receive the incorrect medication or none if an attacker tampers with the data. Their treatment may be postponed or even jeopardized as a result. Hence, the smart healthcare system needs some kind of data sharing control or a mechanism to ensure the transfer of data is secure [49]. For 6G applications to handle a high number of connections efficiently, distributed interference avoidance/mitigation solutions are essential. Flexible spectrum sharing is an appealing concept, and blockchain and deep learning are promising methods for making it a reality. Consequently, it is critical to create new protocols and frameworks for intelligent spectrum sharing.

9.4.2.3 Voluminous Data

Numerous wearable devices fastened to people's bodies gather massive amounts of data. The patient's health status also causes this data to change regularly. It is a daunting endeavor to maintain such a vast and ever-changing amount of data. Additionally, new formats are required for the storage of various types of data. For instance, in order to train an ML model on the EEG data captured by an IoT sensor—which is in picture format—it must first be translated to a CSV format. Therefore, an effective storage system that may alter the file type in response to an application's requirements is required [50].

9.4.2.4 High Power Consumption

Wearable devices require a lot of power from the battery because they constantly track and monitor the patient's health status. Because of this, the user will have to charge it more than once. The solution to this problem is for the user to regularly put their gadgets into sleep mode when they are not checking their health status [51].

Small and linked to multiple sensors, IoT devices used in smart healthcare typically have a minimal physical footprint. A major issue with these gadgets is that they require constant power, which reduces battery life and increases costs. To get around these issues in smart healthcare, devices need to be inexpensive and have minimal power consumption [52]. So, for devices to talk to one other with minimal power consumption, algorithms that are good for the environment are required. Possible advancements in this area include microelectronics, wireless communication, and energy harvesting. For instance, a transparent silicon container housing a Bluetooth-enabled low-energy module allows for in-body sensors to collect sunlight for use in healthcare monitoring. Implants can be further transformed by novel materials like MXenes-based intelligent biosensors, which can determine a wide range of biomarkers and pathogens associated with contagious and deadly diseases without the need for external power.

9.4.2.5 Lack of Standardization

Smart healthcare systems transmit medical records using a network of interconnected devices. The specific protocols and settings that allow each device to communicate this data to healthcare providers vary. Having said that, healthcare organizations do not yet have a standardized framework in place for the communication, implementation, or deployment of IoT devices. Therefore, studies addressing the problem of interoperability amongst IoT devices using various protocols and standards are necessary.

9.4.2.6 Computationally Expensive

It is computationally expensive to integrate ML for smart and safe healthcare. The massive amounts of healthcare data that an ML model must process are the main cause of this. The time it takes for ML to run grows in direct proportion to the dataset size. In the event of an emergency, the medical staff receives a tardy response from the prediction service. To get over this problem, the smart healthcare system needs to use a model that is based on deep learning.

9.4.2.7 Ownership of Data and Ethical Considerations

The information pertaining to healthcare is highly confidential and intimate. There are a number of worries about data ownership, despite the fact that the smart healthcare gadget will enhance quality of life. Take a digital pill with built-in sensors as an example; it can let caregivers and doctors check if the drug is taken on time through a web-based interface. This can help doctors see if their patients are really following their treatment regimens. Nevertheless, insurance companies may have the ability to track patients' medication usage and refuse coverage to those who do not adhere to their prescribed schedule. What is being collected, how often, whether users provide prior informed consent, and whether they have an easy way to refuse collection or stop companies from selling their data are all factors that should be considered when formulating policies.

Emerging traditional digital technology, like the 6GCIoHE approach, can help the healthcare industry stay ahead of the curve and offer the ensuing resolutions to the many problems it is currently facing: (i) 6G TI-powered healthcare apps can revolutionize virtual consultations; (ii) healthcare professionals all over the world can connect through social media platforms made possible by the 6GCIoHE; (iii) improvements to the Medicare EHR (Electronic health record) system can streamline reimbursements; (iv) data management systems can automate inventory oversight; (v) efficient management is made possible by cloud plus data analysis capabilities; (vi) we need to implement blockchain based database answers; (vii) we need to establish prescription-based online medicinal stores; (viii) one typical use case for the 6GCIoHE is remote surgery; and (ix) the 6G TI communiqué system can be used for emotional healing.

The following principles provide stakeholders with the chance to overcome the difficulties posed by the IoHE network.

(i) Design-stage security implementation: smart healthcare brings an original idea that provides patients with the best service to a reality. With the help of innovative healthcare problems, the IoHE is building first-rate systems to aid both patients and doctors. When healthcare stakeholders are aware of the potential outcomes in the event of a device failure, they are better positioned to propose risk-based security measures.

(ii) Encouraging the use of security patches and vulnerability management tools that make use of cryptographic integrity and authenticity safeguards in order to fix software vulnerabilities automatically.

(iii) Establish tried-and-true security procedures that make security by default a reality by requiring login credentials that are both distinct and hard to crack. Incorporating security measures based on potential influence is crucial to avoid reputational and financial losses that could result from insufficient security measures.

(iv) Understanding the context in which an IoHE device will be used allows stakeholders to think about its technical specs and any necessary security measures. Additional security measures can be prioritized with the help of mitigation planning and analysis. The devices that are linked to the network need to be identified and verified.

(v) Investors should involve merchants and dealers in the risk taxation process to promote transparency. This will help raise awareness about potential vulnerabilities in third parties and build trust. It is important to develop a software bill of materials that may help stakeholders trust each other.

9.5 Future Research Directions and Recommendations

At this time, there is a lack of comprehension regarding the radio channel over 140GHz and the future gigabit Wi-Fi with IoT. Therefore, cutting-edge work in proliferation measurements and designing above 140GHz ought to be conducted in order to make progress toward 6G wireless network technology and beyond. One of the most significant new technologies that is now being investigated is known as 6G cell-free MIMO (Multiple Input Multiple Output). This innovation is a revolutionary network structure that aims to eliminate interference amid cells that use higher-frequency gamut bands, with THz bands.

9.5.1 Future Directions

For a high-quality healthcare experience, the IoHE network necessitates immense and intelligent connection, enormous bandwidth, and real-time latency, together with an extremely high data rate. It is anticipated that the forthcoming 6G communication system would be able to deliver intelligent IoT services everywhere and at any time, hence enhancing the quality of life of human beings. The growth of eHealth, which includes SHS, presents a barrier to the ability to meet the stringent quality of service standards that these services have. These needs include continuous connection availability, extremely low-latency, and mobility-support. By combining the sophisticated intelligence of upcoming 6G networks with a wider gamut, it will be possible to pledge key performance indicators and advances in ethereal efficacy that are up to 10 times greater on average.

Researchers in the healthcare industry have a number of challenges when it comes to managing massive amounts of data. These challenges include a high production velocity, a variety of sources, the quality of the data, the reliability of the resources, and many others. The use of CC skills for MDA (main distribution area) in cognitive healthcare can be fascinating for imminent research, and the fact that CC is still in its early phases of development is a promising development. The ever-increasing proliferation of WBS and IoHE devices is bringing about a deep and profound shift in the way healthcare is approached across the world. Data scientists are motivated to construct ANN and DL strategies through the use of biomimicry as a result of the little ML concept. The application of such technologies within the framework of applied clinical research demonstrates how little ML can serve as a tool to backing and magnify hominid cognitive capabilities for medical professionals who are providing care to patients who are becoming increasingly complex. At the moment, the IoE connections are disjointed and cumbersome, and linking gadgets does not generate value in the same way that connecting humans does. A significant issue with the existing architecture of the IoE is that users are compelled to trust platforms.

There is a dearth of a comprehensive perspective on the present status of research and application in the body of literature pertaining to the topic of

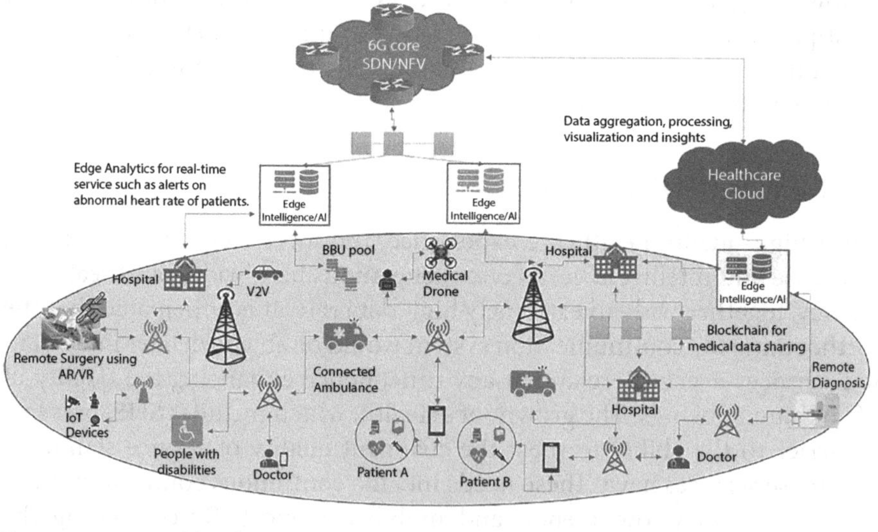

Figure 9.5 6G-enabled future SHS.

cognitive healthcare. For the purpose of ensuring that their methodologies are in line with the cognitive-developmental models, future research ought to take into consideration the philosophical perspectives that underpin theoretical descriptions. The 6G-enabled future SHS is displayed in Figure 9.5.

9.5.2 Recommendations

In this age of unequaled academic research, the cutting-edge technology of today is undergoing a process of evolution. If incantation is supposed to play the part of the supernatural, then cutting-edge technology ought to take on the role of the "instinctive" position. Tactile internet and the internet of human experience are two examples of telecommuting. Because of the incredibly low-latency of 6G structure, the TI will make it possible to manipulate items remotely, such as in the case of remote surgery. This will be accomplished while simultaneously providing the sensation that the remote object is at the user's fingers. This will allow for the provision of real-time thrill. The incorporation of these technologies has the potential to enhance the tactile capabilities of individuals to the extent that they are able to navigate distances that are beyond the typical reach of humans. For this reason, we suggest that the prospect of changing the way in which to participate in a SHS for many aspects of living should be considered. Human-centric mobile communiqués must be one of the significant uses of 6G-enabled TI, and as a result, the wireless research community needs to pay particular attention to this application.

Mobile carriers across the world are speeding up their investments in 5G radio access networks. There will be a certain proportion of the entire radio access network (RAN) market that will be captured by open RAN. A great number of machinists are eager to quicken the speed of open radio network development. We suggest that open RANs become an essential component of the solutions for 6G mobile systems. Compared to 5G, the 6GCIoHE system should be able to meet the requirements of healthcare utilities in terms of latency, reliability, connectivity density, and gaining key performance indicators that are typically 80 to 120 times higher. The CDI needs to acquire the ability to compile pathogenic and patient information in order to examine vast amounts of data in order to provide guidance based on real-time needs.

A more robust level of collaboration is required between the essential parties participating in the solutions for the IoHE in order to ensure the ethical and secure utilization of the IoHE.

1. The user should be made aware of, and trust should be established.
2. Customers should be aware of their rights to the confidentiality of their medical information.
3. From the point of view of the makers, a trustworthy system for IoHE devices ought to be made available in order to establish qualitative and objective standards for reliability.

9.6 Conclusions

This research was able to accomplish the objectives that were outlined in the Introduction (Section 9.1) in a satisfactory manner. In light of the ideas presented in Sections 9.2–9.6 and Sections 9.1–9.5, a novel theoretical framework was developed and submitted for consideration. Among the most important discoveries are the demonstration of the 6GCIoHE paradigm and the connected discussion on the five-layer design, as well as its applications, difficulties, and positive effects on cognitive healthcare. It is anticipated that the forthcoming 6G TI will be deployed on or after the year 2030. This will make it possible to provide end-users with the provision of small ML as a service through the application of pervasive intelligence. For the purpose of minimizing the limitations of the MDA issues, the utilization of cognitive systems is required. Unique insights were bestowed upon the field of CDI as a result of the research, particularly with regard to the characteristics of CC that were plotted with the viewpoints of huge data. These solutions are intended to protect against potential security threats.

References

1. Javaid, M., Haleem, A., Singh, R.P. and Suman, R., 2023. 5G technology for healthcare: Features, serviceable pillars, and applications. *Intell. Pharm.*
2. Suleiman, T.A. and Adinoyi, A., 2023. Telemedicine and Smart Healthcare—The Role of Artificial Intelligence, 5G, Cloud Services, and Other Enabling Technologies. *Int. J. Commun. Netw. Syst. Sci.*, 16(3), pp. 31-51.
3. Tong, C., 2022. Perspectives on 5G and Beyond Applications and Related Technologies. In *Advanced Materials and Components for 5G and Beyond* (pp. 231-258), Cham: Springer Nature Switzerland.
4. Sun, P., 2023. 5G+ Smart Healthcare. In *A Guidebook for 5GtoB and 6G Vision for Deep Convergence* (pp. 217-246), Singapore: Springer Nature Singapore.

5. Yadala, S., Pundru, C.S.R. and Solanki, V.K., 2023, March. A Novel Private Encryption Model in IoT Under Cloud Computing Domain. In *The International Conference on Intelligent Systems & Networks* (pp. 263-270), Singapore: Springer Nature Singapore.
6. Ahad, A., Jiangbina, Z., Tahir, M., Shayea, I., Sheikh, M.A. and Rasheed, F., 2024. 6G and Intelligent Healthcare: Taxonomy, Technologies, Open Issues and Future Research Directions. *Internet Things*, p. 101068.
7. Turab, N.M., Al-Nabulsi, J.I., Abu-Alhaija, M., Owida, H.A., Alsharaiah, M. and Abuthawabeh, A., 2023. Towards fostering the role of 5G networks in the field of digital health. *Int. J. Electr. Comput. Eng.*, (2088-8708), 13(6).
8. Rahman, M.M., Khatun, F., Sami, S.I. and Uzzaman, A., 2022. The evolving roles and impacts of 5G enabled technologies in healthcare: The world epidemic COVID-19 issues. *Array*, 14, p.100178.
9. Delshi Howsalya Devi, R., Naresh, R. and Vinoth Kumar, C.N.S., 2025. Advanced 5G Technology in Healthcare Field. *Resource Management in Advanced Wireless Networks*, pp. 227-245.
10. Devi, R.D.H., Naresh, R. and Kumar, C.V., 2023. Advanced 5G Technology in Healthcare Field. *Resource Management in Advanced Wireless Networks*, 227, p. 227.
11. Pradhan, B., Das, S., Roy, D.S., Routray, S., Benedetto, F. and Jhaveri, R.H., 2023. An AI-Assisted Smart Healthcare System Using 5G Communication. *IEEE Access*.
12. Kanesin, R., Sam, S.M., Sjarif, N.N.A., Abas, H. and Yuhaniz, S.S., 2023, September. Exploring The Role of 5G Networks in Advancing IoT Enabled Smart Healthcare. In *2023 IEEE 2nd National Biomedical Engineering Conference (NBEC)* (pp. 66-71), IEEE.
13. Latif, S., Qadir, J., Farooq, S. and Imran, M.A., 2017. How 5G wireless (and concomitant technologies) will revolutionize healthcare?. *Future Internet*, 9(4), p. 93.
14. Rahman, M.M. and Khatun, F., 2023. Challenges and Prospective of AI and 5G-Enabled Technologies in Emerging Applications during the Pandemic. In *Industry 4.0-Perspectives and Applications*. IntechOpen.
15. Franchi, A., Franchi, L. and Franchi, T., 2021. Digital health, big data and connectivity: 5G and beyond for patient-centred care. *Int. J. Digit.*, 1(1), p. 1.
16. Dash, L., Jain, P. and Albreem, M.A., A Review on Migration from 4G to 5G Network Architecture: Methods to Improve the Bandwidth, Latency, and Data Rate of a Network for Smart Hospitals. *5G-Based Smart Hospitals and Healthcare Systems*, pp. 153-167.
17. Suneel, S., Krishnamoorthy, R., Gopatoti, A. *et al.* Enhanced image diagnosing approach in medicine using quantum adaptive machine learning techniques. *Opt. Quant. Electron.*, 56, 534 (2024), https://doi.org/10.1007/s11082-023-06203-8.

18. Muniyappa, M., Shastri, M., Rohith, S., Nagesh, K.N., Aravinda, K. and Rangappa, D., 2023. 13 Smart Wearable Devices. *5G-Based Smart Hospitals and Healthcare Systems: Evaluation, Integration, and Deployment*, p. 186.
19. Pandiaraj, S., Krishnamoorthy, R., Ushasukhanya, S. *et al.* Optimization of IoT circuit for flexible optical network system with high speed utilization. *Opt. Quant. Electron.*, 55, 1206 (2023), https://doi.org/10.1007/s11082-023-05452-x.
20. Nawaz, N.A., Abid, A., Rasheed, S., Farooq, M.S., Shahzadi, A. and Mubarik, I., 2022. Impact of telecommunication network on future of telemedicine in healthcare: A systematic literature review. *Int. J. Adv. Appl. Sci.*, 9, pp. 122-138.
21. Devi, D.H., Duraisamy, K., Armghan, A., Alsharari, M., Aliqab, K., Sorathiya, V., Das, S. and Rashid, N., 2023. 5g technology in healthcare and wearable devices: A review. *Sensors*, 23(5), p. 2519.
22. Suneel, S., Balaram, A., Amina Begum, M., Umapathy, K., Reddy, P.C.S. and Talasila, V., 2024. Quantum mesh neural network model in precise image diagnosing. *Opt. Quantum. Electron.*, 56(4), p. 559.
23. Padmanayaki Selvarajan, Betty Elezebeth Samuel, Krishnamoorthy Ranganathan, Arvind Kumar Shukla, M Amina Begum and Sundaram Arun, "Mobile edge computing for efficient energy management systems", book title, *Human-Assisted Intelligent Computing*, IOP Publishing Ltd 2023 Pages 16-1 to 16-17, 2023, https://doi.org/10.1088/978-0-7503-4801-0ch16.
24. Prasad, D., Kudva, V., Singh, A., Hegde, R.B. and Rukmini, P.G., 2023. Role of 5G Networks in Healthcare Management System. *Crit. Rev. Biomed. Eng.*, 51.
25. Tanaka, K., Ogura, S., Krishnamoorthy, R., Sugiyama, Ki., Kawahara, M. (2024). Flexibility and Productivity in IoT Programming: A Case Study with Mruby. In: Guarda, T., Portela, F., Diaz-Nafria, J.M. (eds) Advanced Research in Technologies, Information, Innovation and Sustainability. ARTIIS 2023. *Communications in Computer and Information Science*, vol 1936. Springer, Cham. https://doi.org/10.1007/978-3-031-48855-9_2.
26. Ghosh, A., Sarkar, I., Dey, M. and Ghosh, A., 2022. Artificial intelligence and blockchain: Implementation perspectives for healthcare beyond 5G. In *Blockchain Applications for Healthcare Informatics* (pp. 93-116), Academic Press.
27. Ali, N.J., Hamzah, N.A., Ali, A.M., JosephNg, P.S., Tawfeq, J.F. and Radhi, A.D., 2023. An intelligent approach for enhancing the Quality of Service in IoMT based on 5G. *Period. Eng. Nat. Sci.*, 11(3), pp. 58-67.
28. Kiran, A., Rao, T.S., Gopatoti, A. *et al.* Harnessing quantum power using hybrid quantum deep neural network for advanced image taxonomy. *Opt. Quant. Electron.* 56, 574 (2024), https://doi.org/10.1007/s11082-023-06202-9.

29. Singh, D., Singh, D., Manju and Gupta, U., 2023. Smart Healthcare: A Breakthrough in the Growth of Technologies. In *Artificial Intelligence-based Healthcare Systems* (pp. 73-85), Cham: Springer Nature Switzerland.
30. Krishnamoorthy, R., Desai, A., Patel, R. *et al.* 4 Element compact triple band MIMO antenna for sub-6 GHz 5G wireless applications. *Wirel. Netw.*, **27**, 3747–3759 (2021), https://doi.org/10.1007/s11276-021-02734-8.
31. Yang, C., Liang, P., Fu, L., Cui, G., Huang, F., Teng, F. and Bangash, Y.A., 2022. Using 5G in smart cities: A systematic mapping study. *Intell. Syst. Appl.*, 14, p. 200065.
32. R. Krishnamoorthy, Meenakshi Gupta, Gundala Swathi, Kazuaki Tanaka, Ch. Raja, and Janjhyam Venkata Naga Ramesh, "An Intelligent IoT-Based Smart Healthcare Monitoring System Using Machine Learning", A Smart Multimodal Biomedical Diagnosis Based on Patient's Medical Questions and Symptoms" *5G-Based Smart Hospitals and Healthcare Systems*, CRC Press, 1st Edition, 2023, PP. 230-244.
33. Gautam, A., Amin, R. and Jacques, K., 2024. Constraints Due to Regularization of Smart Hospitals: To Study the Impact of 5G Technology on the Financial Sector. In *5G-Based Smart Hospitals and Healthcare Systems* (pp. 63-75), CRC Press.
34. Kumar, A., Jain, R., Gupta, M. and Islam, S.M. eds., 2023. *6G-Enabled IoT and AI for Smart Healthcare: Challenges, Impact, and Analysis*, CRC Press.
35. Satheeshkumar, R., Saini, K., Daniel, A. and Khari, M., 2022. 5G—Communication in HealthCare applications. In *Advances in Computers* (Vol. 127, pp. 485-506), Elsevier.
36. Chhabra, S., Aiden, M.K., Sabharwal, S.M. and Al-Asadi, M., 2023. 5G and 6G Technologies for Smart City. In *Enabling Technologies for Effective Planning and Management in Sustainable Smart Cities* (pp. 335-365), Cham: Springer International Publishing.
37. Diksha Srivastava, R. Krishnamoorthy, Doradla Bharadwaja, Kavyashree Nagarajaiah, Kazuaki Tanaka, and Janjhyam Venkata Naga Ramesh, "A Hybrid Deep Learning–Based Remote Monitoring Healthcare System Using Wearable Devices", *5G-Based Smart Hospitals and Healthcare Systems*, CRC Press, 1st Edition, 2023, PP. 1-14.
38. Eswaran, S. and Honnavalli, P., 2023. Private 5G networks: a survey on enabling technologies, deployment models, use cases and research directions. *Telecommun. Syst.*, 82(1), pp. 3-26.
39. Vijaya Gunturu, R. Krishnamoorthy, M. Amina Begum, R. Jayakarthik, Kazuaki Tanaka, Janjhyam Venkata Naga Ramesh "A Smart Multimodal Biomedical Diagnosis Based on Patient's Medical Questions and Symptoms" *5G-Based Smart Hospitals and Healthcare Systems*, CRC Press, 1st Edition, 2023, PP: 105-119.

40. Alahi, M.E.E., Sukkuea, A., Tina, F.W., Nag, A., Kurdthongmee, W., Suwannarat, K. and Mukhopadhyay, S.C., 2023. Integration of IoT-Enabled Technologies and Artificial Intelligence (AI) for Smart City Scenario: Recent Advancements and Future Trends. *Sensors*, 23(11), p. 5206.
41. Krishnamoorthy, R., Kumar, U., Swathi, G. *et al.* Metamaterial Inspired Quad-Port Multi-Antenna System for Millimeter Wave 5G Applications. *J. Infrared Millim. Terahertz Waves* (2023), https://doi.org/10.1007/s10762-023-00921-6.
42. Kwon, H., An, S., Lee, H.Y., Cha, W.C., Kim, S., Cho, M. and Kong, H.J., 2022. Review of smart hospital services in real healthcare environments. *Healthcare Inf. Res.*, 28(1), pp. 3-15.
43. T.N. Vinuth Raj, Priya A. Hoskeri, H.B. Muralidhara, C.R. Manjunatha, K. Yogesh Kumar, M.S. Raghu.
44. Facile synthesis of perovskite lanthanum aluminate and its green reduced graphene oxide composite for high performance supercapacitors, *J. Electroanal. Chem.*, Volume 858,2020, 113830, https://doi.org/10.1016/j.jelechem.2020.113830.
45. Rao, C.N., Chatrapathy, K., Fathima, A.J., Sathish, G., Mukherjee, S. and Reddy, P.C.S., 2023, October. Intelligent Deep Learning Framework for Breast Cancer Prediction using Feature Ensemble Learning. In *2023 4th IEEE Global Conference for Advancement in Technology (GCAT)* (pp. 1-5), IEEE.
46. Makina, H., Letaifa, A.B. and Rachedi, A., 2023. eHealth: Enabling technologies, opportunities and challenges. *Advances in Computers*, 131, pp. 1-47.
47. Tselios, C., Politis, I., Amaxilatis, D., Akrivopoulos, O., Chatzigiannakis, I., Panagiotakis, S. and Markakis, E.K., 2022. Melding Fog Computing and IoT for Deploying Secure, Response-Capable Healthcare Services in 5G and Beyond. *Sensors*, 22(9), p. 3375.
48. Sector, F., 2023. 5 Constraints Due to Regularization of Smart Hospitals. *5G-Based Smart Hospitals and Healthcare Systems: Evaluation, Integration, and Deployment*, p. 63.
49. Arun Kumar, Aziz Nanthaamornphong, R. Selvi, J. Venkatesh, Mohammed H. Alsharif, Peerapong Uthansakul, Monthippa Uthansakul,Evaluation of 5G techniques affecting the deployment of smart hospital infrastructure: Understanding 5G, AI and IoT role in smart hospital, *Alex. Eng. J.*, Volume 83, 2023, Pages 335-354, ISSN 1110-0168, https://doi.org/10.1016/j.aej.2023.10.065.
50. A. Kumar, M. A. Albreem, M. Gupta, M. H. Alsharif and S. Kim, "Future 5G Network Based Smart Hospitals: Hybrid Detection Technique for Latency Improvement," in *IEEE Access*, vol. 8, pp. 153240-153249, 2020, doi: 10.1109/ACCESS.2020.3017625.
51. Arun Kumar, R. Dhanagopal, Mahmoud A. Albreem, Dac-Nhuong Le, A comprehensive study on the role of advanced technologies in 5G based smart

hospital, *Alex. Eng. J.*, Volume 60, Issue 6, 2021, Pages 5527-5536, ISSN 1110-0168, https://doi.org/10.1016/j.aej.2021.04.016.

52. Ramakrishnan, Balamurali, Arun Kumar, Sumit Chakravarty, Mehedi Masud, and Mohammed Baz. 2021. "Analysis of FBMC Waveform for 5G Network Based Smart Hospitals" *Appl. Sci.* 11, no. 19: 8895, https://doi.org/10.3390/app11198895.

10

Patient Monitoring Using 5G, with MIMO-NOMA for mm-Wave Communications in Heterogeneous Networks

Suprith P. G.[1]*, Mohammed Riyaz Ahmed[2], Mahendra Shridhar Naik[3], Kavitha K. J.[4] and Chaitra S. N.[5]

[1]*School of Electronics and Communication Engineering, REVA University, Bengaluru and GM University, Davangere, India*
[2]*HKBK College of Engineering, Bengaluru, India*
[3]*Department of ECE, New Horizon College of Engineering, Bengaluru, India*
[4]*GMIT, Davangere, India*
[5]*NMAM Institute of Technology, Mangalore and GM University, Davangere, India*

Abstract

Future Internet of Things (IoT) applications are expected to leverage modular computing at the edge (MCE), an approach that is thought to be favorable, to support computation-intensive and time-sensitive tasks. Wireless network areas are defined by their precision in transmitting and receiving data, and they operate either inside or close to the human body. It needs to use less energy and operate for extended periods of time. The short broadcast and receiving distance of less than a few meters is one of its issues. In order to address this issue, researchers focused on a simulation based on a fifth generation (5G) network using multiple-input/multiple-output (MIMO) terminals that enable transport signals to the center (medical center) at 2.4, 2.8, or 5 GHz bands. The power is allocated to the patients through 5G non-orthogonal multiple access (NOMA) topology network. Using Bit Error Rate (BER), achievable total rate, outage likelihood, and the efficiency of the patient's power allocation are assessed. We have seen that devices considerably prolong the life of the nodes, operate better, and consume less energy based on the data acquired, while the reaction time for data transfers was accelerated by 5G devices. Furthermore, the advantage of MIMO antennas is that they increase the long-term reliability of the connection among locations.

**Corresponding author*: pgsuprith@gmail.com

Arun Kumar, Manoj Gupta, Sanjeev Sharma, Er. Himanshu Sharma and Khursheed Aurangzeb (eds.) Smart Hospitals: 5G, 6G and Moving Beyond Connectivity, (195–214) © 2024 Scrivener Publishing LLC

***Keywords*:** Multiple sources of input and output, non-orthogonal multiple access (NOMA), distribution of power, Internet of Things, successive interference cancellation

10.1 Introduction

With the aim of enhancing the standard of healthcare for all people worldwide, the healthcare sector has consistently incorporated the newest technological advancements. The delivery of healthcare services to the public, including those residing in rural areas and developing nations, has been profoundly impacted by the tremendous changes brought about using technology [1]. The identification of complex disorders is now possible because of technological breakthroughs, and complex medical treatments are being performed with simplicity. For example, improvements in medical imaging technologies have improved our knowledge of human physiology inside and have made it possible to diagnose a wide range of illnesses and problems in patients. This rapid treatment transformation is being driven by numerous technological advancements, which are quickly replacing the hospital- and specialist-centered model of healthcare with scattered, patient-centered care [2]. The ability to communicate has rendered remotely and customized treatment achievable, among other advantages. Intelligent healthcare apps make extensive use of the current 4G wireless network along with additional communication methods that are constantly developing to keep up with demands [3]. Communications technology is one of the key applied technologies in healthcare. Over the years, network and communication technologies have brought several improvements to the field of healthcare. Quick and simple communication lines for the exchange of basic diagnostic information, such as patient reports, treatment alternatives, and prescriptions were supported by previous communication technologies, such as wired telephone lines, fax technology, and networking technologies. Healthcare delivery has significantly improved with the introduction of wireless communication and the development of internet and satellite communication technologies [4]. They are essential in reviving primary healthcare because they improve data measurement and management, provide access to healthcare for rural people, and support personalized monitoring of chronic illnesses. Patients are required to attend hospitals; this is typically a labor- and time-intensive procedure in which the patient and medical staff must participate [5]. When the digital healthcare sector develops, more apps will generate a wider range of data formats. Many smart healthcare applications make complicated and continuous demands on existing communication systems, which are not able to handle them. Therefore, it is anticipated that both the 5G and future 6G wireless networks would allow smart healthcare applications that fulfill the majority of the necessary requirements, namely extremely low latency [6].

Future smart healthcare networks are expected to use fog and cloud computing, cloud of things (CoT), 5G and 6G devices, and Internet of Things (IoT) technology [7]. Future intelligent healthcare systems are expected to include 5G, 6G, and IoT devices, fog and cloud computing, and CoT to enhance coverage, network efficiency, and safety. The deployment of 5G innovations has accelerated globally [8]. Because of its components, it is perfect for facilitating significant advancements in the strength and suitability of categorising apps related to human services, including virtualization consideration, remote patient checking, more basic handling of large imaging records, and in-building information management. Soon, an emerging communication technique called 6G will rule the health care industry. An interconnected ecosystem that will create new opportunities for the healthcare and other industries has been made possible by the development of telemedicine, 5G mobile networks, artificial intelligence (AI) methods like device learning, as well as deep learning, as well as big data (BD) and supercomputers, technology for block chains, and the IoT [9].

We will offer a NOMA-MIMO antenna technology design in this study. In order to increase the multi-hop signals' range and lifespan, we also evaluated a number of frequencies for an energy-efficient network of signals that control the outside environment. Giving the NOMA user power to enable remote patient state monitoring is the aim of the work described in this paper. Furthermore, we will concentrate on delivering an appropriate power signal that consists of three primary components: the first component is an automatic case monitoring system that stores all patient data and transmits it to a physician for precise monitoring of condition. To increase the network's lifespan, the second aspect of the system is to offer the quickest path for sending and receiving patient data if the physician is not within the hospital. The final, as well as the largest and most crucial step, is to focus on selecting the optimal frequencies that improves connection stability and widens its transmission capacity for patient data as soon as feasible. Thus, we concentrated on the most crucial factors that gauge the network's performance. These parameters—the power allocation strength, the transmission path losses, and a comparison between the NOMA and orthogonal multiple access (OMA) techniques—are discussed in this study.

10.2 Related Works

To render the declining IoT capability possible electroencephalography (EEG) information, which is lifted out of the cloud, the researchers presented in an article a prototype technique for condensing the whole EEG of the patient information using cloud computing to avoid losing any of the information [10]. The two stages of this technique are data collecting (where data is sorted into hierarchical groups) and data compression (where data is merged in smaller groupings and uploaded above the cloud). The researchers found through a number of studies that the Huffman-based hierarchical clustering approach minimizes the quantity of huge EEG data before uploading transfer it into the web service. Consequently, a 4.33 compressive force ratio generally was obtained using Huffman's method that, for some of the scenarios proposed by other researchers, doubles the strength of compression.

The authors of a different recent study, which was presented in [11], suggested a method for tracking patients' disease risk by placing four sensors and gathering data to track their health. This technology's mechanism gathers patient data at a high pace of adaptability and energy conservation. The suggested strategy minimizes the volume of data collected, which results in providing enough the energy within each and every sensors value implanted on the physique of the person being treated, according to the researchers' simulations of the method. The idea entails a thorough evaluation of NOMA's effectiveness in the context of 5G networks, especially in light of the deployment of many users automatically. Our knowledge of the benefits and application of NOMA in dynamic, daily communication contexts are greatly advanced by this sort of analysis [12–14].

In [15], the primary objective of a model for compressing possible EEG fractal shapes that was presented and put into practice in is to lessen the amount of EEG data that is transmitted between the points of patient gathering (PDA) to the endpoint of the physician. The investigators verified that the suggested model enhances the patient's data flow to the closest medical facility. Furthermore, the researchers verified that the fractal block size is a significant factor in achieving the maximum compression ratio for the sensor data collected, thereby streamlining data flowing via a network and lowering energy consumption to prolong the sensors' operational lifespan.

With this research, we propose a wireless body area network for distant tracking of patient health by implementing an entirely novel scenario. The scenario's three stages were designed to find the quickest way for data to be received or transmitted from the patient to the hospital doctor, or the doctor back the individual in need. The first phase should involve figuring out where the hospital is, and the second should involve figuring out how many people are involved in getting from the doctor to the individual. Finding the patient's location is the third step. Furthermore, we employed three distinct technologies, namely 5G-NOMA and 5G with MIMO, and juxtaposed the acquired outcomes using the OMA methodology. Finding the most effective method with the fewest losses in data transmission or reception between the patient and the physician is the major goal of employing these strategies. The bit error rate, probability, and power allocation in the free space atmosphere are the three characteristics that are used to calculate the effectiveness of these strategies and the suggested NOMA. After closely analyzing different wireless technologies, we found that 5G technology with multiplexing provides the optimum performance for the work with regard to of reliability and consistency. Because MIMO antennas have a group of terminals functioning within separate bands and frequencies, they reduce interference and noise across the pathways, which make 5G with MIMO superior. Thus, the 5G NOMA spectral efficiency improves by finding the suitable patients by allocating power to the users.

The introduction of 5G technology has a significant effect on a number of industries, including healthcare. The integration of IoT, AI, and 5G bring about major advances in the area of smart hospitals. In smart hospitals, the combination of 5G, AI, and IoT offers enormous promise for enhancing patient outcomes, healthcare delivery, and operational effectiveness. For deployment to be successful and widely adopted, it is imperative that issues pertaining to security, interoperability, and regulatory compliance are addressed [16].

Innovative methods are needed to create future 5G-based smart hospitals with lower latency, and a hybrid detection technique can play a key role in reaching this objective. Let us examine the theoretical foundation of a hybrid detection method designed to reduce latency in 5G-based smart hospitals. Future 5G-based smart hospitals will employ a hybrid detection method for latency improvement that combines edge computing, cloud-based AI, dynamic load balancing, predictive analytics, and 5G network slicing integration in a deliberate manner. Through the strategic allocation of computing workloads and the application of modern analytics, smart hospitals can minimize latency and guarantee the prompt and dependable provision of vital healthcare services [17].

A description of 5G technology and its importance for medical care. An overview of smart hospitals' development and how they rely on cutting-edge technology. Problem description and justification for extensive research. Examination of the body of knowledge regarding 5G technologies in healthcare. An overview of the functions of cutting-edge technologies in smart hospitals, including AI, IoT, Edge Computing, and AR/VR. Finding the research's gaps and explaining why it is being done. An explanation in-depth of the research techniques used. An explanation of the methods used to acquire data, such as case studies, questionnaires, and professional interviews [18].

The article outlines the paradigm shift that 5G will bring about in the healthcare industry and stresses the importance of assessing, incorporating, and implementing this technology in smart hospitals. Improving connectivity, real-time data interchange, and cutting-edge healthcare services are the main themes. A detailed analysis of 5G's features include huge device connectivity, reduced latency, and high-speed data transmission. This section assesses the possible advantages and difficulties of integrating 5G technology into healthcare systems, and it focuses on interoperability as it examines the smooth integration of 5G with the current healthcare infrastructure. The potential for a more intelligent and connected healthcare environment is demonstrated by highlighting the cooperative role of 5G with cutting-edge technologies like AI and IoT [19].

The importance of the FBMC (filter bank multi-carrier) waveform in the context of 5G is discussed in the study, along with how it can affect communication in smart hospitals. It highlights how important it is to do a thorough investigation in order to determine whether FBMC is appropriate for supporting advanced healthcare services. A thorough examination of FBMC's features and how they differ from conventional orthogonal frequency-division multiplexing waveforms were made. Aspects like interference reduction and spectrum efficiency are discussed, highlighting the potential benefits of FBMC in the context of 5G networks. The study examined the possible long-term effects of implementing FBMC in smart hospitals and made recommendations for future research and development paths. This includes chances to improve FBMC's capabilities in order to satisfy changing demands for healthcare communication [20].

The importance of hybrid spectrum sensing is discussed, along with how it relates to the changing and dynamic environments of 5G and future 6G technologies. It draws attention to the necessity of sophisticated spectrum sensing methods in order to handle the difficulties brought about by a variety of waveforms and intricate communication settings. A thorough examination of hybrid spectrum sensing approaches with a focus on combining several sensing techniques was done to improve spectrum awareness and utilization; this also includes a review of conventional sensing techniques and the introduction of cognitive radio principles. The uses of hybrid spectrum sensing in relation to expected 5G and 6G waveforms are covered in the study. It discusses the difficulties brought about by various signal formats and modulation techniques, emphasizing how hybrid sensing can change to keep up with the ever-advancing communication technology [21].

In addition to outlining the background of cognitive radio networks, the study emphasizes the importance of NOMA as a multiple access method. It highlights how important it is to do a thorough examination of NOMA's performance evolution and how it affects throughput in Cognitive Radio Network (CRN). An examination of the foundations of NOMA, showing how different power levels and codebooks can be assigned to allow multiple users to share the same time-frequency resources. The potential benefits of NOMA in terms of user fairness and spectral efficiency are highlighted in this section. A thorough examination of how NOMA's performance has changed over time, taking into account variables including shifting user dynamics, channel characteristics, and network conditions. This research investigates how NOMA maintains efficient communication performance in the face of changing conditions [22].

Using non-orthogonal multiple access (NOMA), the research focuses on the introduction of the context of energy efficiency and service delay in 5G networks. As a tactic for reducing energy usage and service latency, it highlights the importance of compute offloading. A look into NOMA technology and how it enables different users with different power levels and codebooks to share the same time-frequency resources. Spectral efficiency and enhanced user fairness are two of the potential benefits of NOMA that are highlighted in this section. A comprehensive examination of the techniques used was done to reduce energy usage in the 5G NOMA system by means of effective compute offloading. This entails taking into account elements like resource allocation plans and power control in order to attain energy efficiency [23].

In order to maximize efficiency and resource use, power allocation in communication systems is a significant problem that is covered in this study. It presents the application of a metaheuristic algorithm called Butterfly Optimization to multi-objective power allocation optimization. The main emphasis is on multi-objective sum rate optimization, highlighting the necessity of improving total data transmission speeds while taking into account a number of competing goals. The study examines the trade-offs associated with concurrently achieving several sum rate-related goals; it describes the butterfly optimization-derived power allocation approach in detail. This entails weighing the trade-offs between competing goals and figuring out the best way to distribute power levels throughout communication channels in order to maximize the total sum rate [24].

The automatic deployment strategy for many users in 5G systems with NOMA support is the main focus. In an effort to maximize system performance, the article examines how this strategy simplifies the user placement and configuration procedure. To evaluate NOMA's efficacy in the automatic deployment scenario, the study uses a set of performance evaluation metrics. System capacity, spectrum efficiency, user fairness, and total network throughput are a few examples of these metrics. Describes the process or algorithm that is utilized in the NOMA system to automatically deploy multiple users. Maximizing the overall performance of the system may entail taking user grouping, power distribution, and other factors into account [25].

The following describes how this paper is organized overall: The related works are included in Section 10.2. In part 10.3, the NOMA architecture is explained in detail. Power allocation is provided to the hospital and 5G equipped NOMA users in Section 10.4. The MIMO-NOMA system to prevent interference is described in Section 10.5. Section 10.6 provides an explanation of the findings and debate. Section 10.7 provides the research work's conclusion.

10.3 NOMA Architecture

Figure 10.1 represents the one base station (BS) that is used, while two individuals – also known as the close user and distant user, in that order – let us examine a downlink NOMA scenario. We designate UE_3 represents the user who is close by, whereas 1 represents the user who is far away. We designate UE_3 as the nearby user and UE_1 as the far user. The signal to be transferred when utilising the superposition transmission strategy is given by:

$$x = \sqrt{P_1}x_1 + \sqrt{P_2}x_2 \tag{10.1}$$

Here, P serves as the overall transmitted strength and P_k is the quantity of transmission strength allotted to the UE_k transmission. $P_1 + P_2 = \mathrm{P}$ in this case, β is the UE_1 power distribution ratio. The signal sent for UE_k is denoted by x_k. The signal that UE_1 and UE_2 are receiving is provided by:

$$\mathrm{y_k} = \mathrm{h_k}\sqrt{\beta \mathrm{P}}\mathrm{x_1} + \mathrm{h_k}\sqrt{(1-\beta)}\mathrm{P}\mathrm{x_2} + \mathrm{n_k} \tag{10.2}$$

for k = 1; 2, here h_k is the unlisten noise additive white (AWGN) at UE_k and h_k is the complex channel coefficient between UE_k and the BS. It is presumption that $|h_1|^2 > |h_2|^2$. By giving UE_2 more power, that is, c < 0:5, the interference that UE_1 signal causes to UE_2 signal is reduced to the

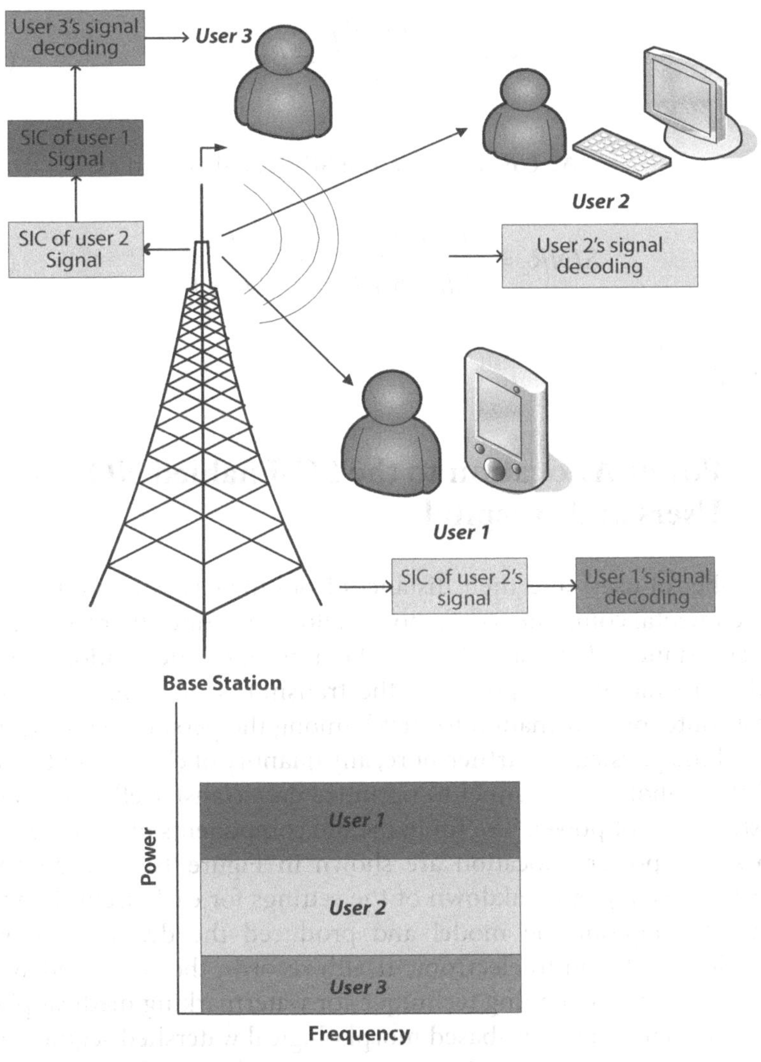

Figure 10.1 NOMA topology.

point that UE_2 can decode its own signal x_1 without using SIC. Since UE_1 channel gain is larger than UE_2, it may decode UE_2 signal in the interim, cancel out UE_2 interference, and then decode its own signal x1. Following SIC, the signal to interference-plus-noise ratio (SINR) at the UE_1 receiver is displayed as:

$$SINR_1 = \frac{\beta |h_1|^2 p}{N_o} = \beta \gamma_1 \tag{10.3}$$

Here, $\gamma_1 = \frac{|h_1|^2 p}{N_o}$. At UE_1 receiver, the SINR is displayed as

$$SINR_2 = \frac{1-\beta |h_2|^2 p}{\beta |h_2|^2 p + N_o} = \frac{(1-\beta)\gamma_2}{\beta \gamma_2 + 1} \tag{10.4}$$

Here, $\gamma_2 = \frac{|h_2|^2 p}{N_o}$.

10.4 Power Allocation to the 5G-Enabled NOMA Users and Hospital

The number of users and their distances from the base station determine the fundamental components of a power allotment. Since there are numerous circumstances that may influence the transfer of information, we have turned to regulating the power of the transmitter and figuring out the shortest route for information to travel among the person receiving treatment and the physician. Furthermore, any quantity of clients can be introduced throughout the channel to optimize data transfer efficiency above the distribution of power. The fundamental components of a wireless area network and power allocation are shown in Figure 10.2. Additionally, Figure 10.3 displays a breakdown of the settings for each scenario, which was run throughout the model and produced the desired outcomes. Specifically in relation to electronic health records, the combined system incorporates a new encoding technique for watermarking medical photographs. It also uses a fusion-based morphological watershed segmentation technique to improve the precision and efficacy of medical image segmentation, which enhances the field of medical imaging's capacity for analysis and diagnosis [25].

10.5 NOMA-MIMO System

We suggest using NOMA in mm-wave vector space massive MIMO structures to further improve availability thickness and range efficiency. Unlike current beam space MIMO frameworks, as shown in Figure 10.2, more

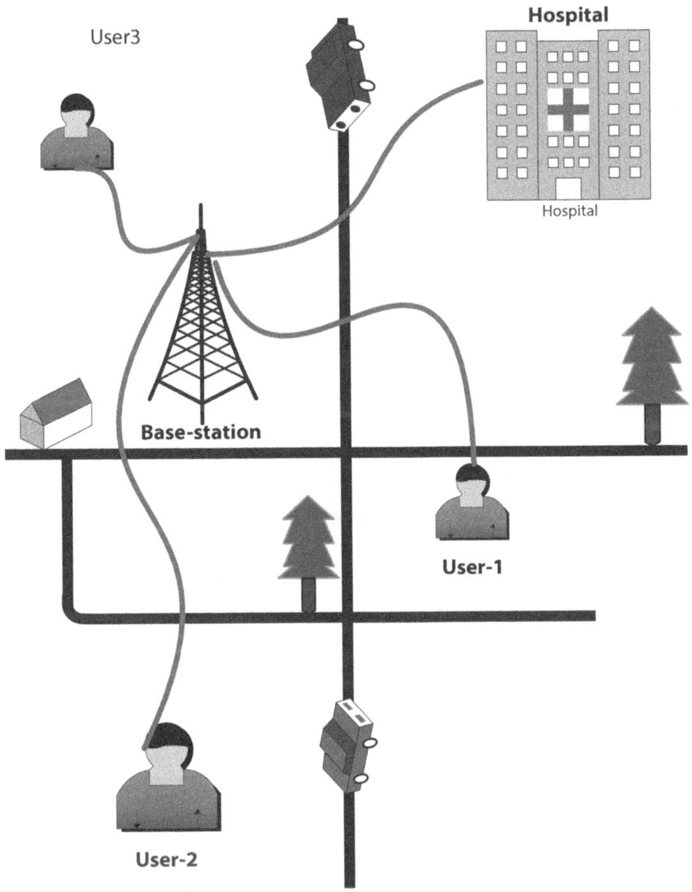

Figure 10.2 A wireless connection is established between the patient and the medical facility to continuously track the health of the individual.

than one customer may be continuously provided within every selected shaft in the suggested beam space MIMO with NOMA graph [26].

Figure 10.4 gives the combination of NOMA-MIMO system to select a single user for every RF link and beam, various algorithms are utilized, like deep learning-based channel estimation and beam space channel estimate. The different clients—who are referred to in this article as "conflicting clients"—will most likely select a pillar that is comparable to one another. In order to completely comprehend the multiplexing gain, we need the number of RF chains (NRF) to match the bar value G. The notion presents a high-tech network of communications that effectively transmits data in the milli-meter-wave frequency band through the use of power control

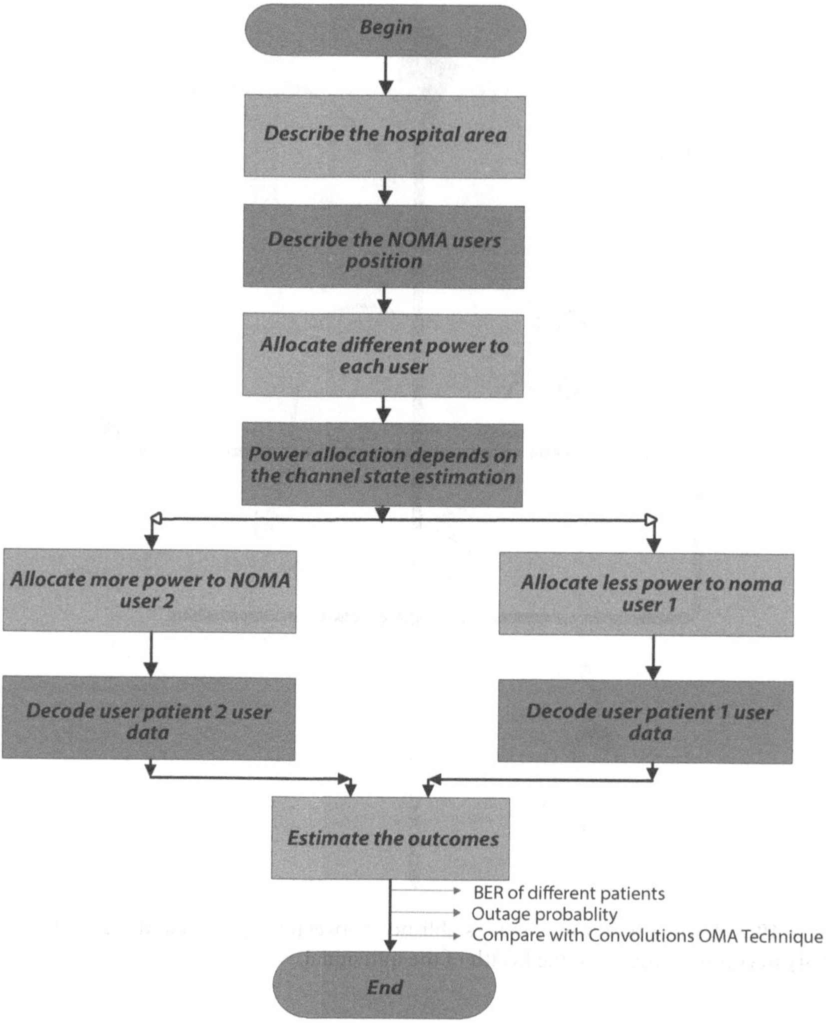

Figure 10.3 The procedures used in the simulation's output between the medical facilities to all three NOMA users via the base station are depicted in the flowchart.

strategies (NOMA) with sophisticated beam forming techniques (beam space MIMO) [27].

$$Y_{n,m} = h_{n,m}^{H} \sum_{j=1}^{G} \sum_{i=1}^{sn} wi\sqrt{p_{i,j}}si, j + vn, m \tag{10.4}$$

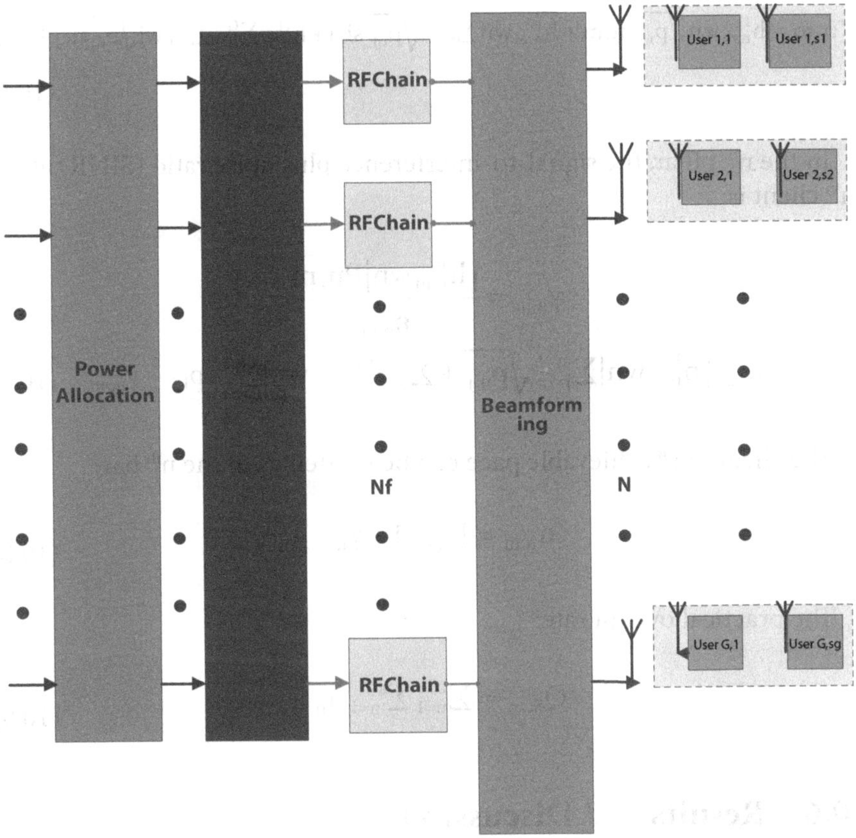

Figure 10.4 Proposed MIMO-NOMA beam space.

$$y_{n,m} = h_{n,m}^{H} wn\sqrt{p_{i,j}}\, s_{n,m} + h_{n,m}^{H} wn \sum_{j=1}^{m-1} \sqrt{p_{i,j}}\, s_{i,j} + h_{n,m}^{H} wn \sum_{i=m+1}^{si} \sqrt{p_{i,j}}\, s_{n,j} + h_{n,m}^{H} \sum_{i\neq n}^{G} \sum_{j=1}^{G} wj\sqrt{p_{i,j}}\, s_{i,j} + v_{n,m} \quad (10.5)$$

Where there is resistance within the bunch and resistance between groups, the precoding vector for the nth pillar is w_n, and the mth client's channel is addressed by $h_{m,n}$ in the nth bar. To reduce the ith client's impedance in the nth (for all i>m) shaft, the serial interference cancellation (SCI) approach is employed by the mth client in the nth pillar. Repurposing the residual sign that the nth client took from the mth shaft is possible [28–30]. Provide an n-layered radio wire to the admission point, which we consider to be an essentially examined uniform straight show for ease of use.

$$\bar{Y}n,m = h^{H}_{n,m} wn\sqrt{p_{i,j}} sn,m + h^{H}_{n,m} wn \sum_{j=1}^{m-1} \sqrt{p_{i,j}}\ si,j + h^{H}_{n,m} \sum_{i\neq n}^{G} \sum_{j=1}^{G} wj\sqrt{p_{i,j}} si,j + v_{n,m} \quad (10.6)$$

In the nth pillar, the signal-to-interference plus noise ratio (SINR) at the mth client is:

$$\gamma_{n,m} = \frac{| h^{H}_{n,m} wn| Pn,m}{\varepsilon_{n,m}}$$

$$\varepsilon_{n,m} | h^{H}_{n,m} wn| \sum_{j=1}^{m-1} \sqrt{p_{n,j}} + \sum_{i\neq n}^{G} | h^{H}_{n,m} wn| \sum_{j=1}^{si} p_{i,j} + v_{n,m} \quad (10.7)$$

The client's m^{th} achievable pace can be written as in the nth bar:

$$u_{n,m} = \log_2(1 + \gamma_{n,m}) \quad (10.8)$$

The practical overall rate:

$$Q_{Sum} = \sum_{n=1}^{G} \sum_{m=1}^{si} u_{n,m} \quad (10.9)$$

10.6 Results and Discussion

The power allocation outcomes of the technique and comments are displayed in this section. The MATLAB R2019a software is used for the power method's development and evaluation. The machine is equipped with an i5 processor and 8GB RAM. This equitable power transfer from the hospital to the patients who live apart is the primary goal. This is to accomplish a suitable power allocation, which will result in a higher sum rate and a lower probability of an outage. In this instance, the three users are communicating via fading Rayleigh channels in a simulation of the NOMA connection.

10.6.1 BER Analysis of Number of Users

In this study, the performance under analysis is the probability of BER calculation represented in Figure 10.5. In this instance, several noise variances

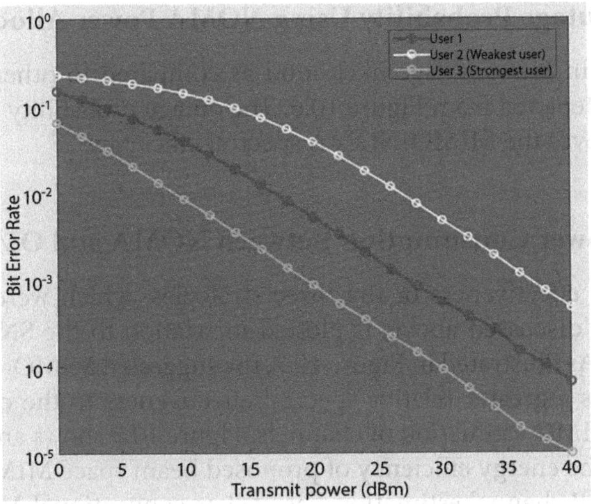

Figure 10.5 Examining of bit error calculation.

are used to analyze the performance. User 3 is the nearest user to the base station; hence, the bit error is less when compared to User 2 who is far away from the base station. The following performance evaluations are given for various noisy variations:

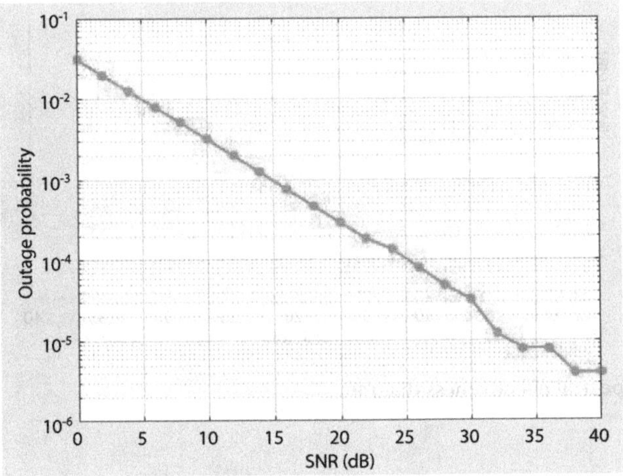

Figure 10.6 Outage probability v/s signal-to-noise ratio (SNR).

10.6.2 Outage Probability Using NOMA Power Allocation

This results in lower outage likelihood as compared to other traditional methods is depicted from Figure 10.6. The outage probability value is less, which improves the MIMO-NOMA spectral efficiency.

10.6.3 Power Consumption Between NOMA and OMA Users

The spectral effectiveness of the three strategies, which were taken into account and discussed above, is plotted in relation to the SNR shown in Figure 10.7. As illustrated in Figure 10.7, the suggested MIMO-NOMA plot demonstrates a greater relative spectral effectiveness to the conventional OMP and MIMO estimation of channels. Figure 10.8 shows an illustration comparing the energy efficiency of proposed beam space MIMO-NOMA, classical OMP channel estimations, as well as conventional MIMO-based channel estimations.

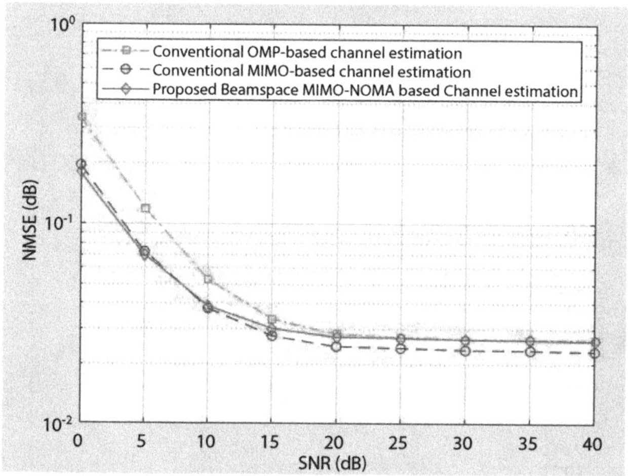

Figure 10.7 Spectral effectiveness diagram.

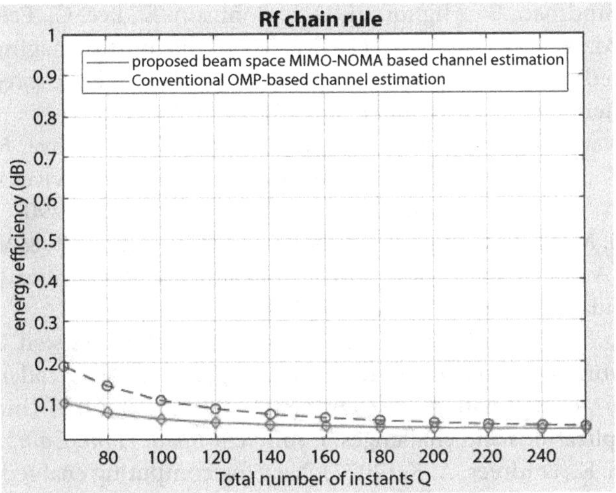

Figure 10.8 Q's energy efficiency graph.

10.7 Conclusion and Future Scope

With the goal to handle the power allocation in a network because of the variations among 5G-NOMA using MIMO connectivity in addition to rapid more efficient data distribution for use in real-time response, this article proposes the optimal techniques for communicating between terminals established by healthcare and their patients. Subsequently, MIMO improved the reliability of the 5G-NOMA utilization approaches. Combining technologies can effectively and considerably minimize the transmitting device's influence. Patients can move around more comfortably by using towers for cell phones to cover more ground and lessen knots. In the next study, researchers will employ an optimizing approach to find the best pathways for mobile sensor networks, thus covering the natural world as effectively as practicable.

References

1. Stefanova-Pavlova, M., Andonov, V., Tasseva, V., Gateva, A., & Stefanova, E. (2016). Generalized nets in medicine: an example of telemedicine for people with diabetes. *Imprecision and Uncertainty in Information Representation and Processing: New Tools Based on Intuitionistic Fuzzy Sets and Generalized Nets*, 327-357.
2. Taleb, H., Nasser, A., Andrieux, G., Charara, N., & Motta Cruz, E. (2021). Wireless technologies, medical applications and future challenges in WBAN: A survey. *Wirel. Netw.*, 27, 5271-5295.

3. Smith-Bindman, R., Miglioretti, D. L., Johnson, E., Lee, C., Feigelson, H. S., Flynn, M., & Williams, A. E. (2012). Use of diagnostic imaging studies and associated radiation exposure for patients enrolled in large integrated health care systems, 1996-2010. *Jama*, 307(22), 2400-2409.
4. Stefanova-Pavlova, M., Andonov, V., Stoyanov, T., Angelova, M., Cook, G., Klein, B., & Stefanova, E. (2017). Modeling telehealth services with generalized nets. *Recent Contributions in Intelligent Systems*, 279-290.
5. Kashani, M. H., Madanipour, M., Nikravan, M., Asghari, P., & Mahdipour, E. (2021). A systematic review of IoT in healthcare: Applications, techniques, and trends. *J. Network Comput. Appl.*, 192, 103164.
6. Ahmed, M. I. B. (2019). Virtual Clinic: A CDSS Assisted Telemedicine Framework. In *Telemedicine Technologies* (pp. 227-238), Academic Press.
7. Alhaidari, F., Rahman, A., & Zagrouba, R. (2020). Cloud of Things: architecture, applications and challenges. *J. Ambient Intell. Hum. Comput.*, 1-19.
8. Idrees, S. K., & Idrees, A. K. (2022). New fog computing enabled lossless EEG data compression scheme in IoT networks. *J. Ambient Intell. Hum. Comput.*, 1-14.
9. Jaber, A. S., & Idrees, A. K. (2021). Energy-saving ultisensory data sampling and fusion with decision-making for monitoring health risk using WBSNs. *Softw.: Pract. Exper.*, 51(2), 271-293.
10. Suprith, P. G., & Mohammed, R. A. (2022). The Performance Evaluation of NOMA for 5G systems using Automatic Deployment of multi Users. *International Journal of Electronics and Telecommunications*, 68.
11. Al-Hussaibi, W. A., & Ali, F. H. (2019). Efficient user clustering, receive antenna selection, and power allocation algorithms for massive MIMO-NOMA systems. *IEEE Access*, 7, 31865-31882.
12. Al-Nassrawy, K. K., Al-Shammary, D., & Idrees, A. K. (2020). High performance fractal compression for EEG health network traffic. *Procedia Comput. Sci.*, 167, 1240-1249.
13. Nalband, A. H., Ahmed, M. R., & Sarvagya, M. (2020). Power Scaling and Antenna Selection Techniques for Hybrid Beamforming in mmWave Massive MIMO Systems Self Driving car View project Advance production technologies in agriculture View project. *Article in International Journal of Electronics and Telecommunications*, 66(3), 529–535.
14. Liang, X., Gong, X., Wu, Y., Ng, D. W. K., & Hong, T. (2018). Analysis of outage probabilities for cooperative NOMA users with imperfect CSI," In *2018 IEEE 4th Information Technology and Mechatronics Engineering Conference (ITOEC)* (pp.1617-1623).
15. Wang, B., Dai, L., Wang, Z., Ge, N., & Zhou, S. (2017). Spectrum and Energy-Efficient Beamspace MIMO-NOMA for Millimeter-Wave Communications Using Lens Antenna Array. *IEEE J. Sel. Areas Commun.*, 35(10), 2370–2382.
16. Kumar, A., Nanthaamornphong, A., Selvi, R., Venkatesh, J., Alsharif, M. H., Uthansakul, P., & Uthansakul, M. (2023). Evaluation of 5G techniques

affecting the deployment of smart hospital infrastructure: Understanding 5G, AI and IoT role in smart hospital. *Alexandria Eng. J.*, 83, 335-354.

17. Kumar, A., Albreem, M. A., Gupta, M., Alsharif, M. H., & Kim, S. (2020). Future 5G network based smart hospitals: Hybrid detection technique for latency improvement. *IEEE Access*, 8, 153240-153249.
18. Kumar, A., Dhanagopal, R., Albreem, M. A., & Le, D. N. (2021). A comprehensive study on the role of advanced technologies in 5G based smart hospital. *Alexandria Eng. J.*, 60(6), 5527-5536.
19. Arun Kumar, Sumit Chakravarty, Aravinda K, Mohit Kumar Sharma (2024). *5G-Based Smart Hospitals and Healthcare Systems Evaluation, Integration, and Deployment.*
20. Ramakrishnan, B., Kumar, A., Chakravarty, S., Masud, M., & Baz, M. (2021). Analysis of FBMC waveform for 5G network based smart hospitals. *Appl. Sci.*, 11(19), 8895.
21. Kumar, A., Venkatesh, J., Gaur, N., Alsharif, M. H., Jahid, A., & Raju, K. (2022). Analysis of Hybrid Spectrum Sensing for 5G and 6G Waveforms. *Electronics*, 12(1), 138.
22. Suprith, P. G., & Ahmed, M. R. *Analysis of NOMA's Performance Evolution and Throughput in Cognitive Radio Network.*
23. Suprith, P. G., & Ahmed, M. R. (2023). Minimization of Energy and Service Latency Computation Offloading using Neural Network in 5G NOMA System. *Int. J. Electron. Telecommun.*, 69.
24. Gangadharappa, S. P., & Ahmed, M. R. (2022). Power Allocation Using Multi-Objective Sum Rate Based Butterfly Optimization Algorithm for NOMA Network. *Int. J. Intell. Eng. Syst.*, 15(4).
25. Kavitha, K. J., & Shan, P. B. (2023). Medical image watermarking based on novel encoding for EHR and fusion based morphological watershed segmentation algorithm for medical images. *Multimed. Tools Appl.*, 1-28.
25. Suprith, P. G., & Mohammed, R. A. (2022). The Performance Evaluation of NOMA for 5G systems using Automatic Deployment of multi Users. *Int. J. Electron. Telecommun.*, 68.
26. Suprith, P. G., & Ahmed, M. R. (2023, June). Power Extracting Beamspace MIMO-NOMA for mm-Wave Communication Uses an Array of Antennas. In *2023 3rd International Conference on Intelligent Technologies (CONIT)* (pp. 1-6). IEEE.
27. T.N. Vinuth Raj, Priya A. Hoskeri, H.B. Muralidhara, C.R. Manjunatha, K. Yogesh Kumar, M.S. Raghu, Facile synthesis of perovskite lanthanum aluminate and its green reduced graphene oxide composite for high performance supercapacitors, *J. Electroanal. Chem.*, Volume 858, 2020, 113830, https://doi.org/10.1016/j.jelechem.2020.113830.
28. Ding, Z., Fan, P., & Poor, H. V. (2016). Impact of User Pairing on 5G Nonorthogonal Multiple-Access Downlink Transmissions. *IEEE Trans. Veh. Technol.*, 65(8), 6010–6023.

29. Islam, S. M. R., Avazov, N., Dobre, O. A., & Kwak, K. S. (2017). Power-Domain Non-Orthogonal Multiple Accesses (NOMA) in 5G Systems: Potentials and Challenges. *IEEE Commun. Surv. Tut.*, 19(2), 721–742.
30. Dai, L., Wang, B., Yuan, Y., Han, S., Chih-Lin, I., & Wang, Z. (2015). Non-orthogonal multiple access for 5G: solutions, challenges, opportunities, and future research trends. *IEEE Commun. Mag.*, 53(9), 74-81.

11

A Review on the Internet of Medical Things

Sowmith Prajwal, Tharun Salgar S.*, Chethana H.T. and Karthik R.

Department of Computer Science & Engineering, Vidyavardhaka, College of Engineering, Mysuru, India

Abstract

As we embark on this exploration of the Internet of Medical Things (IoMT), we find ourselves at the intersection of technology and healthcare, a crossroads where innovation hasthe potential to revolutionize our approach to medical care. The IoMT, a network ofinterconnected healthcare devices that can communicate with each other via the internet, is poised to transform the medical landscape. This chapter delves into the intricacies of the IoMT, exploring its potential to enhance patient care, improve health outcomes, and streamline medical processes. From remote patient monitoring to smart hospitals, we will navigate the complexities and possibilities of this burgeoning field, shedding light on how the IoMT is reshaping the future of healthcare. As we journey through this chapter, we inviteyou to envision a world where technology and healthcare converge to create a moreconnected, efficient, and patient-centric healthcare system.

***Keywords*:** Network architecture, Internet of Medical Things (IoMT), remote healthcare monitoring (RHM), IoMT framework, compound annual growth rate (CAGR), implantable medical devices (IMDs), key generation server (KGS), remote patient monitoring (RPM), GSM (Global System for Mobile Communications)

The major contributions of the research work are as follows:

- To analyze various IoMT architectures and their structured types used in the healthcare system.
- To present a comparative analysis of various data collection techniques and the role of IoMT in healthcare system.

**Corresponding author*: tharunsalgars@gmail.com

Arun Kumar, Manoj Gupta, Sanjeev Sharma, Er. Himanshu Sharma and Khursheed Aurangzeb (eds.) Smart Hospitals: 5G, 6G and Moving Beyond Connectivity, (215–234)

- To present a comprehensive analysis of applications of the IoMT in the healthcare sector in a more convenient manner.
- To explore various health domains of the IoMT framework, including the types of sensors used for each domain.

To propose various research challenges and benefits that need to be considered while creating an IoMT-based smart healthcare system.

11.1 Introduction

Human health is a cornerstone for a serene and prosperous life. As defined by the World HealthOrganization (WHO), health is not merely the absence of diseases or infirmity, but a state of complete physical and mental well-being. Healthcare, therefore, is the practice of preserving or enhancing health through the prevention, diagnosis, and treatment of illness and injury [2]. Traditional healthcare systems often rely on the manual management of patient data, including demographics, case history, diagnostics, medication, billing, and drug stock maintenance [36]. This manual approach can lead to human errors that impact patient care. However, the advent of the Internet of Things (IoT) in healthcare, or smart healthcare, mitigates these errors [2]. It enables physicians to diagnose diseases more accurately and easily by interconnecting all vital parameter monitoring devices over a network with a decision support system [37].

This interconnected network of medical devices, capable of transferring data over a network without requiring human-to-human or human-to-computer interaction, is known as the Internet of Medical Things (IoMT). According to some latest research and advisory company reports, there will be 29 billion things connected to the internet by 2030. Furthermore, according to Fortune Business Insights, the market size is expected to reach USD 3,352.97 billion by 2030, growing at a compound annual growth rate (CAGR) of 26.1% [38].

An IoMT platform is an advanced system that incorporates sensors and electronic circuits designed for capturing biomedical signals from patients. This comprehensive platform consistsof essential components, including a processing unit responsible for analyzing the biomedical signals, a network device for transmitting the acquired biomedical data over a network, and a storage unit, either temporary or permanent [39, 40]. Additionally, it features a visualization platform equipped with artificial intelligence schemes, facilitating data interpretation and decision-making aligned with physicians' expertise. The architecture of IoMT is visually represented in

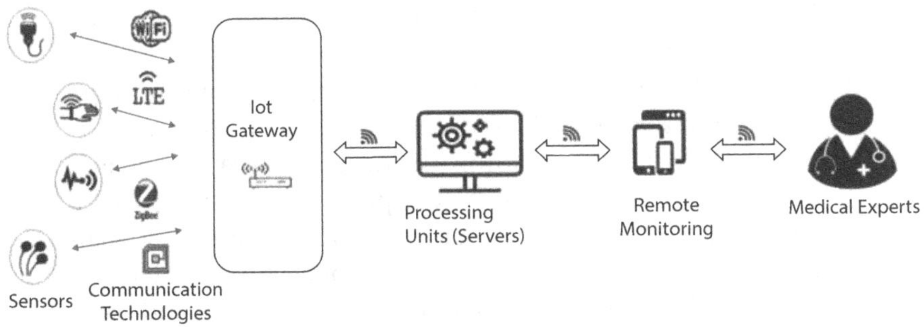

Figure 11.1 The Internet of Medical Things (IoMT) – architecture [1].

Figure 11.1, illustrating the interconnected nature of these components in a unified system [1]. This article emphasizes IoMT-based remote health monitoring, tracking ingestible sensors, smart hospitals, and enhanced chronic disease treatment [41]. It underscores the importance of human health in leading a peaceful and successful life and how the IoMT is revolutionizing healthcare [42].

11.1.1 Definition

The IoMT refers to a network of medical devices and applications that connect to healthcare IT systems through online computer networks. These devices, equipped with sensors and software, can generate, collect, analyze, and transmit health data. From wearable devices to smart hospital equipment, the IoMT is transforming healthcare by enabling remote patient monitoring (RPM), personalized treatment, and enhanced patient care, making healthcare more efficient and patient-focused. It is a key component in the evolution of healthcare delivery.

11.2 Architecture of IoMT

The IoMT is typically structured into four primary layers:

1. *Perception Layer:* This is the foundational layer where data is gathered from various sources.This layer is composed of miniature sensors that are either implanted in the body or worn externally. These sensors gather biometric data from the patient [3]. This data is then wirelesslytransmitted to the next layer using protocols like Wi-Fi or Bluetooth, or via the

Med Radio frequency spectrum that is specifically reserved for implantable medical devices (IMDs) [4].

2. *Gateway Layer:* Given the constraints in processing and storage capabilities of IoMT sensors,the data is relayed unprocessed to the next layer, known as the gateway layer. Devices in this layer, which could be the patient's smartphone or a specific access point (AP), are typically more robust than the sensors. These devices can carry out preliminary operations such as validation, temporary data storage, and basic AI-driven analysis. Furthermore, they transmit the sensor data to the cloud via the internet [3].
3. *Cloud Layer:* The cloud layer plays a crucial role in accepting data from the gateway for purposes of storage, analysis, and secure access. The analysis process might include data processing to identify any shifts in the patient's health status, which are subsequently communicated to physicians or patients for further action. The responsibility of generating IDsand keys for various system nodes lies with the key generation server (KGS). Additionally, this layer facilitates remote management and control over sensor access [3].
4. *Visualization Action Layer:* At this level, the gathered data is made accessible to both doctorsand patients, allowing them to keep track of health progress. This level also includes the physician's suggested actions, which are formulated in response to the patient's health conditions. Such actions could include the prescription of new medicines or the modification ofdosages for current medications [3].

11.2.1 The Role of IoMT in Healthcare

The IoMT is transforming the healthcare landscape by seamlesslyintegrating medical devices, wearables, and sensors into healthcare systems. With IoMT, patients can access top-tier care without leaving their homes. Let us explore the impact and role of the IoMT in the realm of healthcare as shown in Figure 11.2.

11.2.1.1 Data-Driven Decisions

The IoMT in healthcare is a powerfultool for making data-driven decisions, which are essential in the complex world of modern medicine. This

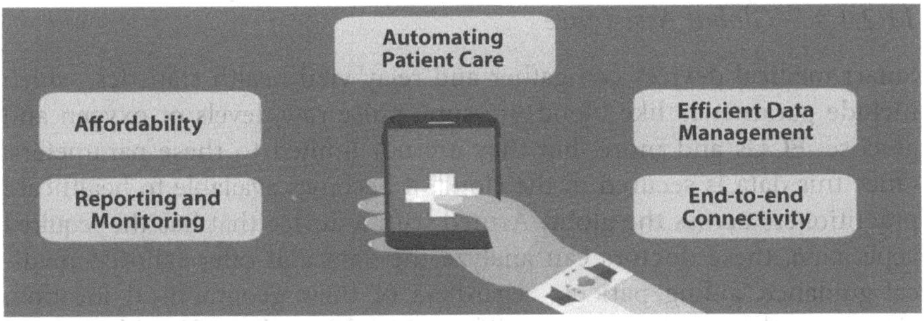

Figure 11.2 The impact of the IoMT on healthcare [5].

technology offers the ability to continuously monitor patients and send reminders for medication, among other features. By leveraging data, healthcare administrators and medical staff can make well-informed decisions that not only benefit patients but also contribute to the digital transformation of the healthcare industry.

11.2.1.2 Smart Medical Devices

Applications of IoMT have revolutionized the tracking of medical components. These devices, whether they are used for managing inventories or monitoring health conditions, play a crucial role in achieving medical goals and enhancing patient experience. Take smartwatches and pillboxes as examples. The former can monitor biometrics, while the latter can serve as a reminder for medication intake. By using this, we can improve the precision of diagnoses and treatments. These healthcare home-based devices are particularly beneficial for patients with disabilities.

11.2.1.3 Efficient Processes

The IoMT offers a beacon of hope for substantial advancements. Take, for instance, True-Access, a product of Koombea. This application empowers healthcare professionals and patients to traverse authorized areas in medical facilities without the need for explicit permission. At its core, it operates akin to an intelligent access card. Its functionality extends beyond mere access. The data it amasses plays a crucial role in operational management. Consequently, it bolsters security protocols and provides valuable insights for data-driven administrative decisions.

11.2.1.4 Global Assistance

Smart medical devices can gather and relay vital health statistics, which include parameters like blood pressure, pulse rate, levels of oxygen and glucose, ECGs and more, but they are not limited to these parameters. Once this data is secured in the cloud, it becomes available to healthcare practitioners across the globe. Armed with a device that has the required application, these doctors can analyze the data and offer tailored medical guidance, aiding patients regardless of their geographical location. Consequently, we observe an upliftment in the quality of healthcare services and benefits, surpassing the constraints of location and time.

11.2.2 Types of IoMT Devices

The domain of the IoMT is overflowing with innovative solutions that hold the promise torevolutionize healthcare provision. The possibilities are boundless, encompassing everything from wearable devices and RPM systems to telemedicine platforms and artificial intelligence-driven analytics.

The types of IoMT devices are:

- On-Body Segment
- In-Home Segment
- Community Segment
- In-Hospital Segment

11.2.2.1 On-Body Segment

On-body segment IoMT devices are revolutionizing the healthcare industry as shown in Figure 11.3. These devices, worn directly on the body, are designed to monitor various health parameters in real time. They include wearables such as fitness trackers, smartwatches, and heart rate monitors.

They collect data on vital signs like heart rate, blood pressure, and oxygen levels, providing valuable insights into the wearer's health. The data can be used by healthcare professionals to make informed decisions about treatment and care. The potential of on-body IoMT devices is vast, from managing chronic conditions to optimizing athletic performance [5].

As technology advances, we can expect these devices to become even more sophisticated, offering a comprehensive view of our health at our fingertips.

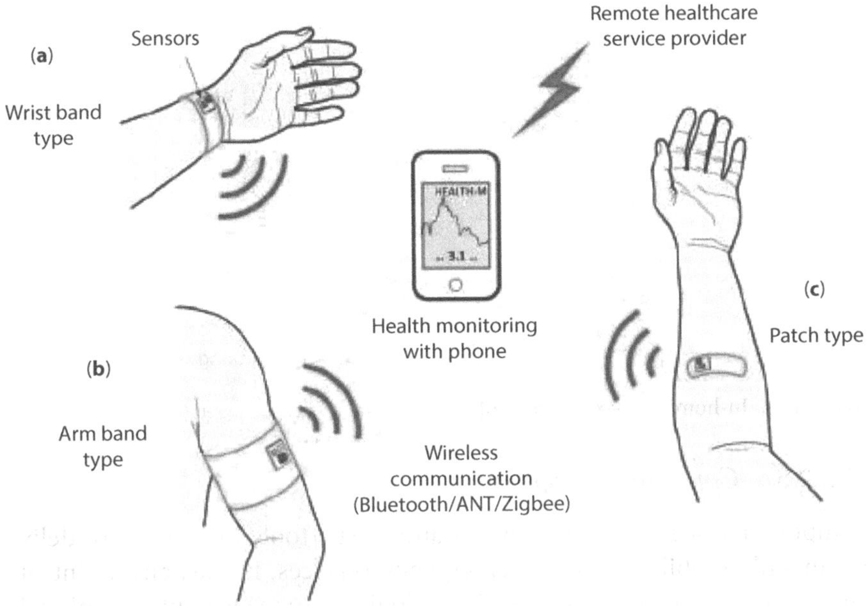

Figure 11.3 On-body segment device [7].

11.2.2.2 In-Home Segment

The home segment encompasses telehealth virtual visits, RPM, and a personal emergency system. This comprehensive package ensures that patients can swiftly access medical assistance during emergencies [5]. Additionally, to impede the progression of chronic diseases, RPM diligently tracks patients' physiological parameters, facilitating the delivery of extended and personalized care over the long term as shown in Figure 11.4.

The IoMT is a transformative concept in the healthcare industry, particularly in the in-homehealthcare segment. The IoMT devices, which include digital tools like wearable fitness trackers, insulin pumps, blood pressure monitors, and smart beds, are designed to provide health services and monitoring over the internet. These devices enable continuous patient monitoring, reducing the need for hospital visits and facilitating timely care [5]. They can collect, analyze, and transmit health data in real time, providing a continuous stream of information to healthcare providers. This data is invaluable for making informed decisions about a patient's care, thereby improving outcomes and reducing costs.

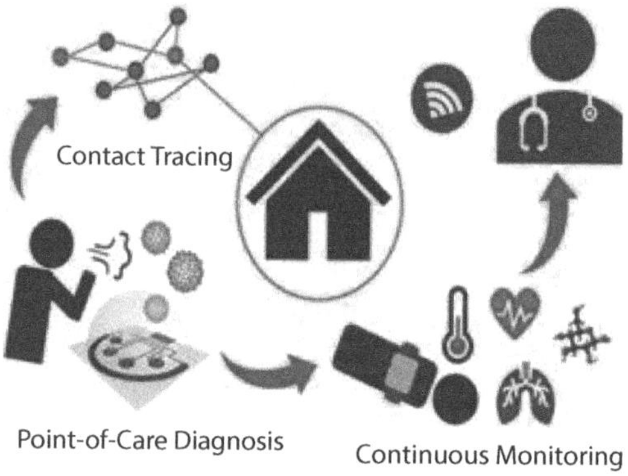

Figure 11.4 In-home segment device [6].

11.2.2.3 Community Segment

Components of segmented sensors and IoMT tools in healthcare delivery include mobility services, emergency services, kiosks, and point-of-care devices. In the realm of healthcare logistics management, the IoMT is exemplified by devices that monitor parameters such as humidity, shock, and temperature during shipment. These devices play a crucial role in ensuring the safe and efficient delivery of healthcare services. Within the community segment of IoMT devices, a transformative wave of innovation is shaping the landscape of healthcare delivery [5].

These interconnected devices are designed to create a communal framework, fostering collaborative approaches to health and well-being.

Smart community health platforms leverage IoMT technology to establish a network of shared health data, promoting real-time information exchange among residents, healthcare providers, and community organizations. Wearable IoMT devices become integral components, not only tracking individual health metrics but also contributing to aggregated data for community healthanalytics. This shared data facilitates early detection of health trends and outbreaks, allowing for proactive community-based interventions. Additionally, these devices play a vital role in preventive care, offering personalized health insights and wellness recommendations at both individual and community levels. Through telehealth features, community members can engagein virtual consultations, enhancing healthcare accessibility and reducing barriers to medical services. The community segment of IoMT devices stands as a testament to the power of technology in building a collaborative health ecosystem, where individuals and healthcare stakeholders work together to promote a healthier and more connected community. As these devices continue to evolve, they hold the potential to revolutionize the way communities approach healthcare, emphasizing proactive health management and fostering a sense of shared responsibility for well-being.

11.2.2.4 In-Hospital Segment

The community segment of IoMT devices encompasses various aspects such as managing patient flow, assets, and inventory, as well as monitoring the environment and energy [5]. The IoMT has significantly transformed the healthcare sector, particularly within the in-hospital segment. This segment includes a wide array of devices such as MRI machines, infusion pumps, and wheelchairs as shown in Figure 11.5.

These IoMT-enabled devices assist hospitals in managing assets, personnel, and patient flow. For instance, monitors can track high-value equipment as they move through the facility. This helps in optimizing resource utilization and improving patient care. In addition to asset tracking,these devices also monitor patient flow and manage inventory, such as pharmaceuticals. This ensures efficient hospital operations and timely delivery of care. Moreover, the in-hospital segment of IoMT devices also includes medical imaging systems such as MRI machines or CT scanners. These devices play a crucial role in diagnosing and treating various medical conditions.

In conclusion, the in-hospital segment of IoMT devices is playing a pivotal role in enhancing healthcare delivery. By optimizing resource utilization, ensuring efficient operations, and improving patient care, these devices are truly revolutionizing the healthcare sector.

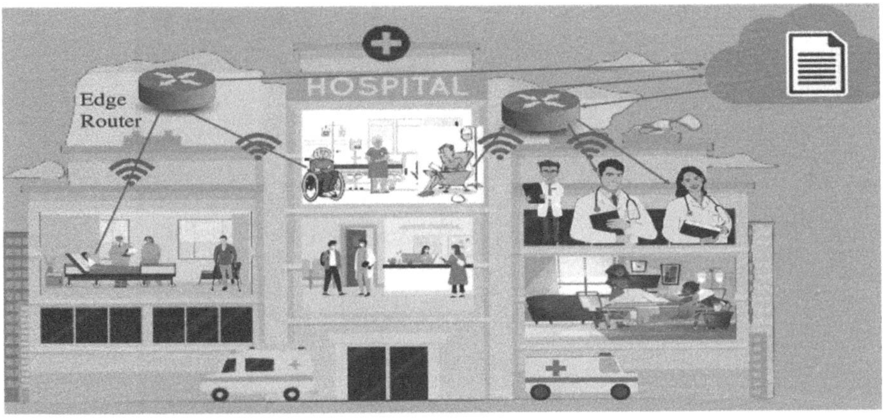

Figure 11.5 In-hospital segment device [9].

11.3 IoMT - Applications, Benefits and Challenges

11.3.1 Applications of IoMT

The implementation of the IoMT in the healthcare sector is revolutionizing the industry, paving the way for increased efficiency, greater accessibility, and a focus on patient-centered care. The wide range of applications across different healthcare areas demonstrates the significant potential of the IoMT to enhance outcomes and elevate the overall experience in healthcare [10] as shown in Figure 11.6.

11.3.1.1 The Sensor Patch Detects Blood Leakage During Hemodialysis

A novel system has been developed that leverages Bluetooth Low Energy (BLE) and Wi-Fi, integrating them with IoMT technologies to form a sensor patch. This system is composed of a sensor designed in a multi-ring shape. As the liquid volume increases, the sensor can detect leaks. A blood leak detector is usually placed in the dialysis circuit in the dialysate outflow line. If a blood leak develops through the dialysis membrane, the blood leaking into the dialysate is sensed by the blood leak detector, and the appropriate alarm is activated [10, 11].

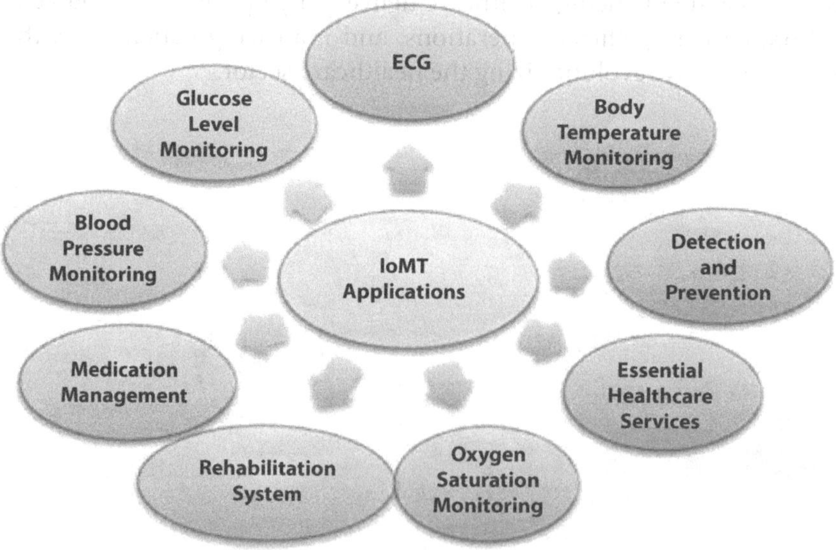

Figure 11.6 Applications of the IoMT [8].

The device also includes a mapping circuit and a Bluetooth low energy module. During its production, a signal line was embedded within the insulating layers, leaving only the sensing point exposed to the environment. The process from blood leakage to detection involves three stages:

1. Absorption: The gauze absorbs the blood, which then diffuses to the patch.
2. Reaction: The blood diffuses into the patch causing an increase in the detection voltage.
3. Saturation: The blood can no longer spread, and the voltage stabilizes [10, 35].

Some of the key benefits of using a sensor patch for blood leakage detection are:

- It can improve patient safety and reduce the risk of mortality from blood loss.
- It can alert the healthcare staff in real-time and enable timely intervention.
- It can enhance work efficiency and reduce the inconvenience of false alarms for thehealthcare staff.
- It can provide accurate and reliable measurements of blood leakage volume and risk level.
- It can be integrated with an IoMT system to enable multi-bed monitoring and data transmission.

11.3.1.2 Disease Surveillance and Tracking

The primary focus in managing the spread of diseases worldwide is on testing and tracking, particularly to slow down transmission. Various devices, based on the IoMT, have been employed to test and monitor individuals infected with the disease, as well as to pinpoint patient locations to track potential disease transmission. Point-of- care testing devices, which are IoMT-based, can enhance the treatment of infectious diseases such as malaria, dengue fever, influenza A (H1N1), human papilloma virus, Ebola virus disease, Zika virus, and coronavirus (COVID-19) [12]. In 2020, Bibi *et al.* developed an IoMT-based system that enabled real-time, fast, and secure testing, along with the diagnosis andmanagement of leukemia using cloud computing. This illustrates the transformative potential of IoMT in healthcare [10, 13, 35].

11.3.1.3 *Digital Biomarkers*

Currently, self-powered diagnostic tools connected to the IoMT are under development. These tools hold the promise of enabling real-time monitoring of biomarkers in various bodily fluids such as sweat, urine, and blood. This could potentially simplify the process of differentiating between bacterial and viral illnesses, which could be highly beneficial. These tools could meticulously track a patient's response to treatment. This would provide insights into whether the patient is positively responding to the therapy or showing signs of resistance. In a recent study, Wessels *et al.* (2021) utilized complex neural networks to develop a new smart biomarker capable of detecting lymph node metastasis. This exemplifies the innovative applications of IoMT in healthcare [14–24].

11.3.1.4 *Wearable Ozone Therapy*

The ozone treatment stands out due to the simplicity of its production process. Ozone can be synthetically produced (via UV light) within compact portable devices carried by patients. This allows for continuous low-dose therapy regimens, while mitigating the adverse effects of increased concentrations on healthy skin cells. Ozonated air aids in wound healing by exposing the wound to oxidative stress [25]. This triggers an increase in the production and migration of components essential for wound healing, as well as an elevation in oxygen levels at the wound site [26].

The development of wearable ozone production technology would empower patients to receive topical ozone therapy outside a clinical setting. The design, production, and testing of a portable and wearable platform could enable localized administration of ozone to the wound site [10].

11.3.1.5 *Seizure Detection*

A seizure is characterized by a sudden electrical disturbance in the brain. Therefore, it is crucial to detect it promptly to provide the necessary care and treatment topatients. An approach based on the IoMT can potentially detect the onset of a seizure using a patient's electroencephalography (EEG) data.

This system analyzes the neurological datacaptured from an EEG sensor and continuously processes it to extract hyper-synchronous pulsesfrom the brain. The collected information is then used to identify the occurrence of a seizure. These IoMT-based systems, such as those leveraging edge machine learning, are being developed for real-time, fast, and secure seizure detection. These systems use hardware-friendly seizure detection algorithms to meet the requirements of edge devices with limited resources [10, 27].

11.3.1.6 Automatic Insulin Injection

This system employs the Raspberry-Pi 3, a device that is not only affordable but also highly adaptable. It gathers information on four crucial bodily vitals and presents them on a website, supplemented by a live video feed from a camera for ongoing observation. To serve the purpose of live tracking, two separate login keys are used: one is assigned to the doctor, and the other is given to the relatives of the patient. If any instability or abnormality is detected by a sensor, a notification is sent to the doctor through the global system for mobile communications (GSM) module. If the doctor deems an insulin injection necessary, a button can be pressed by remotely initiation. This action prompts the delivery of a measured dose of insulin to the patient, enabling treatment to be administered from any location [28, 35].

11.3.2 Benefits of IoMT

11.3.2.1 Improved Patient Experience

Patients involved with the medical IoT within the healthcare system tend to experience superior care, as they are more engaged in their treatment process. Intelligent devices in healthcare deliver valuable patient data, enabling doctors to diagnose health issues with increased precision [34]. The realm of IoT healthcare is filled with endless possibilities. It enhances the accessibility of healthcare and offers doctors invaluable insights into patient's health conditions beyond the confines of a hospital. As a result, patients receive the highest quality of medical treatment, irrespective of their geographical location.

11.3.2.2 Lower Costs

The primary advantage of the IoT in healthcare lies in its real-time health monitoring capabilities. The IoT healthcare solutions and related medical devices allow for continuous health tracking, reducing the need for frequent visits to medical professionals [34]. This typically results in cost savings due to decreased hospital admissions and readmissions.

11.3.2.3 Research and Population Health Management

The IoMT is catalyzing a paradigm shift in the healthcare industry by generating a wealth of data that can be harnessed for research and population health management. The analysis of this data offers us significant insights into disease trends, the efficacy of treatments, and public health trajectories. This information can then be employed to devise evidence-based strategies for disease prevention and the formulation of healthcare policies [34].

11.3.2.4 Reduces Workload on Human Personnel

The IoMT significantly reduces the workload on healthcare personnel. It automates routine procedures such as patient monitoring and data collection, freeing up time for healthcare staff to focus on more critical tasks.

The integration of clinical software systems with IoMT devices minimizes human errors that can occur due to manual data entry. Real-time data and insights provided by IoMT devices enhance operationalefficiency, aiding healthcare personnel in making quick, informed decisions [34].

11.3.3 Challenges of IoMT

11.3.3.1 Privacy and Security of Data

The privacy and security of patient information are of utmost importance as IoMT devices produce and send medical data. To prevent sensitive data from being accessed or breached by unauthorized parties, strong encryption methods, reliable communication rules, and rigorous access policies are necessary [33].

11.3.3.2 Power Consumption

Wearables and sensors are some of the IoMT devices that have low battery capacity. They need to use less power and last longer to avoid frequent interruptions and battery changes [33]. To solve this problem, they need to have design, algorithms, and batteries that are more energy-efficient.

11.3.3.3 Data Management

Patient records, diagnostics, and real-time monitoring data are some of the data types that IoMT produces in large quantities. This data is hard to manage and process effectively [33]. To get valuable insights from this data and keep it intact and accessible, healthcare organizations need strong data management plans that cover storage, processing, and analysis aspects.

11.3.3.4 Interoperability

Different manufacturers make the devices, systems, and platforms that IoMT uses. They may have different ways of formatting, communicating, and standardizing data, which can make it hard for them to talk and share data with each other. To make them work together smoothly, interoperability frameworks and common standards are needed for IoMT ecosystems [33].

11.3.3.5 Environmental Impacts

The production of IoMT devices contributes to electronic waste, as outdated or broken devices are often not recycled properly. This e-waste can leach harmful chemicals into the soil and water, causing environmental damage. Additionally, the energy consumption of these devices and their supporting infrastructure contributes to carbon emissions [33]. Data centers, which store the vast amounts of data generated by IoMT devices, are particularly energy intensive.

11.4 Literature Review

11.4.1 Early Pioneers

Kevin Ashton: Ashton coined the term "Internet of Things" in 1999, laying the groundwork for the broader concept that encompasses the IoMT. His early work emphasized the potential of interconnected devices to revolutionize various industries, including healthcare.
Joseph M. Smith: Smith's research in the early 2000s focused on wireless sensor networks and their applications in healthcare monitoring. His work laid the foundation for the development of wearable medical devices and remote patient monitoring systems, which are key components of the IoMT.

11.4.2 Advancements in Wearable Health Monitoring

Rosalind Picard: Picard's research in affective computing and wearable technology paved the way for emotionally intelligent wearable devices. Her contributions include the development of devices capable of monitoring physiological signals like heart rate variability and skin conductance, which have implications for stress management and mental health monitoring.
John Rogers: Rogers is renowned for his work in flexible and stretchable electronics. His research led to the creation of wearable biosensors that conform to the skin, enabling continuous monitoring of vital signs and biochemical markers. These advancements have significantly enhanced the capabilities of wearable health monitoring devices within the IoMT ecosystem.

11.4.3 Telemedicine and Remote Patient Care

Rashid Bashshur: Bashshur's pioneering work in telemedicine dates to the 1960s. His research laid the groundwork for remote consultations, telemonitoring, and tele-surgery, all of which are integral components of IoMT-enabled healthcare delivery.
Ronald Merrell: Merrell's contributions to telesurgery and robotic-assisted procedures have significantly advanced surgical practices. His research on remote surgical systems has paved the way for IoMT applications in minimally invasive surgeries and remote surgical training, improving access to specialized healthcare services globally.

11.4.4 Data Analytics and Artificial Intelligence

Fei-Fei Li: Li's research in computer vision and machine learning has profound implications for IoMT applications in medical imaging and diagnostics. Her work on deep learning algorithms has led to significant advancements in automated disease detection and image analysis, enhancing the accuracy and efficiency of medical diagnoses.
Atul Butte: Butte's research focuses on translational bioinformatics and data-driven approaches to precision medicine. His work involves leveraging big data analytics and AI techniques to extract actionable insights from healthcare data, thereby enabling personalized treatment strategies and predictive modeling within the IoMT framework.

The limitations of the article are as follows:

This article is restricted to the role of IoMT in the healthcare sector but not its enhanced efficiency and workflow such as automating routine tasks and optimizing resource allocation.

The article provides various applications of the IoMT that are being utilized but does not provide an in-depth implementation of those applications and where they have been used.

The privacy and Security of data, which is major challenge that leads to cyber threats that causes significant risks to patient safety, is not briefed in detail in this article.

The key factors impacting IoMT adoption such as communication protocol and IoMT platform sizing are not included in the article.

11.5 Conclusion

The IoMT refers to the interconnected network of communication-enabled and medical-grade devices, seamlessly integrated into broader health networks. Its primary goal is to enhance patient well- being by leveraging technology [29–32]. The IoMT facilitates remote monitoring, allowing patients to receive care in familiar surroundings. Wearable devices track vital signs, medication adherence, and activity levels, promoting comfort and reducing hospital stays IoMT streamlineshospital workflows. Real-time data exchange between devices and healthcare providers enables prompt diagnosis, personalized treatment plans, and efficient resource allocation. By collectingpatient-specific data, the IoMT tailors interventions. Machine learning algorithms analyze patterns, predict disease progression, and recommend personalized therapies. Despite its potential, the IoMTfaces reliability, safety, and security concerns. Ensuring robustness and privacy is crucial. In summary, the IoMT revolutionizes healthcare delivery, making it more accessible, efficient, and patient-centric.

References

1. Fadi Al-Turjman, Muhammad Hassan Nawaz, Umit Deniz Ulusar. "*Intelligence in the Internet of Medical Things era: A Systematic Review of Current and Future Trends*", https://doi.org/10.1016/j.comcom.2019.12.030.
2. S Vishnu, S R Jino Ramson, R Jegan. "Internet of Medical Things (IoMT) - An Overview". *5th International Conference on Devices, Circuits and Systems (ICDCS)*, 2020.

3. Ali Ghubaish, Tara Salman, Maede Zolanvari, Devrim Unal, Raj Jain, Abdulla Al-Ali. "*Recent Advances in the Internet of Medical Things (IoMT) Systems Security*", 2019.
4. Federal Communications Commission (FCC). "*Medical Device Radio-communications Service (MedRadio).*" [Online]. Available: https://www.fcc.gov/medicaldevice-radiocommunications-service-medradio.
5. How internet of medical things impact on Health care-APPINVENTIV https://appinventiv.com/blog/internet-of-medical-things-in-health-sector/
6. Emerging telemedicine tools for remote COVID-19 diagnosis, monitoring and management ACS publications https://pubs.acs.org/doi/10.1021/acsnano.0c08494
7. On-body segment -https://www.researchgate.net/figure/Applications-of-Internet-of- Medical-Things-IoMT_fig1_367309548
8. Applications of IoMT https://www.researchgate.net/figure/Applications-of-Internet-of- Medical-Things-IoMT_fig1_367309548
9. Pintu Kumar Sadhu ,Venkata P. Yanambaka and Ahmed Abdelgawad, *Physical Unclonable Function and Machine Learning Based Group Authentication and Data Masking for In-Hospital Segments*. Available: https://www.mdpi.com/2079-9292/11/24/4155.
10. Pranay Wal, Ankita Wal, Neha Verma, Rohini Karunakakaran, Anupriya Kapoor. "Internet of Medical Things – The Future of Healthcare", *The Open Public Health Journal*, 2022.
11. Hu HW, Liu CH, Du YC, Chen KY, Lin HM, Lin CC. Real-time internet of medical things system for detecting blood leakage during hemodialysis using a novel multiple concentricring sensor. *Sensors*.
12. Dwivedi R, Mehrotra D, Chandra S. Potential of Internet of Medical Things (IoMT) applications in building a smart healthcare system: A systematic review. *J. Oral. Biol. Craniofac. Res.*
13. Bibi N, Sikandar M, Ud Din I, Almogren A, Ali S. IoMT-based automated detection andclassification of leukemia using deep learning. *J. Healthc.*
14. Stein M, Lipman-Arens S, Oved K, *et al.* A novel host-protein assay outperforms routineparameters for distinguishing between bacterial and viral lower respiratory tract infections. *Diagn. Microbiol. Infect. Dis.*, [http://dx.doi.org/10.1016/j.diagmicrobio.2017.11.011].
15. Shapiro NI, Self WH, Rosen J, *et al.* A prospective, multi-centre US clinical trial to determine accuracy of FebriDx point-of-care testing for acute upper respiratory infections withand without a confirmed fever. *Ann. Med.*, [http://dx.doi.org/10.1080/07853890.2018.1474002].
16. Jain S, Nehra M, Kumar R, *et al.* Internet of medical things (IoMT)- integrated biosensors for point-of-care testing of infectious diseases. *Biosens. Bioelectron.*,[http://dx.doi.org/10.1016/j.bios.2021.113074].
17. Simoens P, Dragone M, Saffiotti A. *The Internet of Robotic Things: A review of concept, added value and applications*, [http://dx.doi.org/10.1177/1729881418759424].

18. Pradhan B, Bharti D, Chakravarty S, *et al.* Internet of things and robotics in transformingcurrent-day healthcare services. *J. Healthc. Eng.*
19. Mišeikis J, Caroni P, Duchamp P, *et al.* Lio-a personal robot assistant for human-robotinteraction and care health application. *IEEE Robot. Autom. Lett.*, [http://dx.doi.org/10.1109/LRA.2020.3007462].
20. Rodriguez-Losada D, Matia F, Jimenez A, Lacey G. Guido, the Robotic SmartWalker for the frail visually impaired. *Seman Scholor.*
21. Automated approach towards robotic real-time interaction with human body. *IEEE Int. Conf. Control. Sys. Comput. Eng.*, [http://dx.doi.org/10.1109/ICCSCE.2017.8284386].
22. Pavón-Pulido N, López-Riquelme JA, Feliú-Batlle JJ. IoT architecture for smart controlof an exoskeleton robot in rehabilitation by using a natural user interface based on gestures. *J. Med. Syst.*, [http://dx.doi.org/10.1007/s10916-020-01602-w].
23. Loureiro RC, Smith TA. *Design of the ROBIN system: whole-arm multi-model sensorimotor environment for the rehabilitation of brain injuries while sitting or standing*, [http://dx.doi.org/10.1109/ICORR.2011.5975511].
24. Dwivedi R, Mehrotra D, Chandra S. Potential of Internet of Medical Things (IoMT) applications in building a smart healthcare system: A systematic review. *J. Oral. Biol. Craniofac. Res.*
25. Fontes B, Cattani Heimbecker AM, de Souza Brito G, *et al.* Effect of low-dose gaseousozone on pathogenic bacteria. *BMC Infect. Dis.*, [http://dx.doi.org/10.1186/1471-2334-12-358].
26. Kulandaivel, I.G. Rahamathullah, A.P. Sathiyagnanam, K. Gopal, D. Damodharan, De Poures Melvin Victor, "EGR on performance, combustion and emission characteristics of a CRDi diesel engine fueled with WHDPE oil/diesel blends", *Fuel*, Volume 278, 15 October 2020, 118304 Sayeed MA, Mohanty SP, Kougianos E, Zaveri HP. eSeiz: An edgedevic for accurate seizure detection for smart healthcare. *IEEE Trans. Consum. Electron.*, [http://dx.doi.org/10.1109/TCE.2019.2920068].
27. Ashfaq Z, [1] Rafay A, Mumtaz R, *et al.* A review of enabling technologies for Internetof Medical Things (IoMT) Ecosystem. *Ain. Shams. Eng. J.*
28. Internet of Medical Things: A Review of Recent Contributions Dealing [https://ieeexplore.ieee.org/abstract/document/8388188].
29. Applied Science, Internet of Medical Things [https://www.mdpi.com/2076-3417/13/15/8869]
30. Journal of Medical Internet Research, The Internet of Things: Impact [https://www.jmir.org/2020/11/e20135/].
31. Internet of Medical Things (IoMT), Based Smart Healthcare ,Hindawi. https://www.hindawi.com/journals/cin/2022/7218113/.
32. Inxee systems private limited https://www.linkedin.com/pulse/challenges-iomt-inxeesystems#:~:text=Seamless%20communication%20and%20data%20exchange,data%20exchange%20in%20IoMT%20ecosystems

33. How internet of medical things impact on human health care *IoMT in Healthcare: A Modern Approach to Patient Care,* (appinventiv.com).
34. Internet Source - https://openpublichealthjournal.com
35. Arun Kumar, Aziz Nanthaamornphong, R. Selvi, J. Venkatesh, Mohammed H. Alsharif, Peerapong Uthansakul, Monthippa Uthansakul, *Alexandria Eng. J.* Evaluation of 5G techniques affecting the deployment of smart hospital infrastructure: Understanding 5G, AI and IoT role in smart hospital-[https://www.sciencedirect.com/science/article/pii/S1110016823009766].
36. Arun Kumar, Mahmoud A. Albreem, Manoj Gupta, Mohammed H. Alsharif, Sunghwan Kim, *Future 5G Network Based Smart Hospitals: Hybrid Detection Technique for Latency Improvement* -[https://ieeexplore.ieee.org/document/9170504].
37. Arun Kumar,R. Dhanagopal,Mahmoud A. Albreem,Dac-Nhuong Le, *Alexandria Eng. J.*, A comprehensive study on the role of advanced technologies in 5G smart hospital- https://www.sciencedirect.com/science/article/pii/S1110016821002581.
38. Arun Kumar, Aziz Nanthaamornphong, R. Selvi, J. Venkatesh, Mohammed H. Alsharif, Peerapong Uthansakul, Monthippa Uthansakul, *Alexandria Eng. J.*, Evaluation of 5G techniques affecting the deployment of smart hospital infrastructure. Understanding 5G, AI and IoT role in smart hospital-[https://www.sciencedirect.com/science/article/pii/S1110016823009766].
39. Arun Kumar, Sumit Chakravarty, Aravinda K, Mohit Kumar Sharma, Routle edge, *5G-Based Smart Hospitals and Healthcare Systems Evaluation, Integration, and Deployment-* https://www.routledge.com/5G-Based-Smart-Hospitals-and-Healthcare-Systems-Evaluation-Integration/Kumar-Chakravarty-K-Sharma/p/book/9781032515274.
40. Balamurali Ramakrishnan, Arun Kumar,, Sumit Chakravarty, Mehedi Masud, and Mohammed Baz, MDPI, *Analysis of FBMC Waveform for 5G Network Based Smart Hospitals,* https://www.mdpi.com/2076-3417/11/19/8895.
41. Arun Kumar, J Venkatesh, Nishant Gaur, Mohammed H. Alsharif, Abu Jahid and Kannadasan Raju, MDPI, *Analysis of Hybrid Spectrum Sensing for 5G 6G Waveforms,* https://www.mdpi.com/2079-9292/12/1/138.

12

6G Networks Technology: An Exhaustive Survey

Nishant Gaur[1], Sumit Chakravarty[2] and Aziz Nanthaamornphong[3]*

[1]Department of Physics, JECRC University, Rajasthan, India
[2]Department of Electrical Engineering Kennesaw State University, GA, United States
[3]College of Computing, Prince of Songkla University, Phuket, Thailand

Abstract

The fifth generation (5G) wireless communications networks have already been executed with high data rates. However, the rapid development in the number of smart devices and the exhibit of the Internet of Everything (IoE) requisition, which require ultra-reliable and low-latency communication, will result in a significant load on the 5G wireless networks. As such, the data rate that could be provided by 5G networks will unlikely support the huge ongoing data traffic crash. This has activated research into continuing to advance the existing wireless networks toward the future generation of mobile systems, known as the sixth generation (6G). Consequently, it is necessary to accommodate a future vision of the 6G and the key enabling technologies for perceived networks. This paper presents an exhaustive survey of the future development of 6G networks. Concretely, the objective of the paper is to provide an exhaustive survey about the key enabling technologies for 6G networks, which include a discussion about the main operation principles of each technology, proposed potential applications, current state-of-the-art research, and the related technical challenges. Comprehensively, this paper contributes useful knowledge for industries and academic researchers and discusses the capability for spreading new research recommendations.

***Keywords*:** 5G, 6G, Wireless communications, Internet of Everything (IoE), network technology, AI, ML, edge computing

**Corresponding author*: aziz.n@phuket.psu.ac.th

Arun Kumar, Manoj Gupta, Sanjeev Sharma, Er. Himanshu Sharma and Khursheed Aurangzeb (eds.) Smart Hospitals: 5G, 6G and Moving Beyond Connectivity, (235–256) © 2024 Scrivener Publishing LLC

12.1 Introduction

The world mobile data transit has escalated appreciably during the past few years. An estimate of the recent analyticals accumulated by International Telecommunication Union (ITU) represent that world mobile data transit is predicted to grow to 607 Exabytes (EBs) per month by 2025 and 5016 EB by 2030 [1]. The amount of data transit per subscriber is predicted to be around 39 EBs by 2025 and about 257 EBs by 2030. Moreover, nearly 70% of the population is predicted to subscribe to mobile services by 2025. Excluding this, 60% out of this 70% are estimated to use mobile internet. The vast data transit request has been accompanied by increasing requirements for variegated services, full coverage, ultra high-speed wireless communications with ultrahigh security and ultra-low latency. The main drivers of the perceptible growth in data transit are personal computers (PCs), laptops, tablets, smart phones, sensors and the Internet of Everything (IoE) devices/implementation. These devices usually consume data capacity (mainly video) rather than voice transit. In addition to this, the number of internet users, mobile subscribers, machine-to-machine (M2M) connections and connected devices worldwide are also predicted to considerably increase in the next few years. As a result of the IoE, many new vertical services and applications have been created to make our lives, society, and industrial processes better. These include mass production, smart transportation systems, smart homes, and virtual reality (VR) technology. There are many different quality of service (QoS) requirements for these vertical solutions, which have a wide range of effects. On the other hand, what current fifth generation (5G) networks can do is not nearly enough to support new vertical applications. Because of this, academics are interested in new ways to design and run sixth generation (6G) networks [2]. Through a shift in service and technology development, integration, and usage, the 6G network seeks to redefine how people view communication networks. The 6G network may address network issues in the future. Future services and applications will leverage complex networks and bio-inspired technologies to meet performance goals and meet rising resource needs [3]. The introduction of 6G networks represents the next crossover in wireless communication technology, contribute extraordinary capabilities, and cover the way for transmute application. As researchers and manufacturing experts look towards the prospective, it becomes crucial to understand what a 6G network is, its key features, and the expectations that need to be dwelled on to unlock its readiness. These 6G networks are envisioned to offer ultra-high data rates, ultra-low latency, massive connectivity, enhanced security, and immersive user experiences. With data rates reaching terabit-per-second levels and latency reduced to sub-millisecond ranges, 6G networks have the potential to enable unconventional applications such as augmented reality (AR), VR, smart cities, and autonomous systems [4, 5]. The perfect integration of these applications into everyday life requires a vigorous and systematic communication framework.

Evidently, the realization of 6G networks is not without its provocation. Spectrum scarcity remains a significant concern, as the ever-increasing demand for bandwidth necessitates inventive approaches to spectrum allocation and utilization. Energy efficiency is another critical aspect that requires attention, as the exponential growth of connected devices and data traffic can strain energy resources. Network densification, utilizing technologies such as small cells and massive multiple-input multiple-output (MIMO), poses challenges in terms of deployment, interference management, and backhaul connectivity. Moreover, the utilization of millimeter-wave (mm Wave) frequencies, while enabling high data rates, presents obstacles such as signal transmission limitations and expand path loss. Intelligent network management and resource allocation become crucial to enhance network performance, ensure QoS, and effectively handle the massive number of connected devices. Moreover, ensuring the security and privacy of user data in 6G networks becomes incumbent, considering the vast amount of sensitive information transmitted and stored. To address these challenges, potential solutions and technologies are being analyzed. Dynamic spectrum sharing, enabling multiple services to coexist and share spectrum resources, is one such approach. Energy-efficient network designs, incorporating techniques like sleep modes and adaptive power control, aim to reduce energy consumption. Advanced antenna technologies, such as beamforming and beam tracking, improve coverage and capacity in mm Wave communications. Machine learning (ML) and artificial intelligence (AI)-driven network optimization techniques offer promising avenues for intelligent and self-optimizing networks. Furthermore, blockchain-based security mechanisms can enhance the trust and privacy aspects of 6G networks [6–9]. Looking beyond 6G, this research paper also presents future directions for next-generation wireless networks. Technologies like terahertz (THz) communications [14–16], satellite networks, reconfigurable intelligent surfaces, edge computing, and AI-driven network optimization are discussed, showcasing the ongoing research and potential innovations beyond 6G [10–13]. By delving into the intricacies of 6G networks and addressing the associated challenges, this research paper aims to provide valuable insights to researchers, industry professionals, and policymakers. By understanding the nature of 6G networks and envisioning their future, stakeholders can make informed decisions and provide the development of robust, efficient, and transmuting wireless communication systems.

These 6G networks will replace 5G cellular technology; they can work at higher frequencies than 5G networks and have a lot more capacity and less latency. The purpose of the 6G network is to make it easier for people to talk to each other by fabricating latency as low as one microsecond. This is 1000 times faster than the throughput of one millisecond. Sixth generation will employ even shorter wavelengths in the THz spectrum, which covers the frequency range of 100 GHz to 3 THz, as opposed to 5G, which employs mm-Wave in the microwave frequency range. While 5G has an important impact on radio access networks (RAN), the impact of 6G networks will be considerably higher due to a significant increase in frequency that will minimize the need for antennas almost everywhere.

12.1.1 Problem Statement and Motivation

The subsist literature survey primarily covers architecture, the technical condition of 6G, and the challenges and problems related to execution. Some surveys also explored various aspects of 6G technologies, each with its special set of parameters. However, these studies did not offer comprehensive coverage of all 6G technologies, focusing on network slicing and security. Some researchers deep dived into THz communication and IoT technologies, while others concentrated on spectrum sharing and radiofrequency (RF) technology.

So, our main aim is to give a detailed study of all the technologies working on the 6G network with security challenges and network slicing in 6G networks. The need for surveying recent advancements in 6G mobile networks and technologies is essential for staying at the forefront of technological progress, guiding research, and development efforts, informing policy decisions, and boosting innovation and collaboration in the 6G domain. The predominant motivation of this survey is to cover the state-of-the-art techniques and recent novel 6G communication and technological developments by researchers. The recent advancement study on 6G will help to accelerate the development and production of the 6G network. This survey provides an umbrella approach to bring multiple solutions and recent improvements in a single place to accelerate the 6G research with the latest key enabling solutions and reviews.

12.1.2 Research Methodology

In order to prepare the literature on the 6G network, we use a search approach and a snowballing approach. However, because of the broad area, we only include research on 6G technologies, security, and network slicing. By comparing the security criteria indicated by various research, we can see how many studies have mentioned them, which risks they are connected to, and what solutions have been suggested. We include the 6G technologies that have been identified together with the characteristics, allowing us to discuss which technologies need more investigation. We have created the following keywords with these requirements: 6G network technology, security, and network slicing. We used the following databases as sources: Elsevier/ScienceDirect, IEEE Xplore, and the ACM Digital Library. Combining these three sources offers a reliable depiction of international research in this field. The search was divided into three phases. First, we searched databases for papers about 6G technology based on their titles. This gave a general summary of the volume of research done in this area. We then restricted our search to include papers addressing 6G security. Finally, we look at research papers on network slicing.

12.1.3 Key Contributions

This article's primary objective is to present the key findings of 6G technologies, network slicing, and security of the 6G network. It also aims to help readers assess how well recent training addressed 6G issues and produced solutions to deal with those issues (i.e., what new approaches need to be used, and how they can solve issues?). The following are some of the highlights of the exploratory composition.

- This survey covers the most recent advances and progress in the 6G age, as well as new benefits received by the experimental group and crucial elements of the 6G evolution.
- The evolution of mobile network technology is the topic of this research. The growth of mobile communications and its many facets are also explored.
- With a comprehensive classification, this study explores the emerging operational and research groups working on 6G and the many exploration domains in 6G wireless communication systems.

- This analysis considers the benefits, features, key technologies, and fundamental concepts of a 6G network. The potential for network slicing and security in the 6G network is also investigated with an eye to future use cases. The 6G IoT-based approaches and optimization techniques were also highlighted in the survey.
- We provide a thorough overview and a summary of recent developments in the emerging technologies of the 6G cellular connection, including wireless communication technology and systems, which also covers THz, next-generation antenna and RF technology, channel coding and modulation technique, spectrum sharing, Internet of Things (IoT), and blockchain technology. By stressing the surroundings of current techniques and accompanying obstacles, a specialized overview is also circulated.
- The improvements in softwarization, agile control, and deterministic services over the 6G armature are explored, and an architectural perspective for network slicing for the 6G network is presented.
- In this study, we examine the potential difficulties and opportunities presented by network security throughout the development of 6G technology. This survey also includes discussions on security considerations, focusing on data processing, threat detection, network monitoring, and data encryption.

12.1.4 Outline of the Survey

The remaining article is structured as follows: wireless networks evolution: 1G to 6G may be found in Section 12.2. Methods has been covered in Section 12.3. Results and Discussion are covered in Section 12.4. Conclusion is explored in Section 12.5.

12.2 Wireless Networks Evolution: 1G to 6G

Beginning from 1980, every 10 years, a latest wireless communication network generation appears [17, 18]. To date, there are 5 generations. Figure 12.1 analyzes the main fingerboard of the five generations (1G to 5G) of wireless communication networks. Additionally, here is a rapid overview of how wireless technologies extend.

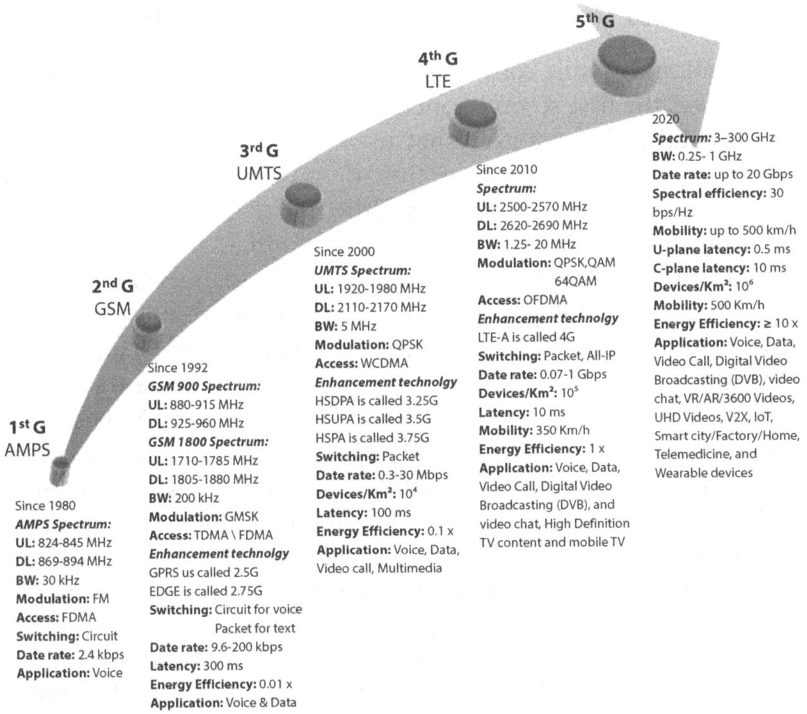

Figure 12.1 Leading communication achievements for several generations (1G to 5G).

12.2.1 First Generation Wireless Communication (1G)

In the 1970s, 1G mobile communications were communicated. North America's advanced mobile phone system (AMPS), Scandinavia's Nordic mobile telephone (NMT), the United Kingdom's total access communications system (TACS), and Japan's total access communications system (JTACS) were the first customers. The 1G technology is a simple analog system with data speeds of up to 2.4 kbps optimized for voice conversations. It has a 30 kHz bandwidth and uses frequency modulation (FM) and frequency division multiple access (FDMA) communication technologies (BW). But 1G has many limitations, such as: i) no encryption, poor quality, and security due to the use of analog modulation; ii) limited customer because of the use of FDMA technology; iii) diffident base station power radiation and lack of shift procedures; iv) supports voice services only; and v) divergent systems because of deficient of consonant international standards [19–21].

12.2.2 Second Generation Wireless Communication (2G)

The international mobile communications (GSM), which was launched in the 1990s, was the first second-generation system. The GSM is an uncomplicated digital cellular system that uses Gaussian minimum frequency shift keying (GMSK) modulation, time division multiple access (TDMA) transmission technology, with bandwidth=200 kHz for voice communications. The features of this generation are: i) a unified international mobile communication standard and the development of international mobile communication technology; ii) improved services; iii) improved network security through coded numbers; and iv) improved the capacity of the system; and v) an extended mobile phone battery because the radio signal uses less power. Although, the lower data rate of GSM has precised improvements in cellular systems that use general packet radio service (GPRS) technology [19–21]. The GPRS is categorized as 2.5G. It employs the GSM's packet switching and circuit switching technologies. Its data rate can be raised by up to 50 kbps, and it uses transmission and modulation that is similar to GSM. Essentially, the GPRS is the first phase on the way to the GSM environment that supports enhanced data (EDGE). EDGE is a radio technology that predates 3G. Customers can transmit and receive data at a rate of up to 200 kbps. The EDGE technology is based on the prior GSM standard, and it employs an identical transmission mechanism and BW as GSM, but it employs eight phase-shift keying (8PSK) and GMSK modulation instead of GSM. The 8PSK has a higher data rate but a narrower coverage area because the GMSK is a genuine model for wide coverage. It was developed to enhance packet-switching services and to enable future applications for high-speed data like multimedia [20, 21].

12.2.3 Third Generation Wireless Communication (3G)

The 3G system employs wideband code division multiple access (WCDMA) and high-speed packet access (HSPA) technology to deliver fast internet access, as well as significantly improved video and audio transmission capabilities. The HSPA combines two mobile phone protocols, high-speed downlink packet access (HSDPA) and high-speed uplink packet access (HSUPA), to enhance and improve the 3G mobile telephony networks performance using the WCDMA protocol. Developed HSPA (commonly known as HSPA+) is an upgraded 3rd generation partnership project (3GPP) standard that was launched at the end of 2008 and was used internationally in 2010. A 3.9G long term evolution (LTE), on the other hand, contains characteristics that go beyond those found in ordinary 3G mobile communications [20, 21]. However, the ITU and the 3GPP eventually concluded that the LTE can be called the 4G technology [22].

12.2.4 Fourth Generation Wireless Communication (4G)

The LTE is a wireless access technology based on orthogonal frequency division multiplexing (OFDM), which allows for a sophisticated multi-antenna transmission, as well as expandable transmission bandwidths of up to 20 MHz. Critical system technology MIMO allows for higher data rates and multi-stream transmission to achieve great spectral efficiency, improve connection quality, and alter radiation patterns for signal gain and mitigation. The antenna's adaptive beamforming is used to create the interference array. The LTE technology boosts data speeds through mobile to 100 megabits per second (Mbps). The wireless technology roadmap has been extended to LTE advanced (LTEA) [22], which can theoretically reach a peak throughput rate of more than 1 gigabit per second, in response to the tremendous increase in demand for mobile broadband communication capacity year after year (Gbps).

By delivering a comprehensive and consistent solution based on the internet protocol (IP), the 4G system improves the current communication network. The wireless community has investigated three primary research topics in-depth to satisfy 4G mobile network capabilities:

- Densification of the network: This technology is used in situations where there are a lot of people, such as stadiums, concerts, public places, and retail malls. By deploying compact, low-power, and low-cost cells, this technique intends to shorten the distance between mobile terminals and base stations (BS), hence increasing spectrum reuse and boosting network coverage. Due to the use of low-loss routing, the small base station has a coverage radius of 50 – 150 m and transmits at low power (0.110 W), which improves energy efficiency and signal interference plus noise ratio (SINR). Furthermore, operators are working to make small base stations plug-and-play, meaning they can configure all the essential parameters themselves and do not need to be maintained regularly [23, 24].
- Improved spectral efficiency: Coordinated transmit/receive methods and solutions to reduce inter-cell interference use

modern signal processing and spatial diversity to reduce co-channel interference and improve spectrum efficiency [25, 26].

- Carrier aggregation is used in LTEA to syndicate separate component carriers, which can be of diverse sizes and are in a non-contiguous spectrum, to facilitate bandwidth increase (up to 100 MHz). Although the combined execution of these technologies can theoretically provide fixed customers with data rates exceeding 1 Gbps, further expansion is limited because of the limited number of frequencies accessible [22, 27].

12.2.5 Fifth Generation Wireless Communication (5G)

The 5G communication standardization process is now complete, and it is being implemented on a global basis [28]. The ITU defines the vision and specifications; 5G should meet eight KPI and three common scenarios [29]. Millions of connections/square kilometers (1 M/km^2) massive machine challenge technology in three scenarios end user like extreme mobile band (eMBB) Gb/s data rate, ultra reliable low latency communications (URLLC) milliseconds (ms) air interface delay, and massive machine challenge technology (mMTC) in three scenarios indicator type communication. Many enabling technologies have been developed, considered in standardization, and implemented in technical trials in order to achieve these KPIs [30]. Dual connectivity architecture, massive MIMO, UDN, sophisticated coding and modulation, millimeter-wave communications, flexible frame structure, non-orthogonal multiple access, and other wireless technologies are only a few examples [31]. As shown in Figure 12.2, the main backbone in the 5G network includes several elements widely fitted all over the network, like multi-access edge computing data center, next generation core, active antenna system (AAS) (with 5G NR support), and source antenna system [32].

The organization employed for the 5G AAS, that is, the RAN fronthaul network of mobile networks, requires the common use of multiple

Figure 12.2 The 5G-infrastructure-fronthault-midhaul-backhaul.

technologies, such as the next generation passive optical network (NGPON), lengthy division of thick wave multiplexing (CWDM), dense wavelength division multiplexing (DWDM), and enhanced common public radio interface (eCPRI). All these techniques necessitate a fiber optic infrastructure that is compatible. Because 5G mobile networks require a lot of bandwidth and speed [33], the infrastructure needs a fiber optic cable to be installed to the antenna. As a result, in addition to boosting the capacity of the backbone fibers [34], it is also required to deploy the 5G mobile network as close to the fiber infrastructure antennas as feasible, as well as to install new fiber optic cable infrastructure for extra antennas when capacity is insufficient. However, due to the substantial growth in the number of associated things, the data traffic has increased exponentially, which can grow to hundreds (s) of devices per m^3; in addition to the rapid increase in new applications, like VR/AR, self-driving cars, integrated three-dimensional communications, and new applications that have yet to be imagined [35], they will still need data rates. Will provide higher and lower latency than 5G networks. These challenges are thought to be the key driving factors for the realization of 6G communication systems. Given the huge potential of 5G networks and their foreseeable evolution, what features of 6G should be included that are not present in 5G? Research, ascademia, and industry have worked on describing and determining the main qualifying technologies that can define 6G; it is expected to be deployed by 2030 [36].

The authors of this study [37] examined the variability of orthogonal time frequency space (OTFS) under the assumption of two-path rectangular waveforms. The OTFS-based matching filter algorithm, which is utilized in radar systems to determine object range and velocity, was evaluated by the authors [38]. It demonstrates that OTFS-based radar processing not only offers improved radar capability but also demonstrates the fundamental benefits that come with multi-carrier modulations. Compared to OFDM, OTFS requires less, resulting in a shorter transmission period. A linear complex iterative technique for rake detector is proposed for OTFS in [39]. In this case, the BER performance of the MRC detector is comparable to that of the MPA detector, but it requires less storage space and complexity.

12.3 Methods

As mentioned in the introduction section, rapid acceleration of global traffic demand is needed for multimedia streaming, online gaming, autonomous driving, and extended reality. As per key performance indicator values, these requirements are shown in Figure 12.3 and include peak data

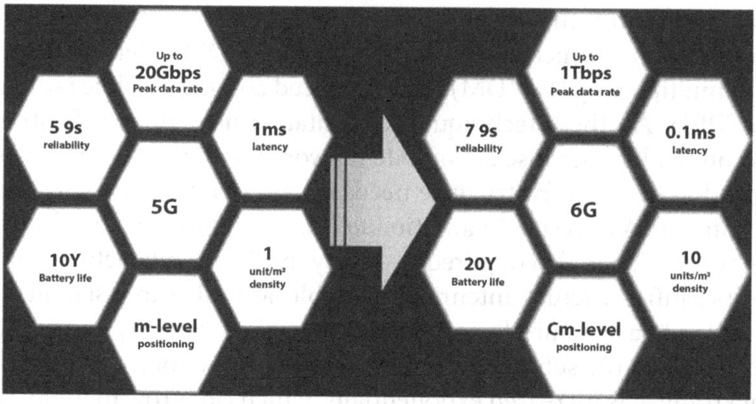

Figure 12.3 5G vs. 6G key requirements comparison.

rate, latency, connection density, positioning precision, battery life, and connection reliability.

Let us review critical technologies that will further augment wireless networks.

12.3.1 Key Enabling Technologies in 6G

Evolution to the next generation of wireless communication would be impossible without technological components that will boost current networks' performance and create new development frameworks.

The first such technology is THz communications (i.e., wireless transmissions in bands defined from 0.1THz to 10THz). These frequencies fall in the gap band between microwave and optical (visible light communications, VLC) spectrum. Hence, it is expected that transmission will take the form of a hybrid electronic-photonic form. Some initiatives in this direction have already been taken, as described in [40, 41]. This technology's main benefit is a vast band even compared with 5G, non-requirement for line-of-sight (LoS) link, and immunity to bad weather conditions. This expects to play an essential role in the uplink transmissions.

In 5G, network slicing has created an incentive for flexible networks and will further evolve. It is expected that the next generation of communications will be cell-free. Therefore, another significant change we can expect in the timeframe of 6G is dynamic deployment and context awareness of networks. These two mechanisms will allow supporting cost-efficient deployment with high operation capability. Specifically, such networks allow an operator to switch performance modes by complementary focusing in either mMTC, eMBB, or URLLC with the same hardware components. Besides, the system should be able to reconfigure itself if environmental conditions would suggest so. For instance, when surveillance operation enters hazardous conditions, the reliability of connection must become the main priority for operation. Context-awareness also can allow machines to operate independently, thus creating a machine-centric perspective.

The most certain technology to power 6G must be AI. Due to advances in ML in recent years and the massive availability of training data, Edge AI will emerge as a new paradigm. So far, there have been many great ideas about the usage of AI in wireless communications: physical layer designs such as channel estimation and precoding, resource allocation, traffic control, cache storage management, authentication and security, and the abovementioned context-aware network operations. As the amount of training data increases and tasks become more time-critical, traditional centralized learning will likely move towards federated [42] and distributed learning and hence is an excellent field for researchers to propose new architectures and algorithms.

Recently, advances in smart metamaterials give us a unique opportunity to take partial control over the communication environment (i.e., channel). Novel intelligent reflective surfaces (IRS) are low-power passive devices [43] including active frequency selection and active/passive reflect arrays. The IRS can provide us access to design the channels we transmit in and create an intelligent environment; it is a low-cost and low-power device and thus can be densely and easily implemented.

The following key technology to enable future technology advance is interterritorial communications. Indeed, to provide drones, aircraft, flying cars, and space stations, the current cellular network is not a suitable candidate. Apart from communications over the sky and on the ground, it is crucial to extend communication networks to the underwater environment, especially considering that most of the Earth's surface is water. This would significantly enhance marine monitoring and create new applications. Underwater communications are likely to exist in acoustic form; however, reliable high-data-rate development is required [44].

Another aspect of the currently existing fiber-optics infrastructure used to connect continents may help be a gateway for basic underwater base stations. Being discussed for decades, Energy harvesting or wireless power transfer is another essential technology in 6G. Due to the network densification, the distance between nodes will become much shorter. Moreover, switching to higher frequencies will have a more considerable power amount transferred over the air and become a valid power source. This technology becomes even more meaningful as users or IoT devices become more power-hungry with the presence of AI at the edge. The improvements in this rely on new networking architectures and operational strategies. It is provisioned that the 6G base station could provide primary power transfer for low-power devices such as implants and sensors [45].

The next enabler of 6G communication is reliable and secure networks, a vital component of the machine-centric network. In recent decades great emphasis was put on data rate, latency, reliability, and coverage, while security has been neglected. Indeed, the current RSA algorithm can increase their security guarantees by simply extending the security key length.

However, given the growth of machines' computational performance, improvements in quantum computing, and the rise of AI technology, alternative approaches need to be investigated. Moreover, physical layer security for VLC and THz communication is a new security challenge for cyber protection.

12.3.2 Driving Trends and Potential Applications in 6G

Evolution and progress in wireless communications are impossible without applications that would convince industry and researchers to explore it. With predicted capabilities, 6G would become a technology that will connect machines to humans and to other machines. Throughout the following applications, it becomes apparent that the main focus is located on non-presence techniques (i.e., remote control, remote presence, and full automation).

The first application of this kind is extended reality (XR). This term combines VR, AR, and mixed reality. The advent of XR with complete human-sense feedback would require high data-rates, extremely low latency, and accurate positioning for precise spatial mapping. Current AR technology [46] requires 55Mbps to support an 8K display that is enough quality of experience (QoE) on mobile display; however, XR media streaming would require nearly 0.9 Gbps throughput is not currently available. One of the potential uses of this application technology is the real estate business. Extended reality makes it simpler for real estate representatives to close a deal by allowing prospective homebuyers to feel the property's authentic feel. Other possible applications can be marketing, healthcare, education, Entertainment, and gaming.

A complementary application to XR is expected to be haptic (tactile) communications, which allow remotely exchanging physical interactions through the tactile internet in real-time. Mainly it will be possible through communications between remotely located mobile nodes and wearable sensors on users. Mobile nodes can form a human-like robot with five basic human senses, while low-latency technology will ensure real-time experience.

This application will be another step that allows accomplishing tasks without human presence using a robot. The importance of it becomes especially clear during the ongoing COVID-19 pandemic when interaction opportunities are limited.

A logical extension of XR and haptic communications is holographic telepresence. Nevertheless, unlike in the previous two technologies, no headset is needed. In such a case, bandwidth requirements will grow to terabits. This technology would allow controlling entire physical space with the use of IRS and similar structures. Using special equipment in a studio or laboratory, projection equipment beams users into one or multiple venues. An example of such technology was shown ARTH Media company as a virtual global stage platform, shown in Figure 12.4. However, at the current stage, physical interaction for the user is impossible.

Combined with tactile communications, a holographic telepresence will bring us new experiences such as holographic calls, meetings, and tourism.

The growing and aging population creates a huge load on the healthcare system. Several ubiquitous health monitoring devices have been created to measure various health indicators such as heart rate, blood pressure, temperature, glucose level, and brain activity to report to medical departments via IoT framework automatically. With this in mind, E-Health applications might become a valid alternative to traditional medicine. The concept assumes sending medical data directly to an AI server that can immediately decide about treatment or suggests visiting a relevant medical department. Given that patients' data is highly private, a high level of secrecy is needed. Another focus should be put on the communication reliability of communication in case of emergencies.

Figure 12.4 An example of a holographic telepresence. Left: presenter's setup. Right: presence at the venue.

Another important concept that can find its application in industry and military is teleoperated driving or intelligent transportation system. The main requirements for this technology are extremely low latency, ultra-reliable connection, and increased security.

Despite total human control, vehicles are required to be equipped with AI technologies that implement a collision-avoidance system coordinated by a combination of multiple sensors. Note that in addition to human-to-vehicle connection, vehicles have to exchange massive amounts themselves to update live-traffic conditions and report hazard information on the road.

Incorporating AI, IoT, and robots into automation and warehouse transportation is crucial for industry advancement. Intelligent automation and manufacturing are perspective direction as it allows to avoid human error, makes faster adjustments, and better monitor. Notably, 5G features industrial internet and industrial IoT to kick off factory transformations. It is expected that the next generation of factories will have an individual radio environment (private 5G/6G) with a very advanced network comprised of hundreds or thousands of robots. The 6G is called to support the next industrial revolution by offering massive URLLC and massive IoT and embedded AI capability. The technology makes it possible to create connections between machines and exchange information per its request to regulate ongoing processes.

Completely, the last key portion of 6G communications is blockchain-enabled security and substantiate. With over 50 billion associated UE and IoT devices, 6G will need to secure data storage and dataflows beyond different platforms. Blockchain technology will be a significant component in securing and substantiating future communication systems thanks to the distributed ledger technology's essential advantage. Some good use cases will include distributed security handling for IoT, offloading in mobile edge computing, network function virtualization, and content caching.

12.4 Results and Discussion

12.4.1 Machine-Centric Communications

The latest and estimated progress of executed 5G networks is expected to reach the restriction in terms of human user QoE. However, recent advances in AI, material science, and the misuse of high-frequency bands create an incentive for further wireless network evolution and become next-generation communications. The performance of 6G is expressed in better internet connection, more reliable and low-latency connection. However, from the users' perspective, it will not create a new application niche; most likely XR, holographic telepresence, and E-health, which already exist in some forms, will evolve and become more spread and low-cost. A different situation is from the machines' perspective. With the increased security level, reliability, and AI onboard, machines will no longer need human intervention to operate, to request, and exchange information with other machines. This is reflected in futuristic applications such as smart manufacturing, intelligent transportation system, and E-health as the closed-loop of interaction can be established to complete tasks without external control during casual operations. Also, certain technologies such as THz and quantum communications are not likely to be carried on smartphones or inside home gadgets. Hence, it is expected that 6G communications will be machine-centric.

12.4.2 Factors Hindering Evolution to 6G

Communication technologies are important but not in every field. In order to promote development, social, economic, technological limitations should be considered. A frequent topic in media nowadays is the "harm" of the 5G base station, which reflects health concerns about radiation in the high-frequency bands. This aspect is likely to get worse as even higher frequency bands will be used. Moreover, since machine-centric communication prevails in 6G, industrial interest will prevail over users and negatively influence social factors. Therefore, industrial investments should prevail. Many examples of promotion schemes and campaigns sponsored by governments and private companies are working to persuade the unconnected, distant areas to be connected and promote the concept of worldwide connectivity in the 6G era.

Current research is focusing on technology and applications while rarely on business models and commercialization. Further network densification improves performance according to the logarithmic curve (i.e., more cost is required to get less performance). Building new base stations is costly, and therefore it is undefined who should pay for it. Moreover, as breakthrough technologies are coming into play, backward compatibility with 4G and 5G remains an open question. The cost evaluation for updating existing infrastructure should be done and compared with building new infrastructures. It should be remembered that ordinary users will refuse to pay several times more for a relatively small QoE gain.

In conclusion, component that delays the development of 6G is a dependency on the basic sciences. While THz communications and VLC are likely-looking theoretically, there are very few works speaking about the constraint of the electronic circuit made by the manufacturing technologies or if commercial chips can process the signal on higher-frequency bands at all.

12.4.3 Major Trade-Offs in the 6G Evolution

During the design of the new engineering systems, it is vital to determine a list of features that will be enhanced. While it is desired to maximize every system parameter, investing resources should be used wisely, and therefore critical trade-offs should be outlined. Moreover, improving certain features automatically leads to the degradation of others. For instance, the trade-off between spectral efficiency versus energy efficiency is traditional performance versus power dilemma. As a longer battery life is required of 6G, energy harvesting must likely release power constraints. Besides, reconfigurable intelligent surfaces can ensure power resource delivery to user devices. The second trade-off is security versus spectral efficiency. To guarantee protection against fraud, part of the radio spectrum is used for encryption algorithms, decreasing the amount of useful information transmitted. Moreover, physical security algorithms such as frequency hopping also decrease spectral efficiency. The third trade-off regulates privacy versus intelligence. Despite a substantial boost in AI algorithms, 6G still relies on training data, which is often private. A potential solution to this issue is introducing differential privacy algorithms, which modify every data point without distorting the global view. Also, performing training in a distributed fashion, such as only local AI models, is exchanged with a centralized server. That creates another trade-off, the cost versus intelligence, as both software and infrastructure advances require new investments. The goal for 6G is to develop highly reconfigurable networks that would balance and fit the industrial and user requirements without rebuilding the overall system.

12.5 Conclusion

In this work, we discussed the evolution of wireless networks at the current stage.

Following the trend of launching a new generation of the internet each decade, 5G implementation has started. At the same time, research and the industrial community have started research about 6G. Its goals are similar to the goals of 5G: higher data-rates, increased reliability, shorter latency, and generally better QoS and QoE. Key enabling technologies, such as THz spectrum, Edge AI, dynamic development, energy harvesting, and context-aware networks, will be used to achieve it. It is predicted that such networks' capabilities will exceed user needs and create a new paradigm – machine-centric networks. As a result, most of the applications will be dedicated to interconnecting machines and remote control for industry and other machine usages. At this stage, many trade-offs and limitation factors will guide future development and provide solutions, which will have a ubiquitous influence on many industries.

References

1. Kumar, Arun, Chakravarty, Sumit and Nanthaamornphong, Aziz. "Analysis of PAPR reduction of optical-OTFS for 256-QAM using companding and clipping–filtering algorithms" *J. Opt. Commun.*, 2024. https://doi.org/10.1515/joc-2023-0369.
2. Kumar, A, Gaur, N., & Nanthaamornphong, A. (2024). Intelligent Signal Identification of NOMA Signal with 256-QAM Modulation Using SVM Algorithm. *Int. J. Intell. Syst. Appl. Eng.*, 12(13s), 257–264.
3. Arun Kumar, Nishant Gaur, Manoj Gupta and Aziz Nanthaamornphong, "Implementation of the deep learning method for signal detection in Massive-MIMO-NOMA systems", *Heliyon*, Volume 10, Issue 3, e25374, 2024.
4. K. B. Letaief, W. Chen, Y. Shi, J. Zhang, and Y.-J. A. Zhang, "The roadmap to 6G: AI empowered wireless networks," *IEEE Commun. Mag.*, vol. 57, no. 8, pp. 84–90, Aug. 2019, doi: 10.1109/MCOM.2019.1900271.
5. Shah, Paritosh Kumar, Kumar, Arun & Masud, Mehedi (2023) A mathematical optimization of the lifetime of the wireless sensor network using ML- based energy dependent clustering and tiered routing algorithm, *J. Interdiscip. Math.*, 26:3, 351-359, DOI: 10.47974/JIM-1666,
6. M. H. Alsharif, M. A. M. Albreem, A. A. A. Solyman, and S. Kim, "Toward 6G communication networks: terahertz frequency challenges and open research issues," *Comput. Mater. Con.*, vol. 66, no. 3, pp. 2831–2842, 2021, doi: 10.32604/cmc.2021.013176.
7. A. Kumar & N. Gaur, "Peak-to-average power ratio reduction using companding algorithm for NOMA waveform," *Radioelectron. Commun. Syst.* (2023), https://doi.org/10.20535/S0021347023040039.
8. H. Elayan, O. Amin, B. Shihada, R. M. Shubair, and M.-S. Alouini, "Terahertz band: the last piece of RF spectrum puzzle for communication systems," *IEEE Open J. Commun. Soc.*, vol. 1, pp. 1–32, 2020, doi: 10.1109/OJCOMS.2019.2953633.

9. N.Gaur, "Reducing latency in optical 6G waveforms using joint detection and channel estimation techniques," *J. Opt. Commun.*, (2023), http://dx.doi.org/10.1515/joc-2023-0274.
10. P. Yang, Y. Xiao, M. Xiao, and S. Li, "6G wireless communications: vision and potential techniques," *IEEE Network*, vol. 33, no. 4, pp. 70–75, Jul. 2019, doi: 10.1109/MNET.2019.1800418.
11. A.Kumar, V. Jayaraman, N. Gaur, Mohammed H. Alsharif, Peerapong Uthansakul and Monthippa Uthansakul, "Cyclostationary and energy detection spectrum sensing beyond 5G waveforms," *Electron. Res. Arch.*, 31(6), 3400-3416, (2023), http://dx.doi.org/10.3934/era.2023172
12. T. S. Rappaport *et al.*, "Wireless communications and applications above 100 GHz: opportunities and challenges for 6G and beyond," *IEEE Access*, vol. 7, pp. 78729–78757, 2019, doi: 10.1109/ACCESS.2019.2921522.
13. A.Kumar, J. Venkatesh, N. Gaur, Mohammed H. Alsharif, Abu Jahid and K.Raju, "Analysis of Hybrid Spectrum Sensing for 5G and6G Waveforms," *Electronics,* 12, 138, (2023), https://doi.org/10.3390/electronics12010138.
14. S. Dang, O. Amin, B. Shihada, and M.-S. Alouini, "What should 6G be?," *Nat. Electron.*, vol. 3, no. 1, pp. 20–29, Jan. 2020, doi: 10.1038/s41928-019-0355-6.
15. A. A. A. Solyman and I. A. Elhaty, "Potential key challenges for terahertz communication systems," *Int. J. Electr. Comput. Eng. (IJECE)*, vol. 11, no. 4, pp. 3403–3409, Aug. 2021, doi: 10.11591/ijece.v11i4.pp3403- 3409.
16. H. H. Attar, A. A. A. Solyman, M. R. Khosravi, L. Qi, M. Alhihi, and P. Tavallali, "Bit and packet error rate evaluations for halfcycle stage cooperation on 6G wireless networks," *Phys. Commun.*, vol. 44, Feb. 2021, doi: 10.1016/j.phycom.2020.101249.
17. J. A. del Peral-Rosado, R. Raulefs, J. A. López-Salcedo, and G. Seco-Granados, "Survey of cellular mobile radio localization methods: from 1G to 5G," *IEEE Commun. Surv. Tutorials*, vol. 20, no. 2, pp. 1124–1148, 2017, doi:10.1109/COMST.2017.2785181.
18. S. Onoe, "1.3 evolution of 5G mobile technology toward 1 2020 and beyond," in *2016 IEEE International Solid-State Circuits Conference (ISSCC)*, Jan. 2016, pp. 23–28, doi: 10.1109/ISSCC.2016.7417891.
19. Arun Kumar *et.al.*, "PAPR reduction using SLM-PTS-CT hybrid PAPR method for optical NOMA waveform" *Heliyon*, Volume 9, Issue 10, October 2023, e20901, https://doi.org/10.1016/j.heliyon.2023.e20901.
20. A. Abrol and R. K. Jha, "Power optimization in 5G networks: A step towards GrEEn communication," *IEEE Access*, vol. 4, pp. 1355–1374, 2016, doi: 10.1109/ACCESS.2016.2549641.
21. A. Gupta and R. K. Jha, "A survey of 5G network: architecture and emerging technologies," *IEEE Access*, vol. 3, pp. 1206–1232,2015, doi: 10.1109/ACCESS.2015.2461602.
22. Arun Kumar *et al.* "Evaluation of 5G techniques affecting the deployment of smart hospital infrastructure: Understanding 5G, AI and IoT role in smart hospital", *Alex. Eng. J.*, Volume 83, 15 November 2023, Pages 335-354.

23. J. Hoydis and M. Debbah, "Green, cost-effective, flexible, small cell networks," *IEEE Commun. Soc. MMTC*, vol. 5, no. 5, pp. 23–26, 2010.
24. J. Xu *et al.*, "Cooperative distributed optimization for the hyper-dense small cell deployment," *IEEE Commun. Mag.*, vol. 52, no. 5, pp. 61–67, May 2014, doi: 10.1109/MCOM.2014.6815894.
25. Kumar, A.; Chakravarthy, S.; Nanthaamornphong, A. Energy-Efficient Deep Neural Networks for EEG Signal Noise Reduction in Next-Generation Green Wireless Networks and Industrial IoT Applications. *Symmetry*, 2023, 15, 2129. https://doi.org/10.3390/sym15122129.
26. L. Lindbom, R. Love, S. Krishnamurthy, C. Yao, N. Miki, and V. Chandrasekhar, "Enhanced inter-cell interference coordination for heterogeneous networks in LTE-advanced: A survey," arXiv preprint arXiv, 1112.1344, Dec. 2011.
27. H. Lee, S. Vahid, and K. Moessner, "A survey of radio resource management for spectrum aggregation in LTE-advanced," *IEEE Commun. Surv. Tutorials*, vol. 16, no. 2, pp. 745–760, 2014, doi: 10.1109/SURV.2013.101813.00275.
28. M. K. Sharma and A. Kumar, "NOMA waveform technique using orthogonal supplementary signal for advanced 5g networks security", *J. Discrete Math. Sci. Cryptogr.*, 2022, https://doi.org/10.1080/09720529.2022.2075088.
29. K. David and H. Berndt, "6G vision and requirements: Is there any need for beyond 5G?," *IEEE Veh. Technol. Mag.*, vol. 13, no. 3, pp. 72–80, Sep. 2018, doi: 10.1109/MVT.2018.2848498.
30. H. Benn, *Vision and key features for 5th generation (5G) Cellular*. Samsung R&D Institute UK, 2014.
31. S. Chen, Y.-C. Liang, S. Sun, S. Kang, W. Cheng, and M. Peng, "Vision, requirements, and technology trend of 6G: how to tackle the challenges of system coverage, capacity, user data-rate and movement speed," *IEEE Wirel. Commun.*, vol. 27, no. 2, pp. 218–228, Apr. 2020, doi: 10.1109/MWC.001.1900333.
32. R.-J. Essiambre and R. W. Tkach, "Capacity trends and limits of optical communication networks," *Proc. IEEE*, vol. 100, no. 5, pp. 1035–1055, May 2012, doi: 10.1109/JPROC.2012.2182970.
33. D. Semrau *et al.*, "Achievable information rates estimates in optically amplified transmission systems using nonlinearitycompensation and probabilistic shaping," *Opt. Lett.*, vol. 42, no. 1, pp. 121–124, Jan. 2017, doi: 10.1364/OL.42.000121.
34. T. Xu *et al.*, "Modulation format dependence of digital nonlinearity compensation performance in optical fibre communication systems," *Opt. Express*, vol. 25, no. 4, pp. 3311–3326, Feb. 2017, doi: 10.1364/OE.25.003311.
35. S. Dang, O. Amin, B. Shihada, and M.-S. Alouini, "What should 6G be?," *Nat. Electron.*, vol. 3, no. 1, pp. 20–29, Jan. 2020, doi: 10.1038/s41928-019-0355-6.
36. E. C. Strinati *et al.*, "6G: The next frontier: from holographic messaging to artificial intelligence using subterahertz and visible light communication," *IEEE Veh. Technol. Mag.*, vol. 14, no. 3, pp. 42–58, Sep. 2019, doi:10.1109/MVT.2019.2921162.

37. Kumar, Arun and Gaur, Nishant. "Enhancement of spectral access of optical OFDM system using cognitive radio" *J. Opt. Commun.*, 2023. https://doi.org/10.1515/joc-2023-0188.
38. Kumar, A. PAPR Reduction in Beyond 5G Waveforms Using a Novel SLM Algorithm. *Natl. Acad. Sci. Lett.* (2023), https://doi.org/10.1007/s40009-023-01289-w.
39. Arun Kumar, N. Gour, N. Gaur, S.K. Yadav ans H. Sharma, "A Comparative PAPR, BER, and PSD for Optical NOMA communication Framework", *Opt. Quantum Electron.*, 2023, https://doi.org/10.1007/s11082-023-05148-2.
40. K.Sengupta, "Study on channel model for frequencies from 0.5 to 100 GHz (release15)," *3GPP TR* 38.901, (2018).
41. Kulandaivel, I.G. Rahamathullah, A.P. Sathiyagnanam, K. Gopal, D. Damodharan, De Poures Melvin Victor, "EGR on performance, combustion and emission characteristics of a CRDi diesel engine fueled with WHDPE oil/diesel blends", *Fuel*, Volume 278, 15 October 2020, 118304).
42. H. Sharma, N. Gour, S. Chakravarty, F. Alraddady, M. Masud, R. Pareek and Arun Kumar*, "Performance Analysis of PTS PAPR Reduction Method for NOMA Waveform", *Intell. Autom. Soft Comput.*, 34(2), pp. 1367-1375, 2022.
43. Q.Wu and R.Zhang, "Towards smart and reconfigurable environment: Intelligent reflecting surface aided wireless network". *IEEE Commun. Mag.* 58.1, pp. 106-112, (2019).
44. Z.Zeng and *et al.* "A survey of underwater optical wireless communications". *IEEE Commun. Surv. Tutorials,* 19.1, pp. 204-238, (2016).
45. W.Saad,M.Bennis and M.Chen, "A vision of 6G wireless systems: Applications, trends,technologies, and open research problems." *IEEE Network,* 34.3, pp. 134-142, (2019).
46. Arun kumar *et al.*, "Intelligent Conventional and Proposed Hybrid 5G Detection Techniques", *Alex. Eng. J.*, Volume 61, Issue 12, pp. 10485-10494, 2022.

13

Smart Hospitals: Integrating Connectivity and Intelligence: A Comprehensive Study and Challenges

Nishi Singh[1]*, Nidhi Gour[2] and Ankit Kumar Tiwari[2]

[1]Squalo Technologies Pvt Ltd., Jaipur, India
[2]Department of CSE, JECRC University, Jaipur, India

Abstract

The smart healthcare concept is gaining more attraction with the development of information technology. Smart healthcare includes the use of new generations of technologies like artificial intelligence, cloud computing, big data, and the Internet of Things (IoT) that transform the traditional system of healthcare. The new technologies make healthcare more personalized, convenient, and efficient. The main purpose of this study is to define the smart and connected healthcare concept with the various key technologies that are used in smart healthcare. This study discusses the different challenges and opportunities of smart healthcare. Different diseases like cardiovascular disease are increasing, and the coronavirus pandemic also creates challenges and increased pressure on current healthcare resources. This study discusses the smart and connected health solutions that help to address these challenges. This system improves healthcare and is more custom-designed, preventive, and strategic, as well as adds value to services. In information and communication technology, the important design characteristics are interoperability and connectivity. The IoT is also an effective technology that has improved the healthcare system and provides on-time, ubiquitous, and cost-effective services. The healthcare system contains different ecosystems like communication technologies, databases, and devices that improve healthcare services. This study includes the different resources and technologies that work with or without the intervention of humans and improve smart and connected healthcare. Different IoT-based healthcare solutions that deliver improved service solutions in healthcare are discussed. The study concludes that the role of advanced technologies in

**Corresponding author*: nishi7796@gmail.com

Arun Kumar, Manoj Gupta, Sanjeev Sharma, Er. Himanshu Sharma and Khursheed Aurangzeb (eds.) Smart Hospitals: 5G, 6G and Moving Beyond Connectivity, (257–286) © 2024 Scrivener Publishing LLC

improving health is effective, and healthcare services, with smart technologies, become better, as well.

Keywords: Smart hospital, 5G, Internet of Things, cloud computing, smart and connected health, networked equipment, smart healthcare

13.1 Introduction

Currently, with advancements in cloud computing and communication technologies, the Internet of Things (IoT) is a term that defines a system where all digital and physical objects communicate with each other and play an important role in efficient building surveillance and control. Smart cities use IoT technology to increase comfort and safety, reduce costs, and create an effective and friendly environment [1]. In any information and communication technology infrastructure, interoperability and connectivity are known as design characteristics. Currently, IoT technologies are combined with different medical systems and provide ubiquitous, cost-effective, and on-time healthcare services to people who require healthcare services [2]. Today, the healthcare system includes a complex ecosystem that contains different communication technologies, databases, and devices that are used together to provide effective healthcare services. These resources and technologies are required in many healthcare information systems to collaborate and interact with humans or without human intervention to support the healthcare system in providing efficient services and achieving its objectives. The IoT technology is effective in providing effective connectivity for billions of devices on a global network; therefore, it has also improved healthcare service delivery and quality [3]. This chapter discusses how IoT-based connectivity improves smart healthcare services and solutions. This chapter discusses the smart hospital, its challenges and opportunities, and the smart hospital system design. Also, discuss small and connected health and different IoT architectures used in smart health services and solutions.

13.1.1 Overview of Smart Hospital

The smart hospital concept has emerged from the use of digitalization in healthcare industries using advanced technologies such as artificial intelligence (AI), data analytics, the IoT, and the availability of personalized services. Smart healthcare's main objective is to utilize information and communication technology to provide the most beneficial affection to the

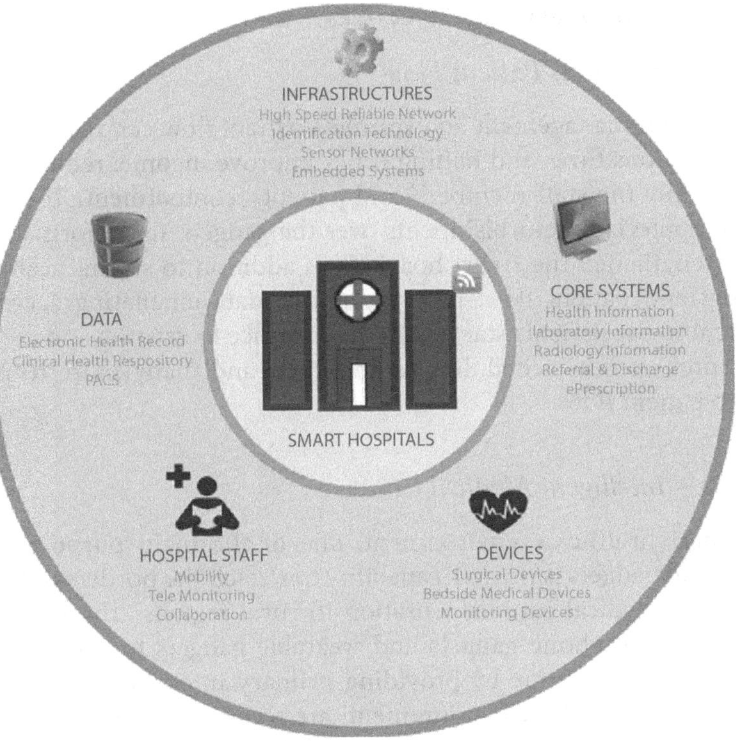

Figure 13.1 A layout of a smart hospital.

patients. When needed, provide internal and external proficiency stores with pertinent information in one place and complete the productive procedures that complete this target with cost productivity and nominal glitch pace. Gadgets, inter-associated systems applications, and accessibility are needed to make smart hospitals. Above Figure 13.1 shows the notion of "Smart Hospitals", demonstrating the integration of multiple infrastructures (high-speed dependable network, recognition technology, connected sensors, embedded systems), data (EHR, PACS), core systems (health, laboratory and clinical health repository), staff (for mobility and monitoring), and devices (surgery, bedside medical, and monitoring). At the end-to-end smart procedures, an indispensable component is system legacy, and this chapter focuses on advanced systems using IoT. Smart hospital ideas consist of computerized and revamped end-to-end processes and IoT technology established in the current process of hospitals and provide different potentials and benefits in patient health maintenance [4].

13.1.2 Smart Hospital Objectives

13.1.2.1 Seamless Patient Flow

Strong health management and seamless patient flow can reduce the hospital detentions time, and halting times improve income, reduce glitches, and multiply the staff members' and patients' contentment. The medical data computerized refurbishments over the gadgets and information systems strengthened the smart hospitals in addition to strong health management and patient flow. In every phase, data emanating accessibility pertinent to the patients starts with the entrance to existing and escalation procedures such as scheduling, admittance, and many more to provide smooth patient flow.

13.1.2.2 Intelligent Medical Care

In a smart healthcare environment, one of the main purposes of IoT devices and gadgets is the IoT capability to stretch the borders of hospitals and ensure medical care dispensation to rural regions. The IoT medical gadgets include phone gadgets and wearable gadgets to support patient supervision in real-time by providing primary important sign measurement. Also, ensure these measurements are accessed by hospital staff easily and the system using gird connections [5]. In remote regions, these medical care abilities are enhanced by using different medical gadgets that show the capability to work on the patient's condition or distant regulation way. Thus, patient admittance to hospitals can be restricted to only important cases, upgrade patient involvement, reduce patient care costs, and patients can receive treatment from their homes.

13.1.2.3 Patient Safety

The patients' and clinical safety were escalated by the effective healthcare deliverance and reinforcing patient flow. However, it is also clear that the healthcare facilities' deliverance and patient flow should not advance at the risk of compromising safety. Information collected by gadgets used for life support supervising machines also provides important patient signs and medicament intake; when used correctly, the result provides patient safety. Below Figure 13.2 illustrates the key objectives of smart hospitals to increase patient safety, such as remote medical care, better trustworthiness, improved diagnostics, and smooth patient flow.

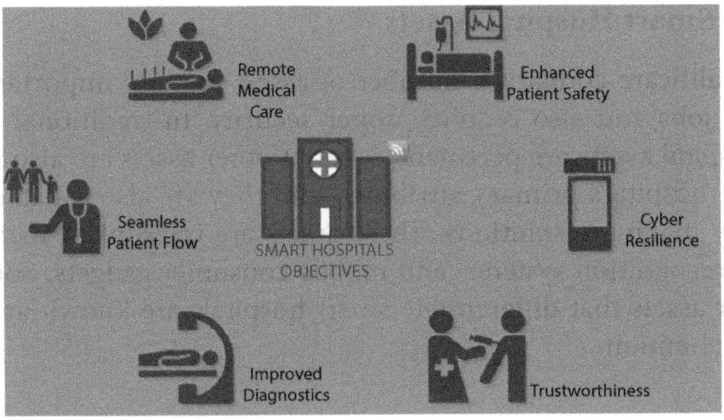

Figure 13.2 Smart hospital objectives.

13.1.2.4 Cyber Facility

It is up to the health center to ensure durability and accessibility towards dispensation that measure on information and communications technology (ICT) resources. More advanced ICT provides higher dependence on ICT, which is followed by increased data security pertinence for smart hospitals. The health division is an important foundation that is required to be secured. In proper healthcare, one needs to reciprocate, be ready, foresee, and acclimate to additive shifts and unforeseen shifts. In smart hospitals, this matter is more common compared to traditional hospitals due to the number of constituents in the former, which results in a shortage of services.

13.1.2.5 Trustworthiness

When there are multiple choices available among disparate providers, achieving a good position and winning faith is an important matter, which includes competition and clashes. Reliability also has a devotion to medical care and medicament that has connotations for health center consequences that will be realized [6]. The utilization of ICT can be effective and secure a good position. It also includes patient safety and confidentiality, not exposed to danger.

13.1.3 Smart Hospital Assets

Smart healthcare contains a number of assets that are important to perform the jobs and also require proper security. In traditional hospitals, some hospital assets are pertinent, too, but other assets are also known as the smart hospital's primary attributes, and they are also capable of independently making resolutions. These assets are interlinked medical data systems, recognition systems, and mobile consumer gadgets. Some of the particular assets that differentiate smart hospitals are known as the chief center of attention.

13.1.3.1 Remote Care System

Automated care system assets support the ICT environment. This environment permits automated hospitals to increase services and health management facilities for patients who live in rural regions:

- ❖ Clinical equipment for telediagnosis, such as blood sugar computation, ECG, blood pressure, ace of heart computation, threshold triggered alarm generators, and other minute corporeal computation and telemonitoring, may come under wearable gadgets and implantable molds.
- ❖ Clinical equipment for medicament dispersion to supervise medical care.
- ❖ Telehealth equipment includes telemedical computer systems, cameras, internet or telephone linkage, and sensors for patients to record their corporeal computation [7].

13.1.3.2 Networked Medical Devices

Network medical devices that use differentiation smart hospitals also provide remote health monitoring services to patients that are primary dispensation compared to classical hospitals and complete the administration of healthcare at a national position. Currently, implantable gadgets such as pacemakers can be updated to reduce the reinstatement requirement. Stagnant gadgets with mobile devices have been brought into application in classical hospitals many times [8]. In the smart hospital, the recognition constituents and medical data system provide the arriving capability at decision and automation degree. These can consist of:

- Wearable extrinsic gadgets such as convenient and compact insulin pumps and wireless temperature counters.
- Mobile gadgets such as blood sugar computation gadgets.
- Adjuvant gadgets such as supportive robots.
- Implantable gadgets such as cardiac pacemakers.
- Stagnant gadget devices such as computer tomography (CT) scanners, chemotherapy furnishing stations, and life support machines.

13.1.3.3 *Mobile Client Device*

In smart hospitals, mobile client gadgets are shrewdly unified to ensure appropriate data accessibility in the appropriate place and time. These devices also provide flexibility for staff members and patients. The mobile client device example consists of developed applications for smartphones, tablets, and laptops, applications of emergency connection for smartphones, tablets, and laptops, and clients for mobile, including laptop computers, tablets, smartphones, and pagers [9].

13.1.3.4 *Identification Systems*

These systems are used in applications for staff members' verification and recording and determining hospital equipment such as beds. The biometric scanners in smart hospital environments are used to recognize systems reading and put in a grid shrewdly with the gadgets and data systems. The system in smart hospitals provides the primary lead to various parts, such as authorization and authentication, which are known as closed-circuit security systems. The example includes:

- Patient resources or staff members supervise analogous shifts, and radio-frequency identification (RFID) devices along with the location services support to appraise.
- Recognition systems components include smart badges, labels, bracelets, and tags.
- Biometric scanners and CCTV with authentication and identification abilities.

13.1.3.5 *Networking Equipment*

Networking equipment provides the associability to smart hospitals over a network basis. The equipment required is the same as the user-accepted equipment used in traditional hospital applications. However, it is identified by their characteristics, like transmitting protocols and bandwidth. For example, interface find cards, transmission media, network backbone gadgets, and IoT portals that evaluate information collected using gadgets and transmit the signals to cloud networking systems and information centers [10].

13.1.3.6 Interconnected Clinical Information System

In an intelligent healthcare center, akin data systems for clinical purposes collectively with recognized constituents and clinical gadgets are set up to provide an end-to-end smart process for patient care. In smart hospitals, set up medical data systems are becoming progressively capable of independently making decisions. For example, pharmacy information systems, radiology information systems, blood bank systems, picture archiving and communication systems, research information systems, laboratory information systems, hospital information systems, and pathology information systems [11].

13.1.3.7 Buildings

It contains smart end-to-end processes that provide diverse operations important for smart hospitals to function properly. Some of the important operations related to patient protection measure upon the amenity supervising systems competence are the clinical gas supply, temperature sensors, supervising systems, smart patient room functioning, smart boards, medical staff members' screens, and patient screens. Also, power regulation and climate systems are included in smart ventilation systems. The smart system is used for door locks and lock tokens provided to the administration, and it also provides the administration and application software for the lock system.

13.1.3.8 Data

Data are considered important resources according to the data safety viewpoint. The smart gadget resolution is established on the collected data scrutiny. For example, managerial and medical patient information such as health records, contact specifications, and test outcomes [12]. Also, hospital financial and other organization information pertaining to vendors' specifications, staff members' Information, and data pertaining to research works.

13.2 Smart Hospital Challenges and Opportunities

13.2.1 Challenges

There are several challenges that may be faced in the transformation process of smart hospitals:

13.2.1.1 Patient Monitoring

Delivering high-quality care, continuous monitoring, regulatory compliance, and patient safety with the decrease in the healthcare staff and fulfilling customer satisfaction can be major challenges. This will need round-the-clock health monitoring through the doctors, as well as alert generations, guided by swift decision-making and fast response. The lack of capability to deploy technologies and IoT solutions for the monitoring of the patient is also a matter of concern.

13.2.1.2 Data Accuracy

If a machine's learning program is fed with the wrong insights, it achieves wrong patterns and may give wrong information, resulting in default treatment for the patients. Hence, the requirement to ensure that only accurate information is fed to the electronic health record (HER) system was identified. The IoT sensors' fed information might not cause problems until the sensors are working correctly. However, information fed by human beings could increase the chance of errors [13].

13.2.1.3 Security and Privacy

Maintaining integrity, availability, and confidentiality of healthcare information is challenging. Storage of health information in untrusted software in hospitals is a cause of concern for patients as it can increase the chances for tampering and abuse of the information. Compromising with healthcare private data can cause implications in real life. Based on Accenture's Cost of Cyber Crime Study 2017, $12.47 million is the cybercrime annualized cost of cybercrime for the healthcare industry. Healthcare information in cloud storage can also cause both compliance and security concerns. Based on the survey conducted in 2018 by Symantec Corporation, utilizing a poorly secure cloud-based database is a weak point for several operations [14].

13.2.1.4 Cost-Effectiveness

Patients face significant challenges as a result of rising healthcare costs. The requirements for performance and compliance also add to the expense of hospitals. The cost and user convenience are subject to trade-offs [29]. One way to lower the initial costs associated with implementing electronic Health Records (EHRs) is through cloud computing. Due to privacy and security concerns, some hospitals have chosen not to implement EHRs. Without an EHR, a hospital is unable to become smart.

13.2.1.5 Data Validations and Intelligent Data Processing

The diversity and heterogeneity of healthcare data also rises with the variation of equipment and devices. Validating and deriving actionable knowledge from it becomes extremely difficult because it includes personal lifestyle data along with a variety of other health data. Only sophisticated algorithms would be able to accomplish this.

13.2.1.6 Interoperability and Standardization

The operating rooms (ORs) of hospitals are usually filled with many supporting systems and freestanding devices that are involved in displaying data. According to the smart hospital expectation, all screens should be prepared with patient information, diagnostic imaging, pre-operative plan, and other information projected onto the desired screens as soon as the doctor enters the operating room. This could be difficult because a lot of hospitals store patient data in various archives and systems, and, likely, many of these tools and programs do not talk to one another. Hence, there is a requirement to integrate all the data systems and their applicability in smart hospitals to enable the display of the patient's relevant information display. The IoT sensor interoperability, or the capacity to receive and modify data from various kinds of IoT sensor devices, presents another challenge [15].

13.2.2 Opportunities

The market value of smart hospitals in 2016 was $13.52 billion, and it is forecasted to reach $63.49 billion by 2023, at a compound annual growth rate of 24.00% from 2017 to 2023. This market is divided according to the application type, wireless connectivity, type of technology, service rendered, service component, and geographical area. Smart hospitals are required to be equipped with smart software, smart hardware, and appropriate smart technologies. The smart technology system compromises the smart system for patients, equipment, and staff, as well as the smart mobility system. The technologies that can contribute to smart hospitals include biotelemetry, blockchain technology, precise medicine and drug development according to big data and genomics, and virtual rehabilitation in orthopedics. Smart hardware can involve active RFID, dashboards, WiFi, IoT sensors, wearables, and many more [16]. The smart hospitals markets of driving factors involve the requirement for healthcare infrastructure modernization, the development of technologies related to IoT in healthcare, the requirement for the implementation of effective solutions in hospitals, the rise in the penetration of connected instruments and devices in hospitals, increasing rate of chronic diseases, etc. The Internet of Healthcare Things, along with its intelligence, equipment, appliances, buildings, and applications, is significantly contributing towards smart hospitals and improving the capability of the hospital to cater to healthcare more effectively, as well as cost-efficiently with better equipment utilization.

The current utilization of technology can be improved with blockchain technology in healthcare. With its distributed ledger technology, enhanced security, interoperability, and immutability, blockchains offer value to smart hospitals [17]. Blockchain technology facilitates more seamless and effective transaction processing between hospitals, patients, insurance companies, and other stakeholders safely and effectively. As the amount and caliber of operational intelligence that smart hospitals have access to grow, they will eventually function like smart machines. Smart machines will use AI, advanced analytics, and machine learning (ML) to extract useful information from operational intelligence. To continuously sustain as smart hospitals, they should continuously learn, enhance, and demonstrate relevant autonomous behavior.

13.3 Smart Hospital System Design

The intelligent building interconnectivity and security theoretically based contribution is used to design a smart hospital system. The main purpose of this new architecture is to secure the sensitive data related to health, the hospital, and interconnect systems and objects in the building.

13.3.1 Energy Efficiency

In a smart building design, a solution is provided for energy efficiency because a major issue is complex security mechanisms applied for patient security and safety. In smart buildings, improving the control system and making the environment more comfortable are more effective solutions. This solution reduces energy usage and costs from the owner's side. In the hospital, the solution is to save energy from construction starts; it covers all the important systems and parameters for energy saving. The systems and parameters include solar energy use and storage, hydroelectric generators, and wind generators. After that, these gained energies must be stored, and the building management system and building automation system can manage and access these energies. The building management system and building automation system contain physical security systems, electrical elements, cooling, elevators, smart lighting, and other smart building components [18]. For example, a building management system, known as open sources in the smart building, provides IoT interoperability. Nowadays, constructing a building from scratch is difficult, and this solution provides for buildings already constructed.

13.3.2 Building Management System

The integrated smart grid is also used in the hospital building for energy efficiency, which is important for energy usage management. A building management system will be an important component of energy management and building actions. The building management system, taken from the decision shown in Figure 13.3, presents the layers of building management system design for smart hospitals [19]. The first layers contain the

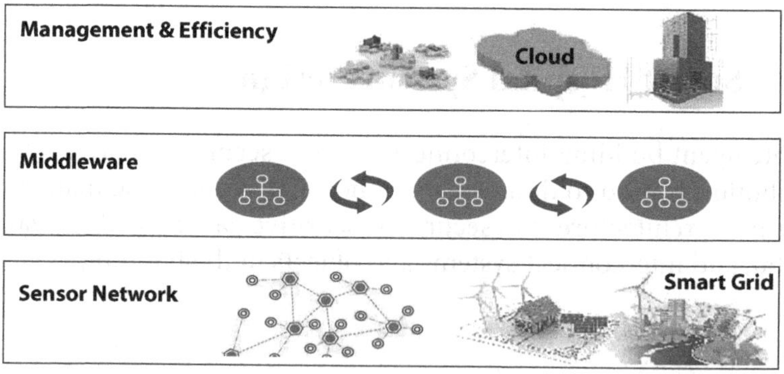

Figure 13.3 The intelligent hospital BMS design layers.

end devices, sensors, and smart grid systems in this layer for integration purposes. The middleware is the second layer that combines the physical system with the cyber system. This other layer is the automation layer, which includes collected data processing, control loop execution, and every alarm activation in the building. The efficient management layer is the last layer, where the aggregations and decisions take place due to the building knowledge, smart grid, and covet of the tenants such as managers, doctors, and patients [20].

13.3.3 Security and Interoperability Solution

The secure smart hospital design includes the benefits of IoT technologies and security solutions for buildings, data, and devices. In this architectural design illustrated in Figure 13.4, a hybrid network topology is made of the integration of mesh and star topology. Actuators and sensor networks (6LoWPANs) are used in every room and every floor and connected to microcontrollers. The data are collected from each microcontroller from each network node and then sent the data to each gateway using the IPv6 communication link [21]. A router and local database are contained in the gateway. The router sends the data to the remote environment, which is also known as the cloud platform. This platform contains a remote cloud

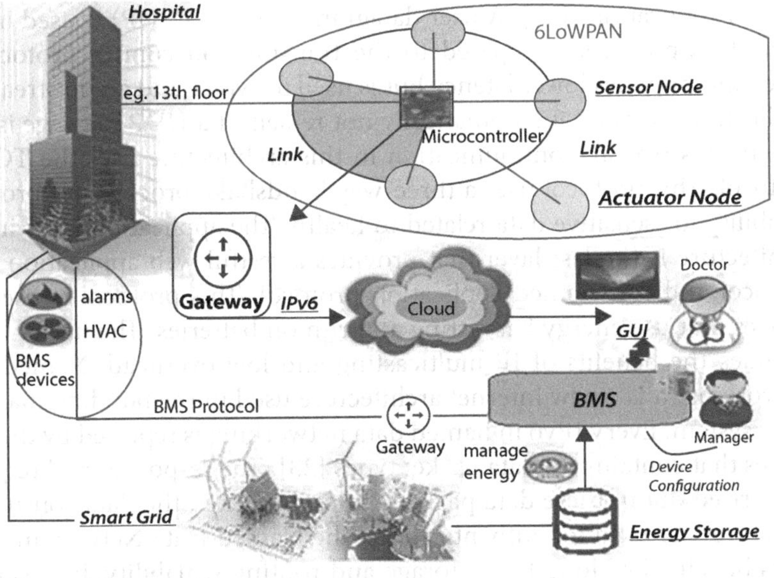

Figure 13.4 Design of an intelligent hospital building.

server and database; the data stored in this database is also analyzed. The real-time data is stored in the cloud server and available for analysis. In the building design, different parts like smoke detectors and fire alarms are combined with the building's devices and stored energy. The building management system can be managed efficiently. The smart hospital building design shown in the figure defines the OSI layers. The first two layers include the IEEE 802.15.4 protocol. These devices are connected using this protocol, and communication starts between them. Devices with limited infrastructure, low-cost communication, low power, and low data rate are provided by the IEEE 802.15.4 standard.

The data link layer is the next layer that contains two sub-layers. The sub-layer is a media access control that contains IEEE 802.15.4 and the IPv6 adaptation sub-layer over a low-power wireless personal area network. This architecture used 6LoWPAN technology for IPv6 data packet encapsulation and header compression so that they can be received and transmitted. This technology provides different benefits like increasing the maximum possible payload, reducing overhead, low cost, mobility, energy efficiency, adaptability, and high reliability. In the network layer, the 6LoWPAN protocol will also be greatly used in the future for every object's authentical and Internet communications. The interoperability and low-cost benefits are provided by the IPv6 protocol using information technology to enable this. The routing data takes place in this layer. The transport layer is the next layer where the communication is produced among the device's applications [22]. A user datagram protocol (UDP) is used in this layer. This protocol, compared to the transmission control protocol, is faster and provides lower latency but is used for voice and audio streaming applications because it automatically not re-sent if a UDP message is lost. Due to this reason, communication in this architecture uses the TCP/IP protocol. This protocol uses a three-way handshake process and provides reliability for sensitive data related to health. The application layer in this architecture is the last layer that provides a restful web application layer protocol and constrained application protocol. This protocol is used for devices that use energy harvesting and run on batteries. The use of CoAp provides the benefits of IP multicasting and low overhead. Named data networking, it is a new internet architecture used in the building management system. Every IPv6 in named data networking is replaced by the data names that contain two data packet types [23]. The responses and requests are carried out in these data packets. In each packet, the data consumers' signatures are used for authentication. The Named Data Networking provides benefits like long-term storage and routing scalability. In hospitals, the whole object system and every object identified has a name instead of an IP address like it is in a named data networking solution.

13.4 Smart and Connect Health

Smart and Connected Health (SCH) systems and solutions for digital healthcare are operated and connected remotely; it is known as a promising and new interdisciplinary research field, including the telecommunication industry, bioengineering, big data, public health, medical informatics,

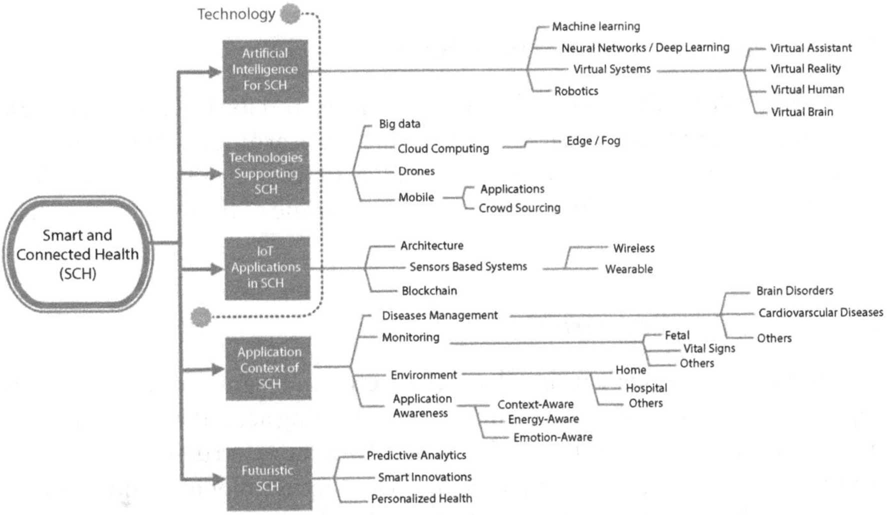

Figure 13.5 Smart and connected health classification.

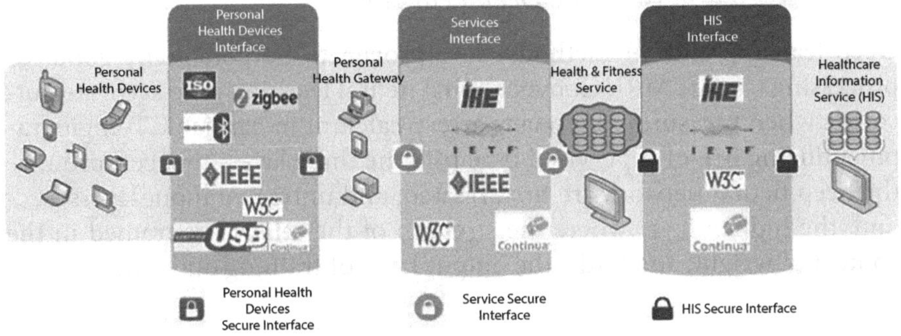

Figure 13.6 Iot-based network architecture.

and many other fields. Figure 13.5 above defines the classification of smart and connected health. The SCH connects with AI and smart devices and provides more personalized and tailored healthcare solutions to healthcare after IoT shapes healthcare governance. The first three clusters of SCH connected with AI, technologies, and IoT applications define the SCH's current trends, advancements, and implementations. The other clusters focus on SCH application context and futuristic work. Above Figure 13.6 shows an IoT-based network architecture for Smart and Connected Health that integrates personal health devices, solutions, and health care information systems (HIS) through safeguarded interfaces and gateways to improve patient care services and quality of life.

13.4.1 Artificial Intelligence for SCH

This field explores the effects of AI on healthcare and its different branches, such as ML, robotics, virtual systems, and deep learning. Artificial intelligence can apply to both unstructured and structured healthcare data. The occurrence of commonalities and variances in some of these settings is also apparent.

13.4.1.1 Machine Learning

Common AI methods can involve ML like neural networks and classical support vectors, as well as modernized deep learning according to the neural networks. Machine learning methods usually analyze structured information like data from genetics, images, and electrophysiological information. The ML techniques utilized in medical applications are done to cluster the features of patients or reason the possibility of disease outcomes [14].

13.4.1.2 Neural Network/Deep Learning

Deep learning and AI methods were proven to be potentially good for processing cardiac MRI. Convocational neural learning gave accurate outcomes when measuring coronary artery calcium in cardiac CT angiography utilizing ML of supervised type [6]. The three layers that compromise the deep neural network are first, treated, and untreated input layers; second, the hidden layer where the strength of the relation is trained in the context of weight; and lastly, the output layer of training outcomes.

13.4.1.3 Virtual Systems

13.4.1.3.1 Virtual Assistance

Virtual assistance or voice-activated assistants have various potential health-care utilization cases involving those in the field of health tracking, education, and monitoring. They can assist in allocating caregivers or healthcare providers. This kind of fitness and health application is available for voice assistance. It comes under the categories of fitness and training, health education, nutrition, health surveillance, brain games, meditation, and motivation.

13.4.1.3.2 Virtual Reality

The use of virtual reality (VR) and augmented reality (AR), two modern technologies that can build an artificial environment and let users interact with it, can undoubtedly improve medical and healthcare standards. These technologies include things like tracking sensors, software, AR glasses, haptic devices, and head-mounted displays.

13.4.1.3.3 Virtual Human

Virtual humans, also known as embodied conversational agents, or ECAs, have been used in clinical face-to-face interviews. Based on the responses provided by patients, an algorithm is used to determine which participants have major depressive disorders (MDD) and which do not, based on DSM-5 criteria.

13.4.1.3.4 Virtual Brain

A neuroinformatics framework called the Virtual Brain allows for thorough brain network models and a replica of brain dynamics at the microscopic scale of the brain organization. It facilitates quick data analysis and visualization of the results [24].

13.4.1.3.5 Robotics

Robotics is currently utilized in different applications, mainly in challenging atmospheres, starting from the handling of material in labs to procedures related to surgery. Multi-agent intelligent healthcare systems allow robots to choose the most beneficial plan for unmanaged conditions and communicate the option with the physician for their approval. Additionally, to enhance surgical workflow, interventions of robotic-assisted surgeries have fostered robotic bone machining, optimized implant positioning and compliance, improved bone implantation, and decreased running time.

13.4.2 Technology Support SCH

This field explores the platforms and data and processing technologies guiding related studies and SCH.

13.4.2.1 Big Data

With the advancement of medical sensors in our daily lives, the healthcare industry has emerged as a major hub for big data users. Although the analysis and processing of healthcare data are domain-specific tasks, general-purpose storage technologies, such as relational and NoSQL databases reinforced by horizontal scaling and data replication, manage the management of big healthcare data relatively successfully.

13.4.2.2 Cloud Computing

The cloud IoT model, which aims to expand both technologies and understand a future generation of smart healthcare apps, was introduced by the convergence of the IoT and the cloud [24].

13.4.2.3 Fog/Edge

Especially in situations requiring real-time processing, like early illness diagnosis or detection, dividing the workload between fog and cloud nodes is the best course of action. This typically means assigning decision-making to the edge and model training to the cloud. Promising is a context-aware solution for edge-event detection in multi-edge cloud-based systems, in-network processing, and multimodal data compression.

13.4.2.4 Drones

Drones show enormous promise for revolutionizing medicine and healthcare in the twenty-first century. The MEDIDRONE was created to offer timely emergency services and health insights to residents of remote villages. The services will involve the timely and economical delivery of necessary medications, such as antivenom for dog and snake bites, to prevent fatalities from these conditions.

13.4.2.5 Mobile Computing

Nowadays, there is an extensive selection of mobile devices in different sizes, ranging from tablets and smartwatches to cell phones and small phones, in addition to integrated gadgets, implants, sensors, and trackers that are based on location.

13.4.2.5.1 Mobile Applications

Intelligent learning systems and user-centered designs are the main concerns in mobile application development when it comes to providing each patient with flexible, individualized, and high-quality care. Mobile apps are used in a variety of contexts, including smart rescue, accident detection, and improving home health.

13.4.2.5.2 Mobile Crowdsourcing

With the widespread use of smart devices and the internet, appropriate data can be accessible for accurate diagnosis and treatment in healthcare mobile crowdsensing (MCS) (HMCS).

13.4.3 IoT Application in SCH

Currently, the fourth industrial revolution has contributed to the growth of the Internet of Robotic Things, IoT, cloud computing, and integrated robotics. In SCH, the IoT is known as the dominant technology for reducing stress on the healthcare system. In SCH, IoT e-health provides many benefits, like availability, real-time analytics, ease of use, interoperability, cost reduction, and lifetime monitoring [25].

13.4.3.1 Architecture

In a smart hospital system, the IoT-aware architecture was developed to monitor a patient's physiological parameters and environmental factors in real time and transmit them to the control center. The IoT architecture contains different parts like RFID, improved wireless sensor network and hybrid sensing network, user interface management and data visualization, and the IoT smart gateway.

13.4.3.2 Sensor-Based Systems

In IoT operations, biometric data, such as identity standards and signatures, are the key biometric characteristics. They cannot be lost, purchased, or borrowed and are difficult to duplicate or replicate. In biometric data applications, a new paradigm is the use of IoT in smart healthcare. Network sensors are used to gather information about the physical and mental health of patients. For example, using wearable accelerometer sensors, a knee injury rehabilitation device was built to measure the angle and position of the knees.

13.4.3.3 Blockchain

In the healthcare system, blockchain is based on peer-to-peer network computers to protect big data management and analysis in healthcare. Blockchain increases IoT security and ensures medical equipment connectivity security.

13.4.4 Application Context of SCH

In SCH, the application context is classified into different categories like disease management, monitoring, environment, and application awareness.

13.4.4.1 Disease Management

In the medical field, SCH plays a major role, from remote diagnosis to complex teleinterventions. It is also effective for disease management and self-monitoring, and it fulfils the increasing demand. In mobile chronic management services used as digital wellness technology, Medtronic works with Canary Health, a medical diagnostic tool used for brain stroke patients for early diagnosis and using a wearable device electromagnetic head imaging [15].

13.4.4.2 Monitoring

Health monitoring includes fetal heart rate monitoring in utero, which tracks the well-being of older people who have a moderate cognitive disability like Alzheimer's disease.

13.4.4.3 Environment

The SCH applicability is suited to different environments involving health index monitoring, smart homes, and smart home rehabilitation networks for patients with brain injuries. In this care, using an IoT system and training is known as another SCH environment that includes medical education that can be delivered and improved through smartphones and telemedicine platforms enabled by AR [24].

13.4.4.4 Application Awareness

In smart health application solutions, context computing evolved, which is the intelligence research branch. The context-based model includes a deep neural network that is used for health risk assessment based on evidence from the health problem of the individual subject to the environmental context. In data flow applications, the IoT device's energy consumption optimization is challenging. An energy-efficient hardware prototype was developed on a microcontroller platform based on IoT. This prototype used the electrocardiogram signal in real-time through the sparse time-frequency domain encoding.

13.4.5 Futuristic SCH

13.4.5.1 Predictive Analytics

In decision-support systems development, predictive analytics play an important role in disease diagnosis and precise prediction. In the healthcare sector, its potential outweighs the challenges. A decision-making model is developed based on the IoT method for type-2 diabetes diagnosis and control.

13.4.5.2 Smart Innovations

Smart personal protective equipment is used with sensor technology to monitor the workforce's health and determine the proximity to hazardous areas and harmful chemicals. A smart mirror provides health indicators like heart rate and body temperature that enable the observation of the changes in the characteristics of the skin, like rashes, moles, texture, and color.

13.4.5.3 Personalized Health

In a system, an autonomous ventilator developed that tracks the response of the patient to ventilation, and changing the ventilator setting that provides patient-administered oxygen optimally is known as a promising system. Also, automated ventilation is developed if professionals are absent in respiratory care, and it also adds AI innovations and significant value to remote environments.

13.5 IoT Design Architecture for Healthcare

The different types of technologies cannot be overfocused to improve the healthcare delivery systems. Among all network devices and systems, strong connectivity is an important part of the healthcare environment [25]. In this section, we discuss the different healthcare system architectures using IoT technologies to provide better healthcare services. These architectures provide different services, define the goals and targeted healthcare solutions for each architecture, and define the design components of architecture and their operation with functional services. These functional services of architectures include notifications that provide an alert or warning, real-time streaming and mobility, data analytics, AI, security, device connectivity and discovery, internet connectivity, and network resource sharing among architecture components.

13.5.1 IoT Healthcare Network Architecture

The goal of IoT healthcare network architecture is to provide personal health and wellness monitoring by providing an end-to-end connected architecture for patient data transmission from health devices to patient information systems, hospitals, and medical offices. This architecture function structure contains WBAN, a data center, wireless wide area networks, and wireless local area networks. In each functional section, the operation of the physical elements includes data storage devices, tablets, smartphones, and wearables devices [8]. These used the 6LoWPAN and IPv6 as main network layer protocols used the 6LoWPAN and IPv6 and the IEEE 802.15.4 protocol used by physical layer transmission (Dwivedi *et al.*, 2022). However, IoT healthcare providers require some services that have access to data for continued patient monitoring instead of seamless communication, real-time continuous, and location. In healthcare, mobility support is critical for the success of IoT. In the IoT healthcare network for communication, mobility support protocols like the 6LoWPAN protocol effectively exchange messages between visited networks, home networks, and mobile patient devices [25].

13.5.2 IoT Architecture for Remote Patient Healthcare

The IoT architecture design for remote patient health care's main purpose is to assist healthcare professionals illustrated in Figure 13.7 in making clinical decisions or depending on patient access to health-related information to prevent acute episodes and emergencies occurring due to the degradation of patient health. This architecture also supports medical students and provides support-based training evidence. During their training, this architecture provides medical students access to view real-life patients. This architecture monitors the activities of the patient, and this data process, sharing and storage help to facilitate scalable, effective, and high-performance data collection. Authorized stakeholders like caregivers, emergency systems, healthcare professionals, patients, and relatives performed the monitoring activity. This architecture supports the non-invasive sensor implementation with cloud computing and big data and allows the high-volume processing of sensor data and data access from other sources. The medical-related patient information is retried and searched with the help of this architecture, and it also provides all stakeholders with an appropriate visualization interface [21]. This architecture supports smartphones from the activity sensors, and wearable devices accept data. A cloud-based infrastructure with an analytic module and data storage generates alarms for patients and caregivers of patients. Message delivery

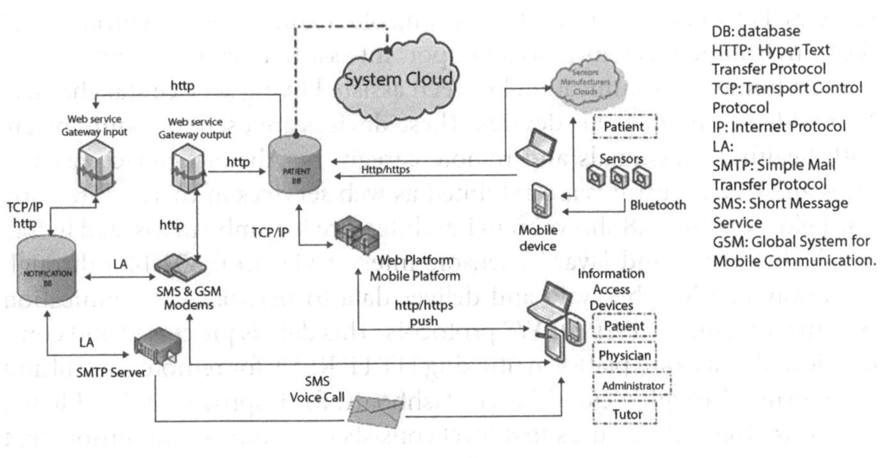

Figure 13.7 IoT architecture for remote patient healthcare.

platforms like voice automated systems, email, short message services, and all PUSH technologies are used to send information to system users. Patient information is accessed in various ways, like websites from mobile devices and desktop computers.

13.5.3 IoT Architecture for Ambient Assisted Living

Ambient intelligence (AmI) systems contain different devices like software applications, wireless networks, computers, medical devices, and sensors that are used to collect data from the environment and users. Generated data enables patient monitoring. Thus, the ambient assisted living (AAL) healthcare application is realized by the ambient intelligence systems. Ambient assisted living facilitates user-dependent services for disabled and older adults. The user-dependent services involved monitoring and controlling vital signs and tracking patient data by analyzing different sensed information and reacting to and detecting abnormal situations [22]. Therefore, ambient intelligence systems must deal with different devices like tablets and smartphones with a medium capacity, actuators, sensors, wearable devices, and consumer electronics with critical resource limitations. Ambient intelligence systems use the smart sensing devices' capability to sense the environment and normal behavior of humans and determine anomalies and critical changes. Create an alert and use the available home automation system enabled by devices communicating with each other if an anomaly exists. Smart sensing devices are used for safety routines at elderly and senior citizen homes to help them and allow a safe and independent lifestyle [22]. The cloud computing, AI, and IoT concept-based architecture deploy the AmI system, and the result provides the realization of AAL health services. Personal communication among older adults, relevant groups, and their environment is known as an important assisted living concept [23]. In a smart home, communication between assisted living service stakeholders is provided through smart devices. These devices are used to communicate with health professionals and remote caregivers. Abstract devices as services and device features are exhibited as web services in this architecture. The below Figure 13.8 shows an IoT architecture for ambient assisted living, in which TinyOS and JavaME sensors interact via IEEE 802.14.5 through a gateway like Raspberry Pi and deliver data to network communication systems utilizing TCP/IP DPWS protocols. This data is processed and communicated to a cloud platform utilizing HTTP REST for remote control and monitoring through a cloud-based dashboard for improved assisted living solutions. The architecture's first level consists of gateways and sensors that transform the message provided by various sensors into devices profile

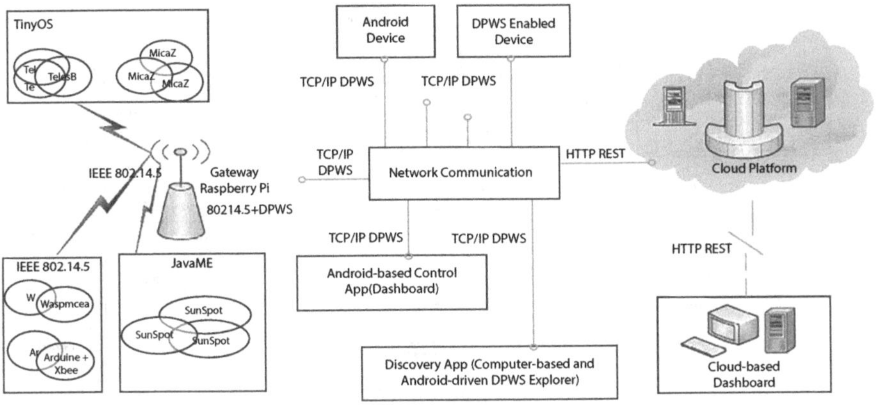

Figure 13.8 IoT architecture for ambient assisted living.

for web services (DPWS)-compliant services. Network communication is the second level that allows heterogeneous devices like Android devices, DPWS-enabled devices, gateways, and sensors to identify and connect. The cloud platform is the last level that uses the network to collect the sensed data and allows users to efficiently access and analyze the available data to react to situations based on collected data. Google Cloud Messages provide push message support for remote monitoring to suggest suitable treatment and diagnosis to medical personnel.

13.5.4 IoT Architecture for Mobile Healthcare

Mobile healthcare is a concept that provides effective healthcare services to highly mobile patients. It integrated communication technologies, sensors, and mobile computing using mobile health devices connected with sensors. Thus, mobility services are also known as the m-health features for providing connectivity with participating stakeholders. Consequently, cellular communication and device-to-device network infrastructure are important components of mobile health service for both current and future use [22]. Figure 13.9 defines the high-level architecture for mobile health services; the components of the m-health architecture are:

Mobile devices of patients: It contains a phone, gateway device, and embedded sensors with an effective installed health services mobile application [23].

Mobile devices of health providers: These include tablets or smartphones that support the healthcare professional in seeing and transmitting the data from the mobile devices of the patient.

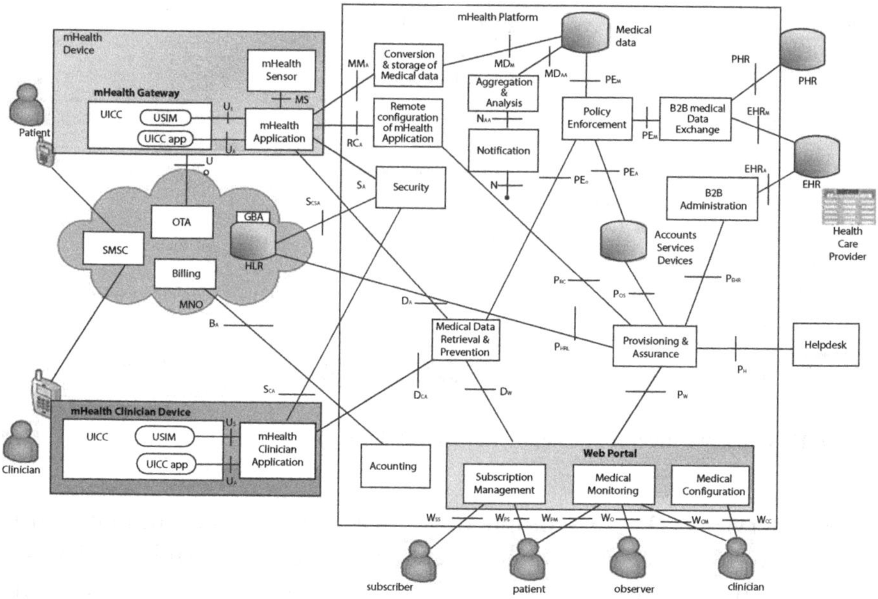

Figure 13.9 IoT architecture for mobile healthcare.

The mobile network and components: It is a cellular mobile network for devices that provides ubiquitous and mobile connectivity. Its components include a home location register, a SIM card, and other cellular network components.

The mobile health platform: This platform uses the mobile operator network for the collection of data and provides mobile health services. This platform's main components perform data storage and conversion through the patient's devices, administrative services, and data synchronization. These components guarantee service level agreement compliance. The mobile health platform provides a web portal interface, and this notification is sent to participants of mobile healthcare and provides thresholds for health-related data.

13.5.5 IoT Architecture for Smart Healthcare Coaching Systems

An IoT architecture for daily activities provided coaching system realization. The human cognition coaching system model addresses the issues of the user as a human [22]. This architecture for cognitively impaired patients assists in caring for, identifying, and dealing with activities ranging

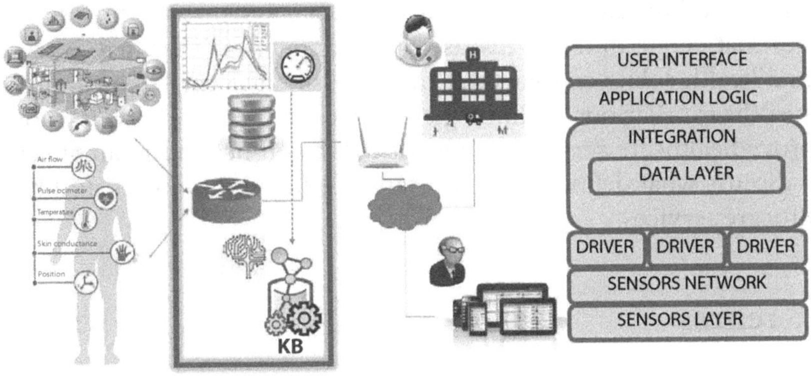

Figure 13.10 IoT architecture for smart healthcare coaching systems.

from dangerous situations to abnormal patient behaviors. These abnormal behaviors are the reasons for alteration or psychotic symptoms in sleep, anxiety, memory impairments, and wake cycles. Above Figure 13.10 shows an Internet of Things architecture for health coaching systems that monitors pulse, temperature, etc. through a network of sensors. User interfaces provide personalized healthcare coaching and feedback for real-time health management and decision-making after multiple layers process and integrate this data. The cognitive architecture components processed and analyzed the data sensed for devices. The framework used in architecture models the brain structure and improves the mind study and their work. This architecture's healthcare goal is to provide coaching and guidance to cognition-impaired patients. The services help the patients avoid incorrect actions or memorizing the correct behavior sequence. The system interprets the sensed data and provides suggestions to the patient to take the correct action [25].

13.6 Conclusion

Smart healthcare prospects are huge, and they provide better health management services. Smart healthcare makes the service more personalized and facilitates appropriate and timely access to health management. Smart healthcare for medical institutions enhances the medical experience, gains information and material management, relieves personnel pressure, and reduces costs. This study discusses smart hospitals, smart assets and resources, and challenges and opportunities for healthcare. There is an increased burden on the current healthcare system and different challenges that create different diseases and pandemics. The smart and connected health solution is effective in addressing the challenges and issues of healthcare. Various technologies and resources also discuss how to improve healthcare services. Different IoT-based healthcare architectures also discuss what defines the importance of IoT technologies in different healthcare services.

References

1. Kumar, Arun, Chakravarty, Sumit and Nanthaamornphong, Aziz. "Analysis of PAPR reduction of optical-OTFS for 256-QAM using companding and clipping–filtering algorithms" *J. Opt. Commun.*, 2024, https://doi.org/10.1515/joc-2023-0369.
2. Kumar, A, Gaur, N., & Nanthaamornphong, A. (2024). Intelligent Signal Identification of NOMA Signal with 256-QAM Modulation Using SVM Algorithm. *Int. J. Intell. Syst. Appl. Eng.*, 12(13s), 257–264.
3. A. Kumar, R. Dhanagopal, M. A. Albreem, and D.-N. Le, "A comprehensive study on the role of advanced technologies in 5G based Smart Hospital," *Alex. Eng. J.*, vol. 60, no. 6, pp. 5527–5536, Dec. 2021, doi:10.1016/j.aej.2021.04.016.
4. M. K. Hassan, A. I. El Desouky, S. M. Elghamrawy, and A. M. Sarhan, "Big Data Challenges and opportunities in Healthcare Informatics and smart hospitals," *Security in Smart Cities: Models, Applications, and Challenges*, pp. 3–26, Nov. 2018, doi:10.1007/978-3-030-01560-2_1.
5. Arun Kumar, Nishant Gaur, Manoj Gupta and Aziz Nanthaamornphong, "Implementation of the deep learning method for signal detection in Massive-MIMO-NOMA systems", *Heliyon*, Volume 10, Issue 3, e25374, 2024.
6. M. K. Gourisaria, R. Agrawal, V. Singh, S. S. Rautaray, and M. Pandey, "Ai and IOT enabled Smart Hospital Management Systems," *Studies in Big Data*, pp. 77–106, 2022, doi:10.1007/978-981-19-5154-1_6.
7. R. Dwivedi, D. Mehrotra, and S. Chandra, "Potential of internet of medical things (IOMT) applications in building a smart healthcare system: A systematic review." *J. Oral. Biol. Craniofac. Res.*, vol. 12, no. 2, pp. 302–318, Mar. 2022, doi:10.1016/j.jobcr.2021.11.010.
8. S. Debdas, C. K. Panigrahi, P. Kundu, S. Kundu, and R. Jha, "IOT application in interconnected hospitals," *Machine Learning for Healthcare Applications*, pp. 225–247, Apr. 2021, doi:10.1002/9781119792611.ch15.
9. V. A. Dang, Q. Vu Khanh, V.-H. Nguyen, T. Nguyen, and D. C. Nguyen, "Intelligent Healthcare: Integration of emerging technologies and internet of things for humanity," *Sensors*, vol. 23, no. 9, p. 4200, Apr. 2023, doi:10.3390/s23094200.

10. G. Acampora, D. J. Cook, P. Rashidi, and A. V. Vasilakos, "A survey on ambient intelligence in Healthcare," *Proc. IEEE*, vol. 101, no. 12, pp. 2470–2494, Dec. 2013, doi:10.1109/jproc.2013.2262913.
11. S. Chakravarty and Arun Kumar, "PAPR Reduction of GFDM Signals Using Encoder-Decoder Neural Network (Autoencoder)". *Natl. Acad. Sci. Lett.*, (2023). https://doi.org/10.1007/s40009-023-01230-1.
12. Arun Kumar, J Venkatesh, Nishant Gaur, Mohammed H. Alsharif, Peerapong Uthansakul and Monthippa Uthansakul, "Cyclostationary and Energy Detection Spectrum Sensing Beyond 5G", *Electron. Res. Arch.*, 2023, Volume 31, Issue 6: 3400-3416. doi: 10.3934/era.2023172, 2023.
13. R. Pedral Sampaio, A. Aguiar Costa, and I. Flores-Colen, "A discussion of digital transition impact on facility management of Hospital Buildings," *Facilities*, vol. 41, no. 5/6, pp. 389–406, Jan. 2023. doi:10.1108/f-07-2022-0092.
14. A. N. Navaz, M. A. Serhani, H. T. El Kassabi, N. Al-Qirim, and H. Ismail, "Trends, technologies, and key challenges in smart and Connected Healthcare," *IEEE Access*, vol. 9, pp. 74044–74067, 2021, doi:10.1109/access.2021.3079217.
15. B. Mohanta, P. Das, and S. Patnaik, "Healthcare 5.0: A paradigm shift in digital healthcare system using Artificial Intelligence, IOT and 5G communication," *2019 International Conference on Applied Machine Learning (ICAML)*, May 2019, doi:10.1109/icaml48257.2019.00044.
16. Arun Kumar, N. Gour, N.Gaur, S.K.Yadav ans H. Sharma, "A Comparative PAPR, BER, and PSD for Optical NOMA communication Framework", *Opt. Quantum Electron.*, 2023, https://doi.org/10.1007/s11082-023-05148-2.
17. S. Tuli *et al.*, "Next Generation Technologies for Smart Healthcare: Challenges, vision, model, trends and Future Directions," *Internet Technol. Lett.*, vol. 3, no. 2, Jan. 2020, doi:10.1002/itl2.145.
18. M. Nasr, Md. M. Islam, S. Shehata, F. Karray, and Y. Quintana, "Smart Healthcare in the age of AI: Recent advances, challenges, and future prospects," *IEEE Access*, vol. 9, pp. 145248–145270, 2021, doi:10.1109/access.2021.3118960.
19. Kumar, A. Analysis of PAPR on NOMA Waveforms Using Hybrid Algorithm. *Wirel. Pers. Commun.*, (2023). https://doi.org/10.1007/s11277-023-10683-y.
20. G. Gardašević, K. Katzis, D. Bajić, and L. Berbakov, "Emerging Wireless Sensor Networks and internet of things technologies—foundations of smart healthcare," *Sensors*, vol. 20, no. 13, p. 3619, Jun. 2020, doi:10.3390/s20133619.
21. S. B. Baker, W. Xiang, and I. Atkinson, "Internet of things for smart healthcare: Technologies, challenges, and opportunities," *IEEE Access*, vol. 5, pp. 26521–26544, 2017, doi:10.1109/access.2017.2775180.
22. S. Zeadally and O. Bello, "Harnessing the power of internet of things based connectivity to improve healthcare," *Internet Things*, vol. 14, p. 100074, Jun. 2021, doi:10.1016/j.iot.2019.100074.

23. M. Ramkumar *et al.* "ECG Cardiac arrhythmias Classification using DWT, ICA and MLP Neural Networks" *J. Phys.: Conf. Ser.,* 1831 012015, 2021.
24. Kumar, Arun, Gour, Nidhi and Sharma, Himanshu. "Analysis of throughput and error rate of 16-QAM, 64-QAM, and 256-QAM O-NOMA waveforms" *J. Opt. Commun.*, 2023, https://doi.org/10.1515/joc-2023-0200.
25. A. Talukder and R. Haas, "Aiot: Ai meets IOT and web in smart healthcare," *13th ACM Web Science Conference 2021*, Jun. 2021, doi:10.1145/3462741.3466650.

14

Exploring the Role of 6G Technology in Smart Healthcare Systems: Challenges, and Future Trends

Sajja Suneel[1]*, Manjula K.[2], Sowmya B. K.[2], Venkateshmurthy B. S.[3], Shams Tabrez Siddiqui[4] and Lakshmana Phaneendra Maguluri[5]

[1]*Department of CSE (Data Science), Institute of Aeronautical Engineering, Dundigal, Hyderabad, Telangana, India*
[2]*Department of CSE, Global Academy of Technology, Bengaluru, Karnataka, India*
[3]*School of EEE, REVA University, Bengaluru, India*
[4]*Department of Computer Science, College of Engineering and Computer Science, Jazan University, Jazan, Saudi Arabia*
[5]*Department of Computer Science and Engineering, Koneru Lakshmaiah Education Foundation, Green Fields, Vaddeswaram, Andhra Pradesh, India*

Abstract

Sixth generation (6G) technology is expected to have a significant impact on several businesses and their goods, particularly in the healthcare sector from 2030. Although the fifth generation (5G) has not yet been thoroughly investigated for commercialization, researchers have begun to envision, plan, and investigate the needs of 6G. The healthcare industry of the future will be powered by AI and 6G. The 6G will aim to overcome the current healthcare system's space and time constraints. It looked like 6G would be a game-changer for the healthcare industry. This view suggests that 6G communication technology may usher in a new age in healthcare in the future. A wide variety of business models, including intellectual wearable tools, the Internet of Medical Things (IoMT), and the hospital-to-home (H2M) services, have been developed to improve people's daily lives beyond the scope of industry 4.0. The 6G is a solution to the severe network needs of smart healthcare treatments, which should have a minimum end-to-end latency of 1 millisecond (ms) and a high service dependability of 99.999%. Achieving such a high level of performance is not without its difficulties. We have covered these

**Corresponding author*: sajja.suneel@gmail.com

Arun Kumar, Manoj Gupta, Sanjeev Sharma, Er. Himanshu Sharma and Khursheed Aurangzeb (eds.) Smart Hospitals: 5G, 6G and Moving Beyond Connectivity, (287–314)

problems and their remedies in this chapter. In addition, telesurgery, epidemics, and pandemics are only a few of the scenarios where 6G has been considered.

Keywords: 6G, smart healthcare, quality of experience, IMoT, artificial intelligence, communication technologies

14.1 Introduction

Today, an exceptional ecosystem for new opportunities is being created at an unprecedented rate by the development of multiple information and communications technologies, which drastically affects the world. The advent of digital technologies has influenced every market imaginable, including healthcare [1]. There is a tremendous prospect to build an united ecology for new possibilities in healthcare and other industries thanks to digital innovations such as the expansion of telehealth, the development of fifth-generation wireless networks (5G), artificial intelligence (AI) techniques like deep learning (DL) and machine learning (ML), big data and supercomputing, Internet of Things (IoT), and digital security competences like blockchain. These advancements can tackle some of the most pressing issues confronting healthcare practitioners and policymakers, such as the need for affordable, accessible, and long-term healthcare [2]. Collectively, these interconnected technologies have the potential to revolutionize disease screening, diagnosis, and monitoring, pave the way for more precise disease progression profiling, and enhance and/or tailor treatments. There will be an emphasis on cutting-edge therapeutic technologies like telesurgery, AI, IoT, and next-generation communications.

The 5G-networks utilize high-frequency millimeter waves to transmit data more quickly than previous networks, and they also boast incredibly low latency—less than one millisecond (ms) contrasted to around 70ms on the 4G-network [3]. Its low power requirements allow it to enhance functionality while simultaneously reducing energy usage by all the linked devices. Signal degradation is more of an issue with 5G, and "base stations" need to be densely inhabited due to the higher frequencies used for transmission [4].

But a word of warning is in order. Not all of 5G's capabilities can be utilized at this time, particularly with the vast array of healthcare-related instruments and devices available on the Internet of Things (IoT), but fundamental scientific considerations pertaining to biology and physiology must be considered when designing and implementing the new opportunities presented by the 5G ecosystem, particularly in telemedicine [5].

Equally important is the need to study the specifics of human interface technology (HIT) in order to maximize people's usage of these new forms of communication; furthermore, there are constraints and difficulties in making full use of the spectrum for these communications. Lastly, the prospects for utilizing the new communication networks are greatly affected by non-internet technologies like AI, database systems (BD), computational analytics (CA), and the factors associated with accessing and storing data in "the cloud" [6].

The intelligent IoMT (IioMT) will develop and fulfill numerous functions for the benefit of humanity under the 6G communication paradigm. The IIoMT are self-determining, AI-powered tools that utilize communiqué technologies to make decisions on their own. Consequently, medical devices will be able to link to the Internet as the IIoMT and the Internet of Everything (IoE) both come to fruition. One example is a computed tomography (CT) scan or an MRI [7]. Using 6G technology, the scanner will scan the devices and transmit the data to distant locations, as shown in Figure 14.1. A pathologist can examine this fact as it happens. Decisions may be made instantly because nearly all medical devices will be able to

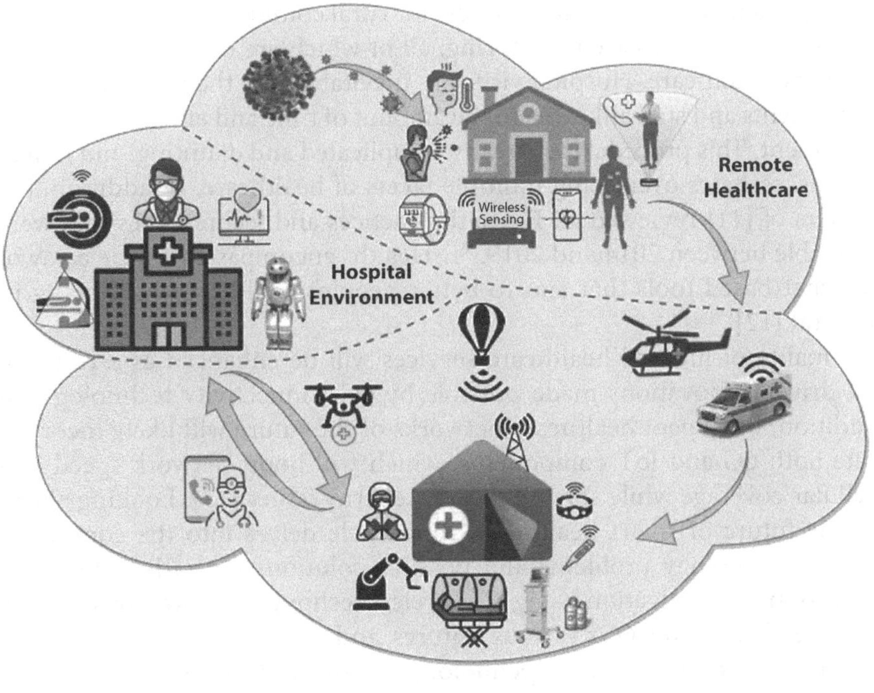

Figure 14.1 Structure of the intelligence 6G-enabled healthcare systems.

connect to the internet. Hence, the IIoMT can transcend the limitations of distance, time, and money. As another example, distant doctors can readily treat cancer patients. Consequently, cancer patients will be preserved by a combination of local doctors and doctors working remotely [8]. If cancer can be detected early, the mortality rate of patients can be reduced to almost zero. Nevertheless, new sensors of this kind must be developed. This circumstance is related to a wide range of illnesses, not only cancer. Treatments for cardiovascular disease are one example.

Technological progress has made it possible to diagnose complex disorders, and modern medicine makes it easier to administer complex therapies. For example, we now know more about the human body's inner workings thanks to medical imaging technology, which has become a crucial tool for identifying a wide range of illnesses and ailments [9]. When it comes to healthcare, communications technology is among the most crucial applied technologies. There are a lot of ways in which healthcare has benefited from the usage of network and communication technology over the years. Traditional means of communication including landlines, fax machines, and computer networks allowed for the rapid and easy transmission of basic diagnostic data like patient reports, treatment alternatives, and prescriptions [10]. They improve data measurement and management, boost healthcare access for rural communities, and help with tailored chronic disease monitoring; all of which are essential to reviving primary healthcare. Hospital visits are inevitable, but they can be a hassle for patients and staff alike due to the amount of time and effort required for treatment. This procedure is already complicated and daunting, and it usually necessitates overseeing multiple facets of healthcare. In addition, the writers of [11] reviewed all E-health practices and technologies that were available between 2014 and 2019. "E-Health" encompasses a wide array of internet-based tools that aim to better people's health and well-being in general [12].

Quality of life and healthcare services will be enhanced as a result of AI-driven innovations made possible by 6G connectivity technology. In addition, intelligent healthcare networks of the future will likely incorporate both 6G and IoT components, which will boost network speed and cellular coverage while solving several security issues [13]. Looking ahead to the future of smart healthcare, this article delves into the communication technology problems and possible solutions for early emergency detection and mitigation using 6G wireless technology. Numerous forums are already debating 6G's various features, and researchers are always looking into 6G communication technology's many needs. In their article [14], the writers addressed the limitations and difficulties of 6G communication technology. Sixth generation communication technology research has already begun in a number of nations in response to various demands and potential applications. Some 6G algorithms have also been developed. Despite the fact that 5G has not yet been fully implemented globally and B5G has not been concluded, there are a number of reasons why these technologies will not be able to revolutionize current ways of life, communities, and industries [15]. The data rate provided by 5G networks, for example, makes holographic communication impractical. Therefore, 6G communication technology capabilities must be evaluated before solutions can be designed. Sixth generation connectivity can only be used in future intelligent healthcare if certain conditions are met: a data rate of at least 1 Tbps, a low end-to-end delay of at least 1 ms, a mobility of at least 1000 km/h, a frequency of at least 1 THz, a dependability of at least 10-9, and a wavelength of at least 300 m [16]. Especially for telesurgery, real-time communication is going to be crucial. The advancement of smart healthcare systems will also benefit from holographic communication and virtual reality (VR).

Intelligent healthcare will be implemented in part by 5G networks. These will not be able to provide holographic communication or telesurgery due to the lofty data rates and very low latency needed for these applications. Another obstacle for 5G communication technology in rural healthcare networks is the availability of connections [17]. When a link is urgently required, drones can be sent out to establish a temporary ad hoc network. Sixth generation communication technology will revolutionize intelligent healthcare, which will rely more and more on communication technologies. We will show how developments in communication technology have triggered a sea change in healthcare.

We believe that the healthcare industry will be well prepared to handle epidemic situations and decrease transience rates by utilizing 6G technology. We are unaware of any other papers that have provided a review on this subject prior to this one. In this work, we offer a comprehensive overview of 6G-enabled healthcare that takes the succeeding factors into account.

- To present a comprehensive evaluation of the ways in which 6G technology has the latency to transform wireless smart-healthcare and to delve into several areas in order to provide a thorough summary of its possible effects.
- Services, communication enhancement, and needs are all covered by a taxonomy for 6G-based healthcare to investigate

the difficulties of healthcare communication systems and to look for ways to improve them.

- The requirements of 6G-enabled and 6G paradigm in healthcare can be met by describing the main technologies that are needed. It also draws attention to the key ideas and parts that are required to make 6G's healthcare potential a reality.
- To offer a complete evaluation of unsettled difficulties and provides intuitions into the future directions surrounding 6G-driven healthcare. In order to improve 6G technology in the healthcare domain, it provides an ample study of unresolved issues and points out areas that need additional exploration and investigation.

The remaining chapter is organized in the following manner. Background of the smart healthcare and 6G communicated described in Section 14.2. Services, communication enhancement, and needs make up 6G healthcare's taxonomy, which are detailed in Section 14.3. In Section 14.4, we cover some of the essential enabling technologies, such as blockchain, the IoE, terahertz (THz) communication, holographic communication, and AI. Open questions and potential avenues for further study are laid out in Section 14.5. The conclusion is then presented in Section 14.6.

14.2 Theoretical Background

This section provides a synopsis of the various components that allowed us to conduct the research investigation. A growing number of countries are embracing healthcare technology that is accessible through mobile devices. Eighty percent of member nations have made attempts to adopt and deploy mobile technologies for health, according to the WHO study on m-healthcare [18]. Information conveyed through mobile health apps may take several forms, including text, images, and videos. The use of medical images and videos for diagnosis has skyrocketed in the last several years. The development of portable scanning devices has simplified the process of creating medical images and movies, thanks to developments in medical imaging technology. Therefore, m-health data increasingly includes medical pictures and videos [19]. The adoption of multimedia technology has made many previously incomplete use cases that affect our daily lives easier to understand and implement. Utilizing the advantages of multimedia technology, systems and services have been created. People with chronic conditions can reduce the need for patient-physician contacts and increase the frequency of doctor appointments using phone, video calls, and the online platform, which allows for the sharing of medical data. The smart medical home often makes use of speech recognition and gesture recognition in addition to telemedicine [20]. Patients must be informed about their diagnosis, surgery, and treatment in order for them to comprehend the medical procedures. To augment the more conventional paper-based material, many patients are now receiving education using visual, auditory, interactive, and internet-based content. This has led medical video streaming to a crucial role in m-health solutions [21].

Intelligent wearable devices (IWD), H2H services, and remote patient monitoring and diagnosis are all essential components of smart healthcare. The patient statistics are transmitted remotely via the internet and analyzed at data centers by these providers. Mobile, high-capacity, low-latency, environmentally friendly communiqué to ensure patient care, and consistently available, reliable association are all essential features of healthcare networks [22]. In light of these considerations, healthcare networks are best hosted by the 6G networks. Intelligent sensing, access, and cloud are the three main deployment tiers shown in Figure 14.2 of the 6G healthcare network architecture. Security, adaptability, and intelligent resource management are just a few of the numerous processes that will be made possible by this 6G architecture. Diverse network slices enable diverse applications, as shown in this diagram, which describes the carving architecture of 6G networks [23]. Sensor nodes collect information and transmit it to higher layers.

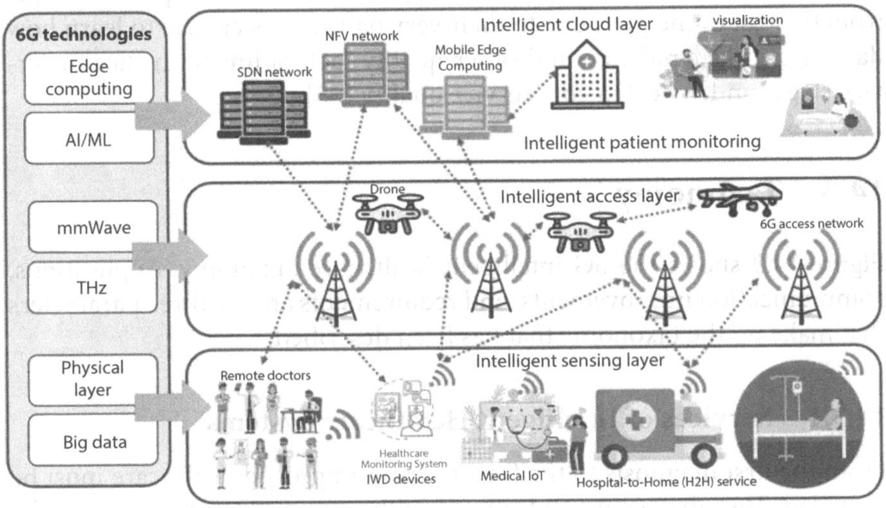

Figure 14.2 Different network layers of 6G.

Connecting nodes, clients, and tools to radio admittance networks is where innovations like sophisticated modulation techniques, tiny cells, and massive MIMO are put into place. The last layer, the cloud layer, is responsible for optimizing networks and intelligently allocating resources. The network is useful for many different kinds of applications, and the various layers allow the system flexibility on many levels. In this diagram, we can see all the levels and the technologies that make them up in this hypothetical situation [24].

In particular, the development of 6G communication technologies guarantees high levels of quality of service (QoS) and quality of experience (QoE) for m-health apps, and it addresses some of the difficulties mentioned in earlier subsections [25]. Mobile broad bandwidth and low latency (mBBLL) and massive low latency machine type (mLLMT) are two criteria that QoS embrace, which have revolutionized numerous applications. In order to attain good quality of experience, 6G technology must execute all needed qualities [26]. With its ability to provide high QoS and QoE, 6G technology will revolutionize numerous industries. It will open the door to new applications like telesurgery, holographic communications, AR/VR, and tangible internet, among many others. Similarly, QoE will be crucial for autonomous vehicles and intelligent transportation services [27]. As a primary objective of 6G, the QoE is used to enable SPs to evaluate the efficacy of their facilities and the role that individual service components play in achieving that efficacy. With this in mind, we want to study the QoE of mobile health multimedia in order to identify the different aspects that affect the QoE of the mobile health app. Mobile health apps are unique from the rest of the pack due to their very nature. It is critical to learn how data, networks, analytics, and other quality factors impact m-health service stages and, by extension, service quality [28].

14.3 Taxonomy

Figure 14.3 shows the 6G intelligent healthcare taxonomy. Applications, communication improvements, and requirements are the three parameters that make up the taxonomy that has been described.

14.3.1 Services of Intelligent Healthcare Systems

From the first diagnosis to the final therapy, improved healthcare must be provided. The advancement of smart healthcare services paves the way for the provision of top-notch medical care.

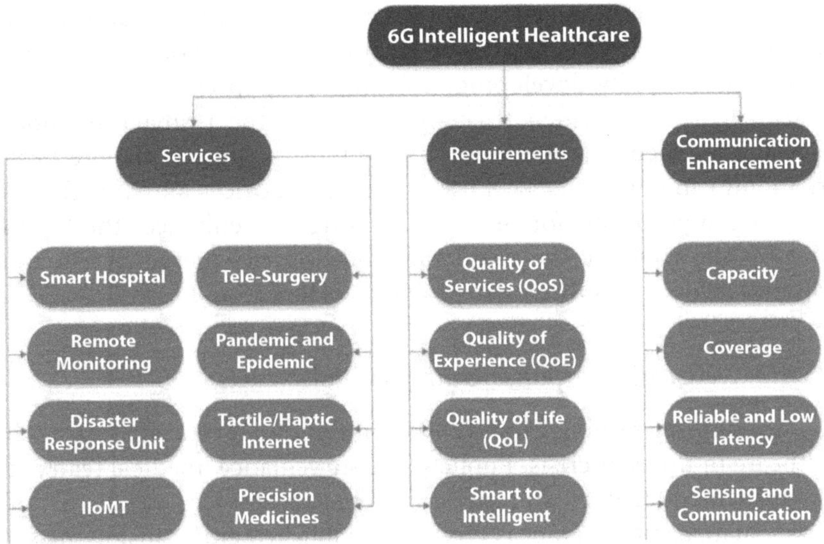

Figure 14.3 Taxonomy of 6G intelligent healthcare.

14.3.1.1 Smart Hospital Service

The hospital has state-of-the-art medical equipment and highly trained personnel to ensure that patients receive the best care possible. It is critical for the smooth operation of the hospital that patients, doctors, staff, and administration can communicate effectively with one another [29]. Email, cell phones, and two-way radios are common forms of hospital-based technology that enable interdisciplinary collaboration. There have been recent innovations in healthcare service delivery that aim to improve hospitals' ability to treat patients. These innovations include: (i) digital health record keeping and information gathering to lessen the likelihood of human mistake; (ii) improved communication between patients and doctors made possible by AI to aid in disease diagnosis; and (iii) the use of surgical robots to aid in precise procedures [30].

14.3.1.2 Remote Monitoring Service

More and more people are opting for remote healthcare as a way to access medical treatment, especially in rural locations or when time is an issue for transportation [31]. Telemedicine and remote health monitoring are the two main means of providing this service. Using telemedicine, medical professionals are able to assess, diagnose, and treat patients remotely [32].

The patient can be watched at anytime, anywhere using healthcare apps and the internet, thanks to remote healthcare. Even though holographic technology is rapidly developing, holographic telepresentation will soon replace high-quality video teleconferencing as the primary method of delivering telemedicine. One use of IoMT technology is remote healthcare monitoring, which makes use of wearable devices and WBANs [33]. Deploying applications for real-time nursing also enhances the QoE for aging by allowing for the rapid identification of emergency situations through sensors and subsequent provision of a response.

14.3.1.3 Disaster Response Unit Service

Having a disaster response unit (DRU) on standby is crucial for providing healthcare in times of crisis. Public space surveillance, medical teams, crisis management centers, and mobile emergency services are all part of it. A crisis management center is typically established either inside the same hospital or at a separate institution to deliver rapid healthcare facilities, departmental communiqué, and consequence reflection [34] whenever a catastrophic event occurs, most notably a pandemic. Field hospitals may play a vital role in these situations by isolating epidemic patients, freeing up beds in other hospitals, and facilitating better use of limited hospital resources. Isolating and treating infected persons is the current use of these facilities. The advent of drones and robots has paved the way for healthcare workers to reduce human engagement with patients and put them to use in emergency response units [35]. Deliveries of food and medication kits, collection of test samples, and sanitization of patient rooms are just a few of the many tasks made possible by these technologies.

14.3.1.4 IIoMT Service

In the context of the 6G communication paradigm, the IIoMT will develop and perform a number of tasks that contribute to human health. Medical devices will soon be able to connect to the web thanks to the formation of an IoE that includes IIoMT, the Internet of Bodies, and other similar networks [36]. With the ability to access the internet from any medical device, quick decisions will be possible. Scans from internet-connected CT and MRI scanners can send data to remote locations via 6G technology [37]. This data can be reviewed by a doctor in real time. Another case in point is the potential ease with which oncologists practicing remotely may indulgence their patients. The current method for identifying cancerous or benign tumors in cancer patients is time-consuming. Nevertheless, 6G will soon allow for the real-time detection of malignancy [38]. Furthermore, specialty hospitals will not be necessary for either the patients or the doctors. Therefore, in order to treat cancer patients, remote doctors will work with local physicians. The mortality rate can be decreased with the early detection of cancer patients. Not only does this predicament apply to cancer, but it also applies to cardiovascular therapy and a host of other disorders.

14.3.1.5 Telesurgery Service

The practice of physician-assisted remote surgery, or telesurgery, is a relatively new area of research [39]. In order for telesurgery to be successful, real-time communication is essential. Because telesurgery involves the exact movement of specialized medical equipment, ultra reliable low latency communication (URLLC) and lofty bandwidth efficacy networks are crucial for the procedure to run smoothly and without data loss. While 5G and B5G can get the job done, 6G will really elevate the telesurgery experience by making the network dependable and cutting latency even more [40]. The doctor can give orders by voice, telepresence, or teleassist. Sixth generation technology enables the possibility of more proactive holographic communication for oral guidance. Using holographic communication, the surgeon may observe the surgery site more clearly and provide guidance as needed. The term "telestration" refers to the practice of remotely displaying a surgical procedure, typically through video, to a potential patient [41]. Augmented and virtual reality have the potential to revolutionize healthcare. In addition, the use of tactile and haptic technologies allows the doctor to support the process.

14.3.1.6 Response in Pandemic Service

The recent COVID-19 pandemic demonstrated the crucial importance of communication technology in times of pandemic or epidemic [42]. In most cases, medical personnel are at danger during pandemics and epidemics because the infections spread from person to person. COVID-19 has killed millions of people, including medical personnel [43]. The use of IIoMT allows for the efficient management of COVID-19 outbreaks. One example is the use of buffer status report (BSR) biosensors, which transport each individual's blood sample to a central laboratory without exposing them to any outside elements. A blood sample will be collected and sent for testing by a BSR biosensor. This makes it easy to separate people and monitor the spread of the pandemic.

14.3.1.7 Tactile/Haptic Internet Service

By utilizing motion, vibration, or force, haptic technology creates the sensation of a virtual touch. For real-time tactile capture via the tactile internet, URLLC and a fast connection are required [44]. Furthermore, it will facilitate doctors' ability to do touch-based diagnoses remotely. Computer, interface, and wearable are the three main types of haptic human-computer interaction (HCI). With desktop HCI, a distant surgeon or doctor can use a virtual instrument to do surgery or provide a diagnosis. The command device, which could be a smartphone or tablet, has a flat screen. Wearable HCI, such a haptic glove, is utilized by the distant doctor in this scenario. Tactile/haptic technology can be useful in healthcare when skilled surgeons are able to do complex surgeries with the assistance of intelligent robots [45]. Robots equipped with perceptible and haptic technology could interact with patients and provide treatment while human doctors and nurses are far away.

14.3.2 Requirements

The need of intelligent healthcare systems for 6G connectivity have been extensively studied and debated by academics. Operating frequency in THz, data rate in gigabits per second, and support for mobility at 1000 km/h are important specifications for 6G communication technology. Furthermore, 6G will be an AI-driven communiqué system that is propelled by various technologies such as software-defined networking, blockchain, and network function virtualization.

14.3.2.1 Quality of Services (QoS)

The QoS metrics offered by 6G technology are bigger to those of 5G and B5G. For instance, QoS encompasses a wide range of communication types, including ultra-massive machine-type communications (umMTC), extremely low-power communications (ELPC), future enhanced mobile broadband (FeMBB), highly dependable and low-latency communications (ERLLC), and long-distance and high-mobility communications (LDHMC). In addition, QoS encompasses mLLMT, MBBMT, and portable broadband with low latency. Holographic communication and telesurgery are only two of the smart healthcare applications that will be made possible by this combination of technologies of the 6G network.

14.3.2.2 *Quality of Experiences (QoE)*

Communication that delivers excellent service is what we mean when we talk about QoE. Experiences for critical procedures and smart health centers must be of a high standard for intelligent healthcare. Internet technologies that need very low latency and high data rates, such as VR, AR, holographic communications, and tactile internet, will improve the quality of the experience. Moreover, QoE is anticipated to transform numerous industries, including smart cars, electronics, medicine, and unmanned aerial vehicles (UAVs). When these characteristics are combined with 6G technology, QoE can be attained. Artificial intelligence will be the true engine behind 6G technology, which will cause massive societal, economic, and lifestyle shifts.

14.3.2.3 *Quality of Life (QoL)*

Health care providers define QoL as an improved standard of living that prioritizes QoE and QoS. Sixth generation communication technology does not necessarily improve people's QoL, but intelligent healthcare systems do; it can meet all of the necessary QoL requirements while still providing a high quality of experience. There are other potential future additions to the key quality of life components, such as remote patient monitoring, smart accident anticipation, connectivity to IWD, diligence medication, and telesurgery. In addition, H2H services are another important component of quality of life. In order to provide H2H services, an autonomous automobile will be outfitted with a m-hospital. Improving modern rescue efforts and quality of life depends on this service. Furthermore, the present healthcare insurance policy will be superseded by a new kind of health insurance at hospitals (HIH). A component of quality of life, HIH will improve trust in hospital care. Hospitals will soon be evaluated based on measures that measure quality of life.

14.3.2.4 *Changeover from Smart to Intelligent*

An AI-driven communication system is what 6G aims to build in order to pave the way for the intelligent era. Devices will thus undergo a metamorphosis in the 6G age, going from smart to intelligent. The evolution of smart gadgets into intelligent ones will be visible as mobile connection and AI continue to advance. When the IoE becomes fully functional in

2030, it will supersede the IoT. Smartphones will be supplanted by intelligent phones in due time. In the future, smart gadgets will be able to access the internet and run on AI. As a result, the smart gadget (which could be quite small) will have the ability to predict outcomes, make selections, and collaborate with other smart gadgets. So, we are entering a new era where intelligence is paramount, thanks to 6G communication technologies.

14.3.3 Communication Enhancement

Capability, coverage, high dependability, low latency communiqué, and sensing are some of the important aspects of intelligent healthcare systems that are discussed in this section.

14.3.3.1 Capacity Enhancement

Operators of the networks began to concentrate on disaster response network infrastructure planning and design after the first wave of COVID-19, with capacity expansion being a major issue. For instance, since the beginning of COVID-19, data utilization has jumped 35% in Turkey. The proliferation of patient data and the widespread usage of IoMT technology have made this trend especially apparent in healthcare systems. However, visible light communication (VLC) has the potential to boost indoor capacity. The current RF-based communications system can be improved with this technology by distributing user load more evenly. Highly efficient data transfer speeds for holographic telepresence in distant hospitals will also be available through THz's ultra-broadband. Furthermore, healthcare system communication links for field hospitals can be expanded with the use of aerial networks like high altitude platforms (HAPs). Emergency medical services can be better provided by UAVs equipped with reconfigurable intelligent surfaces (RIS). In order for IoMT-tools to take benefit of intellectual radios and ambient backscatter technology for ultra-low power transmission and spectrum sharing, cognitive radios with synergetic radios can billet these tools. The linking and energy efficacy can be enhanced simultaneously in this way. But it's not easy to guarantee QoS in such systems.

14.3.3.2 Coverage Enhancement

The intricate design of hospitals and the delicate nature of medical equipment make it imperative that all healthcare institutions have constant, reliable connectivity and coverage. At the moment, the hospital is communicating over Wi-Fi networks. Coverage in sensitive areas is limited, nevertheless, due to significant electromagnetic interference (EMI). To further enhance coverage and safeguard places with RF restrictions, RIS can be strategically installed in certain sections of hospitals, such as on walls and ceilings. When it comes to distant healthcare, there are major coverage issues in rural areas. Consequently, a large section of the population is unable to get telehealth services because of inadequate coverage, which prevents them from connecting. There are comparable coverage concerns in the healthcare industry. The best options for expanding coverage in this regard are HAPs, UAVs, and satellites. By acting as base stations or relay nodes, these networks can aid in coverage expansion. The range offered by non-terrestrial networks (NTNs) is unparalleled by other network types. As a result, disaster scenarios can benefit from the scalability and flexibility offered by hybrid aerial-terrestrial networks.

14.3.3.3 Reliable and Low Latency

In order to provide reliable and low-latency disaster response services and remote healthcare, effective communication is essential. For telesurgery to work, for example, robots driven by AI and ML would require very low latency and dependable connectivity. Therefore, edge intelligence can help move amenities nearer to patients, which could lower the latency of the channel connection. Smart ambulances can provide V2X communication for safe self-driving by utilizing the relatively new concept of joint radar communication (JRC). More so, edge intelligence has the potential to make self-driving ambulances and teleoperated vehicles incredibly mobile. Utilizing NTN platforms with extensive coverage might also improve mobility. Furthermore, with the use of AI-enabled cognitive radios and REM, issues related to handover—specifically, jittery delay—caused by patients' mobility while wearing implanted medical equipment can be resolved. Additionally, low-power, environmentally friendly communication can be achieved indoors and out via the use of hybrid RF-VLC.

Reducing the battery limits of IoMT devices and doing away with the need to clean reusable medical equipment are two further ways it can improve reaction times. In a field hospital, where there is no permanent medical infrastructure, similar methods might be used to track patients' vitals. Furthermore, Wi-Fi sensing can ascertain position and location, which could be essential in a large area with many patients. An additional function of wireless sensing in COVID-19 is the detection of indoor crowding through the use of Wi-Fi signals for the purpose of maintaining social separation. Extra information on social distance implementations can be provided by REM, a more generalized sensing concept. Teleoperated vehicles and unmanned aerial aircraft are two more ways REM can be utilized to keep tabs on those who violate social distance. And as a pre-event signal for disaster scenarios, the odd activity detection system could be useful. Also, REM aided by AI and ML can help with early warning, quick response, and understanding the extent and location of the calamity. Additionally, COVID-19 can be detected non-invasively using sensing technology. By analyzing the amount of water in each image, AI systems and sophisticated DL algorithms can determine whether cells are healthy or diseased. In contrast to previous screening approaches, THz does not harm live cells.

14.4 Key Enabling Technologies for 6G Smart Healthcare

In order to meet the demands of 6G communication technology, ancillary technologies are required. The integration of AI is essential to the communication technology of 6G, which is planned to be an AI-driven communiqué skill. Furthermore, 6G will enable the IoE to speed up numerous industry improvements. In addition, edge tech is essential for 6G tech to lower latency and bring cloud capabilities closer to smart devices and displayed in Figure 14.4.

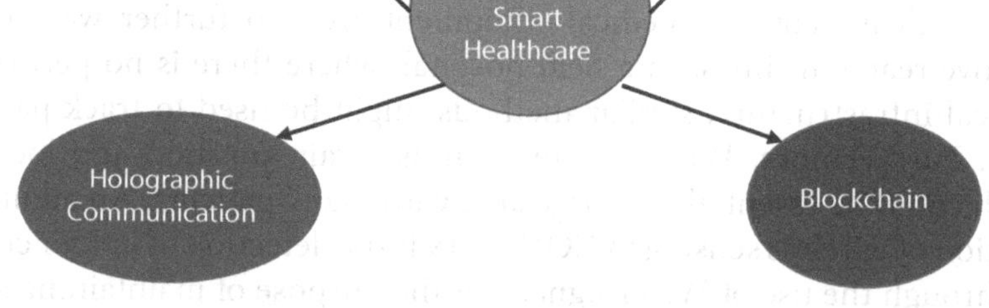

Figure 14.4 Various key-enabled technologies for a 6G-assisted smart healthcare system.

14.4.1 Edge Computing

The storage, processing, and analysis of massive data will be handled by cloud computing in 6G intelligent healthcare systems. Broadband and the ability to communicate with smart devices are necessities for the data transmission and storage process on the cloud server. Technologies like edge computing are being repositioned closer to the data source in response to the meteoric rise of data. The capacity to directly integrate millions of intelligent gadgets will be a high point of 6G. Data collection, evaluation, and real-time analysis are all handled by edge nodes in the network. The edge nodes are positioned near high-tech medical devices. In addition, the edge nodes process health data computationally and analyze it in real-time so that action can be taken. In order to save computing and communication expenses. Additionally, there are privacy, scalability, adaptability, and dependability benefits to using edge technology. These benefits of edge computing will allow 6G to meet its need for delivering high-quality healthcare services, which is essential given the large number of smart devices that will be linked to the 6G internet.

14.4.2 Artificial Intelligence

In healthcare, AI is essential for doing real-time tasks like remote surgery. One form of ML known as DL does not necessitate pre-processing of incoming data. It takes in raw, real-time health data and uses it to do the math. While computing numerous network properties, it also possesses outstanding precision. Another AI method that is gaining traction in the medical field is deep reinforcement learning (DRL). The system uses reinforcement learning to determine the optimal policy based on the current environment state and then executes many actions. The optimal course of action is then determined by recalculating the decision in light of the observation. Combining deep neural networks with reinforcement learning approaches, DRL algorithms maximize their strength. Consequently, DRL results in very good output with very little computational cost. The healthcare industry is currently researching federated learning as a means to improve privacy and security. Edge nodes improve privacy and security by sharing an ML model rather than personally identifiable information. Nevertheless, AI methods are power hogs, necessitating additional data, training time, and computing power.

14.4.3 Holographic Communication

The physical representation of an interference pattern created by light diffraction is known as a hologram. The resulting image keeps all the details, including parallax and depth, of the original item. To create a hologram of an object, holographic communication makes use of many cameras. For accurate control responses and real-time speech, very low latency is also required. Clinicians may have to wait for a diagnosis from a specialist or specialists to be made in an emergency. On the other hand, holographic communication allows the professional doctor(s) to remotely diagnose the condition. In cases of medical emergencies, they may also act as a supervisor to the attending physician. In order to get a proper diagnosis, patients may need to see multiple doctors or even travel to different states or countries. Medical practitioners are now able to diagnose patients remotely using holographic communiqué. Sixth generation holographic communication will improve global healthcare connectivity, just like 6G global coverage. Without changing their schedule or making any travel arrangements, the skilled doctor can provide quick services upon request. In addition, it may connect doctors from different parts of the world so they can monitor and discuss intricate medical issues.

14.4.4 Blockchain

Since 6G systems are typically dispersed and thus subject to greater risks of assaults and threats, attaining a bigger level of privacy and security in IoT networks built on 6G technology is an actual worry. Another concern is the issue of data privacy in multilayer 6G systems, like the intelligent healthcare system, where data is shared openly across multiple tiers. One new and potentially game-changing development in 6G-IoT networks is blockchain technology, which offers novel approaches to old problems like privacy and security. Blockchain technology eliminates the need for a central authority to manage data because it is decentralized, immutable, and transparent. The ability for every entity, like an IoT device, to have equal say over the data stored in the blockchain is made likely by a peer-to-peer network system. When checking medical records, the use of blockchain technology might pave the way for 6G healthcare solutions. Connected to smart contract technology, it does away with middlemen while keeping trust levels high. On the other hand, future 6G-IoT networks that include blockchain technology may have higher energy consumption and latency. Block verification and information sharing are two examples of mining procedures that take a lot of energy and produce a lot of delays in the network.

14.5 Research Challenges and Future Directions

In addition to the improvements already stated, there are still many unanswered questions and potential avenues for further study on the use of 6G in intelligent healthcare.

14.5.1 Challenges

Presented here are some of the unanswered questions surrounding the intelligent healthcare industry's 6G adoption.

14.5.1.1 Security and Privacy

New security measures are required for data gathering from in- and on-body sensors and its transmission to a cloud medical center for processing. It is still in its early days in the field of research into how to enable encrypted communication on and within the body due to the limited computational power and energy consumption of body sensors. The main causes of complexity are as follows:

1. Nanodevices' constrained computational, power, and memory capacities. This makes pre-deployed procedures difficult to execute and on-demand vital distribution methods impractical.
2. Need for a nano-domain network that can scale. Therefore, there is a need for new forms of authentication that make better use of available energy and make use of cryptographic algorithms and security structures with lower key lengths.

A number of researchers looked at molecular communications (MC) to see how well a diffusion-based MC system might keep secrets and to come up with new ways to encrypt data using biological molecules like DNA and RNA. Unpredictable events and spontaneous molecular reactivity, especially at the nanoscale, necessitate additional investigation.

14.5.1.2 Technology Aspect

In the future, the idea of the body as a node in a network will be shaped by the increasing fascination with in-body nano-devices, whether they are dry or wet, and how they can facilitate biological communications.

It is now easy to connect to and interact with biological cells and electrical nano-devices. The idea of the Internet of Bio-Nano Things can include both artificial biological particles on a nanoscale and implants. Since they are all parts of a network, they can communicate with one another through specialized network devices. Integrating nodes both on and within the body allows for the retrieval and transmission of vital data from the depths of the body to the cloud. The requirements for the transmission of data among these nodes, ranging from the smallest to the biggest, are extremely diverse. With 6G technology, all these separate components will be able to function together as one network, allowing for the uninterrupted, dependable, and safe transfer of data. Issues with resource management, cyber-security, pinpointing precise location, and countless more will arise as a result of the need to communicate across numerous channels while collecting data from a wide range of devices, from the nano to the macro.

14.5.1.3 Ethical Aspects

The advent of 6G paves the way for the widespread use of various data-driven, decision-making systems, which in turn will revolutionize healthcare and preventative measures to address people's most basic needs. Problems with equity in healthcare access are brought up by the digital divide at the same time. The less fortunate stand to lose ground in a world where more and more tasks are being handled by computers. Our natural interdependence is strengthened by our increased connectivity. For this reason, minimizing the risks and unintended consequences of digital technologies while maximizing their revolutionary potential requires cross-domain and cross-border cooperation. The challenges of the impending 6G era can only be adequately addressed with a single regulatory framework.

14.5.1.4 Patient Point of View

A new kind of "personalized healthcare" could be greatly aided by 6G, which could have far-reaching effects on patient satisfaction with their treatment, healthcare delivery, and the quality of care overall. Empowering patients to provide the results together with suggested action plans to the patient in a timely manner. Better data collected from a variety of sources should allow doctors and other healthcare providers to analyze "just in time" and administer dealings in a personalized healthcare system. This could be a chance to improve patients' economic stability and mental health while also reducing the need for readmission to the hospital. The efficacy of preventative care will be amplified with 6G because it will allow for better continuous monitoring of patients. Indeed, 6G's ability to enable continuous monitoring will lead to the generation of new data streams, which in turn will enable smart decision-making and the necessity of prognostic analytics.

14.5.1.5 Doctors Point of View

In the eyes of medical professionals, 6G technology could pave the way for unprecedented achievements in healthcare in the future, completely altering the industry as we know it. For instance, enhancing the quality of the home care system through access to patient status information in real-time and pharmaceutical efficiency. Below are some of the points:

1. Taking preventative actions to enhance the patient's QoL.
2. Reducing the use of non-specific, non-targeted analytical pharmacological therapies.
3. Optimizing healthcare spending by doing away with unnecessary medical visits, etc.
4. For a system to be financially and economically viable, it must allow for the home facilitation of chronically and highly individualized patients.
5. The ongoing adaptation of health policies to meet the evolving needs of populations by allocating resources to offer health services to the entire population.

14.5.1.6 Society Point of View

There will likely be a number of social effects stemming from the rollout of 6G. Implementing 6G technology has the latency to revolutionize healthcare by laying the framework for a dependable and personalized system that makes efficient use of available resources through a "win-win" approach that reduces economic and human waste, as well as misallocation. Better management of long-term and chronic illnesses is just one example of how 6G's increased personalization of healthcare may boost productivity and save money for individuals and businesses alike. Further savings might be achieved if 6G enables a move in the location of treatment from hospitals to residences. In addition, 6G's disruptive nature means it might revive old business models and usher in new ones, all while supporting the development of the business ecosystem.

14.5.2 Future Research Directions

Here, we outline the potential avenues for 6G intelligent healthcare research in the future.

14.5.2.1 ML and DL in 6G Intelligent Healthcare

It is necessary to analyze the application's nature in order to choose the appropriate ML strategy for 6G intelligent healthcare, even though ML and DL are parts of this concept. The creation of massive volumes of data in smart healthcare, for instance, necessitates real-time involvement due to the IoE. A single training session can be used to implement centralized ML. The constant influx of fresh data, however, means that the model trained via centralized ML might not deliver satisfactory outcomes. Federated learning outperforms centralized ML in this case. This method trains an ML model on a distributed dataset before sending the model's parameters to the final devices.

Lastly, the end devices refresh the global learning models with data from their local datasets. One advantage of distributed ML is that it eliminates resource fairness issues by sharing learning model parameters in real-time amid end tools and the centralized server. While centralized ML may not compromise user privacy to the same extent, distributed learning does necessitate a dataset stored at a central location that contains enough training data (which may not contain all device data).

14.5.2.2 6G-Enabled Healthcare with Blockchain

An intriguing novel technology, blockchain allows for the secure storage of contacts in a dispersed ledger that cannot be altered. Many smart services are made possible by blockchain technology. Sixth generation networks are known for their extremely low latency and energy consumption, as well as their greater scalability and reliability. Nevertheless, there are issues with the present blockchain consensus algorithms in terms of energy consumption, latency, reliability, durability, and delay. The fundamental goals of 6G-based smart healthcare are continually complicated when blockchain technology is used to accomplish these goals. A novel consensus method that enhances scalability and reliability while balancing latency, security, and latency must be proposed in order to reap the benefits of blockchain implementation.

14.5.3 Enhanced Security

Healthcare 6G-enhanced security metrics should focus on creating advanced, situation-specific security measures. Making encryption methods that are more resistant to 6G-specific cyberattacks is part of this process. The use of sophisticated ML models for real-time threat prediction and neutralization should also be prioritized in order to improve intrusion detection systems. Researching effective privacy-preserving techniques that keep data secure and private without slowing down 6G networks is also very important. To guarantee the safe transfer and conducting of critical healthcare data across upcoming 6G networks, these technological endeavors are crucial.

14.5.4 Terahertz Communiqué

The deployment of 6G healthcare through THz communication is fraught with intrinsic difficulties, and the field is known for its technical rigor. Creating advanced methods of signal creation and detection that are suited to healthcare settings is an essential part of this process. To further address the concerns of signal attenuation and interference, extensive research on the propagation of THz waves in different healthcare environments is essential. An additional critical area for efficient transmission and reception is the development of novel antenna designs optimized for THz frequencies.

14.5.4.1 Self-Sustaining

The administration, optimization, configuration, and planning processes can be expedited with the help of a self-organizing network. In 3GPP Release8, the concept of a self-organizing network was thoroughly outlined. Nevertheless, 6G systems operate in a complex and ever-changing environment, which may render the conventional self-organizing networking architecture impractical. Consequently, it is critical to create a ground-breaking, autonomous 6G network architecture. The ability to adjust to new circumstances is crucial for autonomous 6G systems. Furthermore, in order for the 6G-based healthcare to be self-sustaining, it is necessary to utilize evolving ML algorithms.

14.5.4.2 *Zero-Energy-Enabled*

Data transmission via 6G wireless networks in intelligent healthcare must be fueled by renewable energy sources that harness the power of radio waves (i.e., hybrid energy sources). In contrast, when the amount of energy harvested via radio waves falls short of what is needed to run the system, power must be drawn from the grid station. It is expected that the zero-energy system will feed back into the grid the same quantity of energy that it draws from the grid when there is an excess of radio wave harvesting.

14.5.4.3 *Routing Schemes*

There is a world of difference between conventional IoT healthcare and intelligent healthcare based on 6G. Because 6G has such stringent criteria for a variety of use cases, new routing strategies are required. Because nano and bio-nodes have inadequate computational power, communiqué range, and energy, it is necessary to find routes that do not consume a lot of either. Significant investigation into novel, computationally simple, and energy-efficient routing algorithms is necessary for an intelligent healthcare network based on 6G.

14.6 Conclusion

Due to the increasing occurrence of pandemics and other catastrophic occurrences, substantial advancements in communication technology are required for the management and provision of better healthcare services in the future. One of the most prominent 6G verticals is the healthcare sector. For healthcare providers to carry out their daily tasks more easily and at a lower cost, 6G technology is essential for providing efficient and affordable remote patient services. They will help alleviate the growing patient population and the scarcity of healthcare workers by facilitating at-home treatment. In the event of a pandemic or other catastrophic event, future 6G communiqué networks will be constructed to offer enhanced communiqué capabilities within healthcare systems. In the event of a future pandemic, hospital communication systems equipped with 6G technology can help reduce the impact and respond quickly. In this study, we take a look at 6G technology and how it could help a smarter healthcare system in the future. The essential steps for creating an intelligent healthcare system that can supply all essential services during emergencies or disasters have now been detailed.

References

1. Ismail, L. and Buyya, R., 2022. Artificial intelligence applications and self-learning 6G networks for smart cities digital ecosystems: Taxonomy, challenges, and future directions. *Sensors*, 22(15), p. 5750.
2. Nasralla, M.M., Khattak, S.B.A., Ur Rehman, I. and Iqbal, M., 2023. Exploring the Role of 6G Technology in Enhancing Quality of Experience for m-Health Multimedia Applications: A Comprehensive Survey. *Sensors*, 23(13), p. 5882.
3. De Alwis, C., Kalla, A., Pham, Q.V., Kumar, P., Dev, K., Hwang, W.J. and Liyanage, M., 2021. Survey on 6G frontiers: Trends, applications, requirements, technologies and future research. *IEEE Open J. Commun. Soc.*, 2, pp. 836-886.
4. Kumar, A., Jain, R., Gupta, M. and Islam, S.M. eds., 2023. *6G-Enabled IoT and AI for Smart Healthcare: Challenges, Impact, and Analysis*. CRC Press.
5. Khanh, Q.V., Chehri, A., Quy, N.M., Han, N.D. and Ban, N.T., 2023. Innovative Trends in the 6G Era: A Comprehensive Survey of Architecture, Applications, Technologies, and Challenges. *IEEE Access*.
6. Jawad, A.T., Maaloul, R. and Chaari, L., 2023. A comprehensive survey on 6G and beyond: Enabling technologies, opportunities of machine learning and challenges. *Comput. Netw.*, p. 110085.
7. Sampath, S., Parameswari, R., Prasad, M.L., Kumar, D.A., Hussain, M.M. and Reddy, P.C.S., 2023, December. Ensemble Nonlinear Machine Learning Model for Chronic Kidney Diseases Prediction. In *2023 IEEE 3rd Mysore Sub Section International Conference (MysuruCon)* (pp. 1-6), IEEE.
8. Baskar, S., Nandhini, I., Prasad, M.L., Katale, T., Sharma, N. and Reddy, P.C.S., 2023, November. An Accurate Prediction and Diagnosis of Alzheimer's Disease using Deep Learning. In *2023 IEEE North Karnataka Subsection Flagship International Conference (NKCon)* (pp. 1-7), IEEE.
9. Batista, E., Lopez-Aguilar, P. and Solanas, A., 2023. Smart health in the 6G era: bringing security to future smart health services. *IEEE Commun. Mag.*.
10. Osama, M., Ateya, A.A., Sayed, M.S., Hammad, M., Pławiak, P., Abd El-Latif, A.A. and Elsayed, R.A., 2023. Internet of medical things and healthcare 4.0: Trends, requirements, challenges, and research directions. *Sensors*, 23(17), p. 7435.
11. Reddy, P.C.S., Muller, P.S., Koka, S.N., Sharma, V., Sharma, N. and Mukherjee, S., 2023, November. Detection of Encrypted and Malicious Network Traffic using Deep Learning. In *2023 International Conference on Ambient Intelligence, Knowledge Informatics and Industrial Electronics (AIKIIE)* (pp. 1-6), IEEE.
12. Baswaraj, D., Natchadalingam, R., Rekha, R.S., Sahni, N., Divya, V. and Reddy, P.C.S., 2023, November. An Accurate Stock Prediction Using Ensemble Deep Learning Model. In *2023 International Conference on Research Methodologies in Knowledge Management, Artificial Intelligence and Telecommunication Engineering (RMKMATE)* (pp. 1-7), IEEE.

13. Wang, C.X., You, X., Gao, X., Zhu, X., Li, Z., Zhang, C., Wang, H., Huang, Y., Chen, Y., Haas, H. and Thompson, J.S., 2023. On the road to 6G: Visions, requirements, key technologies and testbeds. *IEEE Commun. Surv. Tutorials.*
14. Ansar, S.A., Samriya, J.K., Kumar, M., Gill, S.S. and Khan, R.A., 2023. Intelligent Fog-IoT Networks with 6G endorsement: Foundations, applications, trends and challenges. *6G Enabled Fog Computing in IoT: Applications and Opportunities*, pp. 287-307.
15. Chillakuru, P., Madiajagan, M., Prashanth, K.V., Ambala, S., Shaker Reddy, P.C. and Pavan, J., 2023. Enhancing wind power monitoring through motion deblurring with modified GoogleNet algorithm. *Soft Comput.*, pp. 1-11.
16. Kumar, K., Pande, S.V., Kumar, T., Saini, P., Chaturvedi, A., Reddy, P.C.S. and Shah, K.B., 2023. Intelligent controller design and fault prediction using machine learning model. *Int. Trans. Electr. Energy Syst.*, 2023.
17. Muthappa, K.A., Nisha, A.S.A., Shastri, R., Avasthi, V. and Reddy, P.C.S., 2023. Design of high-speed, low-power non-volatile master slave flip flop (NVMSFF) for memory registers designs. *Appl. Nanosci.*, pp. 1-10.
18. Imoize, A.L., Adedeji, O., Tandiya, N. and Shetty, S., 2021. 6G enabled smart infrastructure for sustainable society: Opportunities, challenges, and research roadmap. *Sensors*, 21(5), p. 1709.
19. Dang, V.A., Vu Khanh, Q., Nguyen, V.H., Nguyen, T. and Nguyen, D.C., 2023. Intelligent Healthcare: Integration of Emerging Technologies and Internet of Things for Humanity. *Sensors*, 23(9), p. 4200.
20. Al-Ansi, A., Al-Ansi, A.M., Muthanna, A., Elgendy, I.A. and Koucheryavy, A., 2021. Survey on intelligence edge computing in 6G: Characteristics, challenges, potential use cases, and market drivers. *Future Internet*, 13(5), p. 118.
21. Manimegalai, D. and Karthikeyan, M., 2023, November. Exploring the Impact of 5G and the Promise of 6G: Transforming Healthcare Strategies and Technology. In *2023 International Conference on Research Methodologies in Knowledge Management, Artificial Intelligence and Telecommunication Engineering (RMKMATE)* (pp. 1-8). IEEE.
22. Suneel, S., Krishnamoorthy, R., Gopatoti, A. *et al.*, Enhanced image diagnosing approach in medicine using quantum adaptive machine learning techniques. *Opt. Quant. Electron.*, 56, 534, 2024. https://doi.org/10.1007/s11082-023-06203-8.
23. Rao, K.R., Prasad, M.L., Kumar, G.R., Natchadalingam, R., Hussain, M.M. and Reddy, P.C.S., 2023, August. Time-Series Cryptocurrency Forecasting Using Ensemble Deep Learning. In *2023 International Conference on Circuit Power and Computing Technologies (ICCPCT)* (pp. 1446-1451), IEEE.
24. Krishnamoorthy, R., Soubache, I.D. & Jain, S., Wireless Communication Based Evaluation of Power Consumption for Constrained Energy System, *Wireless Pers. Commun.*, 127, 737–748, 2022. https://doi.org/10.1007/s11277-021-08402-6.
25. Patil, S.B., Rao, H.R., Chatrapathy, K., Kiran, A., Kumar, A.S. and Reddy, P.C.S., 2023, August. Ensemble Deep Learning Framework for Classification

of Skin Lesions. In *2023 International Conference on Circuit Power and Computing Technologies (ICCPCT)* (pp. 1550-1555), IEEE.

26. Latha, S.B., Dastagiraiah, C., Kiran, A., Asif, S., Elangovan, D. and Reddy, P.C.S., 2023, August. An Adaptive Machine Learning model for Walmart sales prediction. In *2023 International Conference on Circuit Power and Computing Technologies (ICCPCT)* (pp. 988-992), IEEE.
27. M. Ramkumar *et al.* "ECG Cardiac arrhythmias Classification using DWT, ICA and MLP Neural Networks" *J. Phys.: Conf. Ser.* 1831 012015, 2021.
28. Shen, L.H., Feng, K.T. and Hanzo, L., 2023. Five facets of 6G: Research challenges and opportunities. *ACM Comput. Surv.*, 55(11), pp. 1-39.
29. Mishra, P. and Singh, G., 2023. Internet of medical things healthcare for sustainable smart cities: current status and future prospects. *Appl. Sci.*, 13(15), p.8869.
30. Shahraki, A., Abbasi, M., Piran, M.J. and Taherkordi, A., 2021. A comprehensive survey on 6G networks: Applications, core services, enabling technologies, and future challenges. arXiv preprint arXiv: 2101.12475.
31. Salameh, A.I. and El Tarhuni, M., 2022. From 5G to 6G—challenges, technologies, and applications. *Future Internet*, 14(4), p. 117.
32. Singh, P.R., Singh, V., Yadav, R. and Chaurasia, S., 2023. 6G Networks for Artificial Intelligence-Enabled Smart Cities Applications: A Scoping Review. *Telemat. Inform. Rep.*, p. 100044.
33. Yuvaraj, D., Kumar, V.P., Anandaram, H., Samatha, B., Krishnamoorthy R. and Thiyagarajan, R., Secure De-Duplication Over Wireless Sensing Data Using Convergent Encryption, in: *2022 IEEE 3rd Global Conference for Advancement in Technology (GCAT)*, Bangalore, India, pp. 1-5, 2022, doi: 10.1109/GCAT55367.2022.9971983.
34. Serôdio, C., Cunha, J., Candela, G., Rodriguez, S., Sousa, X.R. and Branco, F., 2023. The 6G Ecosystem as Support for IoE and Private Networks: Vision, Requirements, and Challenges. *Future Internet*, 15(11), p.348.
35. Anand, S.J., Krishnamoorthy, R., Kumar, U.S. & Kamalakkannan, D., An Effective Hybrid Mobility Aware Energy Efficient Low Latency Protocol (HMEL-MAC) for Wireless Sensor Network. *Cybernet. Syst.*, 2022, DOI: 10.1080/01969722.2022.2157598
36. Dao, N.N., 2023. Internet of wearable things: Advancements and benefits from 6G technologies. *Future Gener. Comput. Syst.*, 138, pp. 172-184.
37. Mishra, P. and Singh, G., 2023. *Sustainable Smart Cities: Enabling Technologies, Energy Trends and Potential Applications.* Springer Nature.
38. Abdel Hakeem, S.A., Hussein, H.H. and Kim, H., 2022. Security requirements and challenges of 6G technologies and applications. *Sensors*, 22(5), p. 1969.
39. Zawish, M., Dharejo, F.A., Khowaja, S.A., Raza, S., Davy, S., Dev, K. and Bellavista, P., 2024. AI and 6G into the metaverse: Fundamentals, challenges and future research trends. *IEEE Open J. Commun. Soc.*, 5, pp. 730-778.

40. Mihai, S., Yaqoob, M., Hung, D.V., Davis, W., Towakel, P., Raza, M., Karamanoglu, M., Barn, B., Shetve, D., Prasad, R.V. and Venkataraman, H., 2022. Digital twins: A survey on enabling technologies, challenges, trends and future prospects. *IEEE Commun. Surv. Tutorials.*
41. Ramana, A.V., Bhoga, U., Dhulipalla, R.K., Kiran, A., Chary, B.D. and Reddy, P.C.S., 2023, June. Abnormal Behavior Prediction in Elderly Persons Using Deep Learning. In *2023 International Conference on Computer, Electronics & Electrical Engineering & their Applications (IC2E3)* (pp. 1-5), IEEE.
42. Gera, B., Raghuvanshi, Y.S., Rawlley, O., Gupta, S., Dua, A. and Sharma, P., 2023. Leveraging AI-enabled 6G-driven IoT for sustainable smart cities. *Int. J. Commun. Syst.*, 36(16), p. e5588.
43. Madhavi, G.B., Bhavani, A.D., Reddy, Y.S., Kiran, A., Chitra, N.T. and Reddy, P.C.S., 2023, June. Traffic Congestion Detection from Surveillance Videos using Deep Learning. In *2023 International Conference on Computer, Electronics & Electrical Engineering & their Applications (IC2E3)* (pp. 1-5), IEEE.
44. Rahman, A., Hossain, M.S., Muhammad, G., Kundu, D., Debnath, T., Rahman, M., Khan, M.S.I., Tiwari, P. and Band, S.S., 2023. Federated learning-based AI approaches in smart healthcare: concepts, taxonomies, challenges and open issues. *Cluster Comput.*, 26(4), pp. 2271-2311.
45. Kasinathan, Prabakaran, M. Sangeetha, M. Balamurugan, Shaik Aminabee, B. Dean Beema Rao, and Pundru Chandra Shaker Reddy. "An Early Diabetes Diseases Prediction Using Machine Learning With Optimal Features Selection." In *2023 International Conference on Research Methodologies in Knowledge Management, Artificial Intelligence and Telecommunication Engineering (RMKMATE)*, pp. 1-7, IEEE, 2023.

Index

Also of Interest

Check out these other related titles from Scrivener Publishing

Artificial Intelligence-Based System Models in Healthcare, Edited by A. Jose Anand, K. Kalaiselvi and Jyotir Moy Chatterjee, ISBN: 9781394242498. *Artificial Intelligence-Based System Models in Healthcare* provides a comprehensive and insightful guide to the transformative applications of AI in the healthcare system.

The Impact of Algorithmic Technologies on Healthcare, Edited by Parul Dubey, Mangala Madankar, Pushkar Dubey and Bui Thanh Hung, ISBN: 9781394305469.

Nanoengineered Materials for Medical and Healthcare Applications, Edited by Radhakrishnan E.K, Ashitha Jose and Visakh. P. M, ISBN: 978111979164.

3D Printing in Healthcare: Novel Applications, Edited by Rishabha Malviya and Rishav Sharma, ISBN: 9781394234202.

Artificial Intelligence-Enabled Digital Twin for Smart Manufacturing, Edited by Amit Kumar Tyagi, Shrikant Tiwari, Senthil Kumar Arumugam, and Avinash Kumar Sharma, ISBN: 9781394303571. An essential book on the applications of AI and digital twin technology in the smart manufacturing sector.

Quantum Computing and Artificial Intelligence: The Industry Use Cases, Edited by Pethuru Raj, B. Sundaravadivazhagan, Mariya Ouaissa, V. Kavitha and K. Shantha Kumari, ISBN: 9781394242368.

Artificial Intelligence Enabled Businesses: How to Develop Strategies for Innovation, Edited by Sweta Dixit, Mohit Maurya, Vishal Jain and Geetha Subramaniam, ISBN: 9781394233977.

INTEGRATED DEVICES FOR ARTIFICIAL INTELLIGENCE AND VLSI: VLSI Design, Simulation and Applications, Edited by Balwinder Raj, Suman Lata Tripathi, Tarun Chaudhary, K. Srinivasa Rao, and Mandeep Singh, ISBN: 9781394204359. With its in-depth exploration of the close connection between microelectronics, AI, and VLSI technology, this book offers valuable insights into the cutting-edge techniques and tools used in VLSI design automation, making it an essential resource for anyone seeking to stay ahead in the rapidly evolving field of VLSI design.

DECENTRALIZED SYSTEMS AND DISTRIBUTED COMPUTING, Edited by Sandhya Avasthi, Suman Lata Tripathi, Namrata Dhanda, and Satya Bhushan Verma, ISBN: 978139420436. This book provides a comprehensive exploration of next-generation internet, distributed systems, and distributed computing, offering valuable insights into their impact on society and the future of technology.

EXPLAINABLE MACHINE LEARNING MODELS AND ARCHITECTURES: Real-Time System Implementation, Edited by Suman Lata Tripathi and Mufti Mahmud, ISBN: 9781394185849. This cutting-edge new volume covers the hardware architecture implementation, the software implementation approach, and the efficient hardware of machine learning applications.

MACHINE LEARNING TECHNIQUES FOR VLSI CHIP DESIGN, Edited by Abhishek Kumar, Suman Lata Tripathi, and K. Srinivasa Rao, ISBN: 9781119910398. This cutting-edge new volume covers the hardware architecture implementation, the software implementation approach, and the efficient hardware of machine learning applications with FPGA or CMOS circuits, and many other aspects and applications of machine learning techniques for VLSI chip design.

Printed in the USA/Agawam, MA
September 16, 2026

910661.101